John Mason Neale
and the Quest for Sobornost

John Mason Neale
and the Quest for Sobornost

LEON LITVACK

CLARENDON PRESS · OXFORD
1994

Oxford University Press, Walton Street, Oxford OX2 6DP
Oxford New York Toronto
Delhi Bombay Calcutta Madras Karachi
Kuala Lumpur Singapore Hong Kong Tokyo
Nairobi Dar es Salaam Cape Town
Melbourne Auckland Madrid
and associated companies in
Berlin Ibadan

Oxford is a trade mark of Oxford University Press

Published in the United States
by Oxford University Press Inc., New York

© Leon Litvack 1994

All rights reserved. No part of this publication may be reproduced,
stored in a retrieval system, or transmitted, in any form or by any means,
without the prior permission in writing of Oxford University Press.
Within the UK, exceptions are allowed in respect of any fair dealing for the
purpose of research or private study, or criticism or review, as permitted
under the Copyright, Designs and Patents Act, 1988, or in the case of
reprographic reproduction in accordance with the terms of the licences
issued by the Copyright Licensing Agency. Enquiries concerning
reproduction outside these terms and in other countries should be
sent to the Rights Department, Oxford University Press,
at the address above

British Library Cataloguing in Publication Data
Data available

Library of Congress Cataloging in Publication Data
John Mason Neale and the quest for sobornost / Leon Litvack.
Includes bibliographical references and index.
1. Neale, J. M. (John Mason), 1818–1866. 2. Church of England—
Clergy—Biography. 3. Anglican Communion—Clergy—Biography.
4. Ecumenists—England—Biography. 5. Anglo-Catholicism—
History—19th century. 6. Church—Unity—History of
doctrines—19th century. 7. Anglican Communion—Relations—Orthodox
Eastern Church. 8. Orthodox Eastern Church—Relations—Anglican
Communion. I. Title.
BX5199.N5L57 1994   283'.092—dc20   93–17527
ISBN 0–19–826351–1

1 3 5 7 9 10 8 6 4 2

Typeset by Graphicraft Typesetters Ltd, Hong Kong
Printed in Great Britain
on acid-free paper by
Bookcraft (Bath) Ltd.,
Midsomer Norton

For my parents

Shew us, Lord, Thy work; our sons Thy glory,
   Yet of us, though that be all we ask,
May be said, perchance, in future story,
   These were the men that then did UNION's task.

Men whom satire could not move, and ban not;
   Men who *would* work on, and would not cease;
These were men who never said—'I cannot:'
   These were men who prayed the Church to Peace.
                                (John Mason Neale)

PREFACE

Sobornost is a Slavonic word which means conciliarity, harmony, and unanimity. For the Orthodox it represents an ideal in Christendom: unity in diversity, with individual communions maintaining their originality and autonomy, yet merging into the plural synthesis of the Church.[1] As Sergius Bulgakov says, 'It is unity in multiplicity, a symphony in which many motives and voices are harmonised.'[2] This idea, which was made current in nineteenth-century Russia, is the one which best describes the aim of John Mason Neale (1818–66) in his inquiries into the ways of the Eastern Church.

Neale was a man of many talents; he was simultaneously a hymn-writer, novelist, linguist, liturgist, antiquarian, and priest. His presence may be felt in many developments of the mid-Victorian Anglo-Catholic revival. This book is concerned with the development of Neale's imagination and the literary expressions of his interest in the Orthodox Church: his historical writings on the Eastern Church, his Greek hymn translations and adaptations, and his Eastern religious fiction. Through these three media he reached a diverse audience. His message was this: that the Orthodox Church, with her 'glorious mass of theology' and 'huge treasure of divinity' (HEC, p. xli) could provide valuable lessons for the Anglican Church, a communion which was undergoing momentous changes as a result of the many societal developments in Victorian Britain. The particular aspects of Orthodoxy with which Neale identified, and which he consequently publicized, provide valuable clues concerning the influence of cross-currents within a society on an individual's imagination.

One of the natural consequences of the quest for *sobornost*

---

[1] Kline, lending another shade of meaning, translates *sobornost* as 'organic religious togetherness' (G. L. Kline, 'Russian Religious Thought', in *Nineteenth Century Religious Thought in the West*, ed. N. Smart, J. Clayton, P. Sherry, and S. Katz (3 vols., Cambridge, 1985), ii.218, n. 2).

[2] S. Bulgakov, *The Orthodox Church* (Crestwood, NY, 1988), 60–1, 94.

is Church unity. Although Neale hoped that this goal would eventually be achieved, both through his efforts and those of his contemporaries and successors, he realized that the process was complex and the path uncertain. The best he could hope for was to lay the foundation upon which others could build. The two popular methods he chose—namely, hymnody and fiction—indicate that he wished first to sow the seeds of understanding in people's imaginations, blending Eastern tradition with their own, before tabling any more concrete proposals. By the end of his short life, Neale's project had progressed only as far as guiding his audience through some of the ways of Orthodoxy. The larger question of unity was to be the work of others.

The argument presented here is composed of three parts. Part I looks at why Neale was interested in Orthodoxy. Parts II and III examine the imaginative expression of Neale's fascination with the Eastern Church in hymns and religious fiction, respectively. I have assumed that many readers will not be familiar with either the mechanics of Orthodox hymnody or the plots of the novels and tales selected for discussion, so I have supplied this information in the interests of greater accessibility.

Neale was a proto-ecumenist, who, through his wide-ranging literary activity, did more than any of his contemporaries to bring *sobornost* to the popular mind. The method of investigation adopted here (an examination of the quest as presented in three distinct literary genres—historical narrative, hymns, and novels) is designed to show that Neale exploited each genre in a chronological sequence. The inclusion of an introduction, providing a biographical outline of Neale's life, is intended to complement the thematic analysis which follows and to show how his interest in the Eastern Church was closely related to the rest of his variegated and effective life.

Because my focus is literature and imagination, I do not deal at length with Neale's place in Anglican–Orthodox relations from the angles of theology or church history. I hope, however, that this book may spur others to investigate this topic. I also hope that it will serve as a guide to those interested in how communions with distinct traditions but similar spirituality might make overtures to one another, and that it will in the process make its own small contribution to the quest for *sobornost*.

LEON LITVACK

Belfast, 1993

ACKNOWLEDGEMENTS

I would like to thank the following: Prof. L. Adey, formerly of Dept. of English, University of Victoria; Canon A. M. Allchin, St Theosevia Centre for Christian Spirituality, Oxford; Fr. R. Barringer, St Joseph's College, University of Alberta; Prof. R. Chapman, formerly of the London School of Economics; Ms M. Drabble, London; Dr S. C. M. Drain, Dept. of English, Mount St Vincent University; Dr S. Gilley, Dept. of Theology, University of Durham; the Rt. Revd the Lord Bishop of Oxford, R. D. Harries; Revd Dr W. Horbury, Corpus Christi College, Cambridge; Revd Dr D. Jasper, Centre for the Study of Literature and Theology, University of Glasgow; Dr E. Jay, Westminster College, Oxford; Prof. G. L. Kline, Dept. of Philosophy, Bryn Mawr College; Mr M. J. Leppard, East Grinstead; the late Revd Dr A. G. Lough; Revd Archimandrite J. H. Maitland Moir, Edinburgh; Mr P. Meadows, formerly of Pusey House, Oxford; Revd M. McKenzie, St Margaret's Hope, Orkney; Dom B. Millard, St Augustine's Abbey, Ramsgate; Mrs L. Ormond, Dept. of English, King's College, University of London; Fr. B. Osborne, Oxford; Revd D. Perry, Skirlaugh; Revd Dr G. Rowell, Keble College, Oxford; Dr J. H. Schjørring, Dept. of Theology, University of Aarhus; Dr Ann Shukman, Keston Research, Oxford; Revd Dr K. Stevenson, Guildford; Miss A. Sutherland-Graeme, Holm, Orkney; Prof. T. Tanizaki, Kobe Women's University; Bishop K. Ware, Oxford; Mr M. Walker, Keston College; and Prof. J. R. Watson, School of English, University of Durham.

I am also grateful to the following libraries, associations, and institutions, which were helpful in so many ways: Academic Council, Queen's University of Belfast; the Bodleian Library; the Committee of Vice-Chancellors and Principals in the United Kingdom; Edinburgh University Library; the British Library; the Fellowship of St Alban and St Sergius; the House of St Gregory and St Macrina; the Hymn Society of Great Britain and Ireland; Keston College; Lambeth Palace

Acknowledgements

Library; the National Library of Scotland; the National Register of Archives; New College Library, Edinburgh; Pusey House; Sackville College, East Grinstead; Senatus Postgraduate Studies Committee, University of Edinburgh; St Margaret's Convent, East Grinstead; and the Victorian Studies Association of Western Canada.

The following must be singled out for special recognition, for without them this book could never have been written: Dr Andrew Sanders, Birkbeck College, University of London, who first introduced me to the work of J. M. Neale; my mentors, Mr Geoffrey Carnall and Prof. Ian Campbell, Dept. of English Literature, University of Edinburgh, who helped to develop the original idea into the present study; and my wife, Marianne, whose patience and encouragement ensured a successful outcome.

CONTENTS

Abbreviations	xiv
Introduction: The Life of John Mason Neale	1
Part I. Neale's Orthodox Consciousness	35
1 Anglicans and the Eastern Church	37
2 Neale and the Eastern Church	53
3 Neale's Orientalism	63
4 Neale's *History of the Holy Eastern Church*	75
Part II. Hymnologist of the Eastern Church	89
5 Neale and Orthodox Hymnody	91
6 Neale's Translations	117
7 Neale's Centos and Adaptations	154
Part III. Oriental Novelist	179
8 Neale's Craft of Fiction	181
9 *Theodora Phranza*	207
10 *The Lily of Tiflis*	234
11 *The Lazar-House of Leros*	243
12 Short Stories	260
Epilogue: The Legacy of Neale	265
Glossary	268
Bibliography	273
Index	289

ABBREVIATIONS

ALX   J. M. Neale, *A History of the Holy Eastern Church: The Patriarchate of Alexandria* (2 vols., London, 1847).
ANT   J. M. Neale, *A History of the Holy Eastern Church: The Patriarchate of Antioch*, ed. George Williams (London, 1873).
BWJ   Journal of Benjamin Webb, now in Duke Humfrey's Library, Bodleian Library, Oxford, MSS Eng. Misc. d. 475, e. 406–43, f. 97–9. There is also a copy of the portions of Webb's diary relating to Neale (1839–64) made by Canon P. G. Ward of Peterborough in 1951 in Lambeth Palace Library, London, MS 3595. References to BWJ will be by day, month, and year on which the entry was made.
D&F   E. Gibbon, *The Decline and Fall of the Roman Empire* (6 vols., edn. used: London, 1979).
HEC   J. M. Neale, *Hymns of the Eastern Church* (London, 1862).
INT   J. M. Neale, *A History of the Holy Eastern Church: General Introduction* (2 vols., London, 1850). The page numbering in the two volumes is continuous (vol. 1, 1–526; vol. 2, 527–1243).
LHL   J. M. Neale, *The Lazar-House of Leros: A Tale of the Eastern Church in the Seventeenth Century* (edn. used: London, 1916).
LOT   J. M. Neale, *The Lily of Tiflis: A Sketch from Georgian History* (edn. used: London, 1917).
NJ   Journal of John Mason Neale.[1] Neale's journals are incomplete, and exist today only in transcription. Those for 1836 and 1837, 1 Jan.–10 Aug. 1838, and 1851–1852 exist only

---

[1] It was originally kept primarily for the benefit of Mary Rippingall, to whom Neale had become engaged in 1836; the engagement was broken after three years, but Neale continued to keep the journal. The form of the entries was modelled on that used by the poet George Crabbe (1754–1832), who fell in love with Sarah Elmy, and kept a journal addressed to her.

in the form of copies of copies made by the late Revd Dr A. G. Lough and now in the possession of Leon Litvack. The journal transcriptions for Nov. 1838–Mar. 1840 and Jan. 1842–Apr. 1844 are preserved in Lambeth Palace Library (MSS 3107–8), transferred there from St Margaret's Convent, East Grinstead, in 1979.[2] References to NJ are by day, month, and year on which the entry was made.

SSM   J. M. Neale, 'The Story of S. Metrophanes of Voronej', in *Deeds of Faith: Stories for Children from Church History* (edn. used: London, 1902).

TP   J. M. Neale, *Theodora Phranza; or, The Fall of Constantinople* (London, 1857).

---

[2] The copies in Lambeth Palace Library were probably made by two or three of Neale's daughters: Mary Sackville, who edited and published his letters, and Ermenild or Margaret.

INTRODUCTION

The Life of John Mason Neale

JOHN MASON NEALE was born in Holborn, London, on 24 January 1818.[1] His father was the Revd Cornelius Neale, a committed, pious Evangelical, who, after a distinguished career at Cambridge, took holy orders and was ordained priest in 1822. He died ten months later, aged 34, from consumption. His wife, Susanna, from a similar background, was left to bring up John Mason (who was only 5 years old at the time) and his three younger sisters, Susanna, Cornelia, and Elizabeth.

Life in the Neale household after the father's death was characterized by Evangelical strictness, which sometimes manifested itself as oppressive severity—presumably a consequence of Mrs Neale's concern regarding her children's future. One incident from Neale's childhood, which was to haunt him for the rest of his life, epitomizes the harsh Calvinistic teaching which was inflicted on him and from which he later broke away. The 8-year-old boy was reading from Isaiah 16: 1, 'Send ye the lamb to the ruler from Sela to the wilderness, unto the mount of the daughters of Zion', and pondering the meaning of the text 'Was not the wilderness the world in which God's people still wandered, and the lamb, Jesus the Lamb of God, not his Judge but his Saviour?' When he ventured to exclaim to his mother that it was beautiful to think of Jesus as a lamb, she is said to have retorted: 'Till you are converted it would be far truer if you were to think of Him as a Lion; if you were to die tonight—and who can tell but you may?—He would be in no wise a lamb to you.'[2] In a

---

[1] For biographical information about Neale, I am indebted to the following: E. A. Towle, *John Mason Neale*, D.D. (London, 1906; hereafter Towle); Sr. Miriam, *John Mason Neale* (East Grinstead, 1895; hereafter Sr. Miriam); A. G. Lough, *The Influence of John Mason Neale* (London, 1962); idem, *John Mason Neale* (Newton Abbot, 1976). [2] Quoted in Towle, 248.

sermon in 1858 Neale recalled the rationale behind such statements: 'When I was a child, I was taught, almost as an article of my creed, that the difficulty I felt in doing right, the struggle and pain it cost, was only a proof of an unconverted nature; and that, were I really God's servant, I should feel no such effort necessary, because sin would be in itself so hateful.'[3]

Mrs Neale moved frequently when the children were young; she preferred the mild climate of the south of England because of her delicate health (something which she passed on to her son). From Chiswick, where the family lived when the father died, they moved in 1823 to Shepperton, where Neale was enrolled as a pupil of the rector, William Russell, and in 1829 to Blackheath, where Neale was sent to school for a time. In 1833, when he was 15, he was sent to Sherborne School in Dorset; there he won the Latin and English essay prizes. Two years later the Neales moved to Farnham, Surrey.

From his youth Neale (or 'Mason', as he was called in the family) was shy and sensitive, and spoke in a nasal voice. He was rather tall and angular, with poor eyesight, dark, untidy hair, and an olive complexion. Although never robust in health, and therefore not particularly athletic, he was an enthusiastic walker, thinking nothing of a twenty- or thirty-mile excursion. He was also an avid reader, with a talent for imaginative composition, and delighted in writing poems, stories, and plays. When he was 10, he composed a tragedy, for which he prepared himself by reading all the plays of Seneca. His extraordinary precocity and energy help to explain how he was able to achieve so much in the course of his relatively short life.

Neale made the transition from Evangelicalism to High Church while at Cambridge University (1836–40). During his first undergraduate year at Trinity College, he and his cousin, James Dalton, began to attend Holy Trinity Church, where William Carus, Fellow of Trinity, was curate, and Charles Simeon (1759–1836), leader of the Evangelicals at Cambridge, was vicar. Simeon had been the incumbent since 1782, and by 1836 had preached over 2,500 sermons. That his influence

---

[3] J. M. Neale, 'The Approach of Lent', in *Sermons for the Church Year* (2 vols.; London, 1876), i.117–18.

was so great was partly because he spanned several generations (Neale's father was a Simeonite).⁴ He was reckoned to have moved to a more churchmanly attitude during his career, and by Neale's day he had become respected across party lines.

Neale clearly enjoyed Simeon's preaching. He went to hear him six times in 1836, and although by that time Simeon was well past his prime, each time Neale came away impressed. In his journal he recorded such remarks as 'Mr Simeon preached—that, you know, is as much as saying it was a good sermon' (NJ 10.4.36). The laudatory remarks were short-lived, however; for Simeon died on 13 November 1836. Neale was saddened, and wrote in his journal: 'I cannot tell you how much I am grieved for his loss' (NJ 13.11.36).

While Neale, like many Cambridge undergraduates, embarked on university life as a Simeonite, it was only a passing phase. He spoke highly of the Evangelical preacher, even though his firsthand experience of Simeon was limited; but he would probably have known of Simeon beforehand by reputation, in the course of long Sundays spent either in church or listening to published sermons read to him by his mother. The very qualities which made Simeon a famous preacher were those which Neale rejected in his development from an Evangelical to an Anglo-Catholic.

There is a temptation to compare Neale's youth with that of John Henry Newman, who also grew up as an Evangelical. The comparison should be resisted, however, because of the strength of Neale's later revulsion against a form of religion imbibed at his mother's knee. It must be remembered that Newman said that until he was 15 he had 'no formed religious convictions', but took 'great delight' in reading the Bible in much the same way as he read *The Arabian Nights*.⁵ When he was 15, he adopted a definite creed, and this was a Calvinistic one. The Calvinism wore out within ten years, and he then adopted the doctrine of baptismal regeneration— evidently about the time of his own ordination as priest in 1825—as a mark of his rejection of Calvinist principles.

Although the impetus behind the transformation of Neale

---

⁴ See W. Jowett (ed.), *A Memoir of the Rev. Cornelius Neale, M.A.* (London, 1835), 28. Neale's father was at Cambridge from 1808 to 1811.

⁵ J. H. Newman, *Apologia pro vita sua*, ed. M. Ward (London, 1979), 1.

from an Evangelical to an Anglo-Catholic may have differed somewhat from that for Newman, it was not long before they began to follow parallel paths. In the 1820s and 1830s Evangelicalism underwent a crisis. The clarity and conciseness of Evangelical theology—two features which were highly attractive to those who converted in the eighteenth century from the High Church party—were less appealing to those who, like Neale and Newman, were brought up within the Evangelical tradition. There was a danger in the importance assigned to the Bible in Evangelicalism, which resulted in a tendency to de-emphasize doctrinal interpretation as offered in the traditional development of Church dogma. The spirit of liberalism which marked the Evangelical approach to rationalism meant that the Evangelical party did not stress the authority of tradition; it was this attitude which all the founders of the Oxford Movement found worrying. Newman in particular realized that it was necessary to find proper intellectual roots for the status accorded to the Church. In attempting to find these roots, the Tractarians hoped to counter the Evangelical movement towards liberalism, and in the process to answer questions concerning their own Anglican identities.

Although Neale was an Anglo-Catholic,[6] he should not, strictly speaking, be identified as a Tractarian. He clearly sympathized with various important issues highlighted in the *Tracts for the Times* (1833–41), particularly the emphasis on the historical continuity of the Church of England with Catholic Christianity and a 'high' conception of the authority of the Church. Yet the transition from his initial Evangelicalism seems to have come about not as a direct result of reading the Oxford *Tracts* or the *Library of the Fathers* or the *Library of Anglo-Catholic Theology*, but through his flamboyant antiquarianism and—an important consideration for his work on the Orthodox Church—through his belief that outward symbols of faith, particularly but not exclusively architecture, were exponents of historical facts and eternal verities. It is this which clearly distinguishes Neale from the

---

[6] 'Anglo-Catholic Church', as an epithet in the 19th-cent. Anglican tradition, is discussed in R. Chapman's *Faith and Revolt* (London, 1970), Appendix 1: 'The Nomenclature of the Movement' (280–9).

Introduction: The Life of J. M. Neale

Oxford Anglo-Catholics, and it was through this medium that Neale most clearly made his mark.

Neale professed a deep concern for doctrine and authority—the two features which marked the first twelve years of the Oxford Movement (1833-45); however, his interest in aesthetics points to the complexity of the Catholic revival in Anglicanism. Most of the Tractarians looked to the Caroline divines, the Reformers, and the Fathers to support their case; not so Hurrell Froude, whose *Remains* (1838-9) Neale read, and who conceived a strong enthusiasm for the Middle Ages as the time of the ideal Church. He was hostile to the Reformers, and chided Newman for his fervent disparagements of Rome. The gradual softening of attitudes towards Roman Catholics was partly a result of the Romantic attachment to the Middle Ages. Chapman points out that 'It was not possible to write or paint much on medieval subjects without meeting at least the externals of that Church which was the object of so much scorn'; as a consequence, favourable reactions to Romanism began to emerge, particularly after Catholic emancipation (1829). The novels of Scott also helped to convince readers that 'not all was bad outside Protestantism'.[7]

Froude also differed from the other Tractarians in his concern for architecture; and in the years following his death in 1836—the same year that Neale matriculated at Cambridge—medievalism and architecture were often linked. Architecture was dragged into the theological arena, and was made a rallying-point for many who were discontented with their age for a variety of reasons; the argument also crossed party lines. Augustus Pugin (1812-52), who claimed to have been converted

---

[7] Chapman, *Faith and Revolt*, 228, 229. One thinks particularly of the way in which medieval architecture is venerated by Scott. Chapman adds, concerning the spread of medievalism in the 19th cent., that it 'was developed by the Romantic writers until it became a convenient holdall for anything that could chide the present age. If unrestricted individualism was the ailment, mediaeval collectivism could be produced as the cure; if new factories and schools were ugly, Gothic cathedrals showed how men had built in the old days. The arguments were often specious and historically ill-founded; but the myth was adequate to frame the ideas of great men. Carlyle took a mediaeval stick to beat the present in *Past and Present*. Ruskin wielded it after him, and William Morris also in his turn' (ibid. 228). For Scott's indebtedness to the Middle Ages, see J. Mitchell, *Scott, Chaucer, and Medieval Romance* (Lexington, Ky., 1987).

to Roman Catholicism by the beauty of Gothic architecture, looked for strength to the Middle Ages.[8] For Pugin, for Froude, and for Neale, the architecture and craftsmanship of that period reflected Catholic truth; and in different ways, an appeal to this precedent, which stood around them, in Oxford, Cambridge, and elsewhere, gave each of them a structural basis for his own particular view of the Church.

Neale's medievalism first surfaced while he was preparing for his university entrance examination under Dr James Challis at Papworth Everard, a small village about ten miles from Cambridge. He had occasion to wander among the maze of Gothic buildings which comprised the University, and noted in his journal:

It has struck me that in different styles of architecture we may perhaps find an analogy with the different stages of popular feeling in England. The Norman, heavy, dark, and gloomy, corresponds well enough to the absence of liberty which characterizes the reigns of our kings till John. Then the early English has certainly a resemblance to the far more cheerful and free views introduced by Magna Charta. Still, though there is great beauty in the parts, there is a want of amalgamation and unity in the whole, which, however, we find in the Decorated, the most perfect style, which answers to what was perhaps the happiest age of England, Edward the Third's. Gradually the Commons asserted their own rights, and broke through the symmetry of the Government, and behold! at the same time the Perpendicular mullions cut the beautiful tracery, before unbroken, to pieces. I am disposed to think that there is more than fancy in that. (NJ 1.4.36)

Even at such an early point in Neale's life his guiding principle is manifest. Raised with a sound knowledge of the Bible and its standard typological interpretation, Neale became fascinated by the mystical and symbolic interpretation of Scripture.[9] These hermeneutics he extended to architecture,

---

[8] See M. Trappes-Lomax, *Pugin* (London 1932), 57.

[9] 'Typology', as used in this book, is defined as 'a Christian form of scriptural interpretation that claims to discover divinely intended anticipations of Christ and His dispensation in the laws, events and people of the Old Testament' (G. P. Landow, *Victorian Types, Victorian Shadows* (London, 1980), 3). It should be noted that Landow attributes the Victorian revival of typology to the influence of the 18th-cent. Evangelicals, who adhered to a strict constructionist approach, which preferred one-to-one types and antitypes,

Introduction: The Life of J. M. Neale

which he viewed not simply aesthetically, as supplying an appropriate ornamentation for churches, but as the illustration of liturgical and theological principles. Thus Neale saw church buildings as material aids to faith, on which he laid the foundation for his own Anglo-Catholic structure; his system, which came to be called 'Ecclesiology', clearly distinguished him from Newman, Pusey, and most of the others at Oxford;[10] formed the basis for his contribution to the Catholic revival; and provided some of the motivation for his interest in the Eastern Church.

As an undergraduate, Neale spent his summers examining churches and recording in his journal descriptions of their peculiar features. His first extensive tour was in the summer of 1837, when he visited his friend Edward Boyce; together they travelled through Bedfordshire, examining a total of twenty-nine churches. He embarked on a more ambitious expedition the following summer, visiting the north of England and Scotland. His impressions of Lincoln Cathedral will serve to indicate the pains to which he went to record his findings:

Oh, how shall I describe it to you? The west front is too heavy for my taste, and the N[ave] I do not altogether admire, but the choir, the glorious choir with the E[arly] E[nglish] foliage, the crocketed niches, the elegant and lavish toothed [mouldings], the exquisite triforium, called the Angel's choir, worthy almost to be really so, form an assemblage that no description can give the faintest idea of. But if one part be more beautiful than another, it is the door to the north aisle of the chancel, the porch of the south transept, and the

---

especially those from the Old Testament that foreshadowed Christ. This view has resulted in a flourishing of investigation, mainly concerning the visual art of the Pre-Raphaelites and the writings of Ruskin and Carlyle. Tennyson, however, disputes this localized view, and suggests some signs of a wider dispersal of typology in Victorian culture, pointing to a continuation and reinvigoration of an enduring legacy of Christianity to art. He cites in particular the Tractarian understanding of analogy and reserve, as enunciated by Keble and Isaac Williams. See G. B. Tennyson, ' "So Careful of the Type?"' in *Essays and Studies* (London, 1984), 31–45.

[10] As Towle says, 'It would not be unjust to say that, though Oxford had for the most part provided the letterpress of the movement, Cambridge was furnishing the illustrations.' Neale himself confirmed this dichotomy some years later, when he wrote: 'It is clear to me that the Tract writers missed one great principle, namely, the influence of aesthetics' (Towle, 51).

south transept of the chancel (for there are two sets of transepts). Come now outside, and look at the sublime central tower, and the two small only by comparison, that flank the western front. Now see this rich north door, every niche alive with sculpture, and now the intersecting or trefoiled E[arly] E[nglish] arches, and can anything more grand be imagined? Or more worthy to be called a house of God? ... We stayed at the Minster, and for a short time regaled our eyes with its beauties; we returned and—I love to be particular on great occasions—dined on lamb and peas. (NJ 7.7.38)

Through the teachings of the Fathers and Caroline divines as interpreted by the Oxford Movement and his own ideas on typology, symbolism, and the outward manifestations of faith, Neale combined the spiritual with the material aspects of the nineteenth-century revival in Anglicanism—hence his ability to move easily in the spheres of the Anglo-Catholic movement and the Gothic Revival.

In October 1838 a young man named Benjamin Webb matriculated at Trinity. Like Neale and Boyce, he was interested in church architecture and the catholicity of the Church as advocated by the Oxford *Tracts*. Together they founded a movement whose express aim was to reconstruct visible worship by laying down principles of church architecture and furnishing. In March 1839 Webb noted in his journal that a 'High Church Club' had been founded, and the name 'Ecclesialogical' [*sic*] chosen (BWJ 3.3.39; 15.3.39). The name was later changed to 'Cambridge Camden Society', with Neale as chairman and Webb as secretary and treasurer.

The Camdenians specified the following subjects as being within their scope:

Church Building at home and in the Colonies: Church Restoration in England and abroad: the theory and practice of Ecclesiastical Architecture: the investigation of Church Antiquities: the connection of Architecture with ritual: the science of Musick and all the Decorative Arts, which can be made subservient to Religion: the exposing and denouncing of glaring cases of Church Desecration: criticism upon Designs for and upon new Churches.[11]

[11] E. J. Boyce, *A Memorial of the Cambridge Camden Society* (London, 1888), 11. For a description of the state of church building at the time when the Cambridge Camden Society began its work, see Lough, 'Ecclesiological Conditions', in *Influence of John Mason Neale*, 12–22.

Their meetings were taken up with reports on churches 'taken', which was their way of referring to the recording of minute details about the buildings,[12] and with lectures on such topics as church history, liturgiology, symbolism, music, mechanics, geology, embroidery, and tapestry. The Camdenians developed the study of all these subjects into a science, which they called 'ecclesiology'. Clarke explains, however, that study by itself was insufficient:

Ecclesiology meant understanding the Christian faith and the rubrics of the Prayer Book, and embodying them in a building which should show them forth. The science of church-building as the ecclesiologists understood it was not architectural science: it was the unveiling of the inner mystical meaning of old churches and the infusion of the same meaning into new churches. Its relation to the science of church-building in the most obvious sense was almost that of astrology to astronomy. Astronomy is the serious scientific study of the stars; astrology attempts to find a mystic significance in them. ... This is not made clear in the statement of the objects of the Society. Anyone could study architectural remains or make rubbings of brasses—even heretics or schismatics. But it is clear from the Society's writings that only a good Churchman could appreciate the inwardness of it all, or build new churches as they should be built. Only a good churchman could be an ecclesiologist.[13]

This extra dimension to the definition, which Neale realized, provided the inspiration for much of his later work.

Like Pugin, who was a friend of Neale's and designed the Society's seal, the Camdenians believed that one style of architecture was superior to all others: the fourteenth-century Gothic (Middle Pointed). In their opinion the productions of their 'uncatholic' rivals were abominations. There were churches built in the Norman, Early English, and Perpendicular styles, but hardly any in the Middle Pointed. According to Clarke the Camdenian battle-cry, as it were, was this: 'Let

---

[12] Records of these visits are preserved in the Lambeth Palace Library, MSS 1977-93. These church schemes fill 17 vols.; listed are visits to 348 churches in England and Wales (undertaken in 1839-42), 52 in northern France (1841), and 118 in northern Europe, Spain, and Portugal (1851-3). Most of the reports were compiled by Neale himself, with contributions by Webb, Boyce, and others.
[13] B. F. L. Clarke, *Church Builders of the Nineteenth Century* (New York, 1969), 78.

heretics keep to their own styles—which were either undeveloped or decadent, and therefore suitable to them. An ecclesiologist would use the only style which had not been degraded by modern use—the pure, true, noble and Catholic style of the fourteenth century.'[14] When Neale and his society held up the fourteenth century as the ideal in outward form, so for them it must also have been the ideal in inward faith.[15]

By 1839 Neale had become disillusioned with the sermons of William Carus, Charles Simeon's protégé: 'Went to Trinity [Church] the first time for a very long time. Carus preached. . . . I thought it a poor sermon . . . Oh how my taste has changed' (NJ 3.11.39). Many of the traits he exhibited closely resembled those of the Tractarians. By September he began to date his journal entries according to the fasts and festivals of the English Church. On 18 September, for example, he wrote: 'Wednesday, Ember Day. Kept the fast pretty well, and without the usual accompaniment of a headache' (NJ 18.9.39). On the Feast of St Michael and All Angels he noted with disgust that no reference was made to the festival in the sermon. Neale and his friends also began rising at 4.15 a.m. to say lauds (NJ 18.1.39) and fasting on Fridays. In his journal Neale remarked on the ignorance of Cambridge men on this latter point: 'It is surprising what ignorance exists on the subject of Rubric. Griffiths of Trinity, a man professing High Church principles, asked Webb to wine on Friday. Webb explained the reason why he could not go; and Griffiths frankly acknowledged

---

[14] Ibid. 79. Clarke interestingly notes: 'It would be generally agreed now that fourteenth-century Decorated work is not Gothic at its best. . . . But to the ecclesiologists it seemed very beautiful, and they laid down the dogma that Christian architecture reached perfection in the early days of the Late Middle Pointed' (79).

[15] Cf. E. Burke, who saw the 14th cent. as a classic period of old England, with a congenial social ethos. In speaking of the Hundred Years' War of the 14th and 15th cents., he said: 'Four hundred years have gone over us; but I believe we are not materially changed since that period. Thanks to our sullen resistance to innovation, thanks to the cold sluggishness of our national character, we still bear the stamp of our forefathers. We have not (as I conceive) lost the generosity and dignity of thinking of the fourteenth century' (*Reflections on the Revolution in France*, ed. C. C. O'Brien (Harmondsworth, 1982), 181).

that he had never before heard of the Friday's fast. What shall we come to next?' (NJ 5.12.39).[16]

Various tracts and pamphlets were issued by the Cambridge Camden Society to assist in disseminating their views. Their titles included *Hints for the Practical Study of Ecclesiastical Antiquities* (1840); *A Few Words to Church Builders* (1841); *A Few Words to Churchwardens on Churches and Church Ornaments, No. 1, Suited to Country Parishes*, and *No. 2, Suited to Town and Manufacturing Parishes* (1841); and *Twenty-Three Reasons for Getting Rid of Church Pues* (1841). All were reprinted at least three times; the most popular of all, *A Few Words to Churchwardens, No. 1*, by Neale, went through thirteen editions in two years.

With these publications the reputation of the Society was firmly established. Its membership extended to all parts of Britain and eventually to the colonies; this popularity necessitated a regular medium of communication, which appeared in 1841 under the title of *The Ecclesiologist*. This monthly publication was instigated by Neale, and he proved to be the foremost contributor, particularly on subjects which were not strictly architectural, such as hymnology, liturgiology, symbolism, and ritual. An interesting appraisal of the *Ecclesiologist*'s appeal is provided by Anson in *Fashions in Church Furnishings*, where he notes that Anglican rectory ladies, who produced altar frontals and church embroidery, took to heart the practical advice given in the *Ecclesiologist*, and 'devoured the magazine... as a sort of early Victorian ecclesiastical equivalent of *Vogue*'.[17] The *Ecclesiologist* had a wide circulation both in Britain and overseas; in all, 153 issues appeared, the last one in 1868, two years after Neale's death.

In the publications of the Cambridge Camden Society typological and symbolical interpretation were very important,

---

[16] These disputes also affected Neale's family. In Jan. 1840 he went to Brighton to visit his mother and sisters, whom Webb described as 'very Evangelical & very stiff' (BWJ 9.1.41). Neale's High Church sentiments made his family uncomfortable, and led to heated arguments (NJ 28.1.40).

[17] P. F. Anson, *Fashions in Church Furnishings* (London, 1965), 61. In *Loss and Gain* (1848) Newman has some amusing satire on devout ladies doing ecclesiastical embroidery (pt. 1, ch. 8) and an ecclesiological list of church furnishings (pt. 2, ch. 15).

for they provided a foundation on which to build ecclesiological theories. Neale and his associates adopted allegorical systems that they found in such medieval authors as William Durandus, whose *Rationale Divinorum Officiorum*, book I (a compendium of liturgical knowledge with mystical interpretation), Neale and Webb translated in 1843. They used such books as guides for propriety in matters of church architecture and furnishings. The zest they displayed in such matters was the pleasure of bringing sunken treasure to light. A similar kind of zeal is apparent in Neale's work on the Orthodox Church. Yet, while enthusiasm for the subject certainly motivated him in his work, there arose concurrently the danger of overstatement and misrepresentation, which occasionally crept into his discussions.[18]

In 1843, in a publication entitled *Church Enlargement and Church Arrangement*, Neale argued: 'A Church is not as it should be, till every window is filled with stained glass, till every inch of floor is covered with encaustic tiles, till there is a Roodscreen glowing with the brightest tints and with gold, nay, if we would arrive at perfection, the roof and walls must be painted and frescoed. For it may safely be asserted that ancient churches were so adorned.'[19]

---

[18] The Camdenian exposition of allegorical systems is one example of enthusiasm carried to an extreme. Neale and his followers believed that every item in a medieval church was put there with a symbolic purpose in mind. Isaac Williams (1802–65), one of the contributors to *The Tracts for the Times*, had been an advocate of such 'reading' of architecture in *The Cathedral* (Oxford, 1838), *The Baptistery* (London, 1842), and *The Altar* (London, 1847). But whereas Williams's works were original productions, particularly the poetry, when Neale and Webb wished to demonstrate the symbolic structure of churches, their presentation was through a translation (*The Symbolism of Churches and Church Ornaments*). Their translation of the *Rationale Divinorum Officiorum*, with appended introduction, notes, and illustrations, was an attempt to link religious principles with their physical manifestations; in appealing to a medieval source to expound ecclesiological principles, Neale and Webb hoped to lend greater authority to their statements. Interestingly, the illustrations for the *Rationale* and for Williams's *Cathedral* were both done by the same man: Thomas Orlando Jewitt (1799–1869), who in his day had almost a monopoly of architectural and archaeological drawings and woodcuts, in which he specialized. He was frequently employed by John Henry Parker of Oxford, who published many works by the Tractarians and Camdenians.

[19] J. M. Neale, *Church Enlargement and Church Arrangement* (Cambridge, 1843), 2. The other extreme—that is, failure to appreciate the symbolic

Introduction: The Life of J. M. Neale

Ancient churches may or may not have been decorated thus; but these suppositions point to a pertinacity in Neale and his followers which can only be described as excessive. Anson supports this assessment, particularly concerning Neale's treatment of symbolism, and points out the damaging consequences of such excesses:

> It must be admitted that many of Neale's arguments are more original and entertaining than convincing. Moreover they were dangerous, since they resulted in the destruction of many interesting articles of church furnishing and decoration that had a real historic value, merely because the ancient specimens did not feature correct symbolism, for which reason something new had to be substituted.[20]

This analysis has important implications for Neale's later exploits, particularly his *History of the Holy Eastern Church*, Greek hymn translations, and Oriental novels. In the first and third cases he occasionally altered historical details or fabricated arguments to suit his purpose; in the second he appears deliberately to have misled his readers by excluding the famous Akathist Hymn in praise of the Virgin, in order to avoid accusations of Romanism. In each genre he wished to bring to light what he considered 'sunken treasure'; but in order to be included in his arguments, the details had to fall in line with his preconceived conclusions.

Even though the views of Neale and other members of the Cambridge Camden Society were sometimes singular and went against current trends, Rowell points out that they had an

---

character of ritual and ornament—can also be found in the Victorian Church. Newman cites the case of a Protestant Scripture reader who saw no symbolic significance in the Benediction of the Blessed Sacrament, but only a priest entering 'with a long wand in his hand', lighting candles, taking 'a gold star' from 'a small cupboard on the altar', screwing it on a candlestick, and placing it under a 'beehive' before bowing down before it. Newman laments: 'I am not blaming this person for not knowing a Catholic rite, which he had no means of knowing, but for thinking that he knows it, when he does not know it, for coming into the chapel, with this coxcombical idea ... in his head, that Popery is a piece of mummery, which any intelligent Protestant can see through' (J. H. Newman, *Lectures on the Present Position of Catholics in England*, no. 6: 'Prejudice the Life of the Protestant View'; quoted in T. R. Wright, *Theology and Literature* (Oxford, 1988), 144).

[20] Anson, *Fashions in Church Furnishings*, 73. It is interesting to note that John Sumner, the Archbishop of Canterbury, thought Neale's and Webb's *Durandus* 'awfully Lutheran' (BWJ, 11.12.48).

appreciative and supportive public, to whom their theories of symbolism were acceptable: 'In an age of church building, such as was the mid-nineteenth century, there can be no doubt of the influence of the ecclesiologists' principles, and to their ardent belief in an archetypal symbolism of church architecture we owe the common conceptions of what a proper church building ought to be.'[21]

The Camdenians were certainly influential; but they were not always reasonable. Kenneth Clark confirms this assessment: 'For fifty years almost every new Anglican Church was built according to their instructions; that is to say, in a manner opposed to utility, economy or good sense—a very wonderful achievement in the mid-nineteenth century.'[22] This appraisal suggests that the ecclesiologists, though persuasive in their arguments and apparently principled, were not always practical. Adam Fox, speaking of Neale's place in church history, concurs: 'Ecclesiology led to a comeliness in church within our own times which had not been seen for centuries, though it must be confessed that the path which led to this desirable end was strewn with the products of ignorance, error and want of taste.'[23]

Failed endeavours on the part of the Camdenians may be attributed to youth, inexperience, or unwillingness to embrace ideas other than their own. The excitement of the Anglo-Catholic revival may in some cases have led Neale and his friends to hasty action. In fact, Neale was noted for his ability to put ideas to work. Fox explains:

He was amazingly quick off the mark and would hit upon something new and have the scheme or the book underway in no time; he would be carrying on several activities and conducting several exacting correspondences side by side, and day by day. He was doing all at once things which other people could only do one at a time.... His distinction consisted in having a great many ideas and the impetuous energy, and the needful equipment, to set about to convert the ideas into realities.[24]

[21] G. Rowell, *The Vision Glorious* (Oxford, 1983), 104.
[22] K. M. Clark, *The Gothic Revival* (London, 1928), 226.
[23] A. Fox, 'Keble and Neale', *Hymn Society of Great Britain and Ireland Bulletin*, 6/5 (no. 107) (Sept. 1966), 89. [24] Ibid., 88–9.

Although Neale achieved prominence during his undergraduate years through his ecclesiological endeavours, he was less successful in his academic pursuits. He was acknowledged to be one of the most brilliant classical scholars of his year, but he was very weak in mathematics, and consequently failed the tripos. As a result he was unable to obtain a first class degree, and had to settle, in 1840, for a pass.

In 1841 Neale was made a deacon, and through the efforts of a friend was offered the post of assistant tutor and chaplain at Downing College. Wishing to remain in Cambridge to continue his work for the Camden Society, he accepted the post. To his dismay, however, he did not find it congenial. He was unable to induce the Master and Fellows to attend chapel themselves or to counsel others to do so. After only three weeks he resigned, intimating to Boyce: 'I have made up my mind to take the first suitable curacy that offers, without exercising any choice in the matter.'[25] By the end of the year he was offered a temporary curacy at St Nicholas's, Guildford.

Neale seems to have been happy at Guildford, where he continued to promote his High Church principles. He recorded his sentiments in his journal:

Read some bitter attacks on the good cause [ecclesiology] and could not help thinking—with reference to them—as I walked down the hill, the white tower of my Church at the bottom, glittering in the hazy sunshine, the bell ringing pleasantly for Vespers, and the little congregation going in by twos and threes, how applicable, in spite of all they say of us, are Abijah's words, 'But as for us, the Lord is our God, and we have not forsaken him.' (NJ 1.2.42)

The rector of St Nicholas's, William Pearson, allowed Neale a free hand in the conduct of services and even in the modification of church furnishings. Neale saw this as a personal victory, and was delighted that at last he was being allowed, in his own small way, to put into practice what he had previously only advocated for others through his Camdenian publications.

Others in positions of authority, however, were not as indulgent as Pearson. In February 1842, less than a month after

[25] Letter to Boyce, dated 26 Aug. 1841; quoted in Sr. Miriam, 292.

Neale took up his duties, a letter from Charles Richard Sumner (1790–1874), Bishop of Winchester, informed Neale that his licence had been refused. Neale saw this action as 'a complete destroyer of all the fine prospects I was fond of imagining for myself in this place' (NJ 2.2.42). Bishop Sumner was an Evangelical, who disliked any signs of Tractarianism; he considered Neale and his ecclesiological innovations a danger to his diocese, and Neale had no choice but to leave Guildford.

After being ordained priest in May 1842, Neale accepted the small living of Crawley, in Sussex. Seemingly unperturbed by recent experiences, he was determined to bring about change in this parish as well. He notes on his first Sunday that the parishioners 'seemed to take to the Bidding Prayer very naturally, and were not surprised at the Prayer for the Church Militant'. In the evening, however, things did not go quite as smoothly: 'In the middle of the service judge to my horror when the Churchwarden, wanting to open the east window, got up on the Altar! Really the Protestantism of the people with respect to that is dreadful.'[26] Neale had great plans for liturgical and architectural reform in the parish; however, after only two months his health broke down. The doctor's diagnosis, according to Webb, was that Neale had 'decided, but mild, symptoms of consumption' (BWJ 27.6.42). He was forced to resign, before he had even been instituted to the benefice. It was a severe blow to him, for he dearly cherished the idea of becoming a parish priest. But his dream was not to be fulfilled; and he was never able to undertake such work again.

Neale left Crawley at the beginning of July 1842. Later the same month he married Sarah Norman Webster, to whom he had been engaged since March.[27] She was a constant support to him, and bore him five children: Agnes (born 1844), Vincent (1846), Mary (1848), Katherine (1850), and Margaret (1853). Owing to the precariousness of Neale's health, the couple stayed for a time with Neale's mother in Brighton. It was at this time that, aided by Webb, he undertook the translation

---

[26] M. S. Lawson (ed.), *Letters of John Mason Neale, D.D.* (London, 1910), 36–7 (hereafter *Letters*); to Sarah Webster, dated 29 May 1842.

[27] Even this occasion was overshadowed by disappointment: Neale, ever the ecclesiastical innovator, wished to have a nuptial Eucharist (which was unusual in those days); but the Bishop refused permission.

of the first book of Durandus's *Rationale Divinorum Officiorum*.

By autumn Neale's condition had improved but little; the couple therefore moved to Penzance, where the winter climate was mild. It was there, with ample time on his hands, that he began his literary exploits in earnest, working on a number of projects simultaneously. He wrote a book of *Hymns for Children*; *Songs and Ballads for the People*; *Herbert Tresham* a tale of the Cavaliers and Roundheads; *Agnes de Tracy*, a tale of the times of St Thomas of Canterbury; and *Hierologus*, which purported to be a novel, but was really a thinly disguised ecclesiological discourse.

By the beginning of the new year Neale's health had still not improved. In a letter of 10 January 1843, he wrote: 'To please my wife I saw Dr Montgomery, the first physician here, and his opinion is that, if I wish to prolong my life, I must go to Madeira; but that, going there, I shall only prolong it.'[28] They therefore decided to spend the rest of the winter in Madeira, and left England that February.

On arrival in Funchal, Neale took rooms opposite the cathedral, and arranged to have unlimited access to its library. He occupied himself by writing for the *Ecclesiologist* about the Madeiran churches and by learning Portuguese. He also met the French historian and antiquary Charles Montalembert, who was staying on the island at the time. The latter was of especial interest to Neale because he had a deep interest in the Gothic Revival and was trying to effect in France what the Camdenians were doing in England. Neale said, in a letter to Webb, that he and Montalembert 'seem to have taken to each other';[29] but they later fell out over the Frenchman's ultramontane pronouncements and his derision of the Anglo-Catholic revival.

Neale returned to England in June 1843, after a stopover in Spain. He spent most of the summer at his mother's house in Bristol. He was engaged in various literary undertakings, including *Shepperton Manor*, a novel set near his boyhood home; a collection of *Hymns for the Sick*, which his own fragile

---

[28] Quoted in Towle, 76.
[29] *Letters*, 54; dated 7 Apr. 1843, from Santa Luzia.

condition motivated him to write; and *A History of the Holy Eastern Church*, the plan for which he conceived at this time, and the writing of which was to occupy him on and off for the rest of his life. Some idea of the perceived immensity of the task may be gained from an entry in Neale's journal: 'This Greek History almost terrifies me; the great possibility of my never finishing it; the difficulty and hugeness of the task. But I know not that one could, if called away, be employed in a more generally useful task' (NJ 28.8.43). With the help of Webb and others he collected some of the research material necessary for the project. With this task completed, he set off for Madeira again in October 1843.

On this second trip to the island Neale was primarily occupied with the writing of *The Patriarchate of Alexandria*, the first portion of the 'Greek History', as he called it. His aim was to educate the British public about a communion regarding which they were almost completely ignorant. At the same time, in pursuit of Anglican Church reform, he wished to demonstrate that the Eastern Church—a branch of the Catholic Church which seemed immutable throughout her history—could set an example to which the Church of England would do well to aspire. His discussion embodied history, theology, liturgy, ritual, symbolism, mysticism, and architecture. Concerning this last point he wrote excitedly to Webb from Santa Luzia: 'I am in hopes in the section of the Introductory Essay on the Architectural differences between the Eastern and Western Churches, to strike out something new, and to prove to a dead certainty that our [that is, the ecclesiologists'] views on the final development of architecture are most certainly true.'[30] Throughout his writings on the Eastern Church, Neale kept in mind—and expounded—the various connections he perceived between the Anglican and Orthodox communions. Like his ecclesiological writings, his Eastern works bear his peculiar stamp, and on occasion reveal his tendency towards misrepresentation.

Neale returned to England in early June 1844. Most of the summer was spent in Brighton. The increased financial pressure placed on him by an expanding family forced him to devote less time to his *History of the Holy Eastern Church*

---

[30] *Letters*, 64; dated 27 Nov. 1843.

Introduction: The Life of J. M. Neale

(which he always considered the most important of his writings) and more to immediately remunerative works, such as *Triumphs of the Cross*, a series of tales of Christian heroism, and *English History for Children*, both of which were published in the Juvenile Englishman's Library series.

In October 1844, Neale set out with his family on their last voyage to Madeira. He had two major occupations during this visit: composing tales from Christian history for children and, through heated correspondence, bolstering the faith of his friend Webb in the face of Newman's impending secession from the Anglican Church. On 10 November 1844, Webb wrote to Neale: 'I fancy the last week has been one of unparalleled excitement and fear amongst us Anglo-Catholicks [sic] here. Rumours from many different, and those most authoritative, quarters had been about to the effect that Newman had at last determined to secede. . . . I do not think I am prepared to follow him *now*; but I should feel despair for any revival in our Communion.'[31] Neale quickly replied, in an attempt to reassure his friend: 'I hope and believe that Newman will not leave us; but I should not despair if he did. My sheet anchor of hope for the English Church is, that you cannot point out a single instance of an heretical or schismatical body which after apparent death awoke to life.'[32]

Neale managed to sustain Webb's faith. The exchange points to Neale's unshaken confidence in the Church of England; he remained perfectly calm and unperturbed throughout the crisis. He understood that there were certain aspects of Anglican doctrine and practice which were badly in need of reform, and he set himself the task of effecting the changes which he saw as vital to the survival of his Church.[33]

Neale returned to England in June 1845. His time abroad

---

[31] Quoted in *Letters*, 77–8; from Cambridge.
[32] *Letters*, 80; dated 26 Nov. 1844, from Madeira.
[33] Neale is generally thought of today as a Tractarian, or at least as having Tractarian leanings. He is obviously High Church, but in an antiquarian, picturesque mode. His High Churchmanship is associated with the ecclesiological and liturgical practices of the Church, and he was unsympathetic to Newman's doctrinal emphasis. Neale was especially antagonistic towards the dialectical, doctrinal arguments put forward by Newman to justify his secession in 1845. Neale chastised Newman for abandoning the Church of England, and saw the move as displaying weakness of character. For Neale's thoughts on Newman's conversion and on the *Apologia* and *Essay on Development*, see Towle, 121–6, and Sr. Miriam, 76–90.

had been beneficial not only to his health, but also to his finances: his writings now brought in enough money that he no longer depended on his mother for support. The ecclesiologists, however, were doing less well as a group in their exploits. Their publications had attracted the attention of Francis Close (1797–1882), a disciple of Simeon, who became incumbent of Cheltenham and later Dean of Carlisle; he was hostile to Tractarians and Roman Catholics, and acquired a reputation for running the affairs of his town along the lines of Calvin's Geneva.[34] He was also anti-ecclesiologist, and started a war of words which ended in the dissolution in 1845 of the Cambridge Camden Society as originally constituted.[35]

The root of Close's complaint was that the ecclesiologists advocated extreme modifications to ecclesiastical ritual and ornament, which he saw as Romanist leanings; consequently, he published *The 'Restoration of Churches' is a Restoration of Popery: Proved and Illustrated from the Authenticated Publications of the 'Cambridge Camden Society'* (1845). Based on a sermon delivered at Cheltenham, the text began by explaining the close association which Close believed to exist between the ecclesiologists and the Tractarians: 'As Romanism is taught *Analytically* at Oxford, it is taught *Artistically* at Cambridge,—that it is inculcated theoretically, in tracts, at one university, and it is sculptured, painted, and *graven* at the other.'

Close maintained that 'there is no need of mystic emblems, and mysterious signs, whereby a reconciled God in Christ Jesus may communicate with his people', and he pointed to what he considered 'sickening details' of church restoration, taken primarily from the pages of the *Ecclesiologist*. He quoted from Camdenian calls for the erection of rood-screens, piscinae, sedilia, and hagioscopes,[36] in an effort to show that these modifications were part of an attempt to turn Protestant churches into 'Popish Mass-houses'. He lamented: 'Oh, *Alma*

---

[34] See E. Jay (ed.), *The Evangelical and Oxford Movements* (Cambridge, 1983), 43.

[35] The Society was reorganized as 'The Ecclesiological (Late Cambridge Camden) Society', with headquarters in London.

[36] A hagioscope, as Close defines it, is a hole cut in the wall of the chancel to enable those in the side aisle to observe the priest at the high altar.

Mater Cantabrigia! how thou art fallen, when your fellows of colleges, students, and divines, in this enlightened age, can foster such childish superstitions, and prop them up with such unhallowed corruptions of God's word!'[37]

The success of Close's campaign in temporarily dissolving the Camden Society revealed some of the dangers resulting from perceived excesses in ritualism and adornment, and provided Neale with evidence of what such accusations could do —particularly when linked with charges of Romanism—to damage his work. Yet the Camdenians' mission did not falter; the *Ecclesiologist* continued to be published, and through it and other ecclesiological guides, their mark was left on nineteenth-century church building and adornment.

Although Neale's writings provided him with some income, he was still in need of a permanent position. By January 1846 he had found what he was looking for, and wrote excitedly to Webb: 'I must tell you I have a likelihood of getting a little piece of "preferment", such as it is; but it would suit me. It is the Wardenship of *Sackville College*, East Grinstead—a Caroline foundation with Chapel and Refectory, wretchedly out of order, but capable (I hear) of great things. The Warden's house is in the College, the value £28.'[38] Though previous wardens of this almshouse had not usually been clergymen, Neale was appointed to the post, taking up his duties in May 1846. It suited him well; because of his delicate health, the work of ministering to twelve pensioners and twelve probationers would not prove too taxing, and he would have enough time for his own writing. Moreover, his patron, the fifth Earl De La Warr, was indulgent, and gave Neale a free hand in conducting College affairs.

Neale's first priority was to renovate the chapel, which had fallen into disrepair. This he did according to Camdenian principles: he set up a rood-screen and a vested altar adorned with a cross and candlesticks. Such innovations were seen as evidence of Romanist practice in many mid-nineteenth-century Anglican circles, and were bound to cause problems.

The trouble started in February 1847, when Thomas Palmer

[37] F. Close, *The 'Restoration of Churches' is the Restoration of Popery* (London, 1845), 4, 7, 17, 18, 36.
[38] *Letters*, 95; dated 6 Jan. 1846, from Reigate.

Hutton, an Evangelical preacher who had heard about the irregular furnishings, called on Neale to examine the chapel for himself. On seeing the rood-screen, he told Neale that he would write to the Bishop of Chichester in an effort to have it removed. Hutton's letter proved to be the undoing of Neale, whose only fault was that he was an eager young advocate of a movement which had as its aim a return to pre-Reformation English Church doctrine and a revival of material aids to faith.

Bishop Ashurst Gilbert Turner had been nominated to the see of Chichester in 1842. Prior to this appointment he had been Principal of Brasenose College, Oxford, a High Churchman, and an admirer of Newman and the Tractarian Movement. But by the time he became Bishop, he was opposed to the movement to catholicize England. He tried to steer a middle course, but came down heavily on what he considered to be extreme practices. In his eyes, the reforms instituted by Neale at Sackville College fell into this category.

In May 1847, he visited East Grinstead, and asked to see the College chapel. He was extremely displeased with the alterations Neale had made, and prohibited him from celebrating Divine Service and from exercising clerical functions in the diocese of Chichester. He particularly admonished Neale for the 'frippery with which ... [he had] transformed the simplicity at Sackville College into an imitation of the degrading superstitions of an erroneous Church', and even referred to Neale's innovations as 'spiritual haberdashery'.[39]

Neale was distraught by the censure. After consultation with Earl De La Warr, he resolved to continue to officiate in the College chapel but to abstain from conducting services elsewhere in the diocese. The Bishop took this decision to mean that the prohibition was not being obeyed, and brought the case before the Court of Arches in November 1847. The judgment went against Neale; it was decided that he had committed an ecclesiastical offence by administering the Sacrament and saying the Divine Office without a licence from Turner. He was ordered not to officiate in future without the authority of the Bishop. On top of this distressing verdict, Neale was required to pay the cost of the proceedings. During

---

[39] Quoted in Sr. Miriam, 347a, 351a.

Introduction: The Life of J. M. Neale

the next few years various attempts were made to persuade the Bishop either to state the charge on which the prohibition was founded or to withdraw it. However, the Bishop remained silent.

The Bishop of Chichester's prohibition was not formally lifted until 1863; thus for more than fifteen years Neale was prevented from exercising his priestly function at Sackville College. The fact that he could not legally minister to his elderly group of inmates troubled him deeply; yet he never abandoned them, even when in 1850 he was offered the Deanery of the new Episcopal cathedral in Perth, Scotland, the only opportunity for preferment ever to come his way.[40] The reason Neale gave for staying in East Grinstead was that he had important work to do in his own Church of England.[41]

His attachment to the Church of his birth was strengthened in 1850 by the outcome of the Gorham judgment. In the course of this great ecclesiastical lawsuit (1847–50) the Judicial Committee of the Privy Council declared the High Church understanding of baptismal regeneration an open question. The decision gave great offence to High Churchmen, including Neale, who were appalled by the effect that a secular decision was able to have on the truth preached in the Church

---

[40] For a fuller consideration of this subject, see L. B. Litvack, 'All for Love', *Church of England Historical Society Journal*, 32/1 (Mar. 1987), 5–21.

[41] It should be noted that despite the Bishop's prohibition, Neale did minister to the inmates of Sackville College. While he refrained from conducting services in the chapel, he certainly celebrated Holy Communion for them privately. In an unpublished letter to Eleanor Towle (Neale's biographer), Neale's third child, Mary Sackville Lawson, describes how her father treated Gilbert's prohibition: 'My father obeyed strictly, and as I believe not only at first, but until the inhibition was removed, the Bishop's extraordinary inhibition *in every church* of the diocese and *in Sackville College*, though that was, as many thought, outside the Bishop's jurisdiction. He read prayers and sermons as any lay reader might do, but he never exercised any priestly function there, i.e. he never celebrated, nor read the absolution, nor even wore a surplice or stole till after the inhibition was formally removed (I can remember quite well his first appearing there in surplice and stole and reading the absolution). But as regards S. Margaret's Oratory he undoubtedly took no notice of the Bishop's inhibition.... The Bishop knew he was the Sisters' Chaplain; he knew they did not attend the parish church; he tacitly therefore excepted them from the former sentence, else why did he not fulminate fresh interdicts? I think he was already beginning to regret his action, and waited to see whether this movement were of God or not. (Poor Bishop Gilbert! He will be remembered in the history of his diocese as the man who muzzled one of its greatest men)' (quoted in Lough, *John Mason Neale*, 82).

formularies.[42] He prepared a schedule, in which he declared that 'the Catholic Church from the beginning has ever held that regeneration is conferred in and by Baptism, and that alone' and 'that the English Church, as a branch of the Church Catholic, has ever taught and held the same doctrine in her Offices, in her Catechism, in her Articles'. The document ended with a declaration that if Convocation were to confirm the Privy Council decision, then the signatories would be compelled to regard the Church of England as 'no longer an orthodox branch of the Church of Christ and would leave her accordingly'.[43] Neale himself remained firm; yet he feared that the Gorham judgment would have a detrimental effect on his fellow Anglicans—even more so than Newman's secession. Indeed, it proved the key factor for some prominent Anglicans in their decision to embrace Roman Catholicism, among them Henry Manning (later Archbishop of Westminster) and his friend Robert Wilberforce. As a countermeasure, Neale wrote a pamphlet entitled *A Few Words of Hope on the Present Crisis of the English Church*, in which he assured his readers that there was no cause for despair. His words had a stabilizing influence, and kept many from going over to Rome.

The anxiety passed, and Neale settled down to continue his writing. He resumed work on his *History of the Holy Eastern Church*, publishing a two-volume *General Introduction* in 1850. He also issued more stories from church history for children. At the same time, he began to turn in earnest to hymn writing. It is for his efforts in this field that he has been —and probably will be—chiefly remembered.

Neale wished to extend to another sphere the debate over church furnishings. The various ecclesiological controversies were viewed by some as arcane; but by carrying them over into hymnology, Neale provided a verbal example of this debate in action, seeking to reassert values which were associated with an older—and to some extent more seemly—kind of writing about religion, while maintaining some relevance to an age in which informality and experiment were striking features of literary output. His desire to compose hymns for use

---

[42] For a full account of the Gorham case, see J. C. S. Nias, *Gorham and the Bishop of Exeter* (London, 1951), and J. B. Mozley, *A Review of the Baptismal Controversy* (London, 1862). [43] Quoted in Towle, 177–8.

in the Anglican Church may have come about in the following way. His theology was a by-product of Tractarianism, acquired through a conversion from Evangelicalism while at Cambridge. The Oxford Movement had its greatest appeal not so much in the revolutionizing of Anglican doctrine as in the conduct of pastoral affairs and in changing the perceptions of laymen about the clergy. Neale wanted something more. The Gorham judgment provided the impetus for Neale's belief that the Church of England was about to commit itself to heresy; perhaps he saw himself as the saviour of his Church. He knew, both from his Evangelical upbringing and his familiarity with the state of affairs in other Christian communions, that hymn singing had a popular appeal. Here was an easily accessible, popular method of instilling what he considered to be 'right' Christian doctrine into Anglicans who had been, he thought, isolated by the Establishment. He sought to recover the liturgical disciplines—and with them the hymnody—of the Middle Ages. Neale hoped that the Anglican Church at large would come to appreciate a form of worship which up until his time had been used by Evangelicals, Broad Church, and Dissenters with great effect.[44]

While he did not discount original compositions—some of Neale's own famous hymns had no antecedents—he considered the best hymns to be either translations of, or modelled on, those written in former times; translations of Greek and Latin hymns of old would bring into new prominence the principles and emotions of primitive and medieval Christianity, thus unearthing the ancient 'treasures' which were so central to Neale's particular brand of Anglicanism. Of Neale's translations J. H. Overton says:

It is in this species of composition that Dr Neale's success was pre-eminent, one might almost say unique. He had all the qualifications of a good translator. He was not only an excellent classical scholar in the ordinary sense of the term, but he was also positively steeped in mediaeval Latin. ... Dr Neale's exquisite ear for melody prevented him from spoiling the rhythm by too servile an imitation of the

---

[44] Cf. R. L. Gales, 'A Tractarian Minstrel', which describes Neale rather fancifully as a 'beautiful butterfly bursting from the chrysalis', that state into which he had been transformed by the Oxford Movement (in *Studies in Arcady, and Other Essays from a Country Parsonage*, 2nd ser. (London, 1912), 335).

original; while the spiritedness which is a marked feature of all his poetry preserved that spring and dash which is so often wanting in a translation.[45]

It is for his Latin and Greek hymn translations that Neale is chiefly remembered today. His 'fatal facility of versifying', as Webb said,[46] resulted in the production of over 400 hymns, sequences, and carols, many of which can be found in modern hymnaries and can be heard sung in churches today. There are frequent entries in his journal concerning translations on which he was working. In 1851, a year of great productivity, he noted: 'In the coach, turned "*Sancte Dei Preciose*"' (NJ 11.2.51); 'At night turned "*Christe Salvator Omnium*"' (NJ 22.2.51). The hymns were 'turned' into English quickly and with ease. Towle notes that Neale's ability as a translator developed to such an extent that when in later years he read the lesson to the Sisters of St Margaret in church, he would translate aloud from the Latin in the Vulgate before him into English 'without the slightest hesitation'.[47]

Another often quoted instance of Neale's translating skills dates from 1856, when John Keble was engaged in compiling a hymn-book with the Bishop of Salisbury, and Neale was invited to assist them. He called on Keble, and during the visit the latter left the room to look for some papers, and was unexpectedly detained. When he returned, Neale observed with a touch of reproach that he had always understood his friend's *The Christian Year* to be entirely original. Keble insisted that it certainly was. 'Then how do you explain this?,' said Neale, placing before him a Latin version of one of his hymns. Keble professed himself utterly confounded, and could only protest in distressed astonishment that he had never seen the original before. After a few minutes Neale relieved Keble's anxiety by owning that he had 'turned' the English into Latin in Keble's absence.[48]

Although nineteenth-century Anglican hymn-writers wished to develop the technique of Watts and Wesley for their own purposes—that is, to produce dogmatic statements, in popular language, of the faith as they now saw it—they looked first to

[45] Entry on J. M. Neale in J. Julian (ed.), *A Dictionary of Hymnology* (London, 1907), 787.
[46] *Letters*, 124; dated 1 Sept. 1849, from Brasted, Sevenoaks.
[47] Towle, 212.   [48] Towle, 213.

Introduction: The Life of J. M. Neale

Latin hymns to fashion a new image of hymnody. Neale began this process in 1851, publishing a collection of Latin hymns, entitled *Hymni Ecclesiae* in the original, which made many compositions easily accessible for the first time.[49] This book did not receive much attention, however; nor did its companion volume, *Sequentias ex Missalibus Germanicis, Anglicis, Gallicis, aliisque medii aevi collectae*, published a year later. The Victorians seemed to be much more interested in vernacular hymns to complement the liturgy. Neale responded to this desire, setting to work immediately and compiling a number of collections simultaneously.[50] The first to appear was a collection of hymn translations from Latin entitled *Mediaeval Hymns and Sequences*. Among the most famous pieces in this volume were 'Blessed City Heavenly Salem', 'Christ is made the sure foundation', 'All glory, laud and honour', and 'The Royal Banners forward go'. Overton notes that with this volume Neale was the first to introduce to English readers sequences, the graduals or antiphons sung between the Epistle and the Gospel in the liturgy, ending on festal days with the word 'Alleluia'.[51] This was the first opportunity for Neale to put his hymnological principles to the test. He was not only eager, but excited about the prospect of bringing to the attention of Victorian readers the hymns of the medieval authors he so revered:

It is a magnificent thing to pass along the far-stretching vista of hymns from the sublime self-containedness of S. Ambrose to the more fervid inspiration of S. Gregory, the exquisite typology of Venantius Fortunatus, the lovely painting of S. Peter Damiani, the crystal-like simplicity of S. Notker, the scriptural calm of Godescalus, the subjective loveliness of S. Bernard, till all culminate in the full blaze of glory which surrounds Adam of S. Victor, the greatest of them all.[52]

---

[49] These hymns include 'A qui morte te suscitans', 'Mundo novum Jus dicere', and 'Viri venerabiles sacerdotes dei'. Julian notes that Neale was the only modern source for these three hymns; the others in *Hymni Ecclesiae* appeared in at least one other collection (*Dictionary of Hymnology*, 656–62).
[50] A letter to Webb of 29 Mar. 1851 reveals that Neale was working on no less than 5 collections at once (quoted in Sr. Miriam, 203b–4b).
[51] Julian (ed.), *Dictionary of Hymnology*, 1041.
[52] Preface to 2nd edn. of *Mediaeval Hymns and Sequences*, in M. S. Lawson (ed.), *Collected Hymns, Sequences and Carols of John Mason Neale* (London, 1914), 5.

The next collection of hymns to appear was a co-operative effort by the members of the Ecclesiological Society entitled *The Hymnal Noted*. All the hymns in this book were translations of Latin hymns, and all the music was plainchant, with each hymn being set to its traditional melody—or, as Neale called it, the melody 'of the best books, and the most correct churches'[53]—by Thomas Helmore (1811–90), Chaplain-in-Ordinary to Queen Victoria and compiler of *The Psalter Noted* (1849), who became a close friend of Neale's. He was one of the original compilers of *Hymns Ancient and Modern* and the foremost Anglican exponent of Gregorian chant. He met Neale in the late 1840s through Dr W. H. Mill, Neale's close friend and the father-in-law of Webb. On a Sunday at Webb's home in Brasted, where Frederick Helmore and Mill were guests, Mrs Webb played some old Latin hymn melodies. Mill joined in the singing, and before long remarked that it was a shame that these old hymns were not available to all. 'I have it! I have it!', he cried; 'Helmore, here's your brother coming down in a few weeks to Withyham. You must take him over and introduce him to Mason Neale. We'll bring them together! We'll make Neale do the hymns, and your brother shall arrange the music!' The arrangements were made, and Helmore and the Chapel Royal choirboys who were participating in the choral festival at Withyham marched to East Grinstead, where the project was planned.[54] Since Neale, Mill, and Webb were leaders of the Ecclesiological Society, they were able to present a strong case to the Executive Board, and persuaded them to sponsor the project. Helmore was made a member of the Society in 1849, and joined the Music Committee in 1850. *The Hymnal Noted*, taking its title from Helmore's *Psalter Noted*, was published in two parts in 1851 and 1854.

In the *Ecclesiologist* in 1851 Neale summarized the process involved in compiling *The Hymnal Noted*:

When the attention of the Ecclesiological Society was first turned to the subject of Hymnology, we could only act on the same principles

---

[53] J. M. Neale, 'Proposal for a Noted Hymnal and an Explanation of the Gregorian Note', *Ecclesiologist*, 11 (1850), 175.

[54] These events are recounted by F. Helmore in his sentimental tribute to his brother, *Memoir of the Rev. Thomas Helmore, M.A.* (London, 1891), 65–7.

which we have endeavoured to carry out in all things, that, if we were Catholics in the first place, we were English Catholics in the second. We felt that we could look for our hymns to only one source, the offices,—or rather to use the proper old, as well as modern word,— the *services* of the elder English Church. And of the various uses of that Church, the ritual of Sarum had so incomparably the most authority, that its hymns, we felt, were to be regarded as our especial inheritance.[55]

He believed that *The Hymnal Noted* was the first attempt by Anglicans to produce a collection of indigenous English hymns in the vernacular. He said: 'No translation has yet appeared of our own hymns, and it is with our own hymns that we are concerned.'[56] Of the 105 hymns in the collection, 94 were by Neale.

Neale wanted to improve the quality of English hymnody and to provide his Church with a body of hymns which would meet with the approval of his superiors and which her congregants could call their own. Perhaps, as his daughter suggests, there was a wider aim in his method:

Preserving ... the exact measure of the original may at first glance give an impression of monotony in the hymns ... but the gain is immense, as those of us realize who—strangers in some foreign cathedral—are enabled to join in the *Pange lingua,* Urbs Beata, Vexilla Regis, or some other hymn made familiar to us through [Neale's] translations, and who, therefore, amidst much that is foreign and unfamiliar, recognise in the old Latin hymns the 'Lord's Song in a strange land.' Such recognition leads to a realisation of the oneness of the Church Catholic both here and now, and must make for unity.[57]

Neale himself did not make this claim for desired unity through the Latin hymns; but in light of the translations he produced, there is perhaps some relevance to his daughter's observations.

---

[55] Neale, 'On the History of Hymnology', *Ecclesiologist*, 12 (1851), 241. 'Sarum' originally referred to the medieval modification of the Roman Rite in use at Salisbury Cathedral. In the later Middle Ages the Sarum Rite was increasingly adopted by churches, until by the mid-15th cent. its use extended over most of England, Wales, and Ireland. The Sarum Rite also heavily influenced the Reformers in their choice of material for the first Book of Common Prayer published in 1549 (information from F. L. Cross and E. A. Livingstone (eds.), *The Oxford Dictionary of the Christian Church,* (Oxford, 1974), 1229).

[56] Neale, 'The Hymnal Noted', *Ecclesiologist*, 12 (1851), 11–12.

[57] Introduction to Lawson (ed.), *Collected Hymns*, p. vii.

The period 1850–5 was also when Neale wrote carols. Two collections appeared, *Carols for Christmastide* (1853) and *Carols for Eastertide* (1854); Neale was responsible for the words, Helmore for the music. In the preface to the former, Neale indicated that many of the carols were translations or adaptations from a rare book which had been brought to him from Sweden, *Piae Cantiones Ecclesiasticae et Scholasticae* (1582). His most famous carol, however, was 'Good King Wenceslas', an original composition based on a Bohemian legend.

From 1855 until his death in 1866 there was one other important activity to which Neale devoted his energies: the nurturing of a nursing sisterhood, the Society of St Margaret. Ever since the publication of his novel *Ayton Priory* in 1843, Neale had dreamed of a restoration of the religious life in the Anglican Church. He was not the first to put his ideas into practice. In 1845, under Dr Pusey's aegis, the first Anglican sisterhood was founded at Park Village West; two other communities were established, at Wantage and Davenport, in 1848; in 1851 the Sisters of Mercy at Clewer came into being.[58] Neale made a study of these communities and a number of others in France, in order to determine the shape and direction of the one he proposed to found. His aim, as he intimated to Webb, was to 'have a community of trained Sisters, ready to be sent out at the Superior's discretion *gratuitously* to any Parish Priest within a circuit (say) of twenty-five miles, that may need their services in nursing any of his people.'[59] Neale's plan differed significantly from those of the other founders of sisterhoods: while they were more concerned with penitentiaries, orphanages, and schools, Neale's was specifically conceived with the idea that it would devote its energies primarily to nursing the poor in their homes in the area surrounding East Grinstead.

Neale's charges, originally four in number, established themselves at Sackville College. After formal training (another of Neale's innovations) at Westminster Hospital, they began their work in earnest, very often at considerable risk to

---

[58] For more information on Anglican religious communities, see P. F. Anson, *The Call of the Cloister* (London, 1955), and A. M. Allchin, *The Silent Rebellion* (London, 1958).

[59] *Letters*, 234; dated 1 Feb. 1855, from Sackville College.

themselves. They were constantly exposed to diphtheria, typhus, and scarlet fever. Their work was truly heroic, and it is highly ironic that Bishop Turner of Chichester, despite his prohibition of Neale, publicly recognized the work of the St Margaret's sisters, and bestowed on them his blessing.

The future of the community looked bright. By 1857 there were nine sisters, and a small orphanage, established by Neale's sister in Brighton, was acquired. In the same year, however, the Lewes Riot took place. Emily Scobell (Sister Amy) died from scarlet fever, and left £400 to the community. Her father, an Evangelical clergyman, accused Neale and the sisterhood of putting pressure on his daughter to make the bequest and then engineering her death. At the funeral in Lewes, Neale and the sisters were attacked by a mob, incited by the father. This incident did significant damage to the good name of the sisterhood, and it was only through the Neale's extraordinary efforts that confidence was restored.

Although he came to Sackville College with the idea that life and work there would not prove overly taxing, the added responsibility of the sisterhood—and his writing on top of this—meant that he was pushed to the limit. He outlined his daily routine in a letter to Webb of 15 February 1858:

6:30 Rise
7 Litany, Holy Communion—S. Margaret's
9 Morning Prayers—Chapel
9:30 S. Margaret's (looking over correspondence; seeing any of the Sisters etc.)
10 Eastern History
12 Sext (Chapel), Eastern History
1:30 Dinner
2 Nones (Chapel), Letters
3 Nones (S. Margaret's), Commentary on Psalms
5:15 Vespers (S. Margaret's), Tea
6 Vespers (Chapel), Prepare for Class
6:45 Class (the Sisters)
     Compline (Confession, if any)
8 Story, or article, or accidental work
8:45 Supper
9:15 Matins (S. Margaret's)
10 Reading etc., till 11:30 or 12[60]

---

[60] Quoted in Lough, *John Mason Neale*, 115.

Neale followed this strict regime until the end of his life—and this despite being dogged by increasingly frequent illness. However, he felt himself to be the prime source of support for his sisterhood, and so pressed on with the work. The range of activities expanded: sisters were sent to many parts of England as word of their nursing skills spread; schools were established; houses of refuge for fallen women were opened; and in 1864, St Margaret's, Aberdeen, the first autonomous affiliated house, was founded.

Neale knew that his ill health would sooner or later debilitate him, and so he worked faster, increasing his literary output. In addition to works on liturgy, theology, history, and travel, he wrote novels (a total of ten from 1855 to 1866). He was fond of popular fiction, and among his favourite authors were Jane Austen, Dickens, Trollope, Harriet Martineau, George Eliot, and Charles Kingsley. When it came to finding inspiration for his own writing, though, he deemed the subjects and settings chosen by these novelists unsuitable. He kept those nearest and dearest to him (the sisters, his own children, and those in the orphanage) in mind in the conception of his contributions to fiction. By and large his stories were edifying, Christian tales, either taken from the annals of Church history or designed (as in the case of the allegory *The Two Huts*, 1856) to illustrate an essential Christian principle. Many of them were published in John Henry Parker's series of 'Tales Illustrating Church History'. Of all his productions, by far the most popular was *Theodora Phranza* (1853–4), which John Sutherland, in *The Longman Companion to Victorian Fiction*, describes as 'one of the few successful religious-historical novels of the century', because of its relevance to the Crimean War, in which Britain was involved at the time of writing.[61] Whether he set his tales in central Asia, Europe, Africa, or the Far East, the religious message was clearly emphasized.

As his hymns and other writings were gradually disseminated throughout Britain and beyond, his reputation grew. Because of his extensive knowledge of hymnody, particularly

---

[61] John Sutherland, *The Longman Companion to Victorian Fiction* (London, 1988), 457. In a personal letter to me, Prof. Sutherland has confirmed that it was the currency of Neale's novel which elicited this statement.

Introduction: The Life of J. M. Neale

in the field of translation, Neale's advice was sought by Henry Baker and others in the compilation of *Hymns Ancient and Modern* (trial edition 1860, first full edition 1861). Because of his liturgical, theological, and linguistic expertise, he also received a constant stream of letters, asking him to answer questions in these areas. He took great pains in replying to these queries, which earned him the reputation of a brilliant and dedicated scholar. Officially, there was little public recognition in Britain of his contributions to the life of the Church. In America, however, he was awarded an honorary doctorate in divinity by Trinity College, Hartford, Connecticut, in 1860.

In his last years Neale turned his attention more and more to the Eastern Church and the question of reunion, or at least the achievement of a better understanding between the Anglican and Orthodox communions. With this end in mind he published *Hymns of the Eastern Church* in 1862. These were translations and adaptations of Greek hymns, the most popular of which were 'The day of Resurrection', 'O happy band of pilgrims', and 'The day is past and over'. The year 1863 was also notable for the establishment, on Neale's initiative, of the Eastern Church Association, a society which continues today as the Anglican and Eastern Churches Association. This body had both missionary and ecumenical aims: the members wished to improve the condition of Eastern Christians through the influence of English public opinion and to educate their countrymen in the ways of the Orthodox Church, with a view to intercommunion.[62] Neale did not have much opportunity, however, to join in the work of the Association because of his failing health.

He became increasingly frail, but pressed on with his writing, working furiously on his two monumental works, the

---

[62] The aims of the society, as outlined in 1864, were as follows: 1. 'To inform the English public as to the state and position of the Eastern Christians, in order gradually to better their condition, through the influence of public opinion in England'; 2. 'To make known the doctrines and principles of the Anglican Church to the Christians in the East'; 3. 'To take advantage of all opportunities which the providence of God shall afford for intercommunion with the Orthodox Church, and also for friendly intercourse with the other ancient Churches of the East'; 4. 'To assist, as far as possible, the bishops of the Orthodox Church in their efforts to promote the spiritual welfare, and the education of their flocks' (*First Report of the Eastern Church Association, June 1866* (London, 1866)).

History of the Holy Eastern Church and the *Commentary on the Psalms* (the portions of each which Neale managed to complete were published posthumously by friends). In July 1865 the foundation-stone for the new St Margaret's Convent was laid. The architect was George Edmund Street, who built the complex in a neo-Gothic style. Neale never lived to see the buildings completed, but in his final days he asked to be taken in his wheelchair to the building site, so that he could observe the progress of the work.

On 6 August 1866 he died, aged 48, at Sackville College, and was buried in East Grinstead parish churchyard. During a career which spanned nearly thirty years, Neale had become a leading spirit in the Anglo-Catholic revival. Adam Fox muses on the lasting nature of his achievement: 'You can go to East Grinstead and see the convent; you can easily sing one of Neale's hymns; you can lay your finger on any ornamental object in the church furniture shop or on any kind of vesture in the church tailor's shop, and very likely you can trace it back to Neale.'[63] In all his endeavours it was the extraordinary energy and enthusiasm with which he undertook the task that ensured a lasting place for him in the annals and the ongoing life of the Anglican Church.

[63] Fox, 'Keble and Neale', 97.

PART I

Neale's Orthodox Consciousness

Chapter 1

Anglicans and the Eastern Church

NEALE's interest in the Eastern Church developed in the years following his departure from Guildford in 1842. The reasons for this interest—not only for Neale but for a significant number of mid-Victorian Anglican churchmen—have not been extensively explored. It seems strange that at a time when most Anglo-Catholics were turning their attention to Rome, Neale and others like him turned to the East.[1] A deeper understanding of this phenomenon will help to place Neale's activities in the larger context of nineteenth-century Anglo-Catholicism, where his influence is most apparent.

Anglican approaches to the Eastern Church in the early nineteenth century had been cautious and reserved. Overtures to the Russian Orthodox Church—which was the largest and, because of the favourable political and economic links which existed between Britain and Russia, most approachable of the Eastern communions—could not escape the Shadow cast by the case of the Nonjurors (1716–25). Although this episode occurred long before Neale's time, it is important contextually to a study of early Victorian contacts with the Eastern Church, because of the atmosphere of doubt and distrust of the English Church which it had created in the minds of the Orthodox.[2]

---

[1] The discussion among Anglo-Catholics about the Roman Church did not always lead to secession. As Newman said of his religious opinions in the period 1833–9, 'We had a real wish to co-operate with Rome in all lawful things, if she would let us, and if the rules of our own Church let us; and we thought there was no better way towards the restoration of doctrinal purity and unity' (*Apologia pro vita sua*, 47).

[2] Although the Nonjurors made their first appearance in 1688, it was not until 1716 that they entered into correspondence with the Orthodox Church. For this account I am indebted to G. Williams, *The Orthodox Church of the East in the Eighteenth Century* (London, 1868) and G. Florovsky, 'The Orthodox Churches and the Ecumenical Movement prior to 1910', in *A History of the Ecumenical Movement, 1517–1948*, ed. R. Rouse and S. C. Neill (London, 1967), 190–3.

The Nonjurors were Anglican bishops, priests, and laymen who seceded from the Anglican Church rather than take the required oaths of allegiance to William III and Mary, having already done so to James II. In consequence they suffered deprivation of their benefices. They then organized themselves into a Nonjuring Church, with Jeremy Collier (1650–1726) as the self-proclaimed 'Primus Anglo-Britanniae Episcopus'.[3] Considered schismatics by the Anglican Church, having no recognized titles for their bishops and only a scattered flock, the Nonjurors sought to regularize their position by a concordat with the Eastern Church.

An opportunity for contact arose in 1712. Arsenius, Metropolitan of Thebais, on a visit to England, was persuaded to carry memoranda to Peter the Great, the monarch who had intimated interest in the Nonjurors' plan for contact with the Orthodox Church, and to the Eastern patriarchs. In these documents Collier and his followers, professing themselves to be 'the Catholick remnant' in Britain, applied for official recognition and intercommunion; they supported their proposal with the text of a new Communion office, which was a combination of primitive liturgies and that of the Book of Common Prayer. Florovsky explains that the new liturgy was modelled on an Eastern pattern as the 'best proof and recommendation' of the Nonjurors' 'doctrinal orthodoxy'.[4] The idea of composing a new Communion rite did not, however, find favour with the Orthodox, who insisted on the exclusive use of their traditional liturgy.

In addition to the Communion office, the Nonjurors sent a list of doctrinal points for discussion, including the *Filioque* clause, purgatory, the invocation of saints, the Eucharist, the reverence of icons, and the gradations of the patriarchal thrones.[5] The synodal reply from the Eastern patriarchs was discouraging for the Nonjurors. The Orthodox maintained that their oriental faith was the only true one:

---

[3] Other notable Nonjurors were Nathaniel Spinckes, Henry Gandy, and two Scotsmen, Archibald Campbell and James Gadderar.

[4] Florovsky, 'Orthodox Church', 191.

[5] It should be noted that, theologically, the Nonjurors—like Neale and the Tractarians—upheld the traditions of the Caroline divines, and through them of the Early Church Fathers (Florovsky, 'Orthodox Church', 190–1).

> We preserve the doctrine of the Lord uncorrupted, and firmly adhere to the Faith he delivered to us, and keep it free from blemish or diminution, as a Royal Treasure, and a monument of great price, neither adding any thing, nor taking any thing from it.
> . . . .
> We desire . . . to unite with you, O ye religious remnant of the Britons, . . . that both of us may have one Church, to the glory of God; and that those who for a long time have lost the Orthodox oriental and unspotted Faith may again recover it as formerly in the times of the first and second general Councils, and may be one with us of the Eastern Church.[6]

It is important to note that although the Nonjurors hoped for reunion negotiations, the replies they received from the Orthodox, however courteously phrased, expressed the immovable demand for unconditional submission, so that the Orthodox faith would become the only true one throughout Christendom; this position carried important implications for Anglican–Eastern relations in Neale's day.

By the 1720s the Eastern Church became suspicious of the authenticity of the Nonjurors; the latter proclaimed themselves 'the orthodox and Catholick remnant of the British Churches',[7] yet they never mentioned the Established Church in their correspondence, nor their own historical situation. The *coup de grâce* which brought about the downfall of the Nonjurors was delivered by William Wake (1657–1737) Archbishop of Canterbury, who, when he was informed of the correspondence—which had gone undetected for eight years—immediately wrote to the Patriarch of Jerusalem, exposing the Nonjurors as schismatics:

> Certain schismatical Priests of our Church have written to you under the fictitious titles of Archbishop and Bishops of the Anglican Church, and have sought your Communion with them; who, having neither place nor Church in these realms, have bent their efforts to deceive you who are ignorant of their schism.
> . . . .
> These are the men who have presumed to write to you. These are they, who have endeavoured to withdraw from the communion of

---

[6] Quoted in Williams, *Orthodox Church of the East*, 17, 32. The full texts of the Nonjurors' proposals and the Orthodox patriarchs' reply are found on pp. 4–11 and 15–67 resp.
[7] Williams, *Orthodox Church of the East*, 4.

our Church.... Of these men I pray and beseech your Reverence to beware.⁸

So ended the episode of the Nonjurors. Although the Orthodox were warned by Wake before any significant damage was done, the awkward position in which the Eastern patriarchs were placed as a result of their dealings with the Nonjurors subsequently put them on their guard in communicating—officially or unofficially—with the Anglican Church; and the caution, naturally enough, was reciprocated. This atmosphere persisted well into the nineteenth century.⁹

Initially, early nineteenth-century Anglican interest in the Orthodox Church was of a theological nature, evoked primarily by the Anglo-Catholics. In 1829 Newman preached a sermon entitled 'Submission to Church Authority', in which he said: 'We are the English Catholics; abroad are the Roman Catholics, some of whom are also among ourselves; elsewhere are the Greek Catholics.' This tripartite division of the Catholic Church has since become known as the 'Branch' theory.¹⁰ Newman and the other Tractarians claimed that this was the relation of the Anglican Church—which was the Catholic Church in England—to other Catholic Churches in other parts of Christendom. He explained further in the *Apologia*:

The Catholic Church in all lands had been one from the first for many centuries; then, various portions had followed their own way to the injury, but not to the destruction, whether of truth or of

---

⁸ Quoted in ibid., pp. lvii, lviii.
⁹ Langford notes that the approach of the Nonjurors was further complicated by the case of Cyril Loukaris (1572–1638), the patriarch of Constantinople whose life Neale chronicled in *A History of the Holy Eastern Church*. In his *Confession of Faith* Loukaris displayed Calvinist leanings, which the Orthodox Church authorities considered potentially dangerous. Therefore, according to Langford, the East was 'gravely suspicious of anything that sounded like Protestant ideas' at the time when the Nonjurors addressed their proposals to the Eastern patriarchs (H. W. Langford, 'The Non-Jurors and the Easten Orthodox', *Eastern Churches Review*, 1/2 (Autumn 1966), 125).
¹⁰ J. H. Newman, *Parochial and Plain Sermons* (London, 1875), iii. 191; quoted in G. Florovsky, *Aspects of Church History* (Belmont, Mass., 1975), 222. Florovsky adds that the origin of the theory is uncertain; but something very like it is found in Lancelot Andrewes' prayer for 'the Catholic Church—Eastern, Western, British' (*pro Ecclesia Catholica: Orientali, Occidentali, Britannica*).

charity. These portions or branches were mainly three:—the Greek, Latin and Anglican. Each of these inherited the early undivided Church *in solido* as its own possession. Each branch was identical with that early undivided Church, and in the unity of that Church it had unity with the other branches. The three branches agreed together in *all but* their later accidental errors. Some branches had retained in detail portions of Apostolical truth and usage, which the others had not; and these portions might be and should be again appropriated by the others which had let them slip.[11]

It was Newman's contention that although external communion had been broken, the Greek, Roman, and Anglican Churches were still linked by the invisible ties of a common, Catholic heritage. Schism resulted in the suspension of visible communication and intercommunion; however, unity could be restored once again by mutual recognition of the separated branches.

This theory, which retrospectively seems to be one of the most prominent features of Anglo-Catholic apologetics, became common to most members of the party only after 1845, under the pressures of Newman's secession. While it indicated a softening in the Tractarian attitude towards Rome, it meant a further departure from the Caroline divines' understanding of Anglicanism, which had already been shown—somewhat erroneously—by the writers of the *Tracts*, to hold as immutable the doctrine of episcopal succession: the view that the Church was tripartite effectively excluded—or 'unchurched', to use Cameron's expression[12]—not only English Dissenters but also Continental Protestants.

The branch theory as Newman explained it legitimized for High Churchmen the idea of making contact with the Orthodox. Interestingly, Newman—despite what he said in the *Apologia* and the importance he attached to the Greek Fathers—was not himself interested enough in the

---

[11] Newman, *Apologia pro vita sua*, 47.
[12] J. M. Cameron, 'John Henry Newman and the Tractarian, Movement', in *Nineteenth Century Religious Thought in the West*, ed. N. Smart, J. Clayton, P. Sherry, and S. Katz (3vols. Cambridge, 1985), ii. 75. Cameron adds that this theory had some amusing corollaries; e.g., it was seriously held by some Tractarians that Roman Catholics were schismatics in England but not in France.

Eastern Church to wish to form with her a relationship of any substance.[13]

Most of the early Tractarians did not identify the Church of the Fathers with the contemporary Eastern Church; in fact, they were prejudiced against her, as Florovsky notes: 'In spite of theoretical recognition, the Christian East was not yet recognized as an integral part of Christendom in practice. It was felt to comprise rather a "strange world". The prevailing impression in the Anglican circles was that the Churches in the East were decadent, backward, ignorant or somnolent, and "corrupt".'[14] Shaw supports this view, and believes that early Tractarian indifference to the Orthodox Church was the result of 'insufficient familiarity with the subject'.[15]

There were other Anglicans, however, who believed that what the branch theory required of them was a development of closer relations with the Orthodox Church. Rowell outlines the thinking behind this position and the hoped-for consequences.

It was the Tractarian understanding of the church, expressed classically in the so-called 'Branch' theory, which led Anglicans to recognize in the episcopal, but non-papal, character of the Orthodox Churches a pattern of church order to which they also adhered. As a result of that conviction, romantic at times as it undoubtedly was, the Orthodox came to be drawn into a wider ecumenical movement, and the treasures of Orthodox spirituality came to be shared with Christians in the West.[16]

Information about the Orthodox was becoming available to Anglicans; but renewing contact with the Eastern Church after the Nonjurors episode was a slow, cautious process. One of the first, prudent research expeditions was made in 1839 by

---

[13] The reasons behind Newman's unwillingness are unclear. Perhaps the ignorance, prejudices, and misunderstandings which existed between Anglicans and Orthodox at the time (partly as a result of the episode of the 18th-cent. Nonjurors) made the prospect of communication unattractive. Canon A. M. Allchin has tentatively suggested (in a private conversation) that Newman, through his reading of Gibbon's *The Decline and Fall of the Roman Empire*, had acquired a distaste for everything Byzantine, and that this antipathy contributed to his avoidance of the Eastern Church.

[14] Florovsky, *Aspects of Church History*, 224.

[15] P. E. Shaw, *The Early Tractarians and the Eastern Church* (Milwaukee, 1930), 76.   [16] Rowell, *Vision Glorious*, 217.

George Tomlinson, at the time secretary of SPCK and later Bishop of Gibraltar. He was sent to the Levant to report on the need for English religious publications in the East. He was given letters of introduction by the Archbishop of Canterbury and the Bishop of London, addressed to the 'Bishops of the Holy Eastern Church'. Tomlinson met the Patriarch of Constantinople, and in the course of his discussions outlined the character of the English Church, stressing its Catholic principles and its friendly disposition toward the 'Mother Church of the East'. He made sure to stress that he had no missionary objectives in visiting the Orthodox, but was interested only in fraternal intercourse. On his return to England he published *A Report of a Journey to the Levant* (1841).[17]

Although Tomlinson's trip had official sanction from the see of Canterbury, it was nothing more than a cordial visit. What did more to arouse interest in the East was growing disappointment on the part of some Anglicans in the Church of Rome as a storehouse of ancient Catholic faith. Among these was Pusey, who in 1840 wrote:

It will come as a painful question to many, and to some be a difficulty as to our Church (as they come to see the perfect unity of Antiquity), why are we in communion with no other Church except our own sisters and daughters?—We cannot have communion with Rome; why should we not with the *Orthodox* Greek Church? Would they reject us, or must we keep aloof? Certainly one should have thought that those who have not conformed with Rome would, practically, be glad to be strengthened by intercourse with us, and countenanced by us.[18]

Pusey recognized that renewed discourse with the Eastern Church could bear abundant fruit—not only in alleviating the problems experienced by the Church of England at the time, but also in furthering the ultimate cause of reunion. In 1841 he reiterated the idea:

Why should we ... direct our eyes to the Western Church alone, which, even if united in itself would remain sadly short of the Oneness

---

[17] Information on Tomlinson from Rouse and Neill (eds.), *History of the Ecumenical Movement*, 197.
[18] Quoted in H. P. Liddon, *The Life of Edward Bouverie Pusey, D.D.* (London, 1893–7), iii. 148–9.

she had in her best days, if she continued severed from the Eastern? After a long separation, in which we have not been known by name to the Eastern Church, much less our real character, God seems again to be opening to us ways of kindly intercourse with some portions of her, which must increase love, which will also, under God's blessing, help to restore the holiness and knowledge of her early years, and therewith, make her wish to understand us better, and be united with us.[19]

He pressed the idea of reunion further in an open letter to William Howley, the Archbishop of Canterbury in 1842, in which he said: 'This reopened intercourse with the East *is a crisis in the history of our Church*. It is a wave which may carry us onward, or, if we miss it, it may bruise us sorely and fall on us, instead of landing us on the shore. The union or disunion of the Church for centuries may depend upon the wisdom with which this providential opening is employed.'[20]

Reunion would have been a natural outcome of Tractarian theory; but because interest in the contemporary Eastern Church was growing rather slowly in the 1840s, very few of the early supporters wished to work for the unification of the Church. Nevertheless, ecumenism—not only with the East but also with Rome—must be seen as an integral part of the Catholic revival in Anglicanism. As Miller points out, 'The Oxford Movement was an ecumenical movement. Though this was not the conscious intention of its first members, the Movement's unequivocal assertion of the identity of Anglicanism with the continuing life of the universal Church provided a theological impetus for contact and dialogue with other churches of catholic Christendom.'[21] Thus the Tractarian vision of a unified Church was the motive force behind individual ecumenical contacts with the Christian East.

One of the first Tractarians to show sustained interest in

---

[19] E. B. Pusey, *The Articles Treated on in Tract 90 Reconsidered and their Interpretation Vindicated in a Letter to the Rev. R. W. Jelf, D.D.* (Oxford, 1841), 184.

[20] E. B. Pusey, *A Letter to His Grace the Archbishop of Canterbury, on some Circumstances Connected with the Present Crisis in the English Church* (Oxford, 1842), 118.

[21] E. C. Miller, jun., *Toward a Fuller Vision* (Wilton, 1984), 61. On Anglo-Catholic ecumenism, see Rowell, 'The Catholic Revival and Ecumenical Endeavour', ch. 9 in *Vision Glorious*, 188–219.

the Eastern Church was William Palmer (1811-79), Fellow of Magdalen College, Oxford, who has been described as an 'Ecclesiastical Don Quixote' and the 'Ulysses of the Tractarian Movement'.[22] As a result of a proposal made to the Russian heir apparent, Palmer visited Russia in 1840-1, in order to study Orthodox theology and liturgy, and, should he be found on examination by the Russian ecclesiastical authorities to have orthodoxy of faith and charity of mind, to be admitted to communion in the sacraments. This private venture, which did not carry Archbishop Howley's approval, was Palmer's ideal test for the branch theory as expounded by his Tractarian mentors.

Newman, who later edited Palmer's *Notes of a Visit to the Russian Church*, explained the impression the theory made on this enterprising Fellow of Magdalen:

William Palmer ... was one of those earnest-minded and devout men ... who, deeply convinced of the great truth that our Lord had instituted, and still acknowledges and protects, a visible Church—one, individual and integral—Catholic, as spread over the earth, Apostolic as co-eval with the Apostles of Christ, and Holy, as being the dispenser of His Word and Sacraments—considered it at present to exist in three main branches, or rather in a triple presence, the Latin, the Greek, and the Anglican, these three being one and the same Church, distinguishable from each other by secondary, fortuitous, and local, though important, characteristics. And, whereas the whole Church in its fulness was, as they believed, at once severally Anglican, Greek, and Latin, so in turn each one of those three was the whole Church ... there being no real difference between them except the external accident of place. ... Not to acknowledge the inevitable outcome of the initial idea of the Church, viz., that it was both everywhere and one, was bad logic, and to act in opposition to it was nothing short of setting up altar against altar, that is, the hideous sin of schism, and a sacrilege.

This I conceive to be the formal teaching of Anglicanism ... this

---

[22] Florovsky, *Aspects of Church History*, 227. For the biographical material on Palmer I am indebted to Miller's chapter on 'Orthodoxy and the Tractarians', in *Toward a Fuller Vision*, 61-102; Florovsky's 'Nineteenth-Century Ecumenism', in *Aspects of Church History*, 227-38; and Palmer's own *Notes of a Visit to the Russian Church in the Years 1840, 1841*, ed. J. H. Newman (London, 1882). William Palmer of Magdalen College should be clearly distinguished from William Palmer of Worcester College, who published the first systematic presentation of Tractarian doctrine as *A Treatise on the Church of Christ* in 1838.

is what Mr Palmer intensely believed and energetically acted on when he went to Russia.[23]

On arriving in Russia, Palmer quickly realized that the Russians did not sympathize with his view; his claim to be a member of the Catholic Church was met with astonishment. His hosts were staggered at the idea of one visible Church composed of three communions, which differed in doctrine and rites and in which two of them at least condemned and anathematized the others. They believed that the Eastern Church was the only true, orthodox Church, and saw the Anglican communion as a Protestant body. As for his desiring a communicant status in the Orthodox Church, Palmer was told that this was possible only if he would 'submit absolutely and without restriction to all the doctrine, discipline and ritual of the Orthodox (Eastern) Church'.[24]

Palmer's hopes were frustrated. The Russians could not accept his claim that unity of the Church could be preserved even when there was no longer unity in doctrine. They were also unsure as to what extent Palmer could be regarded as an authentic interpreter of the official teaching and position of the Anglican Church; in fact, he spoke for only one particular trend in Anglicanism.

On a personal level Palmer's mission ended in failure; yet he—and, in a broader sense, his successors—did reap certain benefits from this initial contact with the Russian Church. He had the opportunity to discuss theological matters with some of the major Russian ecclesiastics of the time; but many of them did not understand his position, and dismissed his request to receive the sacraments as frivolous. This was the attitude of Count Protasov, Chief Procurator of the Holy Governing Synod.[25] Protasov was a cavalry officer, whose chief

[23] Introduction to Palmer, *Notes of a Visit to the Russian Church*, pp. vi–vii. Newman was more critical of Palmer's denial of fundamentals than of the branch theory, a fact difficult to reconcile with Newman's own doctrine of the *via media*.

[24] Palmer, *Notes of a Visit to the Russian Church*, 415.

[25] The Holy Governing Synod was formed in 1721 by Peter the Great as an alternative to the Moscow patriarchate. It was composed of the three metropolitans (of Kiev, Moscow, and St Petersburg) and of other bishops appointed for fixed periods by the Tsar. In 1722 Peter created the office of Chief Procurator, who was to be a lay official, with a large bureaucracy under him, reaching down to the full-time lay secretaries of the episcopal consistories. See H. Seton-Watson, *The Russian Empire*, 1801–1917 (Oxford, 1967), 34.

aim seems to have been to serve the Russian empire, relegating the Church to a distinctly secondary place. During his time in office the name of the Orthodox Church officially became 'The Department of the Orthodox Confession', and his own position was transformed from that of State observer to power-wielding first principal.[26] He was also of the opinion—then widespread in Russia—that the Anglican Church was a mixture of Lutheranism and Calvinism. Hence it is not surprising that he found Palmer's arguments perplexing and unconvincing.

More sympathetic than Protasov was his subordinate, the Under-Procurator, Andrei Nikolaievich Muraviev (1806–74), who was also chamberlain to Tsar Nicholas I. He was of the opinion that the days of the early vigour of the Church were over, and that now even the smallest 'landmark' must not be moved. He had heard of the activities of the Oxford Movement, and understood Palmer's motivation; yet he believed that Anglo-Catholicism would find a better ally in Rome than in the East. Muraviev remained unconvinced of the Catholicity of the Anglican Church, and was concerned that continuous explanations and defences on the part of her adherents were signs of a 'bad conscience'. He concluded that Palmer was not a typical representative of the Anglican Church, and that the danger posed by Protestantism prevented the union of the Churches.[27]

[26] Information on Protasov from K. Ridley, 'A Pioneer in Reunion', *Sobornost*, 18 (June 1939), 11.

[27] Information on Muraviev from ibid. 12. Muraviev was looked upon favourably by Neale because he was a kind of Russian ecclesiologist. In one of Neale's scrapbooks there is a report, dated 10 Sept. 1852, of Muraviev's rebuilding a monastery on Mount Athos (MS 3111, fo. 44, Lambeth Palace Library). The same scrapbook contains Neale's own review of Muraviev's *Misle o Pravoslavie Posiechtchenie Sviatine Rousskoe (Thoughts on Orthodoxy, in a Visit to the Holy Places of Russia)* (St Petersburg, 1850). Neale says: '[Muraviev] is intrinsically a popular writer.... Add to this a most profound, and, so to speak, *ultramontane* devotion to the Eastern Church, combined, however, with a deal of bitterness and unfairness as regards Rome, a nationality surpassed even by few Russians, and an elegant, if not forcible, imagination—and we have the elements of such a writer as the Russian Church may well be proud to own.' On the edifying nature of Russian Church history for English readers, Neale says: 'It is not likely that Russ will ever become a popular language in England; but translations of some of the more important books of history and of travels could scarcely fail of being useful, and this more especially with regard to our own ecclesiastical difficulties. We are too apt—we are almost obliged—in summing up our controversy with Rome, to leave out an element which Rome is only too happy to forget—the

There was a third group of Russians who were much more enlightened and open to new ideas, aware of the Catholic movement in England, and not always in agreement with official doctrine as prescribed by the Synod. The most influential of these was Metropolitan Philaret of Moscow (1782–1867). This Russian churchman—despite having been banished from the capital by Protasov in 1842—dominated religious life in nineteenth-century Russia, and has been described as 'the greatest theologian of the Russian Church in modern times'.[28] Martin Jugie, author of the entry on Philaret for *Dictionnaire de théologie catholique* (1933), goes so far as to say that 'no important matter, whether of Church or state, was decided unless he had been invited to give his advice; and his opinion often proved to be final'.[29] Philaret played an active part in the reorganization of Russian theological schools, and was instrumental in preparing a modern Russian translation of the Bible.

He was interested in Orthodox relations with the West. In 1811 he wrote *The Comparison of the Differences betwixt the Eastern and Western Churches*; and it is interesting to note that, while the original Russian was not published until 1870, in 1815 Philaret gave the text to Robert Pinkerton, who included it in his book entitled *Russia, or Miscellaneous Observations on the Past and Present State of that Country and its Inhabitants*, published in London in 1833.

The Metropolitan was also concerned about Church reunion. He wrote in 1815, 'I do not presume to call false any Church which believes that Jesus is Christ'; but at the same time he was convinced that the Orthodox Church was the only one which had not 'mixed with the true and saving teaching of Christ the false and pernicious opinions of men'.[30] Philaret applied the caution implied in this statement to his dealings with Palmer, whom he treated with seriousness and

---

history of the Russian Church.... She is a formidable, a most irresistible, antagonist of the Papal theory' (review of 17 Sept. 1852 (journal unidentified), MS 3111, fos. 40, 42, Lambeth Palace Library).

[28] Florovsky, *Aspects of Church History*, 219.
[29] Quoted in K. Ware, 'Metropolitan Philaret of Moscow (1782–1867)', *Eastern Churches Review*, 2/1 (Spring 1968), 24.
[30] Quoted in ibid. 27.

respect; but because of the latter's views on the preserved unity of the Church despite visible division and his unconfirmed status as an interpreter of Anglican theology and ritual, he neither would nor could grant Palmer's wish for intercommunion.[31]

There was another prominent Russian with whom Palmer made contact: Alexei Stepanovich Khomiakov (1804–60), a layman, poet, scientist, and in his own right an eminent religious thinker, who made current the term *sobornost*. As Florovsky explains, Khomiakov wished to re-state the Orthodox tradition in a new idiom, which would be at the same time modern and traditional, in conformity with the teaching of the Fathers and the continuous experience of the living Church.[32] He was a founder of the Slavophil school, whose members were openly critical of the Russian Orthodox Church as an institution which had been 'bureaucratized' and 'Westernized' by Peter the Great, especially through the St Petersburg institution of the Holy Synod, which replaced the Moscow patriarchate. Such criticisms brought them into occasional sharp conflict with the Tsarist authorities. In fact, as Kline points out, although they were able to subscribe to the official slogan *'Pravoslavie, samoderzhavie, narodnost'* ('Orthodoxy, Autocracy, Nationality'), their allegiance was to the purified, idealized essence of each of these elements, not to their current factual existence, as government spokesmen would have it.[33] The Slavophils struggled against the Westerners—those who ardently believed in man and his power and were for the most part atheists—in the momentous debate about whether the Church or secularized humanitarianism should be the basis of Russian culture.

Khomiakov supported the supremacy of Orthodoxy over Protestantism and Roman Catholicism, as well as the traditional belief that his country was the third and last Rome and would in time reveal to the world the true interpretation of Christianity.[34] Inherent in this ideology was the position of the Russian Church as the protectress of Orthodox Christians

---

[31] For Palmer's record of the encounter, see *Notes of a Visit to the Russian Church*, 349–60.   [32] Florovsky, *Aspects of Church History*, 235.
[33] See Kline, 'Russian Religious Thought', 183–4.
[34] N. Zernov, *The Russians and their Church* (London, 1978), 139.

the world over; this sense of global mission was appreciated by Neale, and manifested itself in his oriental novels, in his support of Russia and her Church during the Crimean War, and more generally in his censure of the Muslims, whom he consistently viewed as the aggressors.[35] For the publication in Britain of Slavophil tracts, Khomiakov was indebted to Palmer.

Other tangible results of Palmer's contact with Khomiakov are difficult to assess. The two corresponded from 1844 to 1854 about the basic doctrine of the Church and its impact on Christian unity. Khomiakov's attitude to Palmer is explored by Zernov:

> Khomiakov loved [Palmer] and treated him as his beloved brother in Christ. He longed to see the Anglican and the Orthodox Churches restored to intercommunion: yet he returned over and over again to his logical position, that if the Church is one and the Eastern Christians are part of it, those who are not in communion with them are outside her fold, and that therefore William Palmer was not a member of the Church, and ought first of all to be baptized.[36]

Although in Khomiakov Palmer found a friend and a willing correspondent, he also found in him a disappointment in his pursuit of intercommunion.

Khomiakov was unable to satisfy Palmer. In words which differed little from those addressed to the Nonjurors by the Eastern patriarchs, he insisted that unions with the Orthodox Church are impossible: there can only be unity within its fold. Khomiakov believed that the unity had been broken by the West, which had acted as a self-contained entity, and that only by the return of those who went their own way could the balance be redressed; this was just the opposite of what Palmer contended.[37]

---

[35] Seton-Watson notes that one 'grotesque distortion of the facts of history' publicized by the Slavophils and 'dear' to their school of thought was the assertion that the Russians, unlike the other major European powers, were not conquerors or oppressors of other peoples (*Russian Empire*, 260–1). In his oriental fiction Neale is seen as agreeing with this view of Russia and extending it to include the whole Orthodox Church.

[36] N. Zernov, 'Alexei Stepanovich Khomiakov', *Sobornost*, 10 (June 1937), 10–11. The letters exchanged between Khomiakov and Palmer were first published in Russian, by A. Ivantzov-Platonov, and then in English, by W. J. Birkbeck, under the title *Russia and the English Church during the Last Fifty Years* (London, 1895). [37] Florovsky, *Aspects of Church History*, 236.

On the official side Palmer did manage, before he left Russia in 1842, to convince the Russian Church of the need for stronger links with England. He was told by Chief Procurator Protasov that a new chaplain would be sent to the Russian embassy in London. Among the duties of the appointee would be the study of English and of Anglican theology and the reporting of ecclesiastical affairs in England. The man appointed to the post was Eugene Ivanovich Popov (d. 1875), who had from 1838 been director of the church at the Russian Embassy in Copenhagen. During his sojourn in England from the mid-1840s onward, he came to be seen as the 'soul of the Russian colony', and developed close ties with Newman and Pusey.[38] His closest associate and friend among the Anglicans, however, was Neale.

In his biographical sketch of Popov in *Khristianskoe chtenie*, Brodsky notes of the Russian·chaplain:

From his first days in London [he] began to study the way in which the different characters of church life in England had developed.... With this aim in mind he struck up close relationships with members of the English clergy, many church organisations and the dons at Oxford and Cambridge. Popov managed to raise the status of the Russian priest in the eyes of the English and held high the banner of Russian Orthodoxy throughout his thirty-two years in London.... He played an important part in all the meetings that shaped society in England and in the committees on the question of the unification of the Orthodox and English Churches.[39]

If the decision to send Popov was made with the advances of William Palmer in mind, then it is an interesting consequence of his visit, and represents the first practical, official step taken by the Russians in the nineteenth century to establish closer ecclesiastical ties with England.

Popov's appointment occurred at the same time as Neale's first expression of interest in the Christian East. The latter

[38] Entry on Popov in *Entsiklopedichesky slovar* (St Petersburg, 1891–1907), xlviii. 562. Popov also corresponded with Christopher Wordsworth, Bishop of Lincoln, concerning questions of Russian Orthodox doctrine and practice. See MS 2908, fos. 111–12, Lambeth Palace Library.

[39] L. Brodsky (ed.), 'Materials concerning the Question of the Anglican Church', *Khristianskoe chtenie*, Apr. 1904, 596–7 (my translation). Brodsky also notes that despite strong prejudice against Russians in Copenhagen, Popov's character was such that he earned the respect of the local people.

was not a consequence of the former; but their contemporaneity points to a growing movement in both Churches for information about—and dialogue with—the other. On the Anglican side this interest grew out of the branch theory of the Church, and, through the work of those like Palmer—and later Neale—allowed the contemporary debate on Catholicity and the Church to be seen in a broader perspective.

Chapter 2

Neale and the Eastern Church

NEALE left few clues as to what sparked his interest in the Eastern Church; when he did mention it for the first time, it was to say that he had begun work on his *History of the Holy Eastern Church* (NJ 1.8.43). Allchin suggests that on first appearances such a concern might seem eccentric:

> What is the real importance of contacts between Anglicans and Orthodox? ... At first sight it might seem that there was little real affinity between the churches of eastern Christendom, and the Anglican communion. So many historical, linguistic, national differences lie between them, without even considering the dogmatic and theological problems which separate them. Is there not something artificial in the interest which many Anglicans have shown in Eastern Orthodoxy?[1]

In answering this question, Allchin offers two alternatives which encapsulate some of the predominant nineteenth-century Anglo–Catholic trends of thought. On the one hand, there were the anti-Romanists, who were spurred by 'a purely controversial desire to find a form of traditional Christianity which is not linked with the Papacy, and which can be used as a counterbalance in reunion discussions to the great confessions of Protestantism'. They recognized a polemical value in Eastern Christianity in their fight against the ascendancy of Roman Catholicism.

On the other hand, there were those who displayed a genuine sympathy and interest in Eastern Christendom; their 'reassertion of traditional views of the Church's hierarchical and sacramental structure, of the sacrificial nature of the Eucharist, and a belief in the Communion of Saints' led them to a

---

[1] A. M. Allchin, 'An Anglican View of Anglican–Orthodox Contacts', *Eastern Churches Quarterly*, 15/1–2 (1963), 56.

desire for contact and communion. Allchin attributes this development in Anglican–Orthodox relations to the effects of the Oxford Movement, and notes: 'While the majority of the Tractarians, like Newman and Pusey, showed little detailed interest in Eastern Orthodoxy, some, William Palmer and J. M. Neale pre-eminent among them, sought eagerly for contacts with the East.'[2] Such a clear distinction cannot be drawn, however.

Neale's Anglo-Catholicism, like Palmer's, led him to an interest in the Church of the Fathers and in the movement to recall their teachings for the Victorian Church. His respect for precedent and tradition accounts for the continuity which he observed between the Eastern and Western Churches; he saw the Orthodox Church as the branch least affected by the Reformation, and therefore as a living witness to the teachings of the Fathers. There were certain Orthodox practices which Neale welcomed and would have liked to see incorporated in Anglican worship. In a letter to Webb he noted that he approved of the Eastern prayers for the dead and the communion of saints, and believed that the time would come when he would 'practically embrace' them.[3] For Neale, the Anglican branch exhibited significant harmony of doctrine with what he called the 'Oriental Branch' (INT 13), which could therefore be seen as a great exemplar for the Anglican Church of true Christian faith.

This explanation conforms to the second of Allchin's hypotheses for nineteenth-century Anglican interest in the East. The first—anti-Romanism—is also apparent in Neale's case, but is not as strong as his desire to promote a Catholic heritage for his Church. When he went to Madeira for health reasons in 1843, he lived opposite the Roman Catholic cathedral in Funchal, attended services there, and used the cathedral library for his research. He noted that, for the first time, he 'felt something of the misery of schism' when he saw the congregation coming out of church, and regretted 'the gulf which the sins of our forefathers have fixed between us' (NJ 14.2.43). Thus, initially, he seems to have had some sympathy for Roman Catholics, in their common plight with all Christians: the lack of unity. Over the next two years,

---

[2] Ibid. 56–7.   [3] *Letters*, 80; dated 26 Nov. 1844, from Madeira.

however, he increasingly turned away from Rome and toward the East.

The year 1845 was a turning-point in relations between Anglo-Catholics and Roman Catholics. The secession of Newman and his followers was considered a setback by Anglicans who had pinned their hopes for a beacon of Catholicity on the Roman Church. Many Tractarians were surprised and bewildered, including Webb, who was a stronger supporter of Newman than Neale was, and had been anxious about the implications of these conversions.[4] Neale, in an effort to allay his friend's fears, had written to him in 1844: 'I hope and believe that Newman will not leave us; but I should not despair if he did. My sheet anchor of hope for the English Church is, that you cannot point out a single instance of a heretical or schismatical body, which, after apparent death awoke to life.'[5] Clearly Neale was referring to the positive effect of the Anglo-Catholic revival on the Church of England as a whole and to the popular notion that the reason for the secessions was the belief that the Church of England was a schismatical, heretical body; but Neale remained steadfast in his Anglicanism.

After Newman's secession, he wrote 'As to Newman's book [*An Essay on the Development of Christian Doctrine*, 1845] I am so thoroughly and morally persuaded of the defensibility of our position, that if I were to feel shaken by its beginning, I would shut up the book. I cannot express to you the firmness of my conviction. It seems to grow upon me the more the others waver.'[6] In an earlier letter to Webb he had written: 'I am quite sure that if we don't desert ourselves, God will not desert us. If you all go, I shall stay.'[7] Neale was

[4] Webb notes in his journal that he discussed with Newman the possibility of his writing the life of St Etheldreda for Newman's *Lives of the English Saints* (BWJ 28.5.44); however, Webb's plan was never carried out.

[5] *Letters*, 80; dated 26 Nov. 1844, from Madeira.

[6] *Letters*, 88; dated 8 Nov. 1845.

[7] *Letters*, 89–90; dated Advent Eve [1844], from Reigate. In the same letter Neale clearly distinguished between the Oxford Tractarians and the Camdenians, and seemed to suggest that the latter's concern with the visible aids to faith was their saving grace—particularly when it came to secession: 'I am more than ever inclined... to believe that the first generation of [Tractarian] reformers may perhaps be absorbed by Rome; but that the second will remain in our Church and renovate it.' Some of what Neale predicted came to be: more first-generation Tractarians seceded than second-, and the latter were more concerned with ecclesiology in the Camdenian sense than their mentors.

unshaken in his devotion to his Church, and did not sympathize with Webb, who experienced a 'vast inward change' as a result of Newman's conversion (BWJ 31.12.45).

Neale's comments to Webb do not amount to antipathy to Roman Catholicism. Although he regretted Newman's secession, this was not why Neale's anti-Romanism developed; rather, it was as a result of discussions while in Madeira with Count Montalembert (1810–70), the French liberal historian. Montalembert was attempting to promote ecclesiology in France along similar lines to the Camdenians in England and the colonies, through the Comité des arts and the Commission des monuments historiques, which Neale called 'the French C[ambridge] C[amden] S[ociety]'.[8] Discussions between the two ecclesiologists remained amicable until the ultramontane Montalembert expressed doubts about the Catholicity of the Anglican Church and, according to Neale, accused Anglo-Catholics of being 'the worst enemies of the Church, more so than infidels themselves', branding the Church of England as 'one of the worst forms of heresy'.[9] Such views surprised Neale, coming as they did from a committed ecclesiologist, and convinced him of the error of ultramontanism, as he disclosed in a letter to Webb: 'Without becoming a shade more Anglican, I do see more and more clearly that High Papal theory is quite untenable.' In the same letter, on the subject of reunion, Neale notes that Montalembert has convinced him that the Roman Catholic Church should not be seen as the focal point: 'I cannot make, as Montalembert does, visible union, or ... the desire for visible union with the Chair of Peter, the key-stone, as it were, of the Church, at least not in the sense in which the Western Church has sometimes done.'[10]

---

[8] *Letters*, 55; dated 7 Apr. 1848, from Santa Luzia.
[9] Letter of 26 Feb. 1843; quoted in Towle, 80, 81.
[10] *Letters*, 69; dated 11 Jan. 1844, from Madeira. 'Ultramontanism' is a word used to describe the tendency in the Roman Catholic Church which favours centralization of authority and influence in the papal Curia, as opposed to national or diocesan independence (Cross and Livingstone (eds.), *Oxford Dictionary of the Christian Church*, 1405). For more information on the peculiarly English manifestations of this tendency, see E. Norman, *The English Catholic Church in the Nineteenth Century* (Oxford, 1984), 234–43. Another comment of Montalembert's which disturbed Neale was made in connection with sacrilege; according to Neale, Montalembert said 'that he

Neale could not support the ultramontane position, and was adamant that Christians should not support claims of papal supremacy. He said precisely this in the introduction to the Portuguese theologian Antonio Pereira de Figueredo's *Tentativa Theologica: Episcopal Rights and Ultra-montane Usurpations* (1847). Portuguese Catholics had always asserted a certain independence from Rome, which allowed Pereira to write a book claiming that the Roman Church had neither in any Council nor in any papal bull advocated what the ultramontanes did: the supremacy of the Pope. In the introduction to the *Tentativa Theologica* Neale outlines the relevance of this idea to Anglican Church, which

had no wish to violate the Apostolic rule, honour to whom honour: She is ready to acknowledge the Primacy, if Rome will drop the Supremacy. But in the present state of things, it is not merely because Rome claims too much, that the Church of England is accused of giving too little: but Rome will not in any way receive what is her due; nor is there any Church under the sun which is able to render it to her. The *Roman* (*i.e.* intruded) Patriarchs of the great Sees of the East are the Pope's slaves.... The real occupants of these Thrones cannot show any deference to Rome, because she refuses deference and claims obedience. This leads to the question what is the true meaning of Primacy and Supremacy.[11]

These comments of Neale's followed from his discussions with Montalembert, and indicate that although he could not be considered anti-Roman in the extreme, his experiences in Madeira in 1843–5 had served to steer him away from the idea of Rome as the axis upon which the Christian Church turned; also, his thoughts on Newman's secession show that he did not look upon Rome with the same interest or sympathy as did many other Tractarian supporters.

To return to Allchin's two categories, Neale in some ways fits into both. He believed that the Anglican Church was a true branch of the Catholic Church, and saw the Orthodox as

could not believe in the curse that followed Sacrilege, because where the Pope had legalised it, it ceased to be sinful' (J. M. Neale and B. Webb (eds.), *The History and Fate of Sacrilege*, by Sir Henry Spelman (London, 1846), introductory essay, p. cxliii).

[11] A. Pereira de Figueredo, *Tentativa Theologica*, trans. E. H. Landon (London, 1847), pp. xviii–xix.

the only other branch which could provide for him a continuity with the Church of the Fathers, but which was also separate from the Church of Rome. Neale was not an out-spoken anti-Roman; but he was opposed to the ultramontanes, who in England included many converts from Anglicanism. Neale also disapproved of the ultramontane fascination with Italianate classical architecture—which was opposed to his own beloved Gothic.[12]

There were other, more personal factors which led Neale to an interest in the Orthodox Church. Some of these stemmed from his association with William Palmer. According to Webb's journal, he and Neale visited Palmer in the latter's rooms in Magdalen in 1846 (BWJ 24.6.46). It appears that Neale was seeking help in compiling his *History of the Holy Eastern Church*, and considered Palmer an authority on Anglican–Eastern relations.[13] Palmer had mastered Russian—as Neale eventually did—and had met Muraviev, whom Neale consulted in the course of his researches.[14] Through Palmer, Neale gained access to many essential contacts and source materials which would otherwise have been denied him. Also traceable to

---

[12] For more information on ultramontane architectural preferences, see Clarke, *Church Builders in the Nineteenth Century*, 48–9, 57.

[13] Neale had respect and admiration for Palmer. In 1849 Palmer promoted a scheme for synodical approval by the Scottish Episcopal Church of Anglican–Orthodox harmony of doctrine, which was published as *An Appeal to the Scottish Bishops and Clergy*. Of this book, which he described as 'remarkable', Neale wrote: 'It will probably stand, in the future history of our Churches, as the most remarkable event that has occurred since the disruption of the Nonjurors' (*The Life and Times of Patrick Torry, D.D.* (London, 1856), 224–5).

[14] There is some doubt about the authority of Muraviev's pronouncements in matters of Orthodox Church doctrine. In 1865 an unknown Russian named B. Pontiatin wrote to Pusey in answer to the latter's request for the official Russian position on the Immaculate Conception. In his reply Pontiatin quotes Popov, whom he considers a 'competent authority' on the subject; but he dismisses Muraviev as having 'no authoritative worth' (letter from B. Pontiatin to E. Pusey, dated 19 Feb. 1865, from Christ Church, Oxford; Pusey Papers, Pusey House, Oxford). It should be noted that Neale, in his preface to *A History of the Holy Eastern Church: General Introduction*, acknowledges the help of a man named Admiral E. Pontiatine [sic] in procuring the ground plan of S. Sophia at Novgorod (p. xxv); this may or may not be the same man who wrote the letter to Pusey. Neale's transliteration of Russian names is usually based on French phonetics ('Mouravieff', 'Pontiatine'), which in certain cases points to the language in which some of his source materials were written; Muraviev, e.g., wrote to Neale in French.

Palmer is Neale's friendship with Popov, who provided him with materials concerning the Orthodox Church, and said that he was 'glad to answer' Neale's questions.[15] Popov reported to Chief Procurator Tolstoy that he had found in Neale a man who enjoyed 'all aspects' of Orthodoxy, 'not only the dogmatic side'; and on visiting Sackville College, he found Neale's rooms 'filled with the spirit of peace, love and unity'.[16] These comments are interesting, because they point to the intuitive feelings which developed in Neale with regard to the Orthodox Church. He had little opportunity to travel to the East, and so gained most of his understanding through books and through personal contacts, primarily Popov. The latter provided encouragement for Neale's work on the Eastern Church in the hope that anything Neale did to instruct Anglicans in the ways of the Orthodox would make for better mutual understanding.

Rowell suggests another personal motivation for Neale's work: the bearing of the Iconoclast controversy on his theories of symbolism.[17] In many of his writings Neale drew attention to this event, and in *A History of the Holy Eastern Church* he chronicled its development (AD 726–843). He referred to it as 'one of the saddest controversies that ever agitated the Church' (ALX ii. 124) and as 'grossly misapprehended' and 'difficult to appreciate' (HEC 43). For Neale it was a key episode in Orthodox Church history, particularly because it sparked what was for him the greatest period in Eastern hym-

---

[15] Unpublished letter from Popov to Neale, from Mr Quilton's, Harrow-on-the Hill, Thursday (n.d.). The original of this letter is now lost. Details of it were given to me by Michael Leppard of East Grinstead, who catalogued it (as no. 12), along with a number of other letters sent to him in 1968 by a Miss Pugh of Ronald's Bungalow, Almesley, nr. Hereford. They were subsequently given to St Margaret's Convent, where most of Neale's papers were kept until 1975, when they were transferred to Lambeth Palace Library. A careful search was made of these and other depositories of Neale's manuscripts; but the letter was not found. Popov is known to have answered 50 of Neale's letters in the course of the latter's compiling *A History of the Holy Eastern Church.* He also supplied Neale with various manuscripts and office-books for what he described to Protasov as 'Neale's great work' (report to Chief Procurator Protasov, dated 7 July 1849, in Brodsky (ed.), 'Materials', *Khristianskoe chtenie*, May 1904, 743).

[16] Report nos. 17 and 18 by Popov to Chief Procurator A. P. Tolstoy, dated 25 Apr. 1859, and 25 Jan. 1860, in Brodsky (ed.) 'Materials', *Khristianskoe chtenie*, July 1905, 129, 131.   [17] Rowell, *Vision Glorious*, 108.

nology: the age of the canon. What is important to note here is the centrality of icons for Orthodox Christians; thereby a better idea may be gained of the reasons for Neale's interest in what he calls 'the neglected half of Catholic Art' (INT 167).

Ware discusses the importance of icons for Orthodox Christians:

> One of the distinctive features of Orthodoxy is the place which it assigns to icons.... An Orthodox prostrates himself before these icons, he kisses them and burns candles in front of them; they are censed by the priest and carried in procession.
> . . . .
> Because icons are only symbols, Orthodox do not worship them, but *reverence* or *venerate them*.... Icons, said Leontius, are 'opened books to remind us of God'; they are one of the means which the Church employs in order to teach the faith. He who lacks learning or leisure to study works of theology has only to enter a church to see unfolded before him on the walls all the mysteries of the Christian religion. If a pagan asks you to show him your faith, said the Iconodules, take him into church and place him before the icons.[18]

The symbolism inherent in icons provided a parallel for Neale's theory of architectural symbolism.

Zernov explains that the Russian reverence for icons is bound up with the Orthodox belief that the whole of God's creation, material as well as spiritual, is to be redeemed and glorified:

> [Icons] were, for the Russians, not merely paintings. They were dynamic manifestations of man's spiritual power to redeem creation through beauty and art. The colours and lines of the obraza [images] were not meant to imitate nature; the artists aimed at demonstrating that men, animals and plants, and the whole cosmos could be rescued from their present state of degradation and restored to their proper 'Image'.... In times of peace, and in moments of danger, at home or on a journey, in the happiest hours of his life, and at the point of death, a Russian wished to see an 'obraz', to touch and kiss it and be comforted by it. The importance attributed to icons seems to be shocking to foreign observers of Russian life, but for Russians the artistic perfection of an icon was not only a reflection of celestial glory—it was a concrete example of matter restored to its original harmony and beauty, and serving as a vehicle of the Spirit.[19]

---

[18] T. Ware, *The Orthodox Church* (Harmondsworth, 1983), 40–1.
[19] Zernov, *Russians and their Church*, 105–6.

The same may be said of Neale's ecclesiology. For him the art and architecture of a Gothic church could serve as expressions of heavenly glory for Anglicans. In his mind the iconoclasts approximated the movement in Europe in the sixteenth and seventeenth centuries to remove from church worship many of the material aids to faith. In his words, 'Till Calvinism, and its daughter Rationalism, showed the ultimate development of Iconoclast principles, it must have been well nigh impossible to realize the depth of feeling on the side of the Church, or the greatness of the interests attacked by her opponents' (HEC 43). Such sentiments were also prevalent in the eighteenth century, which Neale described thus: 'In those old dead times of the eighteenth century, when everything was so flat and stale, when art seemed almost to have come to an end, ... and a deep sleep had fallen upon men, intellectually as well as morally, then the Church did not even hold her own,— poor own that it was.'[20]

Nor did the battle end there: in the Victorian Church there were Anglicans who, by believing that what is spiritual must be non-material, stood against Neale's ecclesiological principles, and thus against his Anglo-Catholicism. He considered such opposition potentially damaging—in the same way as the Iconoclastic Controversy had been a thousand years before. Only a return to worship involving material symbolism could restore true Catholic feeling to Anglicanism. Orthodoxy—and more particularly the reverence of icons— provided for Neale an example of a non-Roman branch of the Catholic Church which employed religious art as an enduring monument of faith. He conducted a detailed examination of Orthodox symbolism in worship, through such media as icons, architecture, and church furnishing, in the *General Introduction* to his *History of the Holy Eastern Church*. Of this study he declared to Webb that he was 'the first Anglican of Catholick principles who has touched the iconoclast controversy'.[21] Rowell, therefore, seems justified in his claim that the Iconoclastic Controversy provided part of the motivation for Neale's researches into Orthodoxy.

---

[20] J. M. Neale, 'The City of David', in *Occasional Sermons, Preached in Various Churches* (London, 1873), 69.
[21] *Letters*, 64; dated 27 Nov. 1843, from Santa Luzia.

Thus there were both popular and personal factors leading to Neale's interest in the Eastern Church. His endorsement of the branch theory of the Church, his contact with William Palmer, his encounter with Montalembert, the congeniality of icon veneration—all helped to bring Neale into contact with the Orthodox communion, and strengthened his resolve to educate the Anglican communion about her.

Chapter 3

Neale's Orientalism

IN addition to the religious and theological factors which led Neale to investigate the Eastern Church, there were also secular, cultural, and historical motivations at work; these factors may be grouped under the general heading of 'orientalism'.

Neale had specific ideas on how the subject of the Orthodox Church should be approached. He believed that those Anglicans who had previously written about the Christian East, including Paul Ricaut (*The Present State of the Greek and Armenian Churches*, 1679) and John Covel (*Some Account of the Present Greek Church*, 1722), were biased in their attitudes. Some had not mastered the languages in which the source materials were written—a fundamental weakness, Neale thought. Others considered the Orthodox Church to be in error, and therefore inferior to their own; they claimed that the Orthodox were in need of instruction in Western practices in order to redeem themselves. This latter view seems to have been based on the idea that the steadfastness of Eastern tradition was synonymous with stagnation, and was presented in the earlier studies in the guise of a comparison between 'undesirable' Orthodox practices and the more attractive, 'acceptable' ways of the Western Church. In order to avoid being accused of doing likewise, Neale established the following general principle for himself in writing about the Orthodox Church: 'The historian should write, not as a member of the Roman, nor as a member of the English Church; but, as far as may be, with Oriental views, feelings and even, perhaps, prepossessions' (ALX i, p. xvi). Thus Neale assayed for himself an Eastern frame of mind, which he believed would enable him to write about Orthodoxy freely, and avoid the shortcomings which he noted in his predecessors.

In spite of Neale's wish to do better than these earlier writers, he laboured under equally debilitating—and perhaps aggravated—deficiencies. The fact that he uses the word 'oriental' places him firmly within a recognized nineteenth-century tradition of scholarly and imaginative writing about the East.

In his book on orientalism, Edward Said describes this phenomenon as 'a kind of Western projection onto and will to govern the Orient'.[1] This view is, of course, closely allied with European expansionist and imperialist tendencies. Since the mid-eighteenth century the Orient has emerged as a locus for anthropological, biological, linguistic, racial, historical, and religious study by Westerners, who were thereby provided with an opportunity to set themselves and their culture off against something which was perceived, in Said's words, to be a 'surrogate and even underground self'.[2]

Oriental study emerged in two modes of expression: scholarly and imaginative. There was a growing systematic knowledge in Europe about the Orient, which was reinforced by colonialism as well as by widespread fascination with the alien and unusual. This resulted in a growing interest in the sciences of ethnology, comparative anatomy, philology, and history and the establishment of learned bodies dedicated to dissemination of knowledge about the East, including the Société Asiatique (founded 1822) and the Royal Asiatic Society (1823). The academic debate gave rise to a sizeable body of imaginative writing about the Orient, by novelists, poets, translators, and travellers. Neale's productions form part of both traditions.

Said, because of his own background, has a heightened awareness of the effects of Western culture on the East, and sees orientalism as 'a sign of European-Atlantic power over the Orient' rather than a 'veridic discourse' (which is what, in its academic form, it claims to be).[3] Europe always speaks about the Orient (whether the Near East, the Levant, India, or the Far East) from a position of strength and, in an imperialist

[1] E. W. Said, *Orientalism* (Harmondsworth, 1985), 95.
[2] Ibid. 3. See also P. Brantlinger, *Rule of Darkness* (Ithaca, NY, 1988), esp. ch. 5, 'The New Crusades', 135–71.
[3] Said, *Orientalism*, 6. Said was born in Jerusalem, into a Palestinian Arab family, and received his primary schooling in Cairo. He is currently Parr Professor of English and Comparative Culture at Columbia University and a member of the Palestine National Council.

context, of domination. This is true not only from the point of view of politics, but also of culture and religion. There is generally a sense that the relationship between West and East is one of 'dominator–dominated', 'we–they', or 'over here–over there'.[4]

This is not true of Neale's work—at least as far as Orthodox Christians are concerned. It must be remembered that he tried, to the best of his abilities and with the best intentions, to bridge the gap between East and West, effectively showing his readers that they had many points in common with the Orthodox. This was a result of his interpretation of the branch theory and his belief that the Eastern Church provided a continuum with the Church of the Fathers. It is precisely on this point of personal association with his subject that Neale can be distinguished from other orientalists of his day, who were acutely aware of the fact of empire. For them Europe was dynamic, powerful, and destined for greatness and cultural domination; the Orient, by contrast, was perceived as static, unchanging (in a pejorative sense), and destined to be governed, controlled, and manipulated. Thus, while orientalist study did nurture dedicated Western scholars, they tended to see the East as something which could be compartmentalized, dissected, and decoded. The previously fearsome, mysterious, exotic East could be made known and 'domesticated' for a Western reading public. Said calls this process the 'orientalization' of the Orient: '[It] not only marks the Orient as a province of the Orientalist but also forces the uninitiated Western reader to accept Orientalist codifications ... as the *true* Orient. Truth, in short, becomes a function of learned judgment, not of the material itself, which in time seems to owe even its existence to the Orientalist.'[5]

Like the academic expounders of the Orient, those who produced imaginative and travel literature engaged in a great deal of decoding for the reader. Important works were produced by Johnson, Beckford, Hugo, Lamartine, Chateaubriand, Nerval, Flaubert, Byron, Scott, Edward William Lane, Harriet

---

[4] Cf. A. S. Ahmed's recent analysis of Western perceptions of the Islamic world, and vice versa, in light of the Salman Rushdie affair and the end of the Cold War in Europe ('Jeans for Me, Robes for You', *Guardian Weekly*, 143/2 (15 July 1990), 21).   [5] Said, *Orientalism*, 67.

Martineau, Kinglake, Thackeray, Disraeli, and Burton.[6] Many of these writers travelled to the East, but with the possible exception of Burton (who, disguised as an Arab, entered Mecca and recorded his experiences as *Personal Narrative of a Pilgrimage to El-Madinah and Meccah,* 1855–6), they remained detached from what they observed in the East, because they insisted on viewing their surroundings from a position of superiority. Most believed that it was unnecessary to 'orientalize' themselves in the way envisioned by Neale, for orientalism was a political vision, whose structure promoted the differences between the familiar West and the 'exotic' East. Because his was the supposedly superior culture, the Westerner was entitled to a certain freedom of intercourse, through which he could penetrate the mysteries of the Orient. In most cases the penetration amounted to the traveller blundering about in the unknown, safe in the belief of his own cultural superiority, then translating and organizing his experiences for his readers. A case in point here is Alexander Kinglake's popular and influential *Eothen, or Traces of Travel Brought Home from the East* (1844). Although Kinglake blithely confesses to no facility in oriental languages, he is not constrained by ignorance from making sweeping generalizations about the Orient, its culture, mentality, and society. *Eothen* was used as a guidebook by Thackeray, who also admitted ignorance of the ways of the East in his *Notes of a Journey from Cornhill to Grand Cairo.* He too domesticates his oriental material, as in his thoughts on first seeing Constantinople, which he compares to a theatrical spectacle at Drury Lane:

[6] Important orientalist works by these authors include the following: Johnson, *Rasselas* (1759); Beckford, *Vathek* (1786); Hugo, *Les Orientales* (1829); Lamartine, *Voyage en Orient* (1835); Chateaubriand, *Itinéraire de Paris à Jérusalem* (1811); Nerval, *Voyage en Orient* (1848–51); Flaubert, *Voyage en Orient* (1849–51), *Voyage à Carthage* (1858), *Salammbô* (1863); Byron, *Childe Harold's Pilgrimage* (1812–18), *The Giaour* (1813), *The Bride of Abydos* (1813); Scott, *The Talisman* (1825), *Count Robert of Paris* (1831); Lane, *An Account of the Manners and Customs of the Modern Egyptians* (1836), *The Thousand and One Nights* (trans. 1839–41); Martineau, *Eastern Life, Past and Present* (1848); Kinglake, *Eothen* (1844); Thackeray, *Notes of a Journey from Cornhill to Grand Cairo* (1844); Disraeli, *Tancred* (1847); Burton, *Personal Narrative of a Pilgrimage to El-Madinah and Meccah* (1855–6), *The Kama Sutra* (1883), *The Book of the Thousand and One Nights* (1885–6), *The Perfumed Garden* (1886).

Well, the view of Constantinople is as fine as any of Stanfield's best
theatrical pictures, seen at the best period of youth, when fancy had
all the bloom on her—when all the heroines who danced before the
scene appeared as ravishing beauties, when there shone an unearthly
splendour about Baker and Diddear—and the sound of the bugles and
fiddles, and the cheerful clang of the cymbals, as the scene unrolled,
and the gorgeous procession meandered triumphantly through it—
caused a thrill of pleasure, and awakened an innocent fulness of
sensual enjoyment that is only given to boys.

The above sentence contains the following propositions:—The
enjoyments of boyish fancy are the most intense and delicious in the
world. Stanfield's panorama used to be the realization of the most
intense youthful fancy. I puzzle my brains and find no better like-
ness for the place. The view of Constantinople resembles the *ne plus
ultra* of a Stanfield diorama, with a glorious accompaniment of music,
spangled houris, warriors, and winding processions, feasting the eyes
and the soul with light, splendour, and harmony.

He goes on to say that 'if you were never in this way during
your youth ravished at the playhouse, of course the whole
comparison is useless'; but perhaps more 'familiar' is his
impression of the seraglio:

The palace of the Seraglio, the cloister with marble pillars, the hall
of the ambassadors, the impenetrable gate guarded by eunuchs and
ichoglans, have a romantic look in print; but not so in reality. Most
of the marble is wood, almost all the gilding is faded, the guards are
shabby, the foolish perspectives painted on the walls are half cracked
off. The place looks like Vauxhall in the daytime.[7]

These books by Kinglake and Thackeray, which continually
reveal both the British imperialist stance and cultural aloof-
ness, were among hundreds of oriental travel books published
in the nineteenth century (including Neale's own *Notes,
Ecclesiological and Picturesque, on Dalmatia, Croatia, Istria,
Styria, with a Visit to Montenegro*, 1861), and while they contributed to a heightened public awareness of the East, they also
helped to render canonical various misconceptions about it.

Foremost, perhaps, among these misrepresentations (and
most interesting as projections of an 'underground self') was

[7] W. M. Thackeray, *Notes of a Journey from Cornhill to Grand Cairo*
(Chicago, n.d.), 642–3, 659. An ichoglan was a page-in-waiting in the palace
of the Sultan.

that of sexual licentiousness—a charge levelled against Muslims and Hindus with almost alarming frequency. Flaubert is a well-known example of some one who made such gross generalizations, through which a prevailing attitude was formed. Like Disraeli and Burton, he undertook his pilgrimage in order to dispel many of the assumptions about the Orient previously acquired through reading books rather than experience. However, the European 'cultural baggage' which these writers brought with them prevented them from seeing the Orient *qua* Orient, and the result was a reduction of it to something queer, perhaps quaint, but certainly non-Western and culturally inferior. Here is Flaubert speaking about the sexual practices of the Egyptians in a letter to Louis Bouillet:

> To amuse the crowd, Mohammed Ali's jester took a woman in a Cairo bazaar one day, set her on the counter of a shop, and coupled with her publicly while the shopkeeper calmly smoked his pipe.
> On the road from Cairo to Shubra some time ago a young fellow had himself publicly buggered by a large monkey—as in the story above, to create a good opinion of himself and make people laugh.
> A marabout died a while ago—an idiot—who had long passed as a saint marked by God; all the Moslem women came to see him and masturbated him—in the end he died of exhaustion—from morning to night it was a perpetual jacking off.... *Quid dicis* of the following fact: some time ago a *santon* (ascetic priest) used to walk through the streets of Cairo completely naked except for a cap on his head and another on his prick. To piss he would doff the prick-cap, and sterile women who wanted children would run up, put themselves under the parabola of his urine and rub themselves with it.[8]

This passage is effective in conveying the strangeness of the East, which pervades Flaubert's work. Through such grotesque anecdotes, a consensus about the sexual behaviour of Muslims was formed. Flaubert was believed because he spoke about the Orient from a position of strength. He was educated, comparatively rich, male, and the citizen of a country which played a central role in European global expansion.[9] He made a

---

[8] F. Steegmuller (trans. and ed.), *Flaubert in Egypt* (London, 1972), 44–5; letter dated 4 Dec. 1849. The portion quoted was a *post scriptum* marked 'For you alone'.

[9] It must be remembered that colonial domination resulted in European control of 35% of the earth's surface by 1815 and 85% by 1914.

detailed study of the Orient, visiting Egypt, Turkey, and Greece (1849–51) and Tunisia (1858); out of these travels emerged *Salammbô* (1862), a romance set in Carthage, as well as two travelogues. In these works Flaubert applies the general principle of the Orient never speaking itself, but always being spoken for. A notable example of this tendency is his description of his encounter with the Egyptian courtesan Kuchuk-Hanem (Ruchiouk Hânem) in Esneh. He orientalized her by representing her as 'une grande et splendide créature', who provides him with 'une petite fantasia' of titillating striptease, followed by sexual gratification.[10] This episode produced in the West a widely influential model of the oriental woman. Thus, in recounting his experiences in Egypt, he makes the oriental—particularly the Muslim—into a general object, so that he can classify and decode; yet he always bears in mind how the oddness of the orientals continually sets them off from Europeans. It is this 'otherness' which is the focus of nearly all nineteenth-century orientalist writers.

Orthodox Christians are also presented as exotic and strange, although orientalists appear to be less fascinated with them than with Muslims. Kinglake, for example, provides glimpses of Greek Orthodox ritual in *Eothen*, and is repulsed by what he sees at Smyrna:

> Never, in any part of the world, have I seen religious performances so painful to witness as those of the Greeks. The horror, however, with which one shudders at their worship is attributable, in some measure, to the mere effect of costume. In all the Ottoman dominions, and very frequently, too, in the kingdom of Otho, the Greeks wear turbans, or other head-dresses, and shave their heads, leaving only a rat's tail at the crown of the head; they of course keep themselves covered within doors as well as abroad, and they never remove their headgear merely on account of being in a church: but when the Greek stops to worship at his proper shrine, then, and then only, he always uncovers; and as you see him thus with shaven skull, and savage tail depending from his crown, kissing a thing of wood and glass, and cringing with base prostrations and apparent terror before a miserable picture, you see superstition in a shape which, outwardly at least, is sadly abject and repulsive.[11]

[10] Flaubert, *Voyage en Orient*, 573–5.
[11] A. Kinglake, *Eothen* (London, 1918), 44.

Thackeray too is disdainful of the Orthodox, and portrays those in Jerusalem as barbaric infidels, whose attitudes and rituals bear almost no resemblance to his brand of Anglicanism. In his description of the holy places he says:

> The Greeks show you the tomb of Melchisedec, while the Armenians possess the Chapel of the Penitent Thief; the poor Copts (with their little cabin of a chapel) can yet boast of possessing the thicket in which Abraham caught the Ram, which was to serve as the vicar of Isaac.... You mount a few steps, and are told it is Calvary upon which you stand. All this in the midst of flaring candles, reeking incense, savage pictures of Scripture story, or portraits of kings who have been benefactors of various chapels; a din and clatter of strange people, —these weeping, bowing, kissing, —those utterly indifferent; and the priests clad in outlandish robes, snuffing and chanting incomprehensible litanies, robing, disrobing, lighting up candles or extinguishing them, advancing, retreating, bowing with all sorts of unfamiliar genuflexions.... and the English stranger looks on the scene, for the first time, with a feeling of scorn, bewilderment, and shame at the grovelling credulity, those strange rites and ceremonies, that almost confessed imposture.[12]

The words 'strange', 'outlandish', 'incomprehensible', and 'unfamiliar' represent Thackeray's—and the British public's—attitude towards the Orthodox Church. Neale's goal was to alter such perceptions.

In his oriental world, Neale clearly sets off the Muslims, or 'Mahometans' (a pejorative term),[13] from Orthodox Christians. The nature of Islam—particularly the tendency towards violence and unbridled sexuality—is summarized by Neale in two pages of his 800-page work, *The Patriarchate of Alexandria*, the second volume of his *History of the Holy Eastern Church*. In book 4 he describes the rise of 'Mahometanism':

> In the meantime it pleased GOD to raise up, as a punishment for the sins of His Church, a more fearful adversary to her doctrine, and a more cruel oppressor of her children, than any with whom she had yet been called to contend. Mahomet had already proclaimed his mission in Arabia, and the Church of Alexandria, ill-recovered from the invasion of the Cosroes, was about to endure a more severe and a more lasting tyranny. (ALX ii. 67)

---

[12] Thackeray, *Journey from Cornhill to Grand Cairo*, 701–2.
[13] See Said, *Orientalism*, 66.

Neale's analysis of Muhammad and his influence was based on the widespread—but incorrect—assumption that the prophet was to Islam what Christ was to Christianity (hence the polemical name 'Mahometanism' given to Islam and the automatic epithet 'impostor' applied to Muhammad). Neale concentrates on the intrigue and cunning which he believes that Muhammad used to gain converts:

That Mahomet was not the enthusiast which some semi-infidel or latitudinarian authors have considered him, is evident from the ingenuity with which, while he panders to the passions of his followers, he also infuses into his religion so much of each of those tenets to which the varying sects of his countrymen were addicted, as to enable each and all to please themselves by the belief that the new doctrine was only a reform of, and improvement on, that to which they had been accustomed. The Christians were conciliated by the acknowledgement of our LORD as the Greatest of Prophets; the Jews, by the respectful mention of Moses and their other Lawgivers; the idolaters, by the veneration which the Impostor professed for the Temple of Mecca, and the black stone which it contained; and the Chaldeans, by the pre-eminence which he gives to the ministrations of the Angel Gabriel, and his whole scheme of the Seven Heavens. To a people devoted to the gratification of their passions and addicted to Oriental luxury, he appealed, not unsuccessfully, by the promise of a Paradise whose sensual delights were unbounded, and the permission of a free exercise of pleasures in this world. To allow that there was some truth intermingled with his falsehood, is only to allow Mahomet sufficient knowledge of mankind to be aware that a system, neither based upon one true, nor supported by one generous principle, would be sure, in a few years, to come to an end. Thus, his inculcation of an entire submission to the Will of GOD is the salt which has for so long a series of years preserved from decay the imposture of which Mahomet was the author. (ALX ii. 68)

Thus Neale dispenses with Islam, and moves on to his main subject. Although he is not party to the graphic sensationalism of Flaubert, his references to 'sensual delights' and the 'pleasures in this world' show that he is aware of popular notions of Muhammad and of the characteristics which the stereotypical Muslim was supposed to embody. As will be shown, 'Mahometans' in Neale's historical narratives and fiction are generally portrayed as cruel, immoral oppressors, whose attitudes toward the innocent, defenceless Orthodox Christians are precursors of terror and doom.

In general, the Western writing out of which a view of the oriental world emerged was governed by a complex amalgam of general ideas about who or what was an oriental and a pattern of individual insight directed by a combination of desire, repression, and projection. The whole field of orientalism is premissed on exteriority; every writer tries to locate himself *vis-à-vis* the Orient, adopting a particular stance, narrative voice, and structure in order to speak on its behalf. Such codification is necessary, because the writer can only represent to his reader something which he knows is not part of his own cultural experience and, hard as he may try to translate the location into his text, he always remains an outsider.

For the most part, Neale's research depended upon careful textual investigation and mastery of the relevant languages.[14] While such scrupulousness may be attributed to other writers as well, Neale's orientalizing was different, primarily because it was bound up with religious and theological motivations: he had a pressing desire to see more clearly a part of the Church long neglected but containing—so it seemed to him— institutions of Christian and Catholic truth since lost in the West. The branch theory taught him to see the Eastern Church as an indispensable participant in any future inter-church dialogue. In a letter to Webb he explained what he meant: 'I know that you are afraid that I shall take an Oriental view, i.e. I suppose so Oriental that it will cease to be Catholick. I hope not.... We *Orientals* take a more general view. The Rock on which the Church is built is S. Peter, but it is a triple Rock, Antioch where he sat, Alexandria where he superintended, Rome where he suffered.'[15] Thus Neale was an 'Oriental', but at the same time a Catholic. He was concerned to present the Eastern Church to his readers with insight, sympathy, and warmth; yet he was also prepared to 'unchurch'

---

[14] Said notes: 'The Orient studied was a textual universe by and large; the impact of the Orient was made through books and manuscripts, not, as in the impress of Greece on the Renaissance, through mimetic artifacts like sculpture and pottery' (ibid. 52).

[15] *Letters*, 69; dated 11 Jan. 1844, from Madeira.

the English Dissenters and Continental Protestants in his idea of the larger framework of a Catholic Church, in which only the Roman Catholic, Anglican, and Eastern Churches played an integral part. He left the study of the Roman Church to others; his primary concern was to outline the affinity, or harmony, which existed between the relatively unknown, unexplored Orthodox Church and his own Church of England.

Neale knew that his familiarity with Orthodox tradition could only extend so far. His knowledge was gained mostly through books and manuscripts, and though he eventually became an authority on the subject, he realized that precisely because he was an Anglican, there were things about Eastern tradition which he could not hope to understand. When it came to writing *A History of the Holy Eastern Church*, he communicated this limitation to his readers:

> It is not to be expected that a history of any Church can be so well written as by one who is a member of that Church; who is imbued with all its feelings, has adopted all its prepossessions, and who is therefore able to look at its actions exactly in the point of view in which they are most clearly to be understood. This being, in the present case, impossible, I have endeavoured, so far as might be, to put myself in an Oriental position, and from that position to review the scenes which pass before us. (INT 8)[16]

---

[16] Neale's orientalism reached its upper limit in his discussion of the *Filioque*, appended to the *General Introduction*. *Filioque* refers to the dogmatic formula expressing the joint procession of the Holy Ghost from the Father and the Son in the Niceno-Constantinopolitan Creed. This creed, which is associated with the Council of Constantinople (381), was meant to be a primary formulation of the common faith of Christians; but the addition by the Western Church to the third article of the words 'and the Son' (*Filioque*) was one of the principal factors leading to schism between East and West in the Middle Ages, and afterwards became a symbol of the rift between the Churches. In his dissertation in the *General Introduction*, Neale adopted the Eastern viewpoint (i.e., omission of the *Filioque*), and in a letter to Webb revealed some of his thoughts on the matter: 'I feel so very strongly on the Eastern side, that I may have spoken more strongly than I want. I wished to seem to pronounce no judgement, but to leave the reader to form his own. . . . In my own mind I am convinced with [William] Palmer that the Latin doctrine, if consistently carried out, would become heresy, and that the Holy Ghost does not proceed from the Son at all, except in the way of Temporal Mission, and then not according to His operations. However, I don't say all this in the book' (*Letters*, 131; dated 23 Jan. 1850, from Sackville College). Neale considered the *Filioque* to be 'the only important doctrinal difference which separates the Eastern from the Western Church', and firmly believed

With his shortcomings frankly acknowledged, Neale then proceeded to decode the mysteries of the Orient for his readers. His particular brand of orientalism was his way of developing an imaginative link with Eastern Christendom, while at the same time remaining unavoidably rooted in the West. Some of the problems involved in writing about the East he overcame by studying the languages in which the source materials were written and by careful research; others he dealt with by adding intuitive motivations to the theoretical ones already considered. The result, he believed, would be a work of insight and feeling, as well as great learning.

that 'no true union—experience has shewn it—can take place till the *Filioque* be omitted from the Creed' (INT 1095, 1168). This is a very brief, incomplete analysis of Neale's stand on a highly complex theological question; but it can safely be said that his favouring the Eastern position indicates the level to which, on occasion, he sympathized with the Orthodox viewpoint. For a fuller explanation of Neale's views on the *Filioque*, see his article, 'The Filioque Controversy', *Christian Remembrancer*, 48 (1864), 468–502.

Chapter 4

Neale's *History of the Holy Eastern Church*

THREE parts of the *History* were published, the first two during his lifetime and the third posthumously: *The Patriarchate of Alexandria* (1847), the *General Introduction* (1850), and *The Patriarchate of Antioch* (1873), edited by George Williams. These volumes provided a carefully researched, though uneven account; at certain points the history chronicled consists of little more than a catalogue of names of successive patriarchs or metropolitans, while at others Neale's prolonged discussions lent greater emphasis to events than was compatible with a balanced survey.

A *History of the Holy Eastern Church* was Neale's peculiar interpretation of Orthodox history, doctrine, and practice. It bore his stamp, as well as that of accepted nineteenth-century orientalist thinking, and in certain instances exceeded the limits imposed by his sources. For example, in his description of Islam as 'a more fearful adversary' to the Church's doctrines and 'a more cruel aggressor of her children than any with whom she had yet to contend' (ALX ii. 64), he recorded the appeals to the Emir in 748 by both Catholic—that is, Orthodox—and Jacobite Christians in Egypt. But in the absence of historical records of these communications, Neale took the liberty of putting into the mouths of the Catholics arguments which he believed they would have used, while simultaneously preserving the words of the Jacobites as recorded by their historians. In a note he justifies his method as follows:

In relating this, and similar disputes, we have given the arguments which, according to the Jacobite historians, were actually used by those of their own sect. But to have assigned to the Catholics the absurd and unworthy answers of which their adversaries accuse them, had been to write with the party spirit of a heretic. Two ways only remained to us. The one, to omit, on all such occasions, the arguments used on both sides, which would reduce the various accounts to little more than a detail of names, and deprive the reader of some curious information: the other to put into the mouths of the Catholic Prelates the arguments which they ought to have employed—and which were certainly employed by the great opposers of the Jacobite heresy, S. Leo, S. Proterius, and others. If this be called a liberty, it would be difficult, we think, to point out any other course which, considering the unhappy state of Alexandrian history, would be more deserving of that name. (ALX ii. 113)

Even though Neale's arguments may have been similar to the ones employed, what he does here borders on intellectual dishonesty. It is surprising in light of his claim that in his analysis of Orthodox history, ritual, and doctrine, he strove for historical accuracy (INT p. xi). He wished to compile a history of the Orthodox communion—based as far as possible on Eastern sources—not for potential travellers or, despite what he had originally thought, for the general public, but for specialists who desired access to Eastern Church history, which had previously been denied them because of language barriers, misconceptions which had become canonical, or confusion in the existing works on the subject (ALX i, pp. vi–xi). What emerged was a work which in some parts displayed the care Neale took in researching Orthodox Church history and practice, but in others clearly exposed Neale's own biases. This second aspect of *A History of the Holy Eastern Church*, which shows what Neale infused of himself into his work, is connected with his Eastern point of view, and further reveals why he went to such lengths to present this communion to a British audience which was almost completely ignorant of her history, doctrine, and ritual.[1]

In the *General Introduction* Neale provided for his readers

[1] Neale's *History* is his major historical work on the Orthodox communion. It should be noted, however, that he had a habit of inserting small amounts of Eastern historical background and improving material into his other works. In *A History of the Church for the Use of Children*, Part I (London, 1853), e.g., Neale included a small section on 'Geographical Divisions of the Church' (120–4); in *Stories of the Crusades* (London, 1905), he interjected: 'It may be necessary to remind the reader of the state of the Church at that time in the East', and followed this with a one-page summary (170–1).

a catalogue of advantages to be gained through a study of the Christian East:

> Theories of the Church, now principally drawn from the Annals of the Western Branch, might be corrected or confirmed by an enquiry into the wonders which the Eastern has been privileged to work, and the trials which she has been strengthened to endure. Details, which in the history of the Latin communion seem isolated or anomalous, will fall into an intelligible system when confronted with the fortunes of the East. Roman developments will be tested by the unbroken traditions of sister communions; Roman arguments strengthened or disproved by a reference to Oriental facts. Uninterrupted successions of Metropolitans and Bishops stretch themselves to Apostolic times; venerable liturgies exhibit doctrine unchanged, and discipline uncorrupted; the same Sacrifice is offered, the same hymns are chanted, by the Eastern Christians of to-day, as those which resounded in the churches of S. Basil or S. Firmilian. I shall write of Prelates not less faithful, of Martyrs not less constant, of Confessors not less generous, than those of Europe; shall shew every article of the Creed guarded with as much scrupulous jealousy; shall adduce a fresh crowd of witnesses to the Faith once for all delivered to the Saints. In the glow and splendour of Byzantine glory, in the tempests of the Oriental middle ages, in the desolation and tyranny of the Turkish Empire, the testimony of the same immutable Church remains unchanged. Extending herself from the Sea of Okhotsk to the palaces of Venice, from the ice-fields that grind against the Solevetsky monastery to the burning jungles of Malabar, embracing a thousand languages, and nations, and tongues, but binding them together in the golden link of the same Faith, offering the Tremendous Sacrifice in a hundred Liturgies, but offering it to the same GOD, and with the same rites. . . . She is now, as she was from the beginning, multiplex in her arrangements, simple in her faith, difficult in comprehension to strangers, easily intelligible to her sons, widely scattered in her branches, hardly beset by her enemies, yet still and evermore, what she delights to call herself, One, Only, Holy, Catholic and Apostolic. (INT 1–2)

Neale compared the Eastern Church, which was unfamiliar, with the Western, which was part of the experience of his readers; he held up the Roman Catholic Church as a standard by which to judge her Eastern sister.[2] He claimed that a

---

[2] This view accounts for Rowell's comments concerning Neale's affinity for the Eastern Church: it placed 'contemporary debates with Rome in a wider perspective' (*Vision Glorious*, 109).

consideration of Orthodox Church history would show that she compared favourably with the Western branch; he also suggested that because of her immutability (which allowed for decoding), the Eastern Church sometimes set an example to which the Western Church would do well to aspire.

Neale narrowed the comparison further to include only the Orthodox and Anglican Churches. He wished to convince his readers that these two branches of the Catholic Church enjoyed an intimacy on certain fundamental points to which the Roman Church was not party. According to Neale, this special relationship between Orthodox and Anglicans made familiarity between them not only attractive, but necessary. He indicated some of the similarities between them—and concurrently the perceived dissimilarities with Roman Catholicism—in *Essays on Liturgiology and Church History*.

> In treating with the East, we come with no pretensions of superiority, with no claims to domination; we come, free from many of the stumbling-blocks which Latin Christianity presents to their eyes— purgatory, indulgences, the denial of the cup to the laity, azymes; and in two of the liturgies out of the three branches of our communion, the Scotch and the American, we approximate very closely; we are identical, on all essential points, with those of S. Chrysostom and S. Basil.[3]

In light of Britain's imperialist political stance in the nineteenth century, such statements seem naïve. But if Neale's words are understood in the context of the Anglo-Catholic revival (with its widespread anti-Roman stance), then he emerges as one who was trying to lead the revival in new directions, and, by a closer association with Eastern Orthodoxy, to strengthen the position of his Church.

In the *General Introduction* Neale explained that the context of relations was not only sororal but also filial; for many aspects of Anglican doctrine, practice, and history he claimed Orthodox roots:

> To write the History of the Eastern Church ought to be a labour of love to an Englishman, not merely because it seems as though the

---

[3] J. M. Neale, *Essays on Liturgiology and Church History* (London, 1863), 281. This essay originally appeared in the *Christian Remembrancer* for 1855 under the title 'Prospects of the Oriental Church'.

future union of the Church were to arise from that quarter... but because, in the history of the past, Britain owes so much to, and is so closely connected with, the East. There appears little doubt, that early British orders were derived from France, as France derived her illuminations from Lyons, and Lyons from Smyrna: thus by S. Polycarp tracing the gift of the HOLY GHOST to S. John. So we find S. Colman, at the conference of Strenaeshalch, quoting S. John as the author of the Paschal Computation then used in Britain; so we shall also see that in some remarkable particulars the English Liturgies approximate to the Oriental: and even in such a comparative trifle as the use of two lights on the Altar, we may trace either the early influence of the East, or more probably that of S. Theodore of Tarsus, when raised to the Archiepiscopal throne of Canterbury. And whatever be the amount of our obligation to S. Augustine, of ever-blessed memory, (himself deriving his consecration through France from Asia), they cannot cancel our debt to the Primeval East, for the first illumination of our country, never lost in Wales, for the thousands of souls saved in ages prior to the Roman Mission, perhaps also in some degree for the readiness with which that mission itself was received. (INT 17)

This passage goes even further than the one from *Essays on Liturgiology and Church History* in its argument for Anglican–Orthodox ties. Throughout his *History of the Holy Eastern Church* Neale sought to draw out instances of perceived Anglican emulation of Orthodox doctrine and practice, as well as examples of co-operation on a historical level between the two Churches. The impression conveyed on these occasions is often misleading, claiming a stronger association than was supported by existing theological or historical sources. Thus while Neale purported to be examining the Orthodox Church with an orientalist eye, his analysis was shaped by his own biases, in order to make the Eastern Church fit into the mould he had created for her.

At times Neale's mould suffered because of genuine ignorance on his part, as in the case of Eastern ecclesiology, which he described in book 2 of the *General Introduction*. He tried to make his research as thorough as possible; but because of ill health and other commitments, he had little opportunity to travel to the East. His only visit took place in 1860, and was chronicled in his *Notes, Ecclesiological and Picturesque, on Dalmatia, Croatia, Istria, Styria, with a Visit to*

Montenegro. Almost all the information on ecclesiology in the *General Introduction*, therefore, was derived from books, and as Every notes, the texts from which Neale industriously reproduced architectural plans and pictures were themselves not always accurate.[4] Although he knew from personal experience the feel and appearances of English cathedrals and parish churches, as well as those of Belgium, France, Germany, Spain, and Portugal, on the subject of Eastern ecclesiology he was on a much less firm footing. But this did not keep him from presenting his perception of Eastern ecclesiology to his readers or from defending Eastern Church architecture from Western criticisms:

> It is curious how strong a prejudice exists against all idea of the beauty of Byzantine architecture. It seems to be regarded as a stiff corruption of heathen art; a 'Jacobean' imitation of Grecian loveliness. That it has itself a breath of Christian life; that it worked out its own developments; that piety of the deepest fervour, and genius of the highest order, were poured forth on its thousand temples; that the sublime dome was its own, that shrine raised to the ALMIGHTY above the din and bustle of the earth ... all this is unknown or forgotten. (INT 166)

Neale tried to present Eastern architecture as something just as valuable, beautiful, and sanctified as the fourteenth-century Middle Pointed which his Cambridge Camden Society had been pressing on church-builders in Britain and her colonies.

Ignorance could not be claimed as the only reason for the singularity of some of Neale's analyses, however. In at least one instance, according to Every, Neale knowingly misled his readers in an attempt to draw a parallel between an Eastern and a Western architectural arrangement. In his description of the iconostasis, Neale was determined to show that the division between the Orthodox nave and sanctuary corresponded exactly to the separation of nave and choir. Every comments on this unfounded claim:

---

[4] G. Every, 'The Legacy of Neale', *Eastern Churches Review*, 1/2 (1966), 143. One of Neale's scrapbooks contains a review which points out his deficiencies in the use of Orthodox liturgical sources (MS 3113, fos. 64–5, Lambeth Palace Library).

[Neale] was well aware that the ikonostasis does not correspond to [the Western division], but he is constantly trying to find one where there is not, and to make it important where it is insignificant. If he possibly can he will locate the angelic doors in the proper place for the Western rood screen. He never saw the liturgical significance of the *naos* as the place where the whole people of God, each in their order, assemble for the synaxis.... Hence the impression which still lingers among Anglicans not well informed about the East... that the ikonostasis effectively divides the Orthodox Church into two churches where two distinct services are going on.[5]

Thus, like Flaubert's presentation of the Islamic world, of which the majority of his readers had little knowledge, Neale's pronouncements became canonical, and fostered deep-rooted misconceptions about the Eastern Church.

In his presentation of Orthodox Church history there is at least one instance of him establishing a connection between the Anglican and Eastern Churches which, according to available historical evidence, was not as strong as he suggested: the case of Cyril Loukaris (1572–1638). This Orthodox prelate, a hero for Neale, was Patriarch of Alexandria and later of Constantinople; his story was given extended treatment in *The Patriarchate of Alexandria*.[6] Neale's aim in producing his 100-page biographical sketch of Loukaris was to develop the Patriarch's special relationship with England, in order to confirm what he perceived to be long-standing historical links between the Anglican and Orthodox Churches. His establishment of such ties as early as 1847 gave him a foundation on which to build later in the quest for *sobornost*.

Loukaris became Patriarch of Alexandria in 1602 at the age of 30. He was known to be an opponent of Roman Catholicism and to be amicably disposed towards the Reformed Churches. He also wanted to effect a reformation within the Eastern Church and to free the sorely oppressed Orthodox Christians from Turkish domination. Although Neale recognized the damage done by Loukaris in bringing Protestant tenets into Orthodox theology, at the same time he saw the

---

[5] Every, 'Legacy of Neale', 143–4. See Glossary.
[6] See *Letters*, 74–5, for Neale's complicated instructions to Webb, who was travelling on the Continent at the time, *re* collecting material on Loukaris.

Patriarch's lifetime as a fruitful period for Anglican–Eastern relations.[7]

Neale admitted that the first ten years of Loukaris's Alexandrian patriarchate—half of the time he spent there—were 'almost entirely unknown to us' (ALX ii. 364). So he focused on the next ten years and the subsequent period in Constantinople, and then almost exclusively on Loukaris's relations with the Anglican Church. Despite the importance Neale attached to this association, its only practical outcome as far as the Orthodox were concerned was the dispatch of a young Beroean monk, Metrophanes Kritopoulos, who later became Patriarch of Alexandria, to Oxford.[8]

Neale might well have spent more time chronicling the journey of Kritopoulos, which did more to forward East–West relations than anything personally attempted by Loukaris. The expedition took Loukaris's emissary through England, Germany, and Switzerland, countries in which the Reformation had had an acute influence on Church doctrine and practice. Though he was an Orthodox Christian who valued his own traditions and tried to teach those around him about them, Kritopoulos also admired some of the teachings of the Anglican and Reformed communions, and saw in them valuable lessons for his own mother Church. He worked through friendship and fellowship, which he believed to be the necessary context for *sobornost*.

In *A History of the Holy Eastern Church*, however, Neale had other ideas. He wished to attest to the privileged position

---

[7] The exact nature of Loukaris's relations with Protestantism has always been a matter of controversy; but it seems clear that while in Alexandria he became deeply interested in the study of Protestant theology, and tended to combine Calvinistic elements with his Orthodox convictions.

[8] The most recent biography of Kritopoulos, C. Davey's *Pioneer for Unity* (London, 1987), confirms that the result of Kritopoulos's 13 years abroad were meagre in terms of solidifying Eastern–Western relations on any official level or of practically promoting Christian unity. This was largely due to the internal state of Europe, the lack of unity between the Protestant Churches, and the lack of any follow-up to Kritopoulos's exploratory journey. Yet he spent much of his time explaining the ways of Orthodoxy to those whom he met, in private conversations, public lectures, sermons, and published works. Davey's book is of interest to the study of Neale for the amount he quotes from Neale's *History of the Holy Eastern Church* and for its confirmation of the close link between Kritopoulos's story and that of Loukaris.

which the Anglican Church enjoyed in its relations with the Orthodox in the seventeenth century. By way of an introduction, he quoted a letter from Loukaris to the Calvinist theologian Uytenbogaert in 1612. In the following extract some of Neale's own thoughts on the Orthodox Church may be discerned:

> Some appear to reproach the Eastern Church with ignorance, inasmuch as the pursuits of literature and philosophy have shifted into other quarters. But, certainly, the East may be esteemed exceedingly happy in this her ignorance. For though, undoubtedly, she is pressed down with many miseries through the tyranny of the Turks, and possesses no facilities for the acquirement of knowledge, she has at least this great advantage, that she knows nothing of those pestilent disputes which, in the present day, pollute the ears of men. To her, innovations are novel signs and prodigies, to be dreaded rather than followed. She is contented with the simple faith which she has learned from the Apostles and our forefathers. In it she perseveres even unto blood. She never takes away, never adds, never changes. She always remains the same, always keeps and preserves untainted orthodoxy. And if any one chose to observe seriously the state of things in the Eastern Church, he would become aware of a highly important and wonderful circumstance; for Christians themselves, since they have been reduced to servitude, though persecuted by the unbelievers as by serpents within their dwellings, even if they see themselves deprived of their substance, their children dragged from their embraces, and themselves afflicted and distressed without intermission, to the utmost limits of endurance, yet think it is not grievous to suffer these things for the faith of CHRIST, and, as has been often proved, when occasion offered, are ready to submit to death itself. And perhaps the almighty power of GOD is by this means rendered more apparent, by which so great grace is bestowed on men, when His strength is made perfect in weakness. Is not this a miracle? Are not these the marks of the LORD JESUS which Paul carried about? For with this the Eastern Christians, setting no store by the advantages of this life, and regarding them as perishable, keep up their hearts to one end—the inheritance of a heavenly kingdom to the glory of GOD. (ALX ii. 367)

This letter embodies elements of Orthodox faith which penetrated Neale's imagination and which he later evoked passionately in his Eastern tales: its simplicity, immutability, and strength in the face of persecution, even unto death.

Neale saw Loukaris's world as troubled by two adversaries: Muslims and Roman Catholics; both, Neale believed, persecuted Orthodox Christians, albeit in different ways. The Turks transformed the Eastern Christians into a suffering, humiliated nation, subject to such persecutions as heavy taxation; 'child-gathering', whereby Christian infants were recruited to be trained as slaves in the seraglio and older boys for eventual service in the janizaries; and forced conversions, which in many cases led to martyrdom. Based on personal experience, Kritopoulos described life under Turkish rule as 'worse than death'.[9]

The Roman Catholics, according to Loukaris, were equally damaging in their approach to the Orthodox. Roman overtures in Eastern countries, made primarily by Jesuits, were at first welcomed; Roman Catholic priests were employed as preachers and confessors, and were enthusiastically received by the faithful. Later, however, they came to be viewed by some Orthodox with suspicion. Among these was Loukaris, who believed that what passed for friendly pastoral work masked an official policy of infiltration as preparation for a takeover of an Orthodox church or patriarchate. The question of Turkish domination was difficult, if not impossible, to settle; but Loukaris believed that the perceived incursion of Romanism could be repelled. In his attempt to deal with this second problem, with its desired goal of preserving the distinct tradition and witness of the Orthodox Church, 'the thoughts of Cyril', according to Neale, 'were much turned to England' (ALX ii. 389).

The Jesuits were originally admitted to the Greek Churches by the Orthodox bishops in order to increase the number of qualified preachers and confessors to an acceptable level. But once intolerance, doubt, and fear had crept into his thoughts, Loukaris saw the need to educate his own clergy to withstand the arguments put to them by the Roman missionaries who travelled about Egypt at the time. In search of a remedy, Loukaris, according to Neale, reasoned thus: 'He was probably unwilling to send them to Venice or Padua, knowing the

---

[9] M. Kritopoulos, *Confession of the Eastern Catholic and Apostolic Church*; quoted in Davey, *Pioneer for Unity*, 4. For a concise survey of Orthodox life under Turkish domination in the 17th cent., see ibid. 2–23.

dangers to which they would there be exposed; and still more unwilling, at this time, to trust them at Geneva, or any of the Dutch universities. He therefore cast his eyes towards England, where Abbot filled the Chair of Canterbury' (ALX ii. 384).

George Abbot (1562–1633) responded favourably to the Patriarch's request for help in educating his clergy in order to combat what Loukaris called 'the tyranny of the Roman Pontiff' (ALX ii. 385). After quoting at length from the courteous and amicable correspondence which passed between Loukaris and Abbot, Neale presented the departure of Kritopoulos in 1617 as the climax to the offer of assistance to the Orthodox by the Anglican Church. His crowning statement was as follows: 'It is plain that at this time the thoughts of Cyril were much turned to England, and that he received pretty accurate information from Metrophanes of what concerned its Church' (ALX ii. 389). While the second part of Neale's claim may be true, the first is an overstatement: he never really established that much significance was attached to this contact.[10]

Loukaris's approach to the see of Canterbury was part of a larger investigation of the ways in which the Orthodox Church might receive support in counteracting the influence and activities of Rome. England was only one of the European Protestant nations which he approached. They were all willing to provide him with printed books, but only from England did he receive the valuable offer of free education for his clergy. This was the only practical outcome of Loukaris's contact with Anglicans which was effected by the Patriarch himself. Metrophanes Kritopoulos, however, reaped other benefits, the foremost of which was firsthand contact with the Reformed Churches, to which he explained the ways of Orthodoxy. Neale did not consider the journey of Kritopoulos in detail, however; he merely quoted letters from Abbot to Loukaris in which Kritopoulos was mentioned, adding the remark, already cited, that Loukaris received from the Greek monk 'pretty accurate information' concerning the Anglican Church.

---

[10] The same lack of evidence may be seen in 'Orthodox Churches', where Florovsky notes: 'Even during his days at Alexandria Loukaris had begun to enter into contact with the Church of England. It was no accident that he sent his Protosynkellos, Metrophanes Kritopoulos, to study theology at Oxford' (184).

The records of Kritopoulos's travels show that during his seven years in England he enjoyed the friendship of many clergymen and scholars, and studied Anglican beliefs and practices. At the same time, according to the evidence collected by Davey, Kritopoulos

> indicated... that the Orthodox had much to teach the Reformed Churches, not least in the matter of respecting the authority of the Fathers and in discovering, through this, a unanimity in doctrine which contrasted strongly with the endless and contentious disputes between the different parties in the Western churches. He could see that they held much in common, and that friendship and study of each other's churches could draw them closer together.[11]

The atmosphere of *sobornost* which surrounded Kritopoulos's work carried with it important considerations for the way in which Christian communions should approach each other.

The cases of Eastern ecclesiology and Cyril Loukaris are just two examples of a general feeling which pervades Neale's *History of the Holy Eastern Church*: the attempt, as part of the well-established orientalist tradition, to domesticate and to familiarize British readers with a Church whose doctrine and practice were less alien to Western Christians than they at first seemed and whose history was at certain points connected with their own. Neale's analyses help to explain the methods he subsequently used in his Greek hymn translations and oriental novels: the casting of characteristically Eastern themes and history in a more recognizable Western form. Hymns were given a characteristically English structure which made them suitable for singing in British churches; the novels and tales, which had an Eastern setting, were blended with certain motifs current in Victorian fiction, such as torture, death, and martyrdom, thereby ensuring their marketability to a British reading public.

Neale's primary aim in *A History of the Holy Eastern Church*, and in the subsequent Eastern hymns and tales, was to bring this ancient branch of Christendom closer to his readers. The ways he chose to do this—and the order in which he employed them—represent a methodical appeal to a gradually expanding audience. The *History* was an academic work, designed for specialists; and after its rather limited success he

---

[11] Davey, *Pioneer for Unity*, 145.

turned to media which had potentially wider appeal and circulation. In all three cases, however, Neale lent a peculiarly English air to his subject.

In writing historical narrative, hymns, or fiction, the wider aim of promoting Christian unity was always at the back of Neale's mind, though to what extent he saw this goal as ultimately attainable is questionable. George Williams, president of the Eastern Church Association and editor of *The Patriarchate of Antioch*, had this to say about Neale's oriental research and its aims:

The sacred cause was, the gradual approximation and ultimate reconciliation of the long-estranged families of Catholic Christendom, on the basis of a better mutual understanding; which he hoped might result in a more just appreciation of the comparative unimportance of the points of difference, when viewed in relation to the vast heritage of Divine Truth which all hold in common. And although he was not permitted to see the consummation of his ardent desires, yet his latter years were gladdened by the unmistakeable evidences of a wider and constantly-increasing interest—both at home and abroad—in the cause of a reunited Christendom, which had been for many years the day-dream of a small and uninfluential section of English Churchmen. How largely his indefatigable industry has contributed to this hopeful progress of opinion, was known to others better than himself; and I can myself bear witness to the fact that while his zeal provoked very many in our own Communion, the exhibition of it in its results, in Russia and the East, was effectual in stimulating a reciprocal interest in various parts of the Orthodox Church. (ANT 10)

Given that Williams was editing the posthumous work of a friend and that he himself was a member of the small group of English churchmen interested in the Eastern Church, his praise of Neale's work might seem inflated.[12] But there was in

---

[12] Neale's *History of the Holy Eastern Church* seems to have pleased the Russians, however. From Tsar Nicholas I he received £100, almost four times his annual salary, for what Popov called an 'arduous and useful work' (letter from Popov to Neale, dated 10 June 1851; quoted in Towle, 175); Metropolitan Philaret sent Neale some icons (which are preserved at St Margaret's Convent, East Grinstead) and a Slavonic service-book; Muraviev wrote to Neale to say, 'It is most pleasing to me to see the true Orthodox spirit of the Orient which pervades the whole work, as if it were written by a Catholic of the Orient' (quoted in the original French in Towle, 174; my translation). Such gestures and words prompted Neale to write happily to Webb: 'I had no idea, until now, how big a man I was in Russia' (quoted in Towle, 286).

Neale's later years a certain 'progress of opinion', which made possible the founding of the Eastern Church Association. The period between the publication of Neale's *History of the Holy Eastern Church* and the formation of this Association (1850–63) was when Neale produced the bulk of his literary expressions of Eastern Orthodoxy: those hymns and tales which reached a greater number of readers and church-goers than his academic, theological, or ecumenical work could have done.

PART II

Hymnologist of the Eastern Church

Chapter 5

Neale and Orthodox Hymnody

IN the years following the publication of his *History of the Holy Eastern Church* Neale had not lost sight of his goal of promoting familiarity with the Christian East among Anglicans. He had written three novels with Oriental settings, *Theodora Phranza* (1853–4), *The Lily of Tiflis* (1859), and *The Lazar-House of Leros* (1859), and several short stories. He had also published, with R. F. Littledale, *the Liturgies of SS. Mark, James, Clement, Chrysostom, and Basil* in English (1859),[1] as well as *Voices from the East: Documents on the Present State and Working of the Oriental Church* (1859). All these received little attention, however, when compared to the *Hymns of the Eastern Church*, first published in 1862.

Neale's interest in Orthodoxy must certainly have been heightened after his first and only visit to the East in 1860, to Dalmatia; as he had intimated to Webb, 'You will easily see how infinitely valuable to me a tour in that country would be.'[2] The purpose of the visit was largely ecclesiological, and Neale had the opportunity to visit churches of a number of denominations, including Protestant, Roman Catholic, and Orthodox. In the tradition of other orientalist travellers, he published a record of his expedition under the title *Notes, Ecclesiological and Picturesque, on Dalmatia, Croatia, Istria, Styria, with a visit to Montenegro* (1861).

---

[1] An edition in the original Greek appeared in the same year.
[2] *Letters*, 311; dated 26 Feb. 1860, from Sackville College. Ideally, Neale would like to have gone to Russia, and it seems that there was a possibility of him going with Alexander Forbes, the Bishop of Brechin, in 1857. At that time he wrote to Webb: 'Did I tell you that Brechinensis is going next year, in all possibility, to confirm at S. Petersburg, Moscow, and perhaps Archangel, and that he has offered to take me as Chaplain? The Russian Company pays all expenses. . . . Just imagine seeing Novogorod!' (*Letters*, 299; dated 31 Aug. 1857, from Sackville College). The plan was never executed.

Neale undertook the journey with Joseph Oldknow, curate of Holy Trinity Chapel, Bordesley, in order to observe the co-existence of the Eastern and Western Churches: 'I had long been desirous, as deeply interested in, and engaged on the history of, the Oriental Church, of observing for myself the mutual action and re-action of the Eastern and Western Communions in their border lands on the east coast of the Adriatic.'[3] The volume is a bit rambling, as Neale digressed at several points to give local history, combining past and present. He also gives an interesting account of the non-Slavonic Glagolita Rite and a curious incident involving his purchase of a full set of Dalmatian women's clothing, for which he engaged in heated bargaining with local residents. There are many minutiae of ecclesiology recorded, as well as some interesting impressions of the Eastern Church as he saw it.

The last point merits some discussion. Until then, Neale's thoughts on the Eastern Church had been based largely on his reading. But now he had the opportunity for some limited personal acquaintance with it. At Zara, for instance, he met the Greek bishop, Steven Knezevitch, who showed his guest over the community. Afterwards Neale concluded: 'I was particularly requested to observe the exceedingly high morality of the people as shown by the authenticated lists of legitimate, and illegitimate births; and certainly it speaks very favourably for the state of the Greek Church in Dalmatia.'[4]

In reporting this 'high morality', Neale might have had as his goal the refutation—or at least modification—of the claims of Flaubert, Kinglake, Thackeray, and others concerning sexual practices in the Orient. At the very least, he was making a distinction between the behaviour of Muslims, who were considered licentious, and Orthodox Christians, who were considered chaste. Nevertheless, like the other Orientalist writers, he was quick to generalize—here about the state of the Orthodox Church in Dalmatia—and from incidents such as this he formed general impressions not only about the four million members of the 'Austro-Oriental Church' as he called it,[5] but

---

[3] J. M. Neale, *Notes, Ecclesiological and Picturesque, on Dalmatia, Croatia, Istria, Styria, with a Visit to Montenegro* (London, 1861), 1. This book was later translated into Russian (see *Letters*, 334).
[4] Ibid. 123.   [5] Ibid. 176.

about the whole of the Christian East; for, aside from his occasional visits to Popov's chapel in London, this was his only firsthand experience of the Orthodox.

Neale had preconceived ideas concerning the relations between the Orthodox and Roman Catholics. His reading of Orthodox Church history had taught him that peaceful coexistence was the exception rather than the rule; this problem he blamed on the Roman Catholics and the Muslims. When he was in Dalmatia, he seized the opportunity of trying to discredit the former; while on Zara, an island inhabited by both Orthodox and Roman Catholics, the former being less numerous, he conducted the following investigation:

> The Church which is in the minority will always be purer than that which is the Establishment: it is very striking to see cottages scattered here and there, tenanted by Orthodox Greeks, who live among a Latin population and who will pass the Latin Church on the way to their own, to go for their sacraments six, or seven, or eight miles away. I asked the Bishop if the extreme severity of the Greek fasts, when brought into contrast with the prodigious laxity of the Latin, did not diminish the number of his people; he told me that he had no reason to attribute any such effect to the difference between the two churches.[6]

Neale expected the opposite to be true, and was greatly reassured by the Bishop's reply, which is important for understanding the tenacious adherence to tradition in Orthodoxy. Incidents such as this point to the biased view he had of East–West church relations. It seems likely that Neale's rather limited experiences form the basis for many of his later opinions and statements about the Eastern Church.

There was another incident in 1860 which might have given Neale's researches into Orthodoxy additional impetus. He described what happened in a letter to Webb:

> I had asked G[eorge] Williams to get for me the liturgy of the Staro-Viertze, which retained, you know, all the *mumpsimuses* that course of years had introduced. After vainly trying elsewhere, he asked Philaret of Moscow where he could procure one. His Holiness sent into his library, gave him one for me, wrote my name in it,—and this: 'God's blessing and help to them who investigate the truth in

---

[6] Ibid. 124.

the ancient books and traditions of the Church for the peace and ultimate Union of the Churches of GOD. Phil. M. Moscow. July 13th, 1860.' It is a very handsome book indeed.[7]

This was the second time that Neale's work had come to Philaret's attention: previously, on the publication of *A History of the Holy Eastern Church*, the Metropolitan had sent Neale a number of small gifts, and had expressed similar sentiments on a 'future union of the Churches'.[8]

It has already been noted that Neale's closest contact with the Orthodox Church was through its Russian branch—more particularly with Philaret, Popov, and their associates and representatives in England. By the early 1860s, however, Neale's fame in Russia was not limited to the clergy, but had spread to the nobility; the latter had presumably been introduced to Neale's work through the Tsar, who had praised Neale in 1851 for his *History*, or through the clergy, who served as confessors to various members of the Russian Imperial Court. The following extract from a letter to Webb attests to Neale's popularity in Russia:

We had last Sunday that Countess Patapoff, of whom I think I told you, at S. Margaret's [Convent]. Her Confessor, one Apollinarius, a monk in the Troitzkoi-Sergievsky Monastery, has told her to come, and to write him a particular account of it. She speaks English very sufficiently well. But the quantity of invitations she brought me from Russia—both at S. Petersburg, Moscow, and Novogorod—is marvellous, and from Prince Gouriel, in Georgia. I do hope some day to go.[9]

All the attention Neale received from Russia would certainly have pleased him, and presumably would have provided additional impetus for his compilation of *Hymns of the Eastern Church*.

Although Neale had no predecessors in Britain who attempted translations of Greek hymns, there was at least one churchman on the Continent who showed a marked interest

---

[7] *Letters*, 326–7; dated 20 Oct. 1860, from Sackville College. Lawson explains that a *mumpsimus* is a stupid or ignorant blunder (*Letters*, 326).
[8] See Sr. Miriam, 9b.
[9] *Letters*, 335; dated 14 Sept. 1861, from Sackville College.

in Orthodox hymnody: the Danish Lutheran Nikolaj Frederik Severin Grundtvig (1783–1872).[10] Almost unknown outside Scandinavia, Grundtvig nevertheless made significant contributions to literature, education, politics, and theology. Allchin, in an attempt to classify him in English terms, says: 'We should do best to imagine a combination of the artistic and social enthusiasms of William Morris, with the theological and philosophical interests of F. D. Maurice, joined to Charles Wesley's gifts as a writer of hymns.'[11] Grundtvig's interest in Orthodox hymnody found expression in a collection of thirty-eight pieces based on Greek originals, published as part of his first volume of *Sang Vaerk til den Danske Kirke* (1836–7).[12]

A number of similarities may be seen between Grundtvig and Neale. The Dane's determination to write hymns (1,400 total) sprang from a dissatisfaction with those then circulating in the Danish Church; he believed that the Danish hymnbook reflected the individualism and moralism of much eighteenth-century religion.[13] To remedy this situation, he began to write original hymns and to make translations from all the great periods of Christian hymnody, in an attempt to strengthen the Christian 'myth', which he believed to be the transcendent reality which bound together the devotion of all

---

[10] A somewhat different version of this discussion of Neale and Grundtvig appeared previously as 'The Greek Hymn Translations and Adaptations of N. F. S. Grundtvig and J. M. Neale', *Hymn Society of Great Britain and Ireland Bulletin*, 12/10 (no. 183) (Apr. 1990), 182–7, and is drawn on here with the kind permission of the Society.

[11] A. M. Allchin, 'The Hymns of N. F. S. Grundtvig', *Eastern Churches Quarterly*, 13/3–4 (1959), 129.

[12] The collection extended to 9 vols. by the time of Grundtvig's death. The title *Sang Vaerk* is interesting in light of what has been said about Neale's hymnological theory. During the English bombardment of Copenhagen in 1807, the spire of the city's main church, the Church of our Lady, was hit, and the 'song-work' (the famous peal of bells that played the old hymn tunes) was destroyed. The church lay in ruins for a number of years, and became for Grundtvig a symbol of both national and Church decay. The *Sang Vaerk* was the rebuilding of the Church with the aid of hymns (C. Thodberg, 'Grundtvig the Hymnwriter', in *N. F. S. Grundtvig*, ed. C. Thodberg and A. Thyssen, trans. E. Broadbridge (Copenhagen, 1983), 175).

[13] The first hymns by Grundtvig entered the Danish hymn-book in 1855; in the current version, he dominates, with some 272 titles out of a total of 754 (Thodberg, 'Grundtvig the Hymnwriter', 160).

ages.[14] Although his translations were often extremely free—more like paraphrases—they nevertheless conveyed the attitudes and teaching of the originals. Neale's desire to write hymns came about in a similar way; but whereas his translations of Latin hymns are in many cases attempts to be faithful to the original, his Greek renderings, like Grundtvig's, are freer.

Another similarity between the two hymn-writers is their rejection of the personal element in hymns in favour of the spiritual. Grundtvig's hymns display an objective and congregational character, making them suitable for Church or community use: 'we-hymns' rather that 'I-hymns'. Grundtvig makes this distinction clear in a letter in which he speaks of the individualizing tendency as a 'chief failing with our Fathers, which we their children must try to correct, that they wished to deal with our Saviour each for himself and to possess him, which can never be the case, as the "Our Father" among other things should have taught them.' Instead, Grundtvig preferred hymns which concerned 'first and foremost, Church, Baptism and Eucharist, and ... our Church festivals, and our Church gatherings in general'.[15] In his own chapel at Vartov Hospital the worship centred on hymns and the Communion service, rather than the sermon.

Neale too objected to what he perceived as the profusion of 'I-hymns' in his day, particularly from Dissenting sources. He believed that the collective essence of worship in these communions was the stylized reiteration of personal spiritual experiences. His objection to this approach was related to his study of liturgy, in which personal experience is subordinate to communal effect. Neale made important observations on this subject in his introduction to *The Liturgies of SS. Mark*,

---

[14] This use of the word 'myth', as opposed to 'image', 'symbol', or 'doctrine', follows Adey, and confines itself to the *mythos*, or sacred story, including the following events: the Fall of the rebel angels, the Creation, and the Fall of Man; the Messiah's advent, Incarnation, Passion, Harrowing of Hell, Resurrection, Ascension, and sending of the Holy Spirit; and his Second Coming, Judgement, and sentence of human beings to hell or heaven (L. Adey, *Hymns and the Christian 'Myth'* (Vancouver, 1986), 2–3).

[15] Quoted in Allchin, 'Hymns of Grundtvig', 135.

James, Clement, Chrysostom and Basil, and the Church of Malabar (1859).[16] In the section entitled 'Mystical Interpretation of the Oriental Liturgies' he said that the introduction of Psalms into the order of worship helps to 'set forth' to the faithful 'the prediction of the Incarnation of the Word to those of old time'; in hymnody, he said, 'the perfect completion of grace is typified to the bystanders, and the SON of GOD incarnate, and all the things which He worked for our sakes.'[17] Neale, then, saw the hymn as of value in so far as it facilitates the objectives of liturgy; and, like Grundtvig, he believed that he could give expression to the liturgy's deeper convictions through hymns, and could thereby take hold of the hearts and minds of church-goers.[18]

Grundtvig undertook his translations in the 1830s. Whether

---

[16] In its review of this book, the Churchman's Companion said: 'The Eastern Church must ever have a claim on the attention and regard of English Churchmen and the various works that have appeared over the last few years on these subjects show that the regard and attention is very much on the increase. The English translation of the Liturgies, now published by Mr Neale, will furnish all reading churchmen with material for a better acquaintance with the public devotions of that ancient branch of GOD's Church. Alexandria, Antioch, Jerusalem, Constantinople, S. Cyril, S. Basil, S. Chrysostom, who can hear these names and not be moved at the trials and triumphs of that Church and those Saints, and seek to know more of them and their successors?' (Churchman's Companion, 26/156 (Dec. 1859), 464–5).

[17] J. M. Neale and R. F. Littledale (eds.), The Liturgies of SS. Mark, James, Clement, Chrysostom and Basil, and the Church of Malabar (London, 1859), p. xxii. In his Lectures on Poetry Keble was speaking along the same lines as Neale concerning poetry and religion. Although Keble was referring to poetry generally, rather than hymns, he claimed: 'Poetry lends religion her wealth of symbols and similes: religion restores these again to Poetry, clothed with so splendid a radiance that they appear to be no longer merely symbols, but to partake (I might almost say) of the nature of sacraments. . . . The very practice and cultivation of Poetry will be found to possess, in some sort, the power of guiding and composing the mind to worship and prayer' (E. K. Francis (trans. and ed.), Keble's Lectures on Poetry, 1832–1841, (Oxford, 1912), ii. 481, 482–3).

[18] In the appeal to liturgy Allchin likened Grundtvig to the men of the Oxford Movement; like them, Grundtvig was committed to affirming that 'especially in [the Church's] worship a way was opened up by which we might discover our solidarity with the earth and with all our human brethren. By rediscovering we share in the life of God the creator, the redeemer, the life-giver, the God who is present and at work in all things' (A. M. Allchin, 'Grundtvig's Catholicity', in N. F. S. Grundtvig (Copenhagen, 1983), 49).

or not Grundtvig influenced Neale is a matter for conjecture.[19] Grundtvig followed the development of the Oxford Movement with great interest, and in a series of articles introduced Tractarianism to Danish readers; his rejection of a biblicist and individualist conception of Christianity paralleled certain developments in Anglicanism.[20] The prominence he assigned to the sacraments and the liturgical confession of faith called for hymns to express this reality; like Neale, he found these themes expressed in the hymnody of the Orthodox Church, and made translations to present these themes to his own communion.

One example of a theme common to the Greek translations of Neale and Grundtvig is Christ's redemptive work, communicated through the Cross and Resurrection, with victory for the participants as a result. In his rendering of St John Damascene's Easter canon, Grundtvig writes, in Allchin's translation of the Danish:

> O Christ our Saviour, both as God and as Man,
> Crucified with thee, buried yesterday,
> May we even here below
> Shine with thee in the land of the living,
> Thou who art rock and support for our heart.[21]

Similar ideas are evoked in Neale's translation of the third ode of the same canon:

> Come, and let us drink of that New River,
>   Not from the barren Rock divinely poured,
> But the Fount of Life that is for ever
>   From the Sepulchre of CHRIST the LORD.

> All the world hath bright illumination,—
>   Heav'n and Earth and things beneath the earth:
> 'Tis the Festival of all Creation:
>   CHRIST hath ris'n, Who gave Creation birth.

[19] It is interesting that both Grundtvig and Neale adopted the Orthodox position concerning the *Filioque*. For more information see A. M. Allchin, 'N. F. S. Grundtvig: The Spirit as Life-Giver', in *The Kingdom of Love and Knowledge* (London, 1979), 87–8.

[20] Allchin, 'Hymns of Grundtvig', 132.

[21] A. M. Allchin, 'Grundtvig's Translations from the Greek', *Eastern Churches Quarterly*, 14/1 (1961), 43. Drawing an Anglican parallel to Grundtvig's difficulty in translating Greek hymns, Allchin quotes from Webb's letter to Neale, considered above, concerning the problems of rendering hymns in the vernacular.

> Yesterday with thee in burial lying,
> Now to-day with Thee aris'n I rise;
> Yesterday the partner of Thy dying,
> With Thyself upraise me to the skies.
>
> (HEC 44)

The emphasis on illumination and the identification of Christ with mankind in a common death and resurrection are present in both translations.

In a freer paraphrase of two conjoined verses, one from the liturgy for Palm Sunday, the other from that of Monday in Holy Week, Grundtvig dwells on the suffering of Christ for the good of man; the latter dies figuratively in baptism so that he can share in eternal life:

> Faithful souls
> Come let us devoutly regard
> The memory of the Saviour's passion,
> To find comfort.
> We will not weep for the pain and death
> Which has yielded us the blessed hope
> But we will worship our Saviour and cry,
> Thanks for the deep, the holy Baptism
> Wherein we are crucified, dead and buried
> With thee, that from thee we may receive life,
> Thou who arose from the dead again
> Thou lover of men.
> We glorify thee as our Lord and God,
> Blessed for ever, praised be thou,
> For that of thy compassion
> Thou sufferedst death,
> And wilt raise us up from death of sin,
> Grant us heaven
> Thou who hast died for us that we might live with thee.[22]

Similar ideas are found in Neale's hymn 'Father of Peace, and God of Consolation', in which he describes Christ as a 'Lover of men',[23] who, through his compassion, allows man to share in the kingdom of heaven:

---

[22] Allchin, 'Grundtvig's Translations', 44.
[23] *Philanthropos*, or 'Lover of men', is a very common epithet for God in Orthodox liturgical material.

> our mortal race
> To sin and Satan slave, from bondage freeing,
> Our poverty in all points didst embrace:
> And by that Union didst combine
> The earthly with the All-Divine.
>
> (HEC 75)

Although Neale met Grundtvig during his ecclesiological tour of Denmark in 1852 (during which he 'bagged churches right and left'[24]), it does not appear that Grundtvig influenced Neale in his decision to translate Greek hymns. Because he was a Lutheran, Grundtvig was regarded with disdain by the established Anglican Church (which he in turn described as 'dry', 'haughty', and 'stiff'[25]); and although he spent some time in Oxford and Cambridge (1830, 1831, 1843), and met Simeon, Hugh James Rose, Newman, Pusey, and William Palmer of Magdalen, he was received more sympathetically by people in other church parties, such as Thomas Chalmers, a leading spirit in the Free Church of Scotland. Neale belittled what Grundtvig was trying to do to revitalize the Danish Church, saying that those involved in the movement 'wish for something better, though they are not agreed on what'. He also noted disapprovingly that the Danish Lutherans defended ordination by presbyters 'tooth and nail', and that Grundtvig stood firm in his conviction that *'nothing* could make him doubt his own orders'. Neale further chastised Grundtvig not so much because he had remarried in his late sixties, but because he was at that age so romantically and unashamedly in love: 'At the age of 69 he lost his wife. Within nine months he married again—a widow—on the avowed principle that he was so much in love he could not help it! and *that* for the leader of the movement! I don't want to be hard on the man, but what sort of a being must he be?'[26]

In spite of the uneasy atmosphere which clouded their personal relations, the comparison between Neale and Grundtvig is relevant because they translated hymns from similar

---

[24] *Letters*, 191; dated 2 June 1852, aboard the Cologne–Ostend line.

[25] P. Lindhardt, *Grundtvig* (London, 1951), 70.

[26] *Letters*, 191; dated 2 June 1852. Neale would certainly have objected to Grundtvig's being made a bishop in recognition of his contribution to the life of the Danish Church, as occurred in 1861.

motives: to provide their respective Churches with expressions of faith which they believed were lacking. Neale viewed his own attempt to correct the deficiency thus:

It is a most remarkable fact, and one which shows how very little interest has been hitherto felt in the Eastern Church, that these are literally, I believe, the only English versions of any part of the treasures of Oriental Hymnology. There is scarcely a first or second-rate hymn of the Roman Breviary which has not been translated: of many we have six or eight versions. The eighteen quarto volumes of Greek Church poetry can only at present be known to the English reader by my little book. (HEC, pp. xi–xii)[27]

Neale had another goal in translating Greek hymns, though he knew that it would be less easily realized than that of education; he wished to further the cause of reunion. By the time *Hymns of the Eastern Church* reached its third edition in 1866, Neale was able to say: 'It is of course a matter of deep thankfulness to me that the Eastern Church should now be more and more widely brought before ordinary congregations by means of some of the following versions. GOD grant that this may be one little help towards the great work of Reunion.'[28]

As Rouse writes, 'The ecumenical implications of our hymn-books are realized by few Christians. Hymnology and ecumenism is an almost unexplored area.'[29] Even Neale himself said little more than the above about forwarding the cause of reunion through his hymns.[30] Perhaps because the ecumenical movement was in its infancy in the 1860s, he

---

[27] C. E. Pocknee notes that the 'chief interest' of HEC is Neale's rendering into English metres of the more famous hymns used in the Orthodox Divine Liturgy (that is, Communion service), as well as in the offices of matins and vespers ('Hymnody in the Eastern Churches', *Hymn Society of Great Britain and Ireland Bulletin*, 7/9 (no. 123) (Jan. 1972), 170).

[28] Neale, Preface to 3rd edn. of HEC (London, 1866), p. xx. Neale included a list of all the musical settings, both English and American, with which he was acquainted (pp. xx–xxi).

[29] R. Rouse, 'Voluntary Movements and the Changing Ecumenical Climate', in *A History of the Ecumenical Movement, 1517–1948*, ed. R. Rouse and S. C. Neill (2nd edn., London, 1967), 333.

[30] It should be noted that there are no journals and very few letters from Neale's pen after 1860; thereafter he devoted much of his energy to building up his Anglican sisterhood, the Society of St Margaret.

thought it best to let his verses speak for themselves—initially, at least.

Neale translated Latin hymns in order to give Anglicans a base on which to build a future corpus. Greek hymns, however, were essentially foreign, and stemmed from a different root from the Latin ones. It seems, however, that Neale saw a connection between Greek hymns and those from his own Western tradition. His aim in some ways mirrored the goals he set in compiling his *History of the Holy Eastern Church*; he wished to show Anglicans that there was much to be learned from their Eastern counterparts, and that the Church of England was an extension of a line which reached as far back as the Orthodox Church. He wanted to use Greek hymns as a model of what he considered religion untainted by the Liberal Protestant theology of his day: 'Those who mourn over the intolerably vague lax theology of modern English preachers, even of those who mean to be orthodox, might well recommend the study of these venerable poems as a corrective of unintentional heterodoxy, and untheological, unscholarlike formulae of expressions. They *will* be known some day.'[31]

A brief survey of Orthodox hymnological history will reveal more about Neale's attitudes to these compositions, which in turn affected his choice of hymns and method of translation. The development of orthodox hymnology falls into three periods: the first to fourth, fifth to seventh, and eighth to eleventh centuries.[32]

The first period began almost with the appearance of Christianity itself. Savas, in his *Hymnology of the Eastern Orthodox Church*, notes two reasons for the introduction of hymns. First, the new faith 'stimulated gifted followers . . . to compose works'.[33] This statement is supported by St Paul, who speaks several times about hymns and spiritual odes in the Apostolic Era.[34] A second reason for hymns was as a reaction to heretical verses by non-Christians. The Gnostics, for

---

[31] J. M. Neale, 'Greek Hymnology', *Christian Remembrancer*, 37 (1859) 315–16.

[32] I am indebted at various points in my discussion to the Revd Archimandrite J. H. Maitland Moir for his practical knowledge of Orthodox hymnody.

[33] S. J. Savas, *Hymnology of the Eastern Orthodox Church* (New York, 1983), 2.   [34] See, e.g., Eph. 5: 19, Col. 3: 16.

example, circulated hymns designed 'to deceive the Christians'; these included verses by the heretic Vardisanis, who composed a psalter containing 150 psalms for Gnostic use.[35] Christians quickly realized the danger inherent in such works, and composed their own hymns to combat them.

The composition of hymns was one thing; their acceptance as part of congregational worship was another. It appears that there was a certain reserve—similar to that of the Victorian High Church—surrounding the general introduction of hymns into the Church; and in some parts they were introduced earlier than in others.[36] Originally there was a predominance of psalmody in Christian worship; in some ways the Psalms epitomized for early Christians the nature of liturgical language. In the fourth century an attempt was made to alter this trend through the introduction of poems in the classical metres. These compositions were shaped by the Hellenistic influence which predominated in Asia Minor; however, precisely because of this stimulus—which the early Church considered non-Christian—these verses were not introduced into worship. Neale said of these early hymnologists: 'Their works have not been employed in the Divine Office, are merely an imitation of classical writers, and, however occasionally pretty, are not the stuff out of which Church-song is made.' (HEC 1).[37]

There were, nevertheless, some noteworthy hymnologists in this period, including Ephraim of Syria; Gregory Nazianzus; Methodius, Bishop of Patara, and Synesius, Bishop of Ptolemais. Neale seems to have dismissed these and other early Greek hymnologists because of the impropriety of their prototypes. His opinion seems too harsh in the light of comments like these by Savas, who appreciates the value of the classical modes: 'Many of the early hymnographers' works . . . were taken by later hymnographers as models for their hymns. Therefore, we can say that there is an indirect connection between ancient and ecclesiastical poetry.'[38]

---

[35] Savas, *Hymnology*, 2.
[36] Julian (ed.), *Dictionary of Hymnology*, 460 (entry on 'Greek Hymnody').
[37] Most of the comments made by Neale on Greek hymnological history in HEC had already appeared in his article 'Greek Hymnology'.
[38] Savas, *Hymnology*, 47.

It seems, contrary to Neale's opinion, that there was merit in the work of these early hymnologists—even though their compositions were not adopted for communal worship.

The second period of Orthodox hymnody, the fifth to seventh centuries, saw the introduction of short *ephymnia* in the Psalms; these interjections are the elements from which the *troparia, stichera, ypakoai, and kathismata* later emerged. Many of these components of the liturgy can be seen in the modern Orthodox *Octoechos, Triodion, Pentekostarion, and Menaion*.[39] They are not in classical metre, and have their roots in the poetry and worship of Judaism. These joyous ejaculations were adopted as hymns, including the following, which are still in use: *Gloria in Excelsis*, the *Trisagion* (the chant 'Holy God, Holy Mighty, Holy Immortal, have mercy on us'), and the Cherubic Hymn.[40]

This second period of Greek hymnology also saw the introduction of scriptural hymns. Although the early Church was reluctant to introduce original compositions into the liturgy, hymns from the Bible were seen as acceptable. Gillet gives the reason for this tradition, thereby illustrating an important principle of Orthodoxy: 'The Word of God present in the holy and divine inspired Scriptures remains the foundation of the whole of Orthodox spirituality.' And again: 'The Orthodox Church can be called a "Biblicist" Church. She has always recommended and encouraged the reading of the Holy Book.'[41] This helps to explain why the Church was receptive to scriptural hymns, including the Songs of Moses (Exod. 15: 1–19; Deut. 32: 1–43); the Song of Hannah (1 Sam. 2: 1–10); the Song of Habakkuk (Hab. 3: 2–19); the Song of Isaiah (Isa. 26: 9–20); the Song of Jonah (Jonah 2: 3–10); the *Benedicite* (S. of III Ch. 35–66);[42] the *Magnificat* (Luke 1: 46–55), and the

---

[39] See Glossary.
[40] The *Ter Sanctus* is also still in use; but it is from a much earlier period.
[41] L. Gillet ['A Monk of the Eastern Church'], *Orthodox Spirituality* (London, 1978), 1–2.
[42] In the Septuagint, Dan. 3: 57–88a (plus 1 or 2 non-biblical verses). It should be noted that the Orthodox Church, like the Roman Catholic Church, considers the Song of the Three Holy Children deutero-canonical; whereas the Anglican Church classes it among the Old Testament Apocrypha. For more information on the positions of various Christian communions on the canonicity of Scripture, see Cross and Livingstone (eds.), *Oxford Dictionary of the Christian Church*, 232 (entry on 'Canon of Scripture').

Benedictus Dominus (Luke 1: 68–79). This reverence for biblical authority was to play an important role in the subsequent development of Orthodox hymnody.

In his introduction to *Hymns of the Eastern Church* Neale hardly mentioned the hymns of the first period, which were in classical metre, or those from the second period, derived from Scripture. In the case of the former he explained that their exclusion from the liturgy prevented him from translating them; the latter would already have been familiar to his readers from previous biblical translations. There was, however, another class of hymns introduced during the second period, of which Neale made no mention—and this without the logical reasoning he applied to the others. This type of hymn may best be described by examining one particular hymnologist and his most famous work: St Romanos the Melodist and his Akathist Hymn.

For some, Romanos (a Jewish convert) is the greatest of all Orthodox hymnologists. According to Bouvy he is the 'Pindar of rhythmical poetry'.[43] He wrote some thousand hymns, of which only eighty or so have survived. They are characterized by a picturesque, almost dramatic treatment of their subject. Romanos is reputed to be the composer of the greatest hymn of the second period, the Akathist Hymn.[44] This composition, despite its being considered by some critics as the 'crown of ecclesiastical hymns',[45] is completely ignored by Neale, presumably because of its subject: the Virgin Mary (or, as she is called in Orthodoxy, the *Theotokos*, or 'God-bearer'). The Akathist Hymn is dedicated to her. It is a narrative, epic poem in twenty-four sections depicting the life of the Virgin Mary by outlining the chronological events of the Incarnation from the Annunciation to the Presentation of Jesus in the Temple, through the words of Gabriel, Mary, Joseph, the shepherds, Herod, and others. It is of great theological and literary importance; some, like Patrinacos, say that the Akathist Hymn occupies 'a place without . . . equal in Orthodox hymnology'.[46]

---

[43] Quoted in Savas, *Hymnology*, 63.
[44] See Savas's arguments for Romanos as composer of the Akathist Hymn (ibid. 83–7).   [45] See ibid. 63.
[46] N. D. Patrinacos, *A Dictionary of Greek Orthodoxy*, (Pleasantville, NY, 1984), 8.

The Virgin Mary as an object of devotion was particularly associated in Anglican minds with Roman practice, so Neale's caution is understandable. The Virgin was never the principal subject of any of Neale's translations, although her presence was sometimes acknowledged. He downplayed—but did not ignore—the strong feminine element in Orthodox hymnody in his praise of the Virgin particularly in her role as *Theotokos*. Neale emphasized her perpetual virginity in such phrases as 'Virgin-honour pure' (HEC 11); and he combined this theme with Christ's redemption of mankind through His adopting man's 'very nature' (HEC 72):

> Who left'st in Birth
> The portals of virginity unbroken,
> And op'st the gates of heaven to sons of earth.
> (HEC 47)[47]

Neale's highest praise of the Virgin, in the hymn 'Father of Peace, and God of Consolation', displays a reserve which does not reflect the authentic spirit of Orthodox reverence for the Mother of God:

> Behold! the Virgin, prophecy sustaining,
> Incarnate Deity conceived and bore;
> Virgin in birth, and Virgin still, remaining;
> And man to GOD is reconciled once more:
> Wherefore in faith her name we bless,
> And Mother of our GOD confess.
> (HEC 75)

How different the Akathist Hymn is in its expression of uncontained joy and exultation concerning the virginity of Mary:

O Theotokos Virgin, You are a fortress protecting Virgins, and all who hasten unto You. For the maker of Heaven and Earth has made you such, O pure One, having entered Your womb and taught all men to call unto you:

Hail! O Pillar of Virginity.
Hail! O Gate of Salvation.

Hail! O Leader of spiritual re-making.
Hail! O Bestower of Divine beneficence.

---

[47] 'And op'st' was changed to 'Opening', and 'Virginity' was capitalized in the 3rd edn.

Hail! For You have regenerated those who were conceived in shame.
Hail! For You gave guidance to the thoughtless.
Hail! To You, Who abolished the corruptor of minds.
Hail! To You, Who gave birth to the Sower of purity.
Hail! O Bridal-Chamber of spiritual wedlock.
Hail! To You, Who bring the faithful to the Lord.[48]

Neale's stanza, by comparison, is cautious and restrained, and was made even more so from the second edition onwards, where it reads:

> Lo, Mary, as the world's long day was waning,
>   Incarnate Deity conceived and bore;
> Virgin in birth, and after birth, remaining;
>   And man to GOD is reconciled once more:
> Wherefore in faith her name we bless,
>   And Mother of our GOD confess.[49]

While Orthodox Christians practise liturgical devotion to the Virgin Mary, they do so differently from their Roman counterparts. As Patrinacos explains, the Virgin Mary is revered by the Orthodox as Mother of the Redeemer, and also as an efficacious intercessor between man and Christ. This latter devotion is very old, going back at least as far as St Gregory of Nazianzus (fourth century), who mentions recourse on the part of believers to her protection.[50] The title *Theotokos* was adopted by the Third Ecumenical Council in Ephesus, in 431.[51] This veneration grew through the centuries in both East and West, but in different ways. The Roman Catholic Church gradually formulated the doctrine of Mary's Immaculate Conception, and formally proclaimed it in 1854. This states that the Virgin Mary, from the moment of her conception, was kept free from all stain of original sin. This doctrine was not acceptable to the Orthodox Church. Neale's *Voices from the East*, a collection of Orthodox essays which Neale translated

---

[48] *Kontakion* of the Akathist Hymn, sec. 19, in Savas, *Hymnology*, suppl. p. 20. It should be noted that Grundtvig too, according to Allchin, 'seems to shrink from drawing out all the consequences of his thought about the Mother of God in his Greek translations' ('Grundtvig's Translations', 41).
[49] Neale, HEC, 2nd edn. (London, 1863), 72.
[50] Patrinacos, *A Dictionary of Greek Orthodoxy*, 246.
[51] K. Ware discusses the theological implications of the word *Theotokos* in *The Orthodox Way* (London, 1979), 101–3.

and published in 1859, includes one entitled 'The Dogma of the Immaculate Conception', in which Neale presented Muraviev's views on the then recently adopted Roman doctrine. These are most concisely summarized in the following words: 'On what is the new Latin dogma founded, contrary as it is to Holy Scripture, Tradition, History? Surely *on nothing.*'[52]

But the Orthodox view is still far removed from that of Protestants, as Muraviev explains:

> We are far from the idea of Protestants, who, while they respect in the person of the Mother of God her virtues, her humility, her submission to the Divine Will, see not, and will not see, her exaltation above all creatures celestial and terrestrial, and her mediation between her SON and the faithful. We agree entirely so far as this; that our duty is to glorify, by every possible means, her whom the Almighty has invested with majesty, and whom, according to the Gospel, all generations must call blessed: we agree that this is a holy work, and the duty of every Christian. This the Orthodox Church does: since the earliest ages of Christianity she has glorified the Blessed Virgin, naming her more precious than the Cherubim, and infinitely more glorious than the Seraphim; supplicating her as the most powerful mediatress with the LORD, and the mightiest advocate of the Christian world; as a token of her profound devotion to Mary, the Orthodox Church gives her image the place next to that of the SAVIOUR, in order that the faithful may be reminded of her powerful intercession with her SON.[53]

By the time Neale published his *Hymns of the Eastern Church*, the subject of the Immaculate Conception had become topical; it became even more so as time passed, and it played a part in the adoption of the idea of papal infallibility in 1870.[54] The doctrine of the Immaculate Conception was publicized in England in Neale's day by the two missionaries sent from Rome to help the Roman Catholic cause: Luigi Gentili and Dominic Barberi. These two were responsible for hundreds of conversions—Barberi himself received Newman into the Roman Church in 1845—and were seen as instigators

---

[52] J. M. Neale (trans. and ed.), *Voices from the East* (London, 1859), 142.
[53] Ibid. 146–7.
[54] For a fuller explanation see Norman, *English Catholic Church in the Nineteenth Century*, 307.

of the wave of secessions which Anglicans, especially those who were overcome with uncertainty, like Webb, came to fear.[55]

By excluding the Akathist Hymn, Neale denied his readers access to one of the most important hymns of the Orthodox Church. However, the external pressures under which he worked should not be forgotten. This omission is also apparent in the hymns of the third period of Orthodox hymnody, from which virtually all Neale's translations are taken.

The third period of Eastern hymnody extends from the eighth to eleventh centuries. Three schools of poets may be distinguished. The first is that of the Savaites, whose centre was the Great Lavra of St Sava in what was then Palestine. Among them were St John Damascene; Cosmas the Melodist; and Andrew, Bishop of Crete. Second is the Studite school, whose status is equal to that of the Savaites. Their centre was the monastery of Studion in Constantinople. Under the able leadership of Abbot Theodore, a school of music was inaugurated, and the monastery eventually became the centre of Orthodox hymnology. Its most famous composers were Theodore and his brother Joseph, who became Archbishop of Thessaloniki, and is believed to have composed 1,000 liturgical canons. The third is that of the Italohellenes, who founded a celebrated school of music at Syracuse. Under these three schools Orthodox hymnody was at its best, and its excellence was sustained until the eleventh century, when the ecclesiastical services and Divine Liturgy reached their final form.[56]

The third period may be characterized as the age of the canon, which Neale called 'the perfection of Greek poetry' (HEC 26). The change to this form of hymnody was largely effected by the Iconoclastic Controversy (c. 725–842). Neale said that the supporters of icons, 'by universal consent,

---

[55] For further information see Sr. Miriam, 335b-68b. It should also be remembered that the Bishop of Chichester's prohibition, imposed on Neale for reputed 'Papist' practices, had only just been lifted when HEC was published.

[56] In the Eastern Church the term 'Divine Liturgy' is specifically applied to the Eucharist. The one most commonly performed is the Divine Liturgy of St John Chrysostom; others are the Liturgy of St Basil the Great (used 10 times a year) and the Liturgy of the Presanctified Gifts. (The Liturgy of St James is now used only once a year, and that of St Mark not officially at all.) For more information, see Elias, *Divine Liturgy Explained*.

numbered amongst their ranks all that was pious and venerable in the Eastern Church' (HEC 44). Their commemorative days filled the Church calendar, and their elaborate doctrinal hymns displaced the more animated, pictorial poems of writers like Romanos the Melodist, and changed the character of the Greek service-books in the seventh to ninth centuries. From that time onward, the canon came to be the highest mode of poetical expression for Orthodox hymnologists.

Canons form by far the largest component of Eastern hymnody. One reason may be the immediate appeal they held for the faithful during the Iconoclastic Controversy because of their doctrinal cast; hence the gradual disuse into which the earlier pictorial, dramatic hymns fell. The character of canons also held an appeal for subsequent generations, however, because of their encapsulation of fundamental Orthodox doctrines. As Savas says, 'The deeper dogmatical truths are taught to the faithful through these verses.'[57] Thus the canons differed significantly from such compositions as the Akathist Hymn. Romanos's hymn had as its primary objective the veneration of the *Theotokos*; canons, however, with their origin in the times of the Iconoclastic Controversy, were more instructional. Savas elaborates; he notes the following of hymns in general: 'It is a fact (unobjectionable) that the hymns of the Orthodox Church ... inspire, uplift and teach the Orthodox Christians and other listening faithful of various confessions.' Of canons in particular, with their dogmatic aspect, he asserts: 'More importantly, the dogmatic contents of some of the hymns conveys the most precise and most accurate formulation of Orthodox teaching.'[58] For Neale, whose plan was to use Orthodox hymnody to teach the faithful in England, canons would have been particularly useful.

In the Eastern Church canons were sung originally at matins. Traditionally, they consist of nine odes, corresponding to the nine scriptural canticles, which are (1) the Song of Moses at the Red Sea (Exod. 15: 1–19); (2) the Song of Moses in Deuteronomy (Deut. 32: 1–43); (3) the Song of Hannah (1 Sam. 2:

---

[57] Savas, *Hymnology*, 28.
[58] Ibid. What Savas means is that the virtue of canons (and of other *troparia*) is that they are theology expressed through prayer.

1–10); (4) the Song of Habakkuk (Hab. 3: 2–19); (5) the Song of Isaiah (Isa. 26: 9–20); (6) the Song of Jonah (Jonah 2: 3–10); (7) the Song of the Three Holy Children (3–34);[59] (8) the *Benedicite* (S. of III Ch. 35–66);[60] and (9) the Song of the *Theotokos* (the *Magnificat*, Luke 1: 46–55), and the Prayer of Zacharias (the *Benedictus Dominus*, Luke 1: 68–79). In practice there are nearly always only eight odes, because the second is omitted except on some days during Lent.[61] At first the biblical canticles were sung by themselves; then in the seventh century *troparia* were inserted between the final verses of the canticles to celebrate particular themes, such as repentance, the feast or saint of the day, the Saviour, the *Theotokos*; or the departed. These sets of eight groups of *troparia* eventually came to comprise the present canon.

In the course of time the practice of reading the actual text of the canticles disappeared for the most part;[62] thus the nine (in practice, eight) odes of the canon, composed of *troparia*, or stanzas, were sung by themselves, with a brief refrain such as 'Glory to Thee, O God, glory to Thee' or 'Most Holy Theotokos, save us' between each *troparion*.[63] This is the form of the canon as it exists today. It should be noted that not all canons contain eight odes: some, especially those on weekdays in Lent, contain either two (*diodia*), three (*triodia*), or four (*tetraodia*).[64]

Before turning to Neale's hymns, it may be useful to describe the structure of an Orthodox canon by way of an example: St Cosmas the Melodist's canon for Christmas Day.[65] The first ode of the canon opens with an *irmos* (Greek for 'chain'), a stanza that links the theme of the biblical canticle, which originally opened the ode, with the *troparia* that follow:

Christ is born, give ye glory, Christ comes from heaven, meet ye Him. Christ is on earth, be ye exalted. O all the earth, sing unto the Lord, and sing praises in gladness, O ye people, for He has been glorified.

---

[59] In the Septuagint, Dan. 3: 26–56.   [60] See n. 42.
[61] When the 2nd ode is recited, it generally has no *troparia*.
[62] It is still carried on by many monastic communities, especially on Mount Athos, though not in full except in Lent.
[63] The text of the *Magnificat*, however, was and is almost always sung in full.   [64] *Triodia* are most common.
[65] The text of Cosmas's hymn is taken from *The Festal Menaion*, trans. Mother Mary and K. Ware (London, 1969), 269–84.

This *irmos*, an example of typology, links the song of Moses in Exod. 15: 1–19, which describes the power and greatness of God, who has saved the Israelites from the Egyptians, with Christ, who is born into the world as the saviour of mankind.[66]

The remaining *troparia* develop the theme of Christ's birth and his purpose on earth:

Man fell from the divine and better life: though made in the image of God, through transgression he became wholly subject to corruption and decay. But now the wise Creator fashions him anew: for He has been glorified.

The Creator, when He saw man perishing, whom He had made with His own hands, bowed the heavens and came down; and from the divine and pure Virgin did He take all man's substance, being made truly flesh: for He has been glorified.

Wisdom and Word and Power, Christ our God is the Son and Brightness of the Father; and unknown to the powers both above and upon the earth, He was made man, and so has won us back again: for He has been glorified.

These *troparia* are followed by a *katavasia*, which forms the concluding stanza of the ode; it is so named from the practice by the members of the two choirs of coming down from their stalls to the centre of the church to sing it. Sometimes, as in the case of the above ode, the *irmos* is repeated as a *katavasia*; on other occasions, including some Sundays and certain feasts, a specially appointed *katavasia* is inserted.

The second ode is omitted in Cosmas's canon, so the third ode follows the first, and adheres to the same pattern.[67] This sequence continues until the end of the ninth ode.[68] The

[66] Usually the *irmos* has much more similarity to the biblical ode than this one has. It should be noted that there are various transliterations of the Greek word *heirmos*; the one adopted here, *irmos*, follows Savas, *Hymnology*, and *Festal Menaion*.

[67] It should be noted that although the method described is the way in which canons were written, the practice of singing them follows a different pattern. Normally more than 1 canon is prescribed to be read at matins: on Sundays, 4; on normal days, 3; on Great Feasts usually 2; and occasionally only 1. Ode 1 of the 1st canon is sung; then ode 1 of the 2nd, 3rd, etc. canons; then ode 3 of the 1st canon, and so on (*Festal Menaion*, 547).

[68] The 3rd ode concludes with *kathismata*, the 6th with a *kontakion* and *oikos*.

canon then concludes with an *exapostilarion*, a term derived from the word meaning 'send out'.[69] Frequently this concluding *troparion* develops the theme of Christ as the light of the world, and is therefore also known by the Slavs as a *photagogikon*, or 'hymn of light'.[70] In Cosmas's hymn it runs as follows:

Our Saviour the Dayspring from the east, has visited us from on high, and we who were in darkness and shadow have found the truth: for the Lord is born of the Virgin.

Because the canon is a predominant form in Orthodox hymnody and, according to Neale, the 'perfection of Greek poetry', it is appropriate to use his translations of canons as representative of his endeavours in the field of Greek hymns.

Neale wished his Greek translations to be used by English congregations in the same way as were his renderings from Latin: as hymns, forming an integral part of church worship. Orthodox hymns, however, were unlike Latin hymns in structure; therefore the method of translation used for collections like *Mediaeval Hymns and Sequences* or *The Hymnal Noted* could not be applied.[71] It was impossible to retain many of the distinguishing characteristics of Orthodox hymnology, such as metre, *isosyllabia, homotonia, homokatalexia* (same ending), or melody, in a translation; likewise the great length of many Greek hymns made them unsuitable for Western worship. Yet Neale was determined to present to Victorian church-goers something of Orthodox tradition in a readily usable form.

He was aware of the difficulties he faced; and these were compounded by his being the first Englishman to attempt to translate Greek hymns. He noted in the preface to the first edition of *Hymns of the Eastern Church*:

Though the superior terseness and brevity of the Latin Hymns renders a translation which shall represent those qualities a work of great

---

[69] Like the *photagogikon*, this word may refer to the sending of a light at dawn, which comes at this point in matins (if sung at the proper time). Cf. 'Glory to Thee Who hast showed us the Light' before the Great Doxology.
[70] In the Greek Church the *photagogikon* is used in Lent, and is slightly different.
[71] For information on technical aspects of Orthodox hymns, such as acrostics, metre, and melody, see Savas, *Hymnology*, 3–38.

labour, yet still the versifier has the help of the same metre; his version may be line for line. . . . Above all, we have examples enough of former translation by which we may take pattern.

But in attempting a Greek Canon, from the fact of its being in prose . . . one is all at sea. What measure shall we employ? why this more than that? Might we attempt the rhythmical prose of the original, and design it to be chanted? Again, the great length of the Canons renders them unsuitable for our churches as *wholes*. Is it better simply to form centos of the more beautiful passages? or can separate Odes, each necessarily imperfect, be employed as separate Hymns? And above all, we have no pattern or example of any kind to direct our labour. (HEC, pp. xii–xiii)[72]

Neale confessed that the Orthodox tradition was so different from his own that he was in a quandary as to how to proceed. Because of the wide divergence of form between Latin (or English) and Greek hymns, it was impossible for him to decode and domesticate them as easily as he did his earlier, Latin hymns. With no guiding principles, Neale experimented, and produced various types of hymns; the result was a highly eclectic collection. Although he said, 'My own belief is, that the best way to employ Greek Hymnology for the uses of the English Church would be by centos' (HEC, pp. xiii–xiv), this is not the method he consistently used. Some, like the canon by Cosmas the Melodist for the Transfiguration, were rendered by Neale as centos; others, like 'Come, ye faithful, raise the strain', St John Damascene's canon for St Thomas's Sunday (the Sunday after Easter), were attempts at exact reproductions of the original; still others, such as 'Art thou weary, art thou languid', 'O happy band of pilgrims', and 'Safe home, safe home in port', by Neale's own admission, 'contain so little that is from the Greek, that they ought not to have been included' in a collection entitled *Hymns of the Eastern Church*.[73]

Neale had thousands of hymns from which to choose for inclusion in his little volume. Some light is cast on the principles according to which he made his choice by drawing a parallel with orientalist Antoine Isaac Silvestre de Sacy (1758–

---

[72] Neale's statement about canons being in prose is not strictly true; see ibid. 20–8 and C. S. Phillips, 'Hymns of the Eastern Church', in *Hymnody Past and Present* (London, 1937), 35.   [73] Preface to 3rd edn. of HEC, p. xxii.

1838), first president of the Société Asiatique, author of various books on Arabic grammar, and the instigator of Arabic studies in France. He forms an interesting comparison with Neale, first of all because he sees his work as having uncovered, brought to light, or rescued a vast amount of obscure oriental matter, and then because, like Neale in his Eastern hymns, he presents the Orient to his readers through extracts or fragments in his book *Chrestomathie arabe* (1826).

Said comments on this method, which was frequently used by orientalists, as follows:

> If the Orientalist is necessary because he fishes some useful gems out of the distant Oriental deep, and since the Orient cannot be known without his mediation, it is also true that Oriental writing itself ought not to be taken in whole. This is Sacy's introduction to his theory of fragments, a common Romantic concern. Not only are Oriental literary productions essentially alien to the European; they also do not contain a sustained enough interest, nor are they written with enough 'taste and critical spirit,' to merit publication except as extracts (*pour mériter d'être publiés autrement que par extrait*). Therefore, the Orientalist is required to *present* the Orient by a series of representative fragments, fragments republished, explicated, annotated, and surrounded with still more fragments. For such a presentation a special genre is required: the chrestomathy, which is where in Sacy's case the usefulness and interest of Orientalism are most directly and profitably displayed. Sacy's most famous production was the three-volume *Chrestomathie arabe*, which was sealed at the outset, so to speak, with an internally rhyming Arabic couplet: 'Kitab al-anis al-mufid lil-Taheb al-mustafid; / wa gam'i al shathur min manthoum wa manthur' (A book pleasant and profitable for the studious pupil; / it contains fragments of both poetry and prose).[74]

The full title of Sacy's work is *Chrestomathie arabe, ou Extraits de divers écrivains arabes, tant en prose qu'en vers, avec une traduction française et des notes, à l'usage des élèves d'Ecole royale et spéciale des langues orientales vivantes*; he claims simply to have exerted himself on behalf of his students so that they could gain some idea of the original from the extracts he chose. Their idea of the Orient was, of course, inextricably linked to his. So too Neale, who wished his hymns to be used—that is, sung—in churches, as part of

---

[74] Said, *Orientalism*, 128–9.

the development of a definitive Anglican hymnal. As straight translations, Greek hymns did not, like Sacy's sources, contain a 'sustained enough interest'; they were long, repetitive, and foreign to the Western experience of hymnody. But Neale was anxious for their dissemination and so he edited, adapted, and transformed—in short, domesticated—Orthodox hymnody in order to ease the process of adoption. In certain cases he limited the decoding, so that what emerged was a complete canon, containing as many elements as possible of the original. In other cases he adapted the originals, perhaps excluding some of the original odes or blending Eastern ideas with elements from his own Western tradition. In still other instances his verses were either loosely based on an Eastern idea or completely original. Interestingly, this third category proved to be the source of his most popular 'Eastern' hymns, some of which still appear in hymn-books. Neale's hope was that *Hymns of the Eastern Church* would be part of the foundation on which, in his words, an 'eclectic superstructure' of Anglican hymnody could be built. He saw his hymnological chrestomathy the best way of contributing to this end.

Chapter 6

Neale's Translations

By the time *Hymns of the Eastern Church* appeared, Neale had firmly secured a reputation as a gifted translator of Latin hymns. He had developed an elaborate theory, which he expounded in the *Christian Remembrancer* for October 1849, in an article entitled 'English Hymnology: Its History and Prospects'. He suggested that in modern languages a translation —particularly from Latin—will fail to convey a true idea of the original unless it adopts the same species of verse. He even went so far as to say that it was desirable for a hymn translation to employ the same tune and rhythm as the original; thus the 'natural concatenation of thought' which peculiarly attaches itself to certain rhythms could be maintained.[1]

In *The Hymnal Noted* (1851, 1854), for which Neale composed most of the hymns, this general principle was followed. In certain cases the original metre, if easily sung, was preserved, as in *'Ad coenam Agni providi'* ('The Lamb's high banquet we await'; long metre, couplet rhyme) and *'Pange, lingua gloriosi'* ('Sing, my tongue, the glorious battle'; 8.7.8.7.8.7). In others, if the Latin metre proved difficult, Neale altered it in translation, as in *'Gloria laus et honor'* ('All glory, laud and honour'; 7.6.7.6.D; the original was in elegiac couplets)[2] and in the extracts from Bernard of Cluny's *Hora*

---

[1] J. M. Neale, 'English Hymnology: Its History and Prospects', *Christian Remembrancer*, 18 (1849), 323.

[2] Neale made an earlier translation of *'Gloria laus et honor'* for *Mediaeval Hymns and Sequences* (1851), in the original metre, in 2-line stanzas; it began 'Glory and honour and laud be to thee, King Christ the Redeemer! / Children before whose steps raised their Hosannas of praise'; both translations were designed to preserve the practice of repeating the opening stanza after all the others.

Novissima, including '*Hic breve vivitur*', '*Urbs Sion aurea*', and '*O bona patria*' ('Brief life is here our portion', 'Jerusalem the golden', and 'For thee, O dear, dear country'; all 7.6.7.6.D).

But Neale came to understand that strict adherence to his hymnological theory did not always result in the best hymns. Routley goes so far as to say that 'when he abandoned his rule of using the original metre he produced many "winners"'.[3] In *A Panorama of Christian Hymnody* he explains:

> It has often been said of Neale, and of those who amended or imitated him, that their translations read stiffly or creakily in places, and we have to admit that Neale is the father of the pedantic 'translator's English' that has brought the Office-hymns and saints-day hymns into disrepute among many. It has to be remembered, of course, that Neale must have worked incredibly fast. To produce the contents of the Hymnal Noted ... (our chief source of his versions from Latin), together with nearly everything else he translated from Latin, well before his fortieth year, he must have worked at high pressure. There were also original hymns and carols in his collection by then; only the Greek originals seem to have occupied him later. But the truth is, as anyone can see, that it is when he can choose his meter that his poetic instinct is allowed the needful freedom.[4]

Neale learned this lesson gradually. As a member of the committee in charge of *The Hymnal Noted*, he came to realize that the quality of his hymns would be improved if they were subjected to closer scrutiny than he himself was capable of. In the publication of *Mediaeval Hymns and Sequences* he had relatively little critical input from others; Webb and a few close friends made suggestions, but Neale, acting as sole composer and editor, was free to dispense with their comments if he so pleased. In compiling this first collection, he had certain ideas about what would appeal to his audience; but because he worked alone, he had no way of knowing if his assessment was correct—at least, not until after publication. In *The Hymnal Noted*, on the other hand, his hymns were subject to scrutiny by a committee of Ecclesiological Society members, who naturally would have expressed a variety of opinions about what was—and what was not—acceptable. Hence, those of

---

[3] E. R. Routley, *Christian Hymns Observed* (Oxford, 1982), 54.
[4] E. R. Routley, *A Panorama of Christian Hymnody* (Chicago, 1979), 59.

Neale's hymns which were included in The *Hymnal Noted* passed a more stringent test than he himself could have imposed, and were therefore, perhaps, superior productions. Neale attests to this difference between the two collections in a letter to his wife: 'Enclosed is a letter from one Harper to you. As he seems to expect you to answer, you can tell him: 1. That he may take anything he likes out of my "Mediaeval Hymns", and may mutilate it in any way he pleases. 2. But that he may not take anything at all out of the "Hymnal Noted"; nor the things in the "Mediaeval Hymns" which are in the "Hymnal Noted".'[5] It seems from Neale's comments that he believed *The Hymnal Noted*, which was the work of a group, as opposed to an individual, to be a superior production to his previous efforts.[6]

In the preface to the second edition of *Mediaeval Hymns and Sequences* Neale acknowledged his debt to the committee which compiled *The Hymnal Noted*:

> Some of the happiest and most instructive hours of my life were spent in the Sub-Committee of the Ecclesiological Society. . . . It was my business to lay before it the translations I had prepared, and theirs to correct. The study which this required drew out the beauties of the original in a way which nothing else could have done, and the friendly collision of minds elicited ideas which a single translator would, in all probability, have missed.[7]

Neale's acceptance of criticism from others thus helped to enhance the quality and popular appeal of his hymns.

There was, however, no committee equipped to deal with his Greek translations; as at the time of *Mediaeval Hymns and Sequences*, he was on his own. In the *General Introduction* to

---

[5] *Letters*, 181; dated 30 July 1851, from Sackville College. Some of Neale's pieces in *Mediaeval Hymns and Sequences* were republished—most altered in some way—in *The Hymnal Noted*.

[6] Neale never paid much attention to the legal notion of copyright; but his desire to protect the product of shared labour is part of the shift in attitude toward hymn texts which enabled the *Hymns Ancient and Modern* proprietors innovatively, successfully, and unpopularly to invoke the law to protect their committee translations.

[7] Preface to 2nd edn. of *Mediaeval Hymns and Sequences*, in Lawson (ed.), *Collected Hymns*, 4. Neale added: 'I have been amused to find, in some reproductions of these hymns, a line given as I had first written it, to the exclusion of our deliberate correction.'

A History of the Holy Eastern Church he attempts to describe the various Orthodox office-books and liturgical languages. Although he (with the help of Popov, INT 820) does a thorough job, the essay is not accessible to the average reader, as Neale himself admits:

> I may observe that the student cannot expect to find a subject, so intrinsically obscure, so treated as to render it light and agreeable reading. I have spared no pains to make it as clear as the nature of the case will admit; and, after a good deal of thought, determined to treat first of the Office-Books, and then of the Offices, of the Eastern Church. . . . Had I reversed the process, the reader would have been so bewildered with the notes which must have been appended to the rubrics, as to lose all the continuity of the offices themselves. As it is, he is not summoned to encounter those rubrics, till the more common terms have already been explained. At the same time I cannot flatter myself that he will thoroughly be master of the present chapter, till after having also read the next, he returns to a second perusal of this. (INT 828)

The structure of Neale's explication does in fact assist the reader in understanding the topics presented, as does his recurrent evocation of parallels between East and West. In the case of the description of the Offices, Neale is more often than not perfectly entitled to perform this operation, as when he compares the *Menaia* to the Western *proprium sanctorum*.[8] The copious notes, however, seem to overwhelm the text, partly owing to their being printed together on the same page. His explications are sound and scholarly; yet at times Neale shown signs of despondency, as when he remarks on the concurrence of festivals in the *Typikon*: 'The confusion is beyond what a Western liturgical scholar would deem possible' (INT 848–9). If Neale, despite assurances to the contrary, can describe his own explications as appearing 'perplexing' to the specialist reader (INT 850), there is little hope for generalists. Thus the gulf between Neale and the average reader is never bridged, and at the time the *General Introduction* was published (1850), little progress had been made towards *sobornost*.

In the *General Introduction* Neale included six translations

---

[8] Ware and Mother Mary draw the same comparision in the appendix to *The Festal Menaion*, 540.

from the Orthodox office-books. His translations in both this volume and *Hymns of the Eastern Church* are almost exclusively from Greek sources, presumably because this was the Eastern language in which he displayed the greatest facility. It is important to note that despite the fact that he had access (again, through Popov) to all the Orthodox service-books, most of his English renderings are from the *Triodion*, which contains the services from the Sunday of the Publican and Pharisee (the Sunday before Septuagesima) to the Saturday of Holy Week, and includes the texts for the Great Fast of Lent; Neale describes it as 'a very important book' (INT 857). He was impressed with the Orthodox observances of Lent and Easter, and took the trouble to transcribe the detailed observations of an unidentified 'modern traveller' to Greece, of the effect produced by the troparion 'Christ hath risen from the dead', sung by the priest during the canon for Easter Day:

There was not a light, not a sound; each individual of that immense multitude, filling even all the adjoining streets, remained still and motionless, so that even the most distant might catch the murmuring voices of the priests, who were reciting the service within the church; troops lined the streets to see that perfect quiet was maintained, but assuredly it was a needless precaution, for there was not one present who did not seem to share in a general feeling of gloom and depression, as though a heavy cloud were hanging over all things; and so complete was the realization of all that these ceremonies are intended to convey, that I am certain the power of death, still so awfully manifest in these last tedious hours, was present with each one of them.

As midnight approached, the archbishop, with his priests, accompanied by the king and queen, left the church, and stationed themselves on the platform, which was raised considerably from the ground, so that they were distinctly seen by the people. Every one now remained in breathless expectation, holding their unlighted tapers in readiness [sic] when the glad moment should arrive, while the priests still continued murmuring their melancholy chant in a low half-whisper. Suddenly a single report of a cannon announced that twelve o'clock had struck, and that Easter Day had begun; then the old archbishop, elevating the cross, exclaimed in a loud, exulting tone, 'Christos anesti,' 'CHRIST is risen!' and instantly every single individual of all that host took up the cry, and the vast multitude broke through and dispelled for ever the intense and mournful silence which they had maintained so long, with one spontaneous shout of indescribable joy and triumph, 'CHRIST is risen,' 'CHRIST is risen.' At the same moment the oppressive darkness was succeeded by a blaze of light from thousands of tapers, which, communicating one from another, seemed to send streams of fire in all directions, rendering the minutest objects distinctly visible, and casting the most vivid glow on the expressive faces, full of exultation, of the rejoicing crowd; bands of music struck up their gayest strains; the roll of drums through the town, and further on the pealing of the cannon, announced far and near these 'glad tidings of great joy;' while from hill and plain, from the sea-shore and the far olive grove, rocket after rocket ascending to the clear sky, answered back with their mute eloquence that CHRIST is risen indeed, and told of other tongues that were repeating those blessed words, and other hearts that leapt for joy; everywhere men clasped each other's hands, and congratulated one another, and embraced with countenances beaming with delight, as though to each one separately some wonderful happiness had been proclaimed;—and so in truth it was;—and all the while, rising above the mingling of many sounds, each one of which was a sound of gladness, the aged priests were distinctly heard chanting forth a glorious old hymn of victory, in tones so loud and clear, that they seemed to have regained their youth and strength to tell the world how 'CHRIST is risen from the dead, having trampled death beneath His feet, and henceforth the entombed have everlasting life'.

It is impossible to give any adequate idea of the effect of this scene. The sudden change of silent sorrow and darkness to an almost delirious joy, and a startling blaze of light spreading its unwonted brilliance through the night was really like magic. (INT 878-9)

This passage, which is repeated in *Hymns of the Eastern Church* (39-41), is significant, for not only does it demonstrate that Neale consulted contemporary Orientalist travelogues; it also shows that his experience of the Eastern Church—and of the Orient in general—was primarily textual. Particularly in the period prior to his own excursion to the East—and it was in this period (the 1850s) that all his Eastern hymns were written (HEC, p. xi)—he depended on others to convey to him the spirit of Orthodoxy. This passage in particular conveys the joy and exultation felt as the Lenten Fast gives way to the Easter Feast; this triumph over death at Easter is a prominent theme in his *Hymns of the Eastern Church*.

The *Triodion* holds a special place in the hearts and minds of the Orthodox. It is a collection of diverse devotional hymns, which help the church-goer to prepare for the Pascha.[9] Ware, in *The Orthodox Church*, tries to convey something of the mood of Orthodox Christians during this most important period in the liturgical year: 'It is during Holy Week that the most moving and impressive moments in Orthodox worship occur, as day by day and hour by hour the Church enters into the Passion of the Lord. Holy Week reaches its climax, first in the procession of the Epitaphion (the figure of the Dead Christ laid out for burial) on the evening of Good Friday; and then in the exultant Matins of the Resurrection at Easter Midnight.' This service, which Neale has described in detail above, is characterized by Ware in similar terms: 'None can be present at this midnight service without being caught up in the sense of universal joy. Christ has released the world from its ancient bondage and its former terrors, and the whole Church rejoices triumphantly in His victory over darkness and death.'[10] Neale believed that the Eastertide service-books were the ones which contained the essence of Orthodox belief. The deep penitence of Great Lent gives way to the boundless exultation of Easter. These are the two predominant moods to be found in Neale's renderings of Greek hymns.

The translations in the *General Introduction*, which predate those in verse in *Hymns of the Eastern Church*, give the reader a somewhat unbalanced picture of Orthodox hymnody. The primary reason for this is that Neale included all six as part of a survey entitled 'The Office-Books of the Holy Eastern Church' (INT 819–90). They are (1) from the *Menaia*, the service for the feast of the Holy Martyrs Proclus and Hilarius on 12 July (INT 829–42); (2) from the *Triodion*, Saturday vespers and Sunday matins of the Sunday before Lent, known as the Sunday of Forgiveness (INT 857–67); (3) from the *Triodion*, the sixty anathemas recited (in various forms) on Orthodoxy Sunday as part of a special 'Office of Orthodoxy' (INT 867–76); (4) from the *Triodion*, four *troparia* from the Great Canon of St Andrew of Crete, sung at matins on Thursday of the fifth week in Lent (INT 876); (5) from the

---

[9] The word *Pascha*, which is commonly used by the Orthodox to refer to Easter, is the approximate rendering by sound of the Hebrew word for 'Passover'. [10] Ware, *Orthodox Church*, 308.

Pentekostarion, part of the service for Easter Sunday, including St John Damascene's canon for Easter Sunday (INT 877–87); (6) from the *Octoechos* (*Parakletike*), some *troparia* for 30 October 1849, in order to demonstrate the method of finding the appropriate variable portion of the daily office for a specific day in the liturgical year (INT 888–9).

Of the six examples chosen by Neale, the first and sixth were included simply to show how the Orthodox worshipper knows of the occurrence of the fixed and variable feasts throughout the year. He translates from the *Menaia* and *Octoechos* because, as he correctly says, they are among the 'most important' service-books (INT 829), and, if only for that reason, require explication by example. Also, in the case of his translation from the *Menaia*, he is able to illustrate the mechanics of the office for a 'simple festival' in what he calls an 'extremely puzzling' book (INT 829); he therefore translates it in its entirety. Some sixty pages later, however, having discussed many of the technical aspects of Orthodox hymnody and having outlined features which many of the offices have in common, he is able to dispose of the *Octoechos* in half a page. One interesting point about Neale's first example from the *Menaia* is his preservation of the acrostic. He writes in the notes:

The acrostich in the present canon, at more pains than it is worth, I have preserved in the text. The number of letters in the English verse,

> To rev'rend athletes pour a rev'rend song,

is the same as that of the Greek . . . and the initials are carefully preserved. (INT 833)

Likewise, in the Greek, the name of the writer, Joseph of the Studium, forms part of the acrostic; Neale reproduces the name 'JOSEF' in ode 9 (INT 941–2). Here Neale the pedantic translator is again in evidence: he sacrifices as little as possible for the most correct rendering he can achieve.

Little more need be said concerning the first and sixth examples, except that Neale did his best to simplify the mechanics of Eastern hymnody for his readers. Far more interesting from the point of view of Neale's own interest in

Orthodoxy are the other examples, which all relate to Easter and reveal something of his sympathies for his subject. The third example, which is not part of a normal Greek canon, comes from the office for Orthodoxy Sunday (the first Sunday in Lent). The special 'Office of Orthodoxy' from which it comes is usually read today in abbreviated form, which varies from place to place. In Neale's rendering, it appears to be no more than a list of names. The catalogue is important, however, for it recalls—and condemns—those who were at the centre of the Iconoclastic Controversy. Orthodoxy Sunday celebrates the 'Triumph of Orthodoxy', marked by the definitive restoration of icons to the churches by the Empress Theodora on the first Sunday in Lent, 11 March 843. The fact that Neale devotes almost ten pages to translating this special office is indicative of the strong affinity he had for icons, those material aids to faith which occupy a special place in the hearts and minds of the Orthodox. Aware of the parallel that could be drawn between the symbolism inherent in icons and in architecture, Neale seized this opportunity in the *General Introduction* to show how the memory of the Iconoclast Controversy penetrated the substance of Eastern Church worship. He clearly appreciated the victory of Orthodoxy and the centrality of this event to the history of the Eastern Church. Thus his painstaking translation in the *General Introduction* of the anathemas—rather than any other portion of the Orthodoxy Sunday office—is justified.[11]

Neale's other translations from the Lenten services are primarily from canons. The second example, from the Sunday of Forgiveness, commemorates Adam's expulsion from Paradise. The central image of the office for this day is a theme which runs throughout the *Triodion*: the longing for a return to Paradise. The sadness felt because of the expulsion of Adam and Eve from Eden, which is evoked during Lent through prayers lamenting the sins which have deprived man of free communion with God, is balanced by the awareness of Christ's approaching death and resurrection, the salvation which is celebrated on Great Friday and Easter Sunday, through which Paradise is reopened. Some idea of the mood may be conveyed

---

[11] A cento from the canon for Orthodoxy Sunday appears in HEC 117–21.

by quoting four *stichera* from vespers on Saturday evening, and, as a check on the accuracy of Neale's translation, by comparing it with the version found in *The Lenten Triodion* by Kallistos Ware and Mother Mary:

Neale, *General Introduction*

My Lord and Maker having taken clay from the earth gave me life by His breath, and gave me a soul, and quickened me, and honoured me as ruler upon earth, of things visible, and the fellow of the Angels: Satan the deceiver, using the serpent as an instrument, beguiled me with the fruit, and separated me from the glory of God, and gave me, on earth, to the death that is in the lowest depth; but, as my LORD, and full of compassion, call me back again.

Miserable man! I was deprived of my GOD-woven vest, when I disobeyed, O LORD, through the guile of the enemy, Thy commands; and now I am girded with the leaves of the fig, and with the coat of skin: I am adjudged to sweat: I must eat the bread of labour; thorns and thistles hath the earth been cursed to bear. But Thou That, in the last times, didst take flesh of a Virgin, bring me back again into Paradise.

Paradise of glory! loveliest in thy beauty! tabernacle raised by GOD! pleasure without end and enjoyment! glory of the just! delight of Prophets! dwelling of Saints! there is the whisper of thy shades.

Ware and Mother Mary (trans.), *The Lenten Triodion*

The Lord my Creator took me as dust from the earth and formed me into a living creature, breathing into me the breath of life and giving me a soul; He honoured me, setting me as ruler upon earth over all things visible, and making me companion of the angels. But Satan the deceiver, using the serpent as his instrument, enticed me by food; he parted me from the glory of God and gave me over to the earth and to the lowest depths of death. But, Master, in compassion, call me back again.

In my wretchedness I have cast off the robe woven by God, disobeying Thy divine command, O Lord, at the counsel of the enemy; and I am clothed now in fig leaves and in garments of skin. I am condemned to eat the bread of toil in the sweat of my brow, and the earth has been cursed so that it bears thorns and thistles for me. But, Lord, who in the last times was made flesh of a Virgin, call me back again and bring me into Paradise.

O precious Paradise, unsurpassed in beauty, tabernacle built by God, unending gladness and delight, glory of the righteous, joy of the prophets, and dwelling of the saints, with the sound of thy

Supplicate the Maker of all things, that He would open to me the gates, which I closed by my transgression; and that I may be counted worthy to partake of the tree of life, and of the joy in which, while in thee, I revelled.	leaves pray to the Maker of all: may He open unto me the gates which I closed by my transgression, and may He count me worthy to partake of the Tree of Life and of the joy which was mine when I dwelt in thee before.
Adam, for his disobedience, hath been cast out from Paradise, and banished from its delights: he sits, deceived by the words of his wife, and naked. Wherefore haste we, to undergo the whole time of the fast, obeying the evangelic traditions, that by means of them, being well-pleasing to CHRIST, we may again receive the abode of Paradise. (INT 857–8)	Adam was banished from Paradise through disobedience and cast out from delight, beguiled by the words of a woman. Naked he sat outside the garden, lamenting 'Woe is me!' Therefore let us all make haste to accept the season of the Fast and hearken to the teaching of the Gospel, that we may gain Christ's mercy and receive once more a dwelling-place in Paradise.[12]

What is immediately apparent in both versions is that the *Triodion* speaks not of 'Adam' but of 'me': 'Supplicate the Maker of all things, that He would open to *me* the gates, which I closed by *my* transgression,' in Neale's translation. Here, as throughout the *Triodion*, the events of sacred history are not treated as a series of past or future events, but as experiences undergone by the individual here and now. Neale sustains the plaintive tone throughout the portions which he translates. He returns to these four *stichera* in *Hymns of the Eastern Church*, as 'The LORD my Maker, as forming me of clay', in which, for the most part, the literal translation is maintained, with the exception of the end of the third stanza:

> And let me taste the holy Tree
> That giveth immortality
> To them that dwell therein!
> Or have I fallen so far from grace
> That mercy hath for me no place?
>
> (HEC 100)

---

[12] *The Lenten Triodion*, trans. Mother Mary and K. Ware (London, 1978), 168–9.

The doubt expressed in Neale's hymn is not present in the Greek original, and it reflects caution on the part of the writer, in order to avoid accusations of boasting of an assured place in the kingdom of heaven. While a similar idea is present in the *Triodion* as the desire to be counted 'worthy', the uncertainty is more pronounced in Neale's hymn.

The beginning of the third stanza is also noteworthy, for it expresses the joy of heaven which is so prominent a feature in Neale's hymn writing:[13]

> O glorious Paradise! O lovely clime!
> O God-built mansions! Joy of every saint!
> Happy remembrance to all coming time!
>
> (HEC 99)

It is the loss of this glorious existence through the Fall which distresses Adam—and, by extension, Neale—in this hymn. The last stanza takes the form of a lament.

> O me! so ruined by the serpent's hate!
> O me! so glorious once, and now so lost!
> So mad that bitter lot to choose!
> Beguil'd of all I had to lose!
> Must I, then, gladness of my eyes,—
> Must I then leave thee, Paradise,
> And as an exile go?
> And must I never cease to grieve
> How once my GOD, at cool of eve,
> Came down to walk below?
> O Merciful! on thee I call:
> O Pitiful! forgive my fall!
>
> (HEC 100)

With a far-reaching sympathy for his subject, Neale suggests: 'The last stanza, Milton, as an universal scholar, had in his eye, in Eve's lamentation' (HEC 98), by which he means *Paradise Lost* xi. 268–85:

> O unexpected stroke, worse then Death!
> Must I leave thee Paradise? thus leave
> Thee Native Soile, these happie Walks and Shades,

---

[13] G. Rowell also notes this characteristic of Neale's hymns in *Hell and the Victorians* (Oxford, 1974), 114.

> Fit haunt of Gods? where I had hope to spend,
> Quiet though sad, the respit of that day
> That must be mortal to us both. O flours,
> That never will in other Climate grow,
> My early visitation, and my last
> At Eev'n, which I bred up with tender hand
> From the first op'ning bud, and gave ye Names,
> Who now shall rear ye to the Sun, or ranke
> Your Tribes, and water from th'ambrosial Fount?
> Thee lastly nuptial Bowre, by mee adornd
> With what to sight or smell was sweet; from thee
> How shall I part, and whither wander down
> Into a lower World, to this obscure
> And wilde, how shall we breath in other Aire
> Less pure, accustomd to immortal Fruits?[14]

It is doubtful whether Milton's erudition extended to Orthodox hymnody (although he does refer to the 'Greek Church' a number of times in his writings). He describes paradise in more minute detail than Neale does, and Eve recalls a multitude of sensual impressions. But the fact that Neale recalls Eve's lamentation from *Paradise Lost* is sufficient to excite the appropriate reaction from the reader: the feelings of loss, isolation, exile, and regret—all of which are present in the *stichera* from the *Triodion*.

The fourth example in the *General Introduction* comes from St Andrew of Crete, who holds an exalted position in the hymnographic life of Orthodoxy, because it was he who systematized the canon. A number of the seventy canons he is said to have composed are still used, on various Sundays and feast-days throughout the year. In the *Triodion*, canons by Andrew include the Great Canon, chanted in its entirety at matins on Thursday in the fifth week of Lent; the evening canon of Friday before Palm Sunday; and the canons of compline and the *triodia* of matins on Holy Monday and Tuesday. The Great Canon is his most important work, not only because of its size, but also because of the spiritual depth of its contents. Although Neale admits that it is 'possessed of considerable beauty, and it is not wonderful that it is regarded as the prince

---

[14] F. A. Patterson et al. (eds), *The Works of John Milton* (New York, 1931), ii.355.

of canons' (INT 876), he does not translate it in full, either in prose in the *General Introduction* or in verse in his *Hymns of the Eastern Church*. While he observes correctly that 'the immense length of the Canon, for it exceeds three hundred stanzas, and its necessary tautology, must render it wearisome, unless devotionally used under the peculiar circumstances for which it is appointed' (HEC 24), one suspects that there are other factors underlying the cursory treatment of this canon by Neale (four *troparia* from the first ode appear in INT 876, and a cento of ten stanzas from the same ode is found in HEC 24–7). Andrew's theme, like that of the canons for the Sunday of Forgiveness, is a melancholy one; the writer feels his earthly life coming to an end, and woefully laments his wretched life. Almost every *troparion* in the canon has two parts: in the first, the writer speaks to his soul, enumerating his sins and pointing out the ways and means of correcting his errors; in the second part, he turns to God with fervent and plaintive prayer, asking for his mercy. The very frank tone of this penitential confession, in which the writer admits to 'murderous thoughts', likens his soul to that of Esau because of his 'raging lust for women', and then cries to God 'like the Harlot',[15] meant, first of all, that if Neale were attempting a literal translation, he would be presenting the Eastern Church in a potentially unfavourable light (contrary to his ultimate goal of *sobornost*); also, these same portions would have been inappropriate as hymns for English congregations. Likewise, verses like 'Holy Mother Mary, pray to God for us', which is repeated at the end of each ode, might lead to accusations of Mariolatry, which Neale desperately tried to avoid (the figure addressed is Mary of Egypt, not the *Theotokos*).[16] In addition, Neale delighted in hymns of glory, and although the Great Canon is of utmost importance to a discussion of Orthodox hymnody and spirituality, its deep, penitential tone and continual self-deprecation rendered it unsuited to use by Neale's audience; although he constructed a cento from the first ode, the hymn 'Whence shall my tears

---

[15] Quotations from the Great Canon are from the translation found in *Lenten Triodion*, 378–415.

[16] It should be noted that while Neale preserved *Theotokia* in translations in INT, none are preserved in HEC.

begin?', it never came into common use. Finally, although Neale was particularly drawn to the Orthodox hymns for Eastertide, it is possible that this canon appealed to him less than others because it contains no direct references to Christ's Passion. As Savas points out, this great canon was not composed specifically for Lent, or for any other feast; it is simply the confession of a sincere penitent.[17] But, since Great Lent is a period of contrition and repentance, and it was deemed suitable for this time of the liturgical year.

The fifth example in the *General Introduction* comes from the *Pentekostarion*, the companion volume to the *Triodion*, which covers the period from Easter Sunday to the Sunday of All Saints (the first Sunday after Pentecost). Its more specific name is the *Pentekostarion Kharmosynon*, or 'Joyful' *Pentekostarion*, and this reflects the character of the book, as well as of Neale's selection, which comes from the service for Easter Sunday. It is the most fully translated of the portions of the Orthodox offices which Neale considers, indicating the importance of Easter to his own experience. After figuratively preparing his readers by leading them through the offices for Great Lent, he ends with the celebration of Easter, the day on which the faithful announce with great rejoicing 'Christ is risen!' The service he translates, which includes St John Damascene's Golden Canon of Easter, may be described as one of the most exultant in Orthodox hymnody, so much so that it is one of only three canons in *Hymns of the Eastern Church* which are fully translated by Neale (HEC 42–52).

The joy of Easter Day, which Neale wished to emphasize, is most strongly conveyed in the first ode, in both his literal translation and in his hymn; the latter, now well known as the altered 'The Day of Resurrection',[18] is a popular Eastertide hymn:

General Introduction	Hymns of the Eastern Church
'On the day of Resurrection let us, O people, be clothed with gladness; it is the Pascha, the	'Tis the Day of Resurrection: Earth! tell it out abroad! The Passover of Gladness!

---

[17] S. J. Savas, *The Treasury of Orthodox Hymnody* (Minneapolis, 1983), 39.
[18] The 1st line was altered by the editors of *Hymns Ancient and Modern* for inclusion in the 1868 edn.

Pascha of the lord: for from death to life, and from earth to heaven, hath CHRIST OUR LORD caused us to pass over, singing the Hymn of Victory.'	The Passover of God! From Death to Life Eternal,— From earth unto the sky, Our CHRIST hath brought us over, With hymns of victory.
Cleanse we our souls, and we shall behold CHRIST, glittering in the unapproachable light of the Resurrection; and we shall clearly hear Him exclaiming, Hail! and singing the Hymn of Victory.	Our hearts be pure from evil, That we may see aright The LORD in rays eternal Of Resurrection-Light: And, listening to His accents, May hear, so calm and plain, His own—*All Hail*—and hearing, May raise the victor strain!
Let the Heavens, as it is meet, rejoice, and let the earth exult: and let the whole universe, visible and invisible, keep festival. For CHRIST hath arisen, and there is eternal joy. (INT 880)	Now let the Heav'ns be joyful! Let earth her song begin! Let the round world keep triumph, And all that is therein: Invisible and visible Their note slet all things blend,— For CHRIST the LORD hath risen,— Our Joy That hath no end.

(HEC 42-3)

As Wellesz notes, in his side-by-side presentation of the Greek text and Neale's prose translation, Neale handles the Greek text with great freedom; but

his translation has the advantage over other attempts at finding English equivalents for the Greek words, since he drew on the language of the Authorized Version of the Bible just as John Damascene drew on that of the Greek New Testament. In consequence the modern reader who does not know Greek is able to see the close connection between the language of John Damascene, and all other hymn-writers, and that of the Scriptures.[19]

What Wellesz says is true. The basis for the first ode is the Song of Moses at the Red Sea (Exod. 15: 1–19), which is itself a hymn of victory. The biblical canticle opens with the words

---

[19] Egon Wellesz, *History of Byzantine Music and Hymnography* (Oxford, 1961), 176. Another Greek hymn-writer who adhered closely to the biblical text was St Andrew of Crete; see Savas, *Treasury*, 37.

'I will sing unto the LORD, for he hath triumphed gloriously', and ends with 'the children of Israel went on dry land in the midst of the sea'. The first stanza of Neale's translation, which is the *irmos* (hence the quotation marks around it), continues with the idea that God's victory should be proclaimed, but, by typological association, connects Moses' leading the Israelites through the Red Sea with Christ's leading man from an earthly to a heavenly existence ('Our CHRIST hath brought us over'). The idea of announcing the event is given added emphasis in Neale's hymn, where what was, metaphorically, joyful raiment becomes a proud exclamation:

> 'Tis the Day of Resurrection:
> Earth! tell it out abroad!

Another parallel between Moses and Christ inherent in the first ode is that just as Moses led the children of Israel from slavery to freedom, so Christ led man's soul from enslavement to redemption.

The prose translation contains one idea which is almost absent from the hymn. In the second stanza Christ is described as 'glittering in the unapproachable light of the Resurrection'. The image is important, for it shows that the glory of Jesus cannot be appreciated by men unless they come before him cleansed of sin. Only then are men delivered from death to eternal life. Ware comments: 'The Crucifixion is itself a victory: but on Great Friday the victory is hidden, whereas on Easter morning it is made manifest. Christ rises from the dead, and by his rising he delivers us from anxiety and terror: the victory of the Cross is confirmed, love is openly shown to be stronger than hatred, and life to be stronger than death.'[20] Although Neale's verse translation makes crystal clear the idea of victory, it fails to articulate strongly enough that the passage from darkness to light is dependent on cleansing one's soul. Only then can the 'Joy That hath no end' find fullest expression.

On Easter Day the second ode is omitted as usual. The third ode derives from the scriptural canticle of the Song of Hannah (1 Sam. 2: 1–10), in which the power of God is catalogued. St

---

[20] Ware, *Orthodox Way*, 111.

John Damascene, and in turn Neale, connect the barren Hannah with the barren rock which Moses smote at Meribah (Exod. 17: 1–7, Num. 20: 1–13):

General Introduction	Hymns of the Eastern Church
'Come, and let us drink the new drink, not produced by miracle from barren rock, but the fountain of immortality, CHRIST having burst from the tomb, in Whom we are established.'	Come and let us drink of that New River, Not from Barren Rock divinely poured, But the Fount of Life that is for ever From the sepulchre of CHRIST the LORD.
Now are all things filled with light; earth and heaven, and that which is under the earth. Now then let all creation keep festival for the Resurrection of CHRIST, in which it is established.	All the world hath bright illumination,— Heav'n and Earth and things beneath the earth: 'Tis the Festival of all Creation: CHRIST hath ris'n, Who gave Creation birth.
Yesterday, O CHRIST, I was buried together with Thee; to-day with Thee arising I arise. Yesterday I was crucified together with Thee: glorify me, O SAVIOUR, together with Thyself in Thy kingdom. (INT 880)	Yesterday with Thee in burial lying, Now to-day with Thee aris'n I rise; Yesterday the partner of Thy dying, With Thyself upraise me to the skies.

(HEC 44)

St John is saying that man no longer needs to drink water which flows from the barren rock, because Christ, the 'New River', has come to supply man's wants. The human race can now drink from him who is the 'fountain of immortality'.

The third stanza of this ode contains an idea which is central to the Orthodox experience of Easter: the identification of the worshipper with the suffering Christ. The Crucifixion must be understood not only as a victory or sacrifice, but as an example for man to follow. The association does not end here, as Ware explains:

The victory of his suffering love upon the Cross does not merely set me an example, showing me what I myself may achieve if by my own efforts I imitate him. Much more than this, his suffering love has a creative effect upon me, transforming my own heart and will, releasing me from bondage, making me whole, rendering it possible for me to love in a way that would lie altogether beyond my powers, had I not first been loved by him. Because in love he has identified himself with me, his victory is my victory. And so Christ's death upon the Cross is truly, as the Liturgy of St Basil describes it, a life-creating death.[21]

The implication of this creative death is that Christ has done for man something that he would be incapable of effecting on his own. The barrenness has been removed through the sacrifice of Christ.

The fourth ode, whose canticle is the Song of Habakkuk (Hab. 3: 2–19), runs as follows, in Neale's translations:

General Introduction	*Hymns of the Eastern Church*
'Upon thy divine watch-tower, Habaccuk, Prophet of GOD, stand with us and shew the Angel of light continually proclaiming, To-day is salvation to the world, for CHRIST, as Almighty, hath risen.'	Stand on thy watch-tower, Habakkuk the Seer, And show the Angel, radiant in his light: To-day, saith he, Salvation shall appear, Because the LORD hath ris'n, as GOD of Might.
CHRIST appeared as a male, opening the Virgin's womb; and, as mortal, He is named a Lamb. Spotless is our Pascha called, as being without taste of blemish, and, as true GOD, He is named perfect.	The male that opes the Virgin's womb is HE; The Lamb of Whom His faithful people eat; Our truer Passover from blemish free; Our very GOD, Whose Name is all-complete.
As a yearling lamb, our blessed Crown, CHRIST, was of His own accord sacrificed as the expiatory Pascha for all; and again shone forth to us from the tomb, the beautiful Sun of Righteousness.	This yearling Lamb, our sacrifice most blest, Our glorious Crown, for all men freely dies: Our cleansing Pascha, beauteous from His rest, Behold the Sun of Righteousness arise.

[21] Ibid. 109.

David, the Divine Father, leapt and danced before the mystic ark; and the holy people of GOD, beholding the forthgiving of the symbols. Let us rejoice in GOD, for that CHRIST, as Almighty, hath risen. (INT 881)	Before the ark, a type to pass away, David of old time danced: we, holier race, Seeing the Antitype come forth to-day, Hail with a shout, CHRIST's own Almighty grace.[22]

(HEC 45)

The Hebrew prophet is invited to stand on the watch-tower with the faithful in order to show them the Angel of light, who proclaims the Resurrection. The emphasis is on the 'salvation' of the world (the word occurs in Hab. 3: 8 and 3: 18 in the Authorized Version), and in the verse translation Christ is clearly identified as 'Salvation'. The ode also accentuates his human side, through the words 'as mortal' in the prose translation. This idea is not emphasized as strongly in the verse translation, which speaks of the 'Lamb' and 'Passover', but in using metaphors does not explicitly point to Jesus's humanity. Christ's full partaking of man's lower nature is central to the concept of salvation, in that he took on not only a human form, but also a human spirit, mind, and soul. Ware reminds us that for the Orthodox sin is not physical in origin, but spiritual: it is man's centre of moral choice—not his body—which is most in need of redemption.[23] By clearly identifying Christ as 'mortal', as having a human mind, it is understood that salvation involves reaching the central point of human need.

The final stanza of this ode depicts David, a type of Christ, dancing before the ark (2 Sam. 6: 14). St John bids the people to celebrate the fulfilment of the type with exultation, thus recalling Hab. 3: 18: 'Yet I will rejoice in the LORD, I will joy in the God of my salvation'. Christ, Who has made a new covenant with man (Heb. 12: 24), supersedes the Hebrew Ark of the Covenant.

The fifth ode, which has as its point of departure the Song of Isaiah (Isa. 26: 9–20), embraces the idea of the first biblical

---

[22] The words of the angel are placed in quotation marks in the 3rd edn. of HEC.   [23] Ware, *Orthodox Way*, 98.

verse, 'With my soul have I desired thee in the night: yea, with my spirit within me I will seek thee early'.

General Introduction	Hymns of the Eastern Church
'Let us arise very early in the morning, and instead of ointment let us bring a hymn to our LORD. And we shall behold CHRIST, the Sun of Righteousness, causing life to spring forth to all.'	Let us rise in early morning, And, instead of ointments, bring, Hymns of praises to our Master, And His Resurrection sing: We shall see the Sun of Justice Risen with healing on His wing.
They that were held by the chains of Hades, when they beheld Thy gentle pity, O CHRIST, hurried onward to light, applauding, with joyful foot, the Eternal Pascha.	Thy unbounded loving-kindness, They that groaned in Hades' chain, Prisoners, from afar beholding, Hasten to the light again; And to that eternal Pascha Wove the dance and raised the strain.
Let us draw near with lamps in our hands, to Him That as a Bridegroom comes forth from the tomb. And let us, with the company that loves the Feast, celebrate together the saving Pascha of the lord. (INT 881–2)	Go ye forth, His Saints to meet Him! Go with lamps in every hand! From the sepulchre He riseth: Ready for the Bridegroom stand: And the Pascha of salvation Hail, with His triumphant band.

(HEC 46)

After the parallel opening, the ode goes off in another direction from the biblical canticle. Instead of the Israelites shutting themselves in their chambers until the 'indignation' of God has passed (Isa. 26: 20), John's addressees are encouraged to go out and meet the Pascha, and to meet Him with dancing and singing (an echo of the fourth ode). They are also to welcome with lamps in their hands the Victor, who has risen from the sepulchre to redeem the faithful.

The image of rising from the tomb is carried over into the sixth ode, which is based on the Song of Jonah in the belly of the whale (Jonah 2: 3–10). The ode describes the Harrowing of Hell, and confirms the type–antitype relationship between Jonah and Christ:

General Introduction
'Thou didst descend into the lowest parts of the earth, O CHRIST; and, having broken the eternal bars which held the prisoners, Thou didst on the third day, as Jonah from the whale, rise again from the tomb.'

Hymns of the Eastern Church
Into the dim earth's lowest
  parts descending,
And bursting by Thy might
  the infernal chain
That bound the prisoners,
Thou, at three days' ending,
As Jonah from the whale,
  hast risen again.

Thou didst preserve inviolate the seals, O CHRIST, when Thou didst rise from the tomb: Thou Who didst not burst the bars of virginity in Thy birth, and didst open to us the gates of Paradise.

Thou brakest not the seal, Thy
  surety's token,
Arising from the tomb, Who
  left'st in birth
The portals of virginity unbroken,
And op'st the gates of
  heaven to sons of earth.

My SAVIOUR, Who didst offer Thyself to the Father, a living and unsacrificed victim, as GOD, Thou didst raise, together with Thyself, Adam and all his race, when Thou didst arise from the tomb. (INT 882)

Thou, Sacrifice ineffable and
  living,
Didst to the FATHER, by
  Thyself atone
As GOD eternal: resurrection
  giving
To Adam, general parent, by
  Thine own.
                        (HEC 47)

The seventh ode returns to Christ's mortality, and takes its theme from the Song of the Three Holy Children (3–34). The connection between canticle and ode can clearly be seen in the first line:

General Introduction
'He That delivered the children from the furnace became man, and suffered as a mortal, and by suffering, endued the Mortal with

Hymns of the Eastern Church
Who from the fiery furnace
  saved the Three,
Suffers as mortal; that, His
  passion o'er,

the beauty of immortality. He, the GOD of our Fathers, That is only blessed and most glorious.'

This mortal, triumphing over death, might be,
Vested with immortality once more.
  He Whom our fathers still confest
  GOD over all, for ever blest.

The holy women followed after Thee with their ointments. But Him Whom they sought with tears as a mortal, they worshipped with joy as the Living GOD, and announced to Thy Disciples, O CHRIST, the glad tidings of the Mystic Pasch.

The women with their ointment seek the tomb,
And Whom they mourned as dead, with many a tear,
They worship now, joy dawning on their gloom,
As Living GOD, as mystic Passover;
  Then to the LORD's Disciples gave
  The tidings of the vanquished grave.

We celebrate the death of death, the destruction of hell, the first-fruits of another and eternal life. And with exultation we hymn the Cause, the GOD of our Fathers, That is only blessed and most glorious.

We keep the festal of the death of death:
Of hell o'erthrown: the first-fruits pure and bright,
Of life eternal; and with joyous breath
Praise Him That won the victory by His might:
  Him Whom our fathers still confessed
  GOD over all, for ever blest.

How truly holy, and all-celebrated is this night of salvation and glory! This night that precedes the splendour-bearing day! in which the Eternal Light burst in His Body from the tomb, and shone upon all. (INT 883–4)

All hallowed festival, in splendour born!
Night of salvation and of glory! Night
Fore-heralding the Resurrection morn!
When from the tomb the everlasting Light,
  A glorious frame once more His own,
  Upon the world in splendour shone.

(HEC 48–9)

This ode too emphasizes the mortality of Christ (the word 'mortal' is repeated in the first stanza of the verse translation, and is found a third time in the second stanza of the prose translation), then celebrates the transformation from gloom to joy, recalled in spectacular fashion, as we have seen, by the Orthodox on Easter morning. The blending of these two ideas in one ode is significant, for it emphasizes that the Orthodox are continually aware of these two themes. Ware explains: 'It would be wrong to think of Orthodoxy simply as the cult of Christ's divine glory.... However great their devotion to the divine glory of Our Lord, Orthodox do not overlook His humanity.'[24]

In all the odes which deal with both themes, it is the overwhelming sense of Christ's divine glory which shines through most powerfully, through images of light, associated with both the Transfiguration and the Resurrection. The importance of the light metaphor may best be understood by noting that the Transfiguration, celebrated on 6 August, is reckoned among the twelve Great Feasts of the Orthodox Church. The *exapostilarion*, repeated three times, from the office for the Transfiguration, clearly illustrates this point:

Today on Tabor, in the manifestation of Thy Light, O Word, Thou unaltered Light from the Light of the unbegotten Father, we have seen the Father as Light and the Spirit as Light, guiding with light the whole creation.[25]

It is important to bear in mind that the light image is also intimately connected with Easter: the Greek Orthodox refer to the Feast as *Lampra*, the brightest day of all. The tapers which are lit at the midnight service carry the Resurrection light to every Orthodox home, as a symbol of the new life of the resurrected Christ.

The eighth ode of a canon, more than the others, focuses on the feast itself, and in this case, is marked as the 'Feast of Feasts' in the verse translation, and 'solemn Festival of solemn Festivals' in the prose:

General Introduction	Hymns of the Eastern Church
'This is the chosen and holy day, the first day of the week, the	Thou hallowed chosen day! that first

[24] Ware, *Orthodox Church*, 231.

[25] *Festal Menaion*, 495.

Feast that is lady and queen of Feasts, and the solemn Festival of solemn Festivals, in which we bless CHRIST for ever and ever.'

O come, and let us participate in the new fruit of the Vine, heavenly joy, in the glorious day of the Resurrection, of the kingdom of CHRIST, honouring Him as GOD, for ever and ever.

Lift up thine eyes round about thee, O Sion, and see; as lights, illumined of GOD, thy children come to thee, from the East and from the West, from the Sea and from the North, blessing in thee CHRIST for ever and ever.

FATHER Almighty, and WORD, and SPIRIT, united nature, and three Persons, super-essential, and GOD Most High, in Thee have we been baptized, and we bless Thee for ever and ever. (INT 884)

And best and greatest shinest![26]
Lady and Queen and Feast of feasts,
Of things divine, divinest!
On thee our praises CHRIST adore,
For ever and for evermore.

Come, let us taste the vine's new fruit
For heavenly joy preparing:
On this propitious day, with CHRIST
His Resurrection sharing:
Whom as True GOD our hymns adore
For ever and for evermore.

Raise, Sion, raise thine eyes! for lo!
Thy scattered sons have found thee:
From East and West, and North and South,
Thy children gather round thee;
And in thy bosom CHRIST adore,
For ever and for evermore!

O FATHER of unbounded might!
O SON and HOLY SPIRIT!
In Persons Three, in Substance One,
Of one co-equal merit;
In Thee baptiz'd, we Thee adore
For ever and for evermore!

(HEC 50-1)

The tone of Neale's hymn is more exultant than that of the prose translation. It not only contains a greater number of exclamations, but takes no account of the word 'solemn'. The prevailing mood on Easter Day, however, is meant to be exultant, and feelings of joy are present in both versions.

The connection between canticle and ode is here more difficult to ascertain than in the previous ones. The third stanza

---

[26] From the 2nd edn. onwards these two lines were altered to 'Thou hallowed chosen morn of praise, / That best and greatest shinest!'

contains the phrase 'as lights, illumined of GOD, thy children come to thee', which may be an allusion to the Song of the Three Holy Children. What the canticle and ode have in common is their universal participation in praise and celebration, which is sustained here through the repetition of 'for ever and ever' in the prose translation and 'For ever and for evermore' in the verse translation; these endings of the stanzas provide a connection between canticle and ode.

The theme of the last ode of an Orthodox canon usually derives from praise of the *Theotokos*, based on the ninth canticle, the *Magnificat* (Luke 1: 46–55), which begins, 'My soul doth magnify the Lord, and my spirit hath rejoiced in God my Saviour,' and the *Benedictus Dominus* (Luke 1: 68–79). Here, however, St John Damascene continues to praise the feast-day, and, it seems, to pay more attention to it than to the *Theotokos* because of the centrality of Easter to Christian tradition:

General Introduction	Hymns of the Eastern Church
'Arise and shine, New Jerusalem; for the glory of the LORD hath risen upon thee. Rejoice and exult, O Sion! and thou, pure Mother of GOD, joy in the Resurrection of thy SON!'	Thou New Jerusalem, arise and shine! The glory of the LORD on thee hath risen! Sion, exult! rejoice with joy divine, Mother of GOD! Thy Son hath burst His prison.
O heavenly and dear and most sweet word! Thou hast promised, O CHRIST, to be with us, and Thou canst not lie, until the end of the world! We, the faithful, exult, holding that Thy word is an anchor of hope.	O Heavenly Voice! O word of purest love! 'Lo! I am with you alway to the end:' This is the anchor, steadfast from above, The golden anchor, whence our hopes depend.
O great and most holy Passover, CHRIST! O Wisdom and Word and Power of GOD! grant us more expressly to partake of Thee, in the day of Thy kingdom that hath no evening. (INT 884–5)	O CHRIST, our Pascha! greatest, holiest, best! GOD's Word and Wisdom and effectual Might! Thy fuller, lovelier presence manifest, In that eternal realm, that knows no night! (HEC 52)

There are several interesting inconsistencies between the prose and verse translations. In the verse no mention is made of Christ's inability to lie (that is, to break his promise, which, of course, he will never do) because of the fear of misrepresentation; rather, Christ himself speaks, confirming his promise to be with man until the end of the world. Also, in the verse translation, points are reinforced by variations on words or repetition—for example, 'rejoice with joy divine' and the repetition of 'anchor'. At the end, the verse translation does not evoke the image of partaking of Christ, which includes both a sharing in the Eucharist and an imitation of Christ's life, which lies at the centre of the canon's theology. In its place is a passive manifestation of Christ's presence; it thereby loses the force which St John Damascene intended.

This discussion of the translations of St John Damascene's Golden Canon clearly shows that Neale had sympathy for his subject and that he revelled in the Orthodox celebration of Easter, the feast which he correctly perceived as pre-eminent among all Eastern Church festivals. The examination also shows the difficulty—for both Greek and English hymn-writers —of sustaining the praise through eight odes, which, ultimately, are all variations on one theme. It is important, however, to note the mechanics of concatenation of these odes into a canon, as well as the difficulty of using more than one at a time as a hymn in a Western church service. In the case of the Golden Canon of Easter, only 'The Day of Resurrection', a translation of the first ode, came into common use; this may be partly the result of its being the only hymn of the eight to be written in 7.6.7.6.D, the metre of many of Neale's best hymns.

In following this analysis, the reader may have felt that St John—and Neale—were running out of images and words with which to celebrate Easter Day. In Eastern hymnody, the ability to vary modes of praise based on a single theme is thought to be a great strength (Neale applied this principle in *Hymns of the Eastern Church* by varying the metres of his eight hymns). Because of the rigidity of form, with each ode corresponding to a specific biblical canticle, the scope for invention, as Neale recognized, seems very narrow, and can produce an image, in the mind of the reader or hearer (whether Orthodox or Western), of a hymn that is repetitive and tedious. The above analysis has shown, however, that each ode is a complete unit, different from every other in the canon, yet intimately connected to it to produce an overall sensation of the almost limitless joy associated with the Orthodox celebration of Easter.

A closer look at *Hymns of the Eastern Church*, which Neale calls 'my little book' (HEC, p. xii), reveals that, as in the *General Introduction*, there is a concentration on hymns relating to Lent and Easter. From the point of view of sheer volume, there are over three times as many verses, or poetic stanzas, connected with Eastertide than Christmastide; furthermore, Easter hymns outweigh those devoted to other festivals by more than fifty per cent (including Theophany and Pentecost, both of which are traditionally regarded as greater than Christmas—although Neale seems to be unaware of this peculiarly Orthodox emphasis, and therefore incorrectly makes Christmas the second great 'pole' in the Orthodox Church year). If, as in tables 1–3, the compositions in *Hymns of the Eastern Church* are divided into the three categories (those for Advent and Christmastide, Lent and Eastertide, and other festivals)—as opposed to Neale's chronological classification by author—these results are confirmed. The tables clearly demonstrate that Neale wished to give greater prominence to the hymns of Lent and Eastertide (table 2) than to those of any other single feast in the Orthodox liturgical year. In light of what has been said about the Eastern Church's own attitude to this period in the Church year, Neale's stress was perfectly correct. It is also interesting to note that of the twenty-three Lent and Eastertide hymns he presents, only two are centos; this points to Neale's wish to preserve the theology and divinity as communicated in the Greek original (the same is true of Advent and Christmastide, though the selection is smaller). Although Neale had no control over the alterations or stanzaic rearrangements introduced by hymn-book editors, it is significant that 'Christian, dost thou *see* them', 'The abyss of many a former sin', and 'The Day of Resurrection' appeared almost unchanged in hymnals. All three are easy-to-follow congregational hymns, which communicate clear messages and serve to complement the liturgy, which was the reason why Neale wrote hymns in the first place. 'Christian, dost thou

TABLE 1. Hymns for Advent and Christmastide

First line of hymn	Original author	Office-book source	Liturgical classification and occasion for use	Page no(s). in HEC
The Lord and King of all things	St Anatolius	*Menaion*	*Doxastikon* of *stichera* on 'Lord I have cried' for St Stephen's Day[a]	7–8
A great and mighty wonder	St Anatolius	*Menaion*	*Aposticha* for first vespers of Christmas Day[b]	11–12
In Bethlehem is He born	No Greek original[c]	——	Said by Neale to be *idiomelon* for Christmas	13
CHRIST is born! Tell forth His fame!	Cosmas the Melodist	*Menaion*	Ode, canon for Christmas Day	69–70
Him, of the FATHER's very Essence	Cosmas the Melodist	*Menaion*	Ode, canon for Christmas Day	71–2
Rod of the Root of Jesse	Cosmas the Melodist	*Menaion*	Ode, canon for Christmas Day	73–4
Father of Peace, and GOD of Consolation!	Cosmas the Melodist	*Menaion*	Ode, canon for Christmas Day	75
As Jonah, issuing from his three days' tomb	Cosmas the Melodist	*Menaion*	Ode, canon for Christmas Day	76–7
The Holy Children boldly stand	Cosmas the Melodist	*Menaion*	Ode, canon for Christmas Day	78–9
The dewy freshness that the furnace flings	Cosmas the Melodist	*Menaion*	Ode, canon for Christmas Day	80–1
O wond'rous mystery, full of passing grace!	Cosmas the Melodist	*Menaion*	Ode, canon for Christmas Day	82–3

Note: Hymns which came into common use are given in bold type.

[a] Said by Neale to be *stichera* for St Stephen's Day.
[b] Said by Neale to be *stichera* for Christmastide.
[c] Said by Neale to be by St Anatolius.

TABLE 2. Hymns for Lent and Eastertide

First line of hymn	Original author	Office-book source	Liturgical classification and occasion for use	Page no(s). in HEC
O the mystery, passing wonder	St Andrew of Crete	*Triodion*	*Stichera* in the 9th ode of the *triodion* at compline of Great Wednesday[a]	20–1
JESUS, hastening for the world to suffer	St Andrew of Crete	*Triodion*	*Troparia* from the *Triodion* at compline of Palm Sunday	22–3
Whence shall my tears begin?	St Andrew of Crete	*Triodion*	Cento from the Great Canon, Thurs., 5th wk. of Lent	24–7
Christian, dost thou *see* them	No Greek original[b]	—	Said by Neale to be *stichera* for 2nd wk. of Lent	28–9
'Tis the Day of Resurrection	St John Damascene	*Pentekostarion*	Ode, canon for Easter Day	42–3
Come and let us drink of that New River	St John Damascene	*Pentekostarion*	Ode, canon for Easter Day	44
Stand on thy watch-tower, Habakkuk	St John Damascene	*Pentekostarion*	Ode, canon for Easter Day	45
Let us rise in early morning	St John Damascene	*Pentekostarion*	Ode, canon for Easter Day	46

Into the dim earth's lowest parts descending	St John Damascene	*Pentekostarion*	Ode, canon for Easter Day	47
Who from the fiery furnace saved the Three	St John Damascene	*Pentekostarion*	Ode, canon for Easter Day	48–9
Thou hallowed chosen day!	St John Damascene	*Pentekostarion*	Ode, canon for Easter Day	50–1
Thou New Jerusalem, arise and shine!	St John Damascene	*Pentekostarion*	Ode, canon for Easter Day	52
Come, ye faithful, raise the strain	St John Damascene	*Pentekostarion*	Ode, canon for St Thomas's Sunday	53–4
On the rock of Thy commandments	St John Damascene	*Pentekostarion*	Ode, canon for St Thomas's Sunday	55–6
Christ, we turn our eyes to Thee	St John Damascene	*Pentekostarion*	Ode, canon for St Thomas's Sunday	57–8
Hither, and with one accord	St Theophanes	*Triodion*	*Stichera* on 'Lord, I have cried' for Fri. before Sunday of Forgiveness[c]	95–7
The LORD my Maker, forming me of clay	St Theophanes	*Triodion*	*Stichera* on 'Lord, I have cried' of vespers on Sunday of Forgiveness[d]	98–100
That fearful day, that day of speechless dread	Theodore of the Studium	*Triodion*	Ode, canon for Sunday of the Last Judgement	107–8
God comes;—and who shall stand before His fear?	Theodore of the Studium	*Triodion*	Ode, canon for Sunday of the Last Judgement	109–10

TABLE 2. (Cont.)

First line of hymn	Original author	Office-book source	Liturgical classification and occasion for use	Page no(s). in HEC
The Day is near, the Judgment is at hand	Theodore of the Studium	*Triodion*	Ode, canon for Sunday of the Last Judgement	111–13
The LORD draws nigh, the righteous Throne's Assessor	Theodore of the Studium	*Triodion*	Ode, canon for Sunday of the Last Judgement	114–15
A song, a song of gladness!	Theodore of the Studium	*Triodion*	Cento from canon for Orthodoxy Sunday	117–21
The abyss of many a former sin	Joseph of the Studium	*Triodion*	Ode + 2 *troparia* from canon for Sunday of the Prodigal Son	128–9
Thee, O CHRIST, we, very early rising[e]	St John Damascene	*Pentekostarion*	Ode, canon for St Thomas's Sunday	2nd edn., 63

Note: Hymns which came into common use are given in bold type.

[a] Said by Neale to be *stichera* for Great Thursday.
[b] Said by Neale to be by St Andrew of Crete.
[c] Said by Neale to be *idiomela* for the same day.
[d] That is, Saturday evening.
[e] Not in 1st edn.; added in 2nd edn. Altered to 'Reconciliation's plan devising' in 3rd edn.

TABLE 3. Hymns for Other Festivals, etc.

First line of hymn	Original author	Office-book source	Liturgical classification and occasion for use	Page no(s). in HEC
Fierce was the wild billow	St Anatolius	*Octoechos*	*Stichera* for Sun. in wk. of 1st tone	4
The day is past and over	St Anatolius	*Horologion*	Evening hymn at Great Compline	5–6
Exult, ye Gentiles! mourn, ye Hebrews!	St Andrew of Crete	*Pentekostarion*	Ode, canon for mid-Pentecost	30–2
By fruit, the ancient Foe's device	St Germanus	*Octoechos*	*Stichera* on the Beatitudes for Sun. in wk. of 1st tone	35–6
Take the last kiss, the last kiss for ever	St John Damascene	*Euchologion*	Funeral office	60–4
Those eternal bowers	No Greek original[a]	—	Said by Neale to be *idiomela* for All Saints	65–6
The choirs of ransomed Israel (shortened to 'In days of old, on Sinai')	Cosmas the Melodist	*Menaion*	Cento from canon for the Transfiguration	84–6
Art thou weary, art thou languid	No Greek original[b]	—	Said by Neale to be *idiomela* in wk. of 1st oblique tone	88–9

TABLE 3. (Cont.)

First line of hymn	Original author	Office-book source	Liturgical classification and occasion for use	Page no(s). in HEC
Are thy toils and woes increasing?	Said by Neale to be by St Methodius	Octoechos	*Idiomela* for a Sun. of 4th tone	123–4
O happy band of pilgrims	No Greek original[c]	—	Said by Neale to be a cento from canon of SS. Chrysanthus and Daria (19 Mar.)	130–1
Safe home, safe home in port!	No Greek original[c]	—	Said by Neale to be a cento from canon of St John Climacos	132–3
Let our choir new anthems raise	Joseph of the Studium	*Menaia*	Cento from canon for SS. Timothy and Maura (3 May)	134–5
And wilt thou pardon, LORD	Joseph of the Studium	Octoechos	Cento from canon for Mon. in wk. of 1st tone	136–7
Stars of the morning	No Greek original[c]	—	Said by Neale to be a cento from canon for Tues. in wk. of 4th tone	138–40
After three days Thou didst rise	Joseph of the Studium	*Pentekostarion*	Ode, canon for Ascension Day	141–2
Exalt, exalt, the Heavenly Gates	Joseph of the Studium	*Pentekostarion*	Ode, canon for Ascension Day	143–4

JESUS, LORD of Life Eternal	Joseph of the Studium	*Pentekostarion*	Ode, canon for Ascension Day	145–6
Now that Death by death hath found its ending	Joseph of the Studium	*Pentekostarion*	Ode, canon for Ascension Day	147–8
Rain down ye heav'ns, eternal bliss!	Joseph of the Studium	*Pentekostarion*	Ode, canon for Ascension Day	149–50
Wafting Him up on high	Joseph of the Studium	*Pentekostarion*	Ode, canon for Ascension Day	151–2
Of twofold natures, CHRIST, the Giver	Joseph of the Studium	*Pentekostarion*	Ode, canon for Ascension Day	153–4
Holy gift, surpassing comprehension!	Joseph of the Studium	*Pentekostarion*	Ode, canon for Ascension Day	155–6
JESU, **Name all names above**	Theoctistus of the Studium	*Horologion*	Cento from the Suppliant Canon to Jesus	157–9
O Unity of Threefold Light	Metrophanes of Smyrna	*Octoechos*	Cento from canon for Sun. of 2nd tone	161–2

Note: Hymns which came into common use are given in bold type.

[a] Said by Neale to be by St John Damascene.
[b] Said by Neale to be by Stephen the Sabaite.
[c] Said by Neale to be by Joseph of the Stadium.

see them', a hymn for Lent in 6.5.6.5.D metre, concerns the interior battle against sin which Christians are constantly waging. The italicizing of the verbs serves to encourage man to play an active part in warding off sin by recognizing it within himself, and then smiting it 'by the virtue / Of the Lenten fast' (HEC 28). 'The abyss of many a former sin', in 88.88.88 metre, again emphasizes the plight of the individual, this time by recalling the parables of the Pharisee and the publican and of the prodigal son, the themes of the Gospels for the tenth and ninth Sundays respectively before Easter. Like 'Christian, dost thou *see* them', this hymn recalls Christ's earthly nature in the line 'O Thou, Who freely wast made poor' (HEC 129). In 'The Day of Resurrection', it is easy to see why this 7.6.7.6.D hymn, with its festive spirit, set to the tune *Ellacombe*, has remained unchanged since Neale's time. It is the hymn that, more than any other in Neale's entire collection, encapsulates the essence of Orthodox theology about Easter; the pre-eminence of this feast among the Orthodox is based on a particular verse from St Paul's First Epistle to the Corinthians (15: 14): 'If Christ be not risen, then is our preaching in vain, and your faith is also vain'.

A similar sentiment is communicated in the fourth of Neale's Eastertide hymns to come into common use: 'Come, ye faithful, raise the strain'. The first three stanzas of this 7.6.7.6.D hymn (which originally appeared in 1859 in the *Christian Remembrancer*) have been preserved without alteration by the compilers of major hymnals. The final stanza, however, has been changed, from describing the transformation of Christ from mortal to immortal to a sustained praise of the Heavenly King ('Alleluia' is repeated three times) by the editors of *Hymns Ancient and Modern*, whose version has become the standard one:

Neale, *Hymns of the Eastern Church*	Hymns Ancient and Modern

Neither might the gates of death
  Nor the tomb's dark portal
Nor the watchers, nor the seal
  Hold Thee as a mortal;
But to-day amidst the Twelve
  Thou didst stand, bestowing
	Alleluia now we cry
	  To our King immortal,
	Who triumphant burst the bars
	  Of the tomb's dark portal;
	Alleluia, with the Son
	  God the Father praising

That Thy peace, which evermore Passeth human knowing.	Alleluia yet again To the Spirit raising.[27]

(HEC 54)

Part of the Orthodox theology of Easter is lost through this alteration, yet another part is maintained: the exultation which encourages Orthodox Christians to exclaim, 'Christ is risen from the dead having conquered death by death' at the Easter vigil service and throughout Eastertide. Western Christians can experience something of this through singing Neale's hymns.

[27] M. Frost (ed.), *Historical Companion to Hymns Ancient and Modern*, (London, 1962), 214.

Chapter 7

Neale's Centos and Adaptations

MOST of the other hymns from Neale's collection which came into common use were not literal translations. Standard Orthodox theology, is communicated, both in the *General Introduction* and in *Hymns of the Eastern Church*, through the line-by-line, *troparion*-by-*troparion* correspondence between Greek original and English translation. While this may have been appreciated by some of his readers, the majority—including compilers of important hymnals like *Hymns Ancient and Modern*—were looking for hymns which they could incorporate into their own services.[1] Sometimes, as we have seen, a literal translation suited very well; but Neale realized that many of his translations were perceived to be pedantic and that they contained references to Orthodox theology or less well-known books of the Bible which would be dismissed as obscure or inappropriate for use by English congregations. He therefore included centos (compositions made up of quotations from other authors[2]), which he deemed to be the most appropriate form of Greek hymn translation.

The best one for consideration might be 'The choirs of ransomed Israel', which is perhaps better known as the shortened 'In days of old, on Sinai'. The original on which these verses are based is an eight-ode canon for the Transfiguration by Cosmas the Melodist.[3] Neale noted that Cosmas 'holds the second place amidst Greek ecclesiastical poets' after St John Damascene, and that Cosmas is 'the most learned of

---

[1] For information on the inclusion of Neale's Greek hymns in *Hymns Ancient and Modern*, see S. Drain, *The Anglican Church in Nineteenth Century Britain* (Lewiston, NY, 1989), 253–7.
[2] Defintion from *OED*.
[3] The Transfiguration, commemorated on 6 Aug. in both Eastern and Western Churches, is a major feast in the former, but not in the latter.

the Greek Church poets' (HEC 80). The best way to examine Neale's translations is to consider the stanzas individually and compare them with the odes of the canon from which they come.

Neale, *Hymns of the Eastern Church*	Ware and Mother Mary (trans.), *The Festal Menaion*
The choirs of ransomed Israel The Red Sea's passage o'er, Uprais'd the hymn of triumph Upon the further shore: And shouted, as the foeman Was whelm'd beneath the sea,— 'Sing we to Judah's Saviour, For glorified is He!' (HEC 84)[4]	The choirs of Israel passed dry-shod across the Red Sea and the watery deep; and beholding the riders and captains of the enemy swallowed by the waters, they cried out for joy: 'Let us sing unto our God, for He has been glorified'.[5]

Neale's stanza displays the 7.6.7.6.D metre which Neale favoured when he allowed himself the freedom to choose. It corresponds approximately to the *irmos* of the first ode in Cosmas's canon, which links the succeeding *troparia* to the biblical canticle which forms the thesis of the ode: the Song of Moses at the Red Sea (Exod. 15: 1–19).

This *irmos* is intended as a linking device, taking as its subject the Hebrew scriptural account of the crossing of the Red Sea. The main subject of the canon as a whole, however, is the Transfiguration, and because its length had to be limited if it were to be adopted for use in English Churches, Neale packed more into his stanza than the original *irmos* suggested in order to elicit the same meaning; thus his first stanza differs from that of Cosmas.

In this Greek translation Neale allowed himself considerable freedom in order to achieve this condensation. His first alteration to the *irmos* is the addition of the word 'ransomed', which in this context carries with it a number of biblical allusions, such as Isaiah 43: 1–3: 'O Israel, fear not: for I have redeemed thee. I have called thee by thy name; thou art mine.

---

[4] All quotations from 'The choirs of ransomed Israel' are taken from HEC 84–6.

[5] All quotations from Cosmas's canon are taken from *Festal Menaion*, 482–95.

When thou passest through the waters, I will be with thee; and through the rivers, they shall not overflow thee.... For I am the LORD thy God, the Holy One of Israel, thy Saviour: I gave Egypt for thy ransom, Ethiopia and Seba for thee.'

There may be other echoes of Isaiah 35: 10, which embodies the idea of joyful singing.[6] The Christian scriptural antitype is Christ as the ransom for mankind, as described in Matthew 20: 28[7] and Mark 10: 45.[8] Thus, through the addition of one word, Neale has evoked a number of scriptural images relating to Christ as the Redeemer. The word 'ransomed' serves as an example of how a small addition—even one word—can bring to mind a wealth of biblical allusion in order to give a hymn a range of meaning beyond the original.

There are, of course, many scriptural images in Cosmas's original; Neale himself pointed out that this Greek writer was particularly adept at applying typology in his hymns: 'His fondness for types, boldness in their application, and love of aggregating them, make him the Oriental Adam of St Victor' (HEC 68).[9] Because of the importance of typological interpretation of Scripture to Victorian culture, Orthodox hymnody, with its emphasis on scriptural allusion, was well suited to the times. The subject of Neale's first type, the exodus, was a favourite of Victorians, and not only in an abstract religious context, as Landow notes:

> The use of typology derived from the Exodus was a commonplace of nineteenth-century political discourse, and one encountered such political applications of types not only in Carlyle and Kingsley but also in working-class poets, such as Gerald Massey, and in the speeches of strikers imploring their fellows not to return to 'Egyptian slavery'. Had the parish authorities chosen thus to make a political statement, they would not have been making an arcane theological

---

[6] 'And the ransomed of the Lord shall return, and come to Zion with songs and everlasting joy upon their heads: they shall obtain joy and gladness, and sorrow and sighing shall flee away.'

[7] 'Even as the Son of man came not to be ministered unto, but to minister, and to give his life a ransom for many.'

[8] 'For even the Son of man came not to be ministered unto, but to minister, and to give his life a ransom for many.'

[9] Adam of St Victor (12th cent.), of whom Neale greatly approved, was one of the foremost sacred Latin poets on the Middle Ages, and was particularly known for his accurate knowledge of Scripture and its typology.

point unintelligible to many working men and women. Rather, they would have been employing a favourite convention of contemporary political discourse.[10]

Hence in the exodus Neale introduced a familiar—and topical—theme.

Whereas the Red Sea crossing was already present in Cosmas, Neale departs from the original in his next type. Where Cosmas depicts 'the riders and captains of the enemy'—continuing the Exodus theme—Neale substituted 'the foeman', meaning the adversary, or Satan. This too was a favourite Victorian typological image, based on Genesis 3: 15, where God tells the serpent: 'And I will put enmity between thee and the woman, and between thy seed and her seed; it shall bruise thy head, and thou shalt bruise his heel.' This prophetic type alludes to the fundamental battle between good and evil, and announces the coming salvation by, as Neale put it, 'Judah's Saviour'. The word 'foeman' alludes to Acts 2: 35 ('Until I make thy foes thy footstool') or, in its more common biblical form, 'adversary', to Numbers 22: 22,[11] 1 Kings 11: 14,[12] and Luke 18: 3.[13]

The second stanza of Neale's hymn is based on the second *troparion* of Cosmas's first ode; both begin to develop the theme of the Transfiguration, which is the overall subject of the canon. Cosmas's stanza runs as follows:

Delivering to his friends words of life concerning the Kingdom of God, Christ said to them: 'When I shall shine forth with unapproachable light, ye shall know that the Father is in Me, and shall cry out for joy: Let us sing unto our God, for He has been glorified.'

Neale renders it thus:

> Amongst His Twelve Apostles
> CHRIST spake the Words of Life,
> And shew'd a realm of beauty
> Beyond a world of strife:

[10] Landow, *Victorian Types*, 129–30.
[11] 'And God's anger was kindled because he went: and the angel of the Lord stood in the way for an adversary against him.'
[12] 'And the Lord stirred up an adversary unto Solomon, Hadad the Edomite: he was of the king's seed in Edom.'
[13] 'And there was a widow in that city; and she came unto him, saying, Avenge me of mine adversary.'

'When all My FATHER's glory
Shall shine express'd in Me,
Then praise Him, then Exalt Him,
For magnified is He!'

Neale's ideas differ somewhat from those of Cosmas. The latter uses the word 'friends' to describe the Apostles. The reason seems to be to emphasize the earthly nature of Jesus. Christ's humanity is as important for the Orthodox as his divinity, and it is perhaps through a better understanding of the two natures of Christ that man's suffering on earth can be eased. Ware, in *The Orthodox Way*, considers the two natures in Christ from an Eastern perspective:

However far I have to travel through the valley of the shadow of death, *I am never alone*. I have a companion. And this companion is not only a true man as I am, but also true God from true God. At the moment of Christ's deepest humiliation on the Cross, he is as much the eternal and living God as he is at his Transfiguration in glory upon Mount Tabor. Looking upon Christ crucified, I see not only a suffering man but *suffering God*.[14]

It seems that by this change Neale has missed the idea of Jesus as a companion—not only to the Apostles, but to all Christians. Whereas Cosmas presents both the human and divine natures of Jesus, Neale chooses to concentrate on the divine, thereby making it more difficult for the singer of the hymn to make the imaginative leap from the human to the divine Jesus.

In the second line of the translation, Neale, emphasizes 'the Words of Life'. In Cosmas these words refer to the kingdom of God. In Neale they also allude to the celestial realm; but their capitalization and position at the end of the line suggest that they allude as well to the whole Gospel, which contains the words of Christ spoken 'Amongst His Twelve Apostles'. It seems that Neale is here highlighting Scripture as a whole—perhaps as a sign of his times, which the Bible held an important cultural position. This idea complements the Orthodox view of Scripture. As Ware says, 'At each step upon the path [of life], we turn for guidance to the voice of God speaking

---

[14] Ware, *Orthodox Way*, 106.

to us through the Bible'; and, as Philaret, the Metropolitan of Moscow in Neale's day, wrote, 'The only pure and all-sufficient source of the doctrine of the faith is the revealed word of God, contained in the Holy Scriptures.'[15]

Although Neale does not point directly to the humanity of Jesus, he does allude more generally to the suffering of men in the phrase 'a world of strife'. Neale's introduction of these words is characteristically Victorian, and shows him using stock images, or types, with which his audience would readily associate.

The words spoken by Jesus in Cosmas's hymn are not based on any of the accounts of the Transfiguration, but rather on the words of Jesus in the Last Discourse, at John 14: 10: 'Believest thou not that I am in the Father, and the Father in me? The words I speak unto you I speak not of myself: but the Father that dwelleth in me, he doeth the works.' Neale's words approximate those of Cosmas: both wish to emphasize the divinity of Christ—particularly after the Transfiguration.

Cosmas's second *troparion* ends with the same words as the first: 'Let us sing unto our God, for He has been glorified'. Neale concludes with a variation on the ending of the first stanza: the first concludes with 'For glorified is He!', the second with 'For magnified is He!' It seems that similar or identical endings for *troparia* were favoured by the Greeks; another example is found in St John Damascene's canon for the Transfiguration, where his *troparia* for the first ode all end with 'Let us sing unto our Deliverer and our God'.[16] Neale used his own form of this device in other Orthodox hymn translations, such as the evening hymn 'The day is past and over', where the stanzas end as follows: 'And save me through the coming night!' (1 and 2); 'And guard me through the coming night!' (3); 'Nor guard them through the hours of night!' (4); 'And guard and save me from them all!' (5).[17] Other examples are 'Christ is born!! Tell forth His fame!' and 'Take the last kiss,— the last for ever!' (HEC 82-3, 69-72). This repetition, or partial repetition, is for the purposes of emphasis and unity.

Neale's third stanza is a compilation of ideas from the first, third, and fourth of Cosmas's odes.

---

[15] Ibid. 146, 147.   [16] See *Festal Menaion*, 482-3.
[17] See HEC 5-6.

> Upon the Mount of Tabor
> The promise was made good;
> When, baring all the Godhead,
> In light itself He stood:
> And they, in awe beholding
> The Apostolic Three,
> Sang out to GOD their Saviour,
> For magnified was He!

From the first ode Neale took the idea of Christ's promise before the Transfiguration—'There be some standing here, which shall not taste of death till they see the Kingdom of God' (Luke 9: 27)—fulfilled on Mount Tabor:

> Today as He has promised, Christ, shining on Mount Tabor, dimly[18] disclosed to His disciples the image and reflection of the divine brightness; and filled with godlike and light-bearing splendour, they cried out for joy: 'Let us sing unto our God for He has been glorified'.

From Cosmas's third ode, for which the biblical canticle is the Song of Hannah (1 Sam. 2: 1–10), Neale borrowed the idea of Christ's sanctification of the body through adopting human form:

> Thou hast put Adam on entire, O Christ, and changing the nature grown dark in past times, Thou hast filled it with glory and made it godlike by the alteration of Thy form.

Finally Neale introduced the episode from the Transfiguration where Moses and Elijah appear and confer with Jesus on Tabor. Cosmas does not introduce the two Old Testament figures until ode 4, *troparia* 5 and 6:

> Those with whom Thou hast conversed of old in fiery vapour, in darkness and the lightest of winds,[19] stood before Thee in the manner of servants, O Christ our Master, and talked with Thee. Glory to Thy power, O Lord.

> Moses who in past times foresaw Thee in the fire of the burning bush, and Elijah who was taken up in a chariot of fire, were present on Tabor and made known there Thy decease upon the Cross.

In the longer canon Cosmas can afford to give each theme a much fuller treatment than can Neale, who must fit these

---

[18] The Slavonic text reads 'clearly' instead of 'dimly' (note in *Festal Menaion*, 482).
[19] See Exod. 19: 18–19; Deut. 4: 11; 1 Kgs. 19: 12.

ideas into a cento if he wants them to be adopted into English church worship. In the space allotted him within the confines of English hymnological form, Neale needs to condense these images, relying on the familiarity of his audience with the biblical narrative and typological imagery. His listeners would recognize the 'promise' made good on Mount Tabor, the revelation of the divine light, and the meeting with Moses and Elijah.[20]

The typological significance of Neale's third stanza rests on this convocation, which serves as a testimony of the Jewish Law and the prophets to the Messiahship of Christ, and as such may be seen by Christians as a proof of the typological nature of Scripture. Newman, in a sermon entitled 'Moses the Type of Christ', shows how this key figure in the Hebrew Scriptures prefigured Jesus as redeemer, prophet, and intercessor for guilty man; as he says, 'The history of Moses is valuable to Christians, not only as giving us a pattern of fidelity towards God, of great firmness, and great meekness, but also as affording us a type of our Saviour Christ.'[21] Moses, of course, is, associated with the idea of redemption; and Christ can be seen as a second Moses, leading Christians out of the slavery of sin to the Promised Land of eternal life, and giving the new Law on the Mount of the Beatitudes.

Elijah too plays an important role in typological interpretation. It was he who was to announce the coming of the Messiah; and when the Apostles asked Jesus about the fulfilment of the prophecy he answered that Elijah had already come, in the guise of John the Baptist (Matt. 17: 10–13). Thus the connection between Hebrew and Christian Scripture is made. There is also an association between the lives of Elijah and Jesus: Elijah's fiery chariot prefigures Christ's ascension in the presence of his disciples.

In the first three stanzas of 'The choirs of ransomed Israel' Neale's rendering of the Transfiguration canon manages not only to echo individual *troparia* from Cosmas, but also to cement the typological connection between Hebrew and Christian Scriptures which the worshippers he had in mind

---

[20] Although Mount Tabor is never mentioned by name in the Gospel accounts, tradition has located the Transfiguration there (Cross and Livingstone (eds.), *Oxford Dictionary of the Christian Church*, 1390).

[21] Quoted in Landow, *Victorian Types*, 23.

would take for granted. Typology allowed Neale to condense various episodes from the biblical narrative without having to chronicle them fully. There is also a gradual movement away from the Greek original. The first stanza follows Cosmas's *irmos* for the first ode quite closely; the second approximates to the second *troparion* of this ode, but with greater freedom than the first; the third is a blending of ideas from *troparia* of at least three odes, and indicates a movement away from the literalness with which he began, while at the same time including standard typological images from the original. What began as a cento—has developed into an original composition, which uses familiar images.

The typological association is further developed in Neale's fourth stanza. Although the starting-point is Cosmas's fourth ode, the accompanying biblical canticle is the prayer in Habakkuk 3: 1–19, whose theme is the power of God, and particularly his wrathful nature, for which the motivation is ultimate good: 'Thou wentest forth for the salvation of thy people' (Hab. 3: 13). Neither Cosmas nor Neale dwell on this wrathful divine nature; but the description of God's power is put to different purposes by the two hymn-writers. This divergence may be illustrated by quoting the fourth ode of Cosmas's canon in its entirety, followed by Neale's corresponding fourth stanza.

Cosmas has the following:

(Irmos) I have heard of Thy glorious Dispensation, O Christ our God: how Thou wast born of the Virgin, that so Thou mightest deliver from error those who cry aloud to Thee: Glory to Thy power, O Lord.

Thou, O Christ our God, hast delivered the written Law upon Mount Sinai, and hast appeared there riding upon the cloud, in the midst of fire and darkness and tempest. Glory to Thy power, O Lord.

As a pledge of Thy glorious dispensation, Thou hast ineffably shone forth on Tabor, O Christ our God, who wast before the ages and whose chariot is the clouds.

Those with whom Thou hast conversed of old in fiery vapour, in darkness and the lightest of winds, stood before Thee in the manner of servants, O Christ our Master, and talked with Thee. Glory to Thy power, O Lord.

Moses who in past times foresaw Thee in the fire of the burning bush, and Elijah in a chariot of fire, were present on Tabor and made known there Thy decease[22] upon the Cross.

Neale's stanza runs as follows:

> In days of old, on Sinai,
>   The LORD Jehovah came,
> In majesty of terror,
>   In thunder-cloud and flame:
> On Tabor, with the glory
>   Of sunniest light for vest,
> The excellence of beauty
>   In JESUS was express'd.

In a cento it was not necessary for Neale to follow the original closely. What he concentrated on was the perception of God in Hebrew and Christian Scriptures, juxtaposing the image in Habakkuk with the image in the account of the Transfiguration.[23] The wrathful God is placed alongside the God of light and beauty, presumably to show the reader which is more desirable. Perhaps it is not fair to present such a dichotomy, because it gives the mistaken impression that anger characterizes God throughout the Hebrew Scriptures; this is not, however, Neale's intention. Hebrew and Christian images of God are each allotted four lines, in order to strike a balance between the two. 'Thunder-cloud and flame' give way to 'excellence of beauty' so as to evoke the typological climax of the Old Testament presentation. The types are Moses on Sinai and Elijah in his fiery chariot; the antitype is Jesus on Tabor. The reason for the more benign imagery in the second half of the stanza is to show Jesus in the 'sunniest light', as the fulfilment of the prophecies. The balance achieved by devoting four lines to each subject also alludes to the

---

[22] The Greek word in this Gospel is *exodos*.
[23] This hymn echoes Keble's verses for Pentecost, 'When God of old came down from Heaven', from *The Christian Year* (1827), particularly in the following lines:

> The fires that rushed on Sinai down
>   In sudden torrents dread,
> Now gently light, a glorious crown,
>   On every sainted head.

(John Keble, *The Christian Year* (London, 1895), 143)

proclamation in the Transfiguration by God the Father[24] (the subject of the first four lines) of the sonship of Jesus (the subject of the next four lines).

The above explanation points to the aim of Neale's hymn: to present Jesus as the typological culmination of the Old Testament prophecies. The Transfiguration is the occasion for the hymn; but a celebration of this event does not seem to be the hymn's ultimate purpose. This interpretation is borne out in another hymn which Neale wrote for the Transfiguration: a translation of the fifteenth-century Latin hymn *'Coelestis formam gloriae'*. The first stanza runs as follows:

> A TYPE of those bright rays on high
> For which the Church hopes longingly,
> CHRIST on the holy mountain shows
> Where brighter than the Sun He glows.[25]

The key word is 'TYPE', and it is in this guise that Jesus is portrayed. The idea is perhaps more clearly presented in a somewhat altered version of Neale's hymn in the third edition of *The Church Hymnary*:

> O Wondrous type, O vision fair
> Of glory that the Church shall share,
> Which Christ upon the mountain shows,
> Where brighter than the sun he glows![26]

Both these renderings of the Latin hymn attest to Neale's emphasis on Christ's typological character at the Transfiguration.[27] In 'The choirs of ransomed Israel' there is a similar emphasis. In the fourth stanza, type and antitype have been given equal treatment, in an effort to show that the Hebrew prophecies, delivered in 'thunder-cloud and flame', have now been fulfilled in Jesus, clothed in divine light and epitomizing the 'excellence of beauty' on Tabor in the Transfiguration.

Neale says that he took his inspiration 'principally from the

---

[24] Whereas in Cosmas it is the second Person of the Trinity who delivers the Law on Sinai.
[25] Lawson (ed.), *Collected Hymns*, 150.
[26] Church Hymnary Revision Committee (eds.), *The Church Hymnary*, 3rd edn. (Oxford, 1973), no. 217.
[27] It must be noted, however, that in the Latin hymn Christ is the type, not the antitype.

first four odes' of Cosmas's original (HEC 84); but the fifth stanza is derived from the fifth ode, and continues with the praise of Jesus, who has been revealed in the divine light. Cosmas writes:

The seasons bowed down before Thy face: for at Thy feet the sun laid its light and its bright rays which fill the heavens, when Thou, O Christ, vouchsafed to change Thy mortal form.

'Behold the Saviour', cried Moses and Elijah on Tabor the Holy Mountain, and their words rang in the ears of the disciples. 'Lo, here is Christ whom we in ancient times proclaimed as God.'

Neale condenses these ideas into the following:

> All hours and days inclin'd there
> And did Thee worship meet,
> The sun himself adored Thee,
> And bow'd him at Thy feet:
> While Moses and Elias,
> Upon the Holy Mount
> The co-eternal glory
> Of CHRIST our GOD recount.

The description of the sun conveys the same idea as Cosmas's *troparion*. The second half of Neale's stanza turns to human praises, in the persons of Moses and Elijah. While the natural world humbles itself before the Saviour, the human world glorifies his name. The choice of Moses and Elijah further develops the theme of typological fulfilment: two of the greatest figures from the Hebrew Scriptures come to foretell the greater glory for which he, who is at once human and divine, is destined.

The final stanza does not correspond to any *troparia* from Cosmas's ode. It is a foretelling of heavenly glory, not for Jesus, but for man:

> O holy, wond'rous Vision!
> But what, when this life past,
> The beauty of Mount Tabor
> Shall end in Heav'n at last?
> But what, when all the glory
> Of uncreated light
> Shall be the promis'd guerdon
> Of them that win the fight?

Here what began as a cento of an eighth-century hymn goes on to include characteristically Western themes. The portions of Cosmas's hymn quoted above all display the objectiveness and sustained praise which characterize Orthodox hymnody. Cosmas delights in the Transfiguration itself; and the effect of the event on human emotions is to some extent subordinated. Even the *exapostilarion*, the final *troparion* of Cosmas's canon, which has as its theme Christ as the light of the world, does not attempt any spiritual analysis:

Today on Tabor in the manifestation of Thy Light, O Word, Thou unaltered Light from the Light of the unbegotten Father, we have seen the Father as Light and the Spirit as Light, guiding with light the whole creation.[28]

By contrast, Neale's final stanza is reflective, or self-regarding, in its mode of praise. This is not to say that the individual is excluded from Cosmas's canon, only that the point of view is different. Eastern hymns, as Savas says, 'express the feelings and thoughts of the dedicated, pious soul': the place of the individual is understood.[29] In Neale's hymn, however, the relation of the individual to the person or event being praised is more in the forefront.

The publication history of 'The choirs of ransomed Israel' attests to the appeal of Neale's concluding stanza. Julian notes that centos have been made from Neale's hymn: *The People's Hymnal* adopted stanzas 1, 2, and 6; the SPCK's *Psalms and Hymns*, 1, 4, 5, and 6; Palmer's *Supplementary Hymnal*, 1, 3, 4, and 6; and *Hymns Ancient and Modern*, which gives its cento the title 'In days of old on Sinai', adopted 4, 5, and 6. But they have all retained Neale's last stanza.[30]

As one would expect, Neale's translation has one glaring omission: Cosmas's celebration of the Virgin Mary. We have seen already how important the *Theotokos* is for Eastern Christians. Her honour and power are highlighted in almost every Greek hymn.[31] The final ode of Cosmas's canon has as its accompanying biblical canticle the *Magnificat*, or Song of

---

[28] *Festal Menaion*, 495.   [29] Savas, *Hymnology*, 29.
[30] Julian (ed.), *Dictionary of Hymnology*, 224.
[31] The final *troparion* of each ode and each set of *troparia* is normally a *Theotokion* in praise of the Virgin.

the *Theotokos*, which is usually sung even when the other canticles are omitted, thereby attesting to its importance. The *irmos* of the ninth ode is as follows:

Thy birthgiving was undefiled: God came forth from thy womb, and He appeared upon the earth wearing flesh and made his dwelling among men; therefore we all magnify thee, O Theotokos.[32]

The omission of this theme from 'The choirs of ransomed Israel' underlines Neale's reserve with respect to the Virgin in his translations.

In 'The choirs of ransomed Israel' we have a hymn with roots in both the past and present. At times Neale attempted a literal translation; at other times he constructed a cento; and at still other times he departed from the original in favour of original verses. Several trends are apparent: first, Neale used the Greek hymn as the basis and occasion for a hymn of his own; second, he used typological imagery familiar to his audience, almost all of whom were steeped in biblical narrative and typological interpretation; third, he related the ancient hymn to his own tradition. Thus he tried to bring to the attention of his audience previously unknown Orthodox hymns, but in such a way as to make them relevant and 'Western'.

As another example of the dual nature of Neale's Greek hymns, we will examine a very different hymn from his collection: the popular 'Art thou weary, art thou languid'. In the first edition of *Hymns of the Eastern Church* Neale attributed the original to St Stephen the Sabaite, calling it *'Idiomela* in the week of the first oblique tone', and added this note: 'These stanzas, which strike me as very sweet, are not in all the editions of the Octoechus. I copy from a dateless Constantinopolitan book' (HEC 88). In subsequent editions he deleted the second sentence concerning the Constantinopolitan source. As Julian notes, 'This omission has caused fruitless searches for the [original] text in the authorized editions of the Octoechus. The Constantinopolitan book referred to by Dr Neale cannot be found amongst Dr Neale's books, nor has a copy corresponding thereto been as yet discovered.'[33] Neale further complicated the search by admitting, in the third

---

[32] *Festal Menaion*, 493.   [33] Julian (ed.), *Dictionary of Hymnology*, 632.

edition of *Hymns of the Eastern Church* (1866) that 'Art thou weary' and two other hymns in the book 'contain so little that is from the Greek that they ought not to have been included in this collection; in any future Edition they shall appear as an Appendix'.[34] These hymns—'Art thou weary', 'O happy band of pilgrims', and 'Safe home, safe home in port'—became three of the most famous in his collection; in fact, 'Art thou weary' appeared in most hymnals in Britain and America by the turn of the century.[35] Claims to an authentic ancient model were evidently less important for the majority of Neale's readers than they were for him. It may be of interest to take a closer look at 'Art thou weary' to see what Neale was trying to achieve by using an ancient idea, but developing it in accordance with 'modern' hymnological practice.

Since there are no corresponding Greek *troparia*, it may be best to quote the hymn in its entirety at the outset.

> Art thou weary, art thou languid,
>   Art thou sore distrest?
> 'Come to me'—saith One,—'and coming
>   Be at rest!'
>
> Hath he marks to lead me to Him,
>   If He be my Guide?
> 'In His Feet and Hands are Wound-prints,
>   And His Side.'
>
> Is there a Diadem, as Monarch,
>   That His Brow adorns?

---

[34] HEC, preface to 3rd edn., p. xxii. The same may be said of 'Christian, dost thou *see* them', the original for which Neale attributed to St Andrew of Crete; but no Greek source has ever been discovered. Neale confounded such searches for the originals with his own words: in a sermon in 1862 he referred to 'Safe home, safe home in port' as an 'old Greek hymn', which does not seem to be the case (J. M. Neale, 'The Potters and their Work', in *Occasional Sermons*, 76).

[35] Julian (ed.), *Dictionary of Hymnology*, 632. Pocknee confirms that 'O happy band of pilgrims' and 'Art thou weary' were the two from HEC which found 'widest vogue' with 19th-cent. congregations (C. E. Pocknee, 'Hymnody since the Oxford Movement', *Hymn Society of Great Britain and Ireland Bulletin*, 3/2 (no. 59) (Spring 1952), 25). D. W. Perry notes that today 'Art thou weary' is found in 14 major hymnals in Britain, and 'O happy band of pilgrims' in 15 (*Hymn Tunes Indexed by First Lines, Tune Names, and Metres, Compiled from Current English Hymnbooks* (London and Croydon, 1980), 7, 72).

Neale's Centos and Adaptations 169

> 'Yea, a Crown, in very surety,
>   But of Thorns!'
>
> If I find Him, if I follow,
>   What His guerdon here?
> 'Many a sorrow, many a labour,
>   Many a tear.'
>
> If I still hold closely to Him,
>   What hath He at last?
> 'Sorrow vanquish'd, labour ended,
>   Jordan past!'
>
> If I ask Him to receive me,
>   Will He say me nay?
> 'Not till earth, and not till Heaven,
>   Pass away!'
>
> Finding, following, keeping, struggling,
>   Is He sure to bless?
> 'Angels, Martyrs, Prophets, Virgins,
>   Answer, Yes!'
>
>   (HEC 88–9)[36]

The hymn seems more Western than Eastern because of its subjective emphasis on the individual, as opposed to the more reserved, objective celebration of the Transfiguration in Cosmas's ode. The words appear to stem from Jesus's preaching. In Matthew 11: 28–30 he says: 'Come unto me, all ye that labour and are heavy laden, and I will give you rest. Take my yoke upon you, and learn of me; for I am meek and lowly in heart: and ye shall find rest unto your souls. For my yoke is easy, and my burden is light.' The idea of finding in Christ rest from labour and heavy burden is the point of departure for Neale's hymn. The theme is common in Victorian hymnody, as in 'Another six days' work is done' (1732, often reprinted) and 'O where shall rest be found' (1818, 1853).[37]

Neale does not stick to this one idea, however; instead, he

---

[36] Routley notes that the metre of this hymn (8.5.8.3), mixing short and long lines, often has an effect of pathos, and was one to which Victorian English women writers were often partial (*An English-Speaking Hymnal Guide* (Collegeville, Minn., 1979), p. xi).

[37] See L. Adey, *Class and Idol in the English Hymn* (Vancouver, 1988), 26–7.

blends it with a familiar Eastern Orthodox hymnological theme: the suffering Christ. This is not to say that such images are absent from Western hymnody; only that several Greek echoes may be heard. While there does not appear to be any exact Greek parallel to Neale's lines, in the Orthodox liturgy for Holy Week and Easter there are clues which may assist in placing 'Art thou weary' in an Eastern context.

At Easter the emphasis in Orthodox hymnody is on the redemptive power of Christ and his ability to relieve suffering. For instance, on Great Wednesday evening, the following *kontakion* is appended to the sixth ode of the canon for the day:

Being, O exceedingly good One, a fountain of mercy: Deliver Thou from every adversity those who with fervent faith adore Thy ineffable mercy; O compassionate One. And taking away their maladies, vouchsafe Thou unto them Divine Grace from on High.[38]

A different kind of echo may be heard in the *troparia* on the Beatitudes, sung during matins of Great Friday.[39] This part of the liturgy is composed of a series of promises of a personal state of blessedness for those who follow the way of life required for their attainment. One Beatitude, 'Blessed are the peacemakers; for they shall be called the children of God', is followed by these words:

Thou wast crucified, Christ, for my sake, that Thou mightest pour forth forgiveness for me. Thy side was pierced with a spear that Thou mightest cause rivers of life to flow for me. Thou hast been fastened with the nails, that so realizing the depth of Thy Passion and the height of Thy might, I may cry unto Thee, Glory to Thy Cross and to Thy Passion, O lifegiving Saviour.[40]

---

[38] G. L. Papadeas (ed.), *Greek Orthodox Holy Week and Easter Services* (Daytona Beach, Fla., 1985), 117. As Archimandrite Moir pointed out to me, Papadeas's book is useful, though full of mistakes; the words quoted here have been somewhat altered by Moir for the sake of the literal correctness of translation.

[39] Papadeas includes these *troparia* as part of the service of Holy Thursday evening, which is not strictly true. What he means is that in practice matins of each day in Holy Week is sung the night before; thus matins of Great Friday is in practice sung on Thursday evening.

[40] Papadeas (ed.), *Greek Orthodox Holy Week and Easter Services*, 242 (with alterations by Moir)

'Art thou weary' focuses on the Passion and its implications for the individual. The message seems to be that Christ saves man through an identification with him. This idea calls for a physical depiction of the suffering Christ. Such a portrayal is not unusual for Neale, as the second stanza of his 'Raise thine eye a little way', a translation from the Latin, demonstrates:

> Look on the Head, with such a Crown
> Of bitter thorns surrounded;
> Look on the Blood that trickles down
> The Feet and Hands thus wounded![41]

The images in 'Art thou weary' are not as vivid as those above, although both point to the physicality of the Passion. The difference seems to lie in the reason for the suffering. In 'Raise thine eye' Christ suffers greatly so that man may not suffer; by contrast, in 'Art thou weary' the suffering of man on earth parallels that of Christ: when he asks what his 'guerdon' shall be, the answer is 'Many a sorrow, many a labour, / Many a tear'. The promised reward—that is, rest—is not bestowed until after man's death; while on earth, labour and suffering will be man's lot, as they were Christ's.

Ware explains the value of Christ's suffering and death for Orthodox Christians as follows: 'We should not say that Christ has suffered "instead of us", but rather that he has suffered *on our behalf*. The Son of God suffered "unto death", not that we might be exempt from suffering, but that our suffering might be like his. Christ offers us, not a way *round* suffering, but a way *through* it; not substitution, but saving companionship.'[42]

Herein lies the message of Neale's hymn, and its peculiarly Orthodox flavour. The invitation is to partake of the proffered 'rest', but only after a life of suffering. This idea makes 'Art thou weary' particularly Victorian: physical work, with its related sorrow and tears, was praised as a virtue, and, says Houghton, it became the 'actual faith' of many Victorians.[43]

---

[41] Lawson (ed.), *Collected Hymns*, 78.
[42] Ware, *Orthodox Way*, 109.
[43] W. E. Houghton, *The Victorian Frame of Mind*, 1830–1870 (New Haven, Conn., 1979), 251. Cf. W. M. Clow's 'A Hymn of the Cross', a sermon (based on 'Art thou weary') which evokes many of Neale's ideas about work. Clow describes an incident in a New Hampshire village in a service of song. During a moment of silence a man suddenly exclaimed: 'Thou didst say that if we

In *Past and Present* Carlyle reinforces the idea that the sorrow and tears of Neale's hymn can be beaten back through work: 'Doubt, Desire, Sorrow, Remorse, Indignation, Despair itself, all these like helldogs lie beleaguering the soul of the poor day-worker, as of every man: but he bends himself with free valour against his task, and all these are stilled, all these shrink murmuring far off into their caves.'[44] Yet there is also something alien to the work ethic in Orthodox hymnody: labour as weariness, which relates to other-worldly attitudes of Eastern religion. There is a hint of industrial society as an awful thing in Neale; and he is not as strong in his advocacy of work as Carlyle.

Hymns of the Eastern Church represents the only time Neale turned his hand to translations—or rather, as has been shown, adaptations—of Greek hymns. The collection went through three editions in his lifetime and a further five afterwards. The most popular hymns from it were 'Art thou weary', 'O happy band of pilgrims', and 'Safe home, safe home in port'—all of which contained very little from the Greek—as well as 'Christian dost thou see them?', 'The day is past and over', 'The Day of Resurrection' and 'Fierce was the wild billow'. There were other nineteenth-century hymnologists who attempted Greek hymn translations, including Neale's friend Richard Littledale, who in 1863 published *Offices of the Eastern Church*, and Allen William Chatfield, who in 1876 produced *Songs and Hymns of the Earliest Greek Christian Poets*. Neale, however, was the first and the only Victorian

---

would come to Thee we should have rest. Give us rest, O Lord! Amen!' At this point the congregation spontaneously broke into the hymn 'Art thou weary'. Of this remarkable occurrence Clow says: 'There was something very moving, very thrilling, in the utterance of the hymn by that group of country people. They were one and all men and women to whom life is the perpetuation of the curse—labour, for bread. There was all the eloquence of which the human voice is capable in the way they sang, with suppressed, inquiring, almost doubting voice, the question of the hymn. There was a swelling of assurance as they poured out the response of the answers' (*in The Cross in Christian Experience* (London, 1909), 305). Duffield records another New England association with 'Art thou weary': in Sally Pratt McLean's story *Cape Cod Folks*, George Olver and Benny Cradlebow sing Neale's hymn as a duet immediately prior to Benny's heroic death at sea (S. W. Duffield, *English Hymns* (London, 1886), 40–1).

[44] T. Carlyle, *Past and Present* (London, 1978), 189.

hymn-writer whose Eastern hymns were widely used. Although he did not publish his collection until 1862, he had written most of the hymns in the early 1850s, thereafter keeping most of them by him, as he said, 'for at least the nine years recommended by Horace' (HEC 13).[45] He holds the distinction of introducing Orthodox hymnody to the English church-going public; in some cases his renderings are the only ones available in English.

The popularity of individual hymns is very difficult to judge.[46] One possible key is their appearance in various hymnals; Neale's Eastern hymns are included in the twentieth-century surveys by Routley[47] and Perry.[48] Their continuous appearance since 1862 would certainly indicate that they were and are popular—not only with editors, but also with choirs and congregations. Routley considered a total of thirty representative hymn-books published between 1906 and 1979;[49] Perry conducted a wider—though less detailed—survey of thirty-six collections from the period 1927–80.[50] The 'pool' of Greek hymns from which selections were made include 'A great and mighty wonder', 'Art thou weary, art thou languid', 'Christian, dost thou see them', 'Come, ye faithful, raise the strain', 'Fierce was the wild billow', 'In days of old, on Sinai', 'Jesu, Name all names above', 'Let our choir new anthems raise', 'O happy band of pilgrims', 'Safe home, safe home in port', 'Stars of the morning', 'The abyss of many

---

[45] Sr. Miriam suggests another reason for the delay in publishing the Greek hymns: until 1862 Neale's search for a publisher proved fruitless (215d). A few of the hymns were, nevertheless, published in the *Ecclesiastic* as early as 1853.

[46] The psychology of hymn singing, which is only one of a number of factors contributing to the appeal of hymns, is briefly discussed in L. B. Litvack, ' "Come, Ye Faithful, Raise the Strain",' in A Collection of Treatises on Language and Literature, Tokushima Bunri University, 6 (Mar. 1989), 41–66.

[47] Routley, English-Speaking Hymnal Guide, 1. Routley noted all the occurrences he could find of Neale's hymns from the Greek in modern denominational hymnals in Britain and North America, together with major textual variations. See nos. 2, 51, 117, 192, 364, 390, 520, 662, 686, 687.

[48] Perry, *Hymns and Tunes Indexed*, nos. 1, 7, 15, 18, 25, 50, 55, 72, 88, 95, 98.

[49] The *terminus a quo* for Routley's study was the publication of *The English Hymnal*.

[50] Perry's *terminus a quo* was the publication of *The Church Hymnary*, rev. ed.

a former sin', 'The Day of Resurrection', 'The day is past and over', and 'Those eternal bowers'. This test of popularity, however, is not in itself proof that the ideas expressed in the hymns were accepted by congregations; for in many cases, either the text was altered or stanzas were omitted or rearranged. Moreover, much of a hymn's effect depends on the music (which in all these cases was Western), so it is difficult to know whether it is the language or the tune which appeals most to the church-goer. Neale's ultimate dream was the congregational use of his hymns in order to promote *sobornost*; as he wrote in the preface to the third edition of the Greek hymns, 'God grant that this may be one little help towards the great work of Re-union' (HEC 16). Although this was his stated aim, it is difficult to gauge the extent to which the publication of *Hymns of the Eastern Church* succeeded in fulfilling it.

A significant gauge of the success of Neale's Eastern hymns in terms of educating the English reader is provided by Popov, who helped Neale at the composition stage and later sent a copy to the Holy Governing Synod in Russia. In 1859—three years before *Hymns of the Eastern Church* was published—Popov told Procurator Tolstoy that he wanted to teach Neale about Orthodox hymnology because 'it is completely unknown to present-day readers' in Britain.[51] In the process Popov introduced Neale to Cosmas the Melodist's Christmas canon, and translated it into English for him.[52]

Popov and Neale disagreed about what should be included in *Hymns of the Eastern Church*. As a Russian and a Slavophil, Popov would have liked Neale to touch on Russian hymns; but he understood that inclusion of same would have been contrary to the form which Neale had chosen for the collection and the introductory essay.[53] Despite this bone of contention, the Russian chaplain's overall impression of the work was favourable, as the following assessment shows:

[51] Report no. 17 to Procurator Tolstoy, dated 25 Apr. 1859, in Brodsky (ed.), 'Materials', *Khristianskoe chtenie*, July 1905, 129.
[52] Report no. 16 to Procurator Protasov, dated 3 Jan. 1853, in Brodsky (ed.), 'Materials', *Khristianskoe chtenie*, June 1904, 884. Popov originally translated the canon to help Neale with his essay on 'Greek Hymnology', published in the *Christian Remembrancer* in 1859. [53] Report no. 16.

This little book, as the learned author said, is the fruit of hours of his labour, for the last twenty years. He also says that it is the first acquaintance of the West with the enormous number of hymns contained in the services of the Holy Eastern Church. Therefore any inadequacies in his work can be forgiven, the author continues. But at the same time, shouldn't we excuse ourselves before the public, as we take it on ourselves to criticise the work? for there are no precedents with which to compare it. And it is clear that just one single choice of pattern must have cost the translator great effort: the ecclesiastical books of the Greek Church consist of 50 volumes in quarto — that's about 50,000 pages!

. . . .

Dr Neale says that he hopes others will follow his example. But we only fear that a person who can compare with Neale in his learning and genius will not soon be found. We hope and will hope that people in general will turn their attention to the sources of spiritual wealth towards which he directs us.[54]

It was not only Neale who hoped that British readers would direct their attention to the 'glorious mass of theology' and 'huge treasure of divinity' contained in Eastern hymns (HEC, p. xli); it was also the aspiration of Orthodox churchmen, like Popov, who were interested in the prospects of the Anglican Church.

An interesting modern Orthodox appreciation of Neale's work comes from the late Fr Lev Gillet, chaplain of the Fellowship of St Alban and St Sergius, who, as 'A Monk of the Eastern Church', wrote: 'In the Church of England, John Mason Neale was deeply sensitive to the innermost Greek piety, and interpreted it beautifully in his hymnodic translations. He seems to have been, to a large extent, a Greek soul.'[55] Such an assessment attests to Neale's success, perhaps in furthering the cause of Church union, but certainly in understanding the Orthodox hymnological tradition, and—through a process of 'orientalizing' himself—in communicating this understanding to others through his *Hymns of the Eastern Church*.

The ecumenical movement has gained in strength since Neale's day; his efforts helped to set the process in motion.

---

[54] Report no. 31 to Procurator Tolstoy, dated 8 Jan. 1862, in Brodsky (ed.), 'Materials', *Khristianskoe chtenie*, Sept. 1905, 406–7.
[55] Gillet, *Orthodox Spirituality*, p. xi.

He was a pioneer in bringing Eastern Orthodoxy to the popular mind. The question of why he spent so much time on the history and hymnology of the Eastern Church, when everyone around him was discussing the Roman Church, has inevitably been asked. Part of the answer lies in what Turner calls 'Victorian humanistic Hellenism'.[56] He explains that the extensive nineteenth-century fascination with ancient Greece was a result of the dissatisfaction among Europeans with the values, ideas, and institutions inherited from their Roman and Western Christian past. The search for new cultural roots and alternative cultural patterns developed out of the need to understand and articulate the disruptive political, social, and intellectual experience that Europeans confronted in the wake of the Enlightenment and of revolution. The path led to Greece, whose heritage was for Victorians ampler, finer, deeper-rooted in history than anything Roman—or even Christian.[57]

Neale's interest in the Greek heritage stemmed from the same root as, for example, that of Matthew Arnold, though it matured in a different way. Naturally Greek formed part of Neale's education, and the pre-Christian elements of that culture found expression in two of his early publications: *A History of Greece for Young Persons* (Juvenile Englishman's Historical Library, 1845) and *Stories from Heathen Mythology and Greek History for the Use of Christian Children* (same series, 1847). In his introduction to the latter volume, Neale says that the study of Greek is necessary because 'it is the most perfect of all languages,—and, better than any other, teaches us the principles of speech; also, because it is the language in which the New Testament is written.'[58]

Neale, ever the Anglo-Catholic, forms a tenuous connection between Greek culture and the Christian tradition in what he sees as their common attitude to great men:

We may learn from mythology . . . that man feels his need, in some form or other, of the blessed doctrine of the Communion of Saints. Even the Greeks could not endure that men whom they believed to

---

[56] F. M. Turner, *The Greek Heritage in Victorian Britain* (New Haven, Conn., 1981), 15.   [57] Ibid. 2, 9–12.
[58] J. M. Neale, *Stories from Heathen Mythology and Greek History for the Use of Christian Children* (London, 1905), 10.

have been great and good in past ages, should be forgotten as though they had never been. They loved to talk of them, to think of them, to look for their help, to feel that they had a kind of connection with them; and so, at last, they ended by worshipping them. So it was with many, but with Hercules more especially. He is set forth by the poets as the perfect image of a good and brave man, struggling with all kinds of troubles and misfortunes, and doing the will of the gods;—as the fullest representative of what the Church calls a confessor.[59]

Concerning his interest in the Orthodox Church, one could argue that Neale was aware of Greek Christianity as a noble combination of Hebraism and Hellenism. His obsession with martyrdom is clearly a manifestation of the 'fire and strength'—associated above with Hercules—which Arnold opposed to 'sweetness and light'.[60]

In his Eastern hymn translations and adaptations Neale chose to consider only those from Greek, the 'perfect' language which reflected his schoolroom and common room, rather than, for example, Slavonic, the liturgical language which he was urged by Popov to consider for *Hymns of the Eastern Church*[61] and to which he had more exposure in his firsthand experience of the Orthodox tradition. Neale's choice is significant, for it indicates something of the importance attached to Greek culture in the nineteenth century and his—and his potential readers'—familiarity with it. He wrote about Greek hymns, and published Greek liturgies in the original, in the hope that others would learn from them about the Eastern Church. Pocknee considers the closer attention which he believes these elements of Orthodox tradition should receive and the implications their study has for the quest for *sobornost*:

In these days of oecumenical dialogue there is a tendency to concentrate too closely on relations between Protestant and Reformed Churches, or else to consider the matter one of Protestant–Roman Catholic relations. A much wider survey and conspectus is desirable if Oikoumene is to be truly relevant since the Eastern Orthodox

---

[59] Ibid. 14.
[60] For more on Arnold's ideas of Hellenism and Hebraism, particularly as presented in *Culture and Anarchy* (1869), see Turner, *Greek Heritage*, 18–24, and R. Jenkyns, *The Victorians and Ancient Greece* (Oxford, 1980), 264–74.
[61] Report no. 16 to Procurator Protasov, 884. Neale omits Russian hymns despite his deeming Slavonic to be 'more complete a Church language than any other' (INT 822).

Church is the second largest Church in Christendom. The study and appreciation of Orthodox worship and hymnody is an important one.[62]

In publishing *Hymns of the Eastern Church* Neale reached the apogee of his hymnological development. He began with a rigid theory, which he rigorously applied to many of his Latin translations. The Greek hymns, however, led him in a different direction, providing greater scope for originality. He gave the English Church her first taste of Orthodox hymnody, in accordance with his Anglo-Catholic belief in ancient Christian tradition. He also brought the Eastern Church a little closer to his countrymen. Most of the hymns were based on those by famous composers of canons from the eighth, ninth, and tenth centuries; but these were blended with modern themes to make them relevant to nineteenth-century concerns and tastes. It must be remembered that while fostering a better understanding of Orthodoxy among his readers, Neale entertained the private hope of ultimate Church reunion, which he hoped his volume, in some little way, would hasten. The manner of his Greek translations and their content are an essential element in his quest for *sobornost*.

[62] Pocknee, 'Hymnody in the Eastern Churches', 172.

PART III

Oriental Novelist

Chapter 8

Neale's Craft of Fiction

NEALE helped to bring the Orthodox Church to the popular mind through oriental fiction. At least five of Neale's works were of this type: three novels—*Theodora Phranza; or, The Fall of Constantinople* (1853–4), *The Lazar-House of Leros* (1859), and *The Lily of Tiflis* (1859)—and two shorter pieces—'Erick's Grave' (1845) and 'The Story of S. Metrophanes of Voronej' (1850). Neale's fiction, comprising thirty novels and collections of short stories, was popular, especially among younger readers; and many of his works were reprinted well into the twentieth century.[1] His work formed part of a larger tradition: the Victorian religious historical novel. Neale concentrated on certain themes while working within this genre, in order to assist his portrayal of the Orthodox Church; Christian heroism, death, and martyrdom were all employed to produce fictionalized religious affirmation. By laying the foundations of these central issues in a wider nineteenth-century context, a complete

---

[1] For much of my bibliographical information on Neale I am indebted to Mr Michael Leppard of East Grinstead, who has privately been compiling a Neale bibliography since 1969. For a possible sixth oriental tale by Neale, see Anon., 'The Conversion of St Vladimir'; or, *The Martyrs of Kief: A Tale of the Early Russian Church*, *Tales Illustrating Church History*, 5: *Eastern and Northern Europe* (London, 1871). A diligent search, with the kind assistance of Dr D. Jasper, was made to discover the author of this tale; however, nothing definite could be established. It should be noted that the tales considered in this part are not the only ones set in the Christian East; *De Hellingley*, in *Stones of the Crusades*, e.g., has an oriental setting, as does much of part I of *A History of the Church for the Use of Children*. The former, however, concentrates on the Crusaders, with short explications of Eastern Church history inserted where appropriate; the latter, being more in the tradition of 'history' than 'stories' or 'tales', follows Neale's *Patriarchate of Alexandria* in many of its details (*A History of the Church for the Use of Children*, part I, pp. vii–viii), and contains little in the way of plot development or characterization. The tales considered here, by contrast, were specifically designed to illustrate various aspects of the Eastern Church.

picture of Neale the novelist may be developed, and an understanding may be gained of the atmosphere surrounding his tales of the Eastern Church and their substance.

Neale's obsession with the past was related to a keen sense of present needs and challenges. Most of his fictional works were set in former times, but written in the belief that just as in theology, ritual, art, and architecture the past could influence and enhance the present, so historical novels and short stories—particularly when describing deeds performed for the Church Militant—could provide useful models in nineteenth-century Britain. Edifying tales, Neale believed, might be found in every epoch of church history; and by bringing the characters to life, he could teach useful lessons. Neale explained this aim in the preface to the collection entitled *Deeds of Faith: Stories for Children from Church History* (1850): the stories were designed 'to lead children to take an interest in Ecclesiastical History, as members of that One Church which produced the Martyrs of Primitive Times, the Saints of the Middle Ages, and which at the present day is rousing herself in this land, to emulate (as we may trust) the brightest periods of earlier centuries. For this reason these stories stretch from Apostolic times to our own.'[2]

It was the appeal to history that had set Neale on the course of Anglo-Catholicism in the late 1830s; he believed that if it produced such a radical change in him, it could work on others as well.

Neale's antiquarianism was characteristic of his time. As Sanders puts it,

The nineteenth century was an acutely historical age; it believed in the efficacy of the study of the past; avidly collected the relics and art of the past; and it rejoiced . . . in the idea of being enveloped by Time, past, present, and future. If the century witnessed change on an unprecedented scale, in society and politics as much as in science and invention, a good deal of its art and thought looked back, sometimes nostalgically, to traditions and to alternative forms.[3]

[2] J. M. Neale, *Deeds of Faith* (London, 1902), 7. It is interesting to note that this collection was translated into German by a Dr Pelldram, and appeared in 1860 as *Werke des Glaubens* (information from 'Notices of Books', *Christian Remembrancer* 40 (1860), 484).

[3] A. Sanders, *The Victorian Historical Novel, 1840–1880* (London, 1978), 1.

While perhaps too general, this analysis helps us to understand some sentiments of the age concerning the past; yet nostalgia is not the word which best describes either Neale's— or the Victorian—historical sense. It was the link between past and present which fascinated and motivated him.

The Victorians saw themselves as caught up in the forward movement of time; their present had an additional significance because it appeared to form part of an observable trend out of the past. Houghton, in *The Victorian Frame of Mind*, concurs, adding that for the Victorians history was not a 'stop-and-go' process, in which advance waited upon particular events, but a 'natural and organic development, in which each age was the child of the previous one'.[4]

In the 1830s and 1840s writers such as Mill and Carlyle, influenced by the writings of Auguste Comte (1798–1857, founder of positivism), were writing of history as a cyclic process; Mill thought in terms of alternations of destruction, reconstruction and doubt, while Carlyle juxtaposed ages of belief and unbelief.[5] In their own time they saw a transition taking place: society was entering a period of reconstruction and belief. This was Neale's attitude, particularly concerning the Church of England. He was caught up by Tractarianism, and gave it his own peculiar Camdenian stamp; he believed that his reforms in ecclesiology and hymnology were helping to change the face of the Church of England, which, he said, was once again 'rousing herself in this land'.[6]

---

[4] Houghton, *Victorian Frame of Mind*, 29.

[5] Comte, who subsisted on financial aid secured by Mill, belonged to the French St Simonian school, with which Mill became acquainted in 1829–30, just after the crisis in his 'mental history'. Mill outlined this group's influence on him in his *Autobiography*: 'I was greatly struck with ... the natural order of human progress; and especially with their division of history into organic periods and critical periods. During the organic periods (they said) mankind accept with firm conviction some positive creed, claiming jurisdiction over all their actions, and containing more or less of truth and adaptation to the needs of humanity. Under its influence they make all the progress compatible with the creed, and finally outgrow it; when a period follows of criticism and negation, in which mankind lose their old convictions without acquiring any new ones, of a general or authoritative character, except the conviction that the old are false' (J. S. Mill, *Autobiography*, ed. J. Stillinger (Oxford, 1971), 98–9). Mill looked forward to a future which would unite the best qualities of the critical and organic periods (100). See also Houghton, *Victorian Frame of Mind*, 29–33.   [6] Neale, *Deeds of Faith*, 7.

In order to fulfil this cyclic process in history Neale believed that it was necessary to teach people about the past; thus they would become attuned to the parallels between previous ages and the contemporary one. We have already seen how he attempted to make the past live in the present through his adaptations of ancient hymns; fiction also answered this purpose.

The kind of religious historical novel which Neale wrote is an amalgamation of two separate genres: the religious novel and the historical novel. The first of these was used in the nineteenth century for religious instruction as well as for polemical purposes. In the 1820s the 'War of the Novels', to use Maison's term, began.[7] The first tales written either praised or derided Roman Catholics; these were quickly followed by Tractarian and anti-Tractarian novels, Evangelical and anti-Evangelical novels; later in the century there appeared Broad Church novels, and finally novels of doubt.[8] The second type, the historical novel, is today the most widely known, and had a greater influence on Neale than the novels of faith and doubt; its practitioners include Dickens (*Barnaby Rudge, A Tale of Two Cities*), Thackeray (*The History of Henry Esmond, The Virginians*), Charles Kingsley (*Hereward the Wake*), George Eliot (*Romola*), Mrs Gaskell (*Sylvia's Lovers*), and Hardy (*The Trumpet Major*).[9] All these historical novelists have one thing in common: they all owe their inspiration to the influence of Sir Walter Scott.

Scott was the progenitor of what Lukács calls the 'classical form' of the historical novel, in which the reader is made to perceive the connection between past and present.[10] The range of his influence is sketched by Sanders:

[7] M. M. Maison, *The Victorian Vision* (New York, 1962), 29.
[8] For an idea of the range of religious novels circulating in the 19th cent., see the categorized survey by R. L. Wolff, *Gains and Losses* (New York, 1977).
[9] In the case of Eliot it should be noted that *Romola* was her only novel set in the distant past; her other works, excluding *Daniel Deronda*, were set in the past of her readers' own experience.
[10] Georg Lukács, *The Historical Novel*, trans. H. and S. Mitchell (Harmondsworth, 1981), 15. He also categorizes the historical novels of Manzoni, Pushkin, and Tolstoy as 'classical'. I am indebted to Lukács's book for some of the points made about the historical novel in general, and Scott in particular.

As any student of literature knows, Scott's impact on European culture was immense, for a time exceeding even Shakespeare's, and it proved to have an influence that was as popular as it was lasting. Scott alerted his readers to history, and, by looking at politics, society, regionalism, or landscape in a new way, he made them aware of the vital links between past and present. . . . It is still acknowledged that Waverley gave the European novel profitable new bearings.[11]

The realistic novel in a historical setting is something which Scott virtually invented. His tales were not simply an easy way of familiarizing oneself with history: they went below the surface, acquainting readers with the habits, conditions, and opinions of former times.[12] Even Carlyle, who was no admirer of fiction, admitted in an essay on Scott (1838), that

Historical Novels have taught all men this truth . . . that the bygone ages of the world were actually filled by living men, not by protocols, state-papers, controversies and abstractions of men. Not abstractions were they, not diagrams and theorems; but men, in buff or other coats and breeches, with colour in their cheeks, with passions in their stomach, and the idioms, features and vitalities of very men. . . . It is a great service, fertile in consequences, this that Scott has done; a great truth laid open by him;—correspondent indeed to the substantial nature of man.[13]

Scott's method involved the depiction of certain historical personalities who were representatives of historical movements embracing large sections of the populace; however, he was not prompted by what Lukács calls 'a feeling of romantically decorative hero-worship *à la* Carlyle.'[14] It is not the important historical figures who are central to the action: they are merely embodiments of historical movements, and are not Scott's protagonists. His heroes are minor figures, through whose joys

---

[11] Sanders, *Victorian Historical Novel*, p. ix. The assessment of Scott in this book is largely based on Lukács's appraisal in *Historical Novel*.
[12] J. C. Simmons notes that these aspects were absent from formal history written in the 1820s and 1830s. Also, historical instruction had not yet entered the curricula of most English schools (it was first taught at Cambridge in 1848 and at Oxford in 1852) (*The Novelist as Historian*, Studies in English Literature 88 (The Hague, 1973), 28).
[13] T. Carlyle, 'Sir Walter Scott', in *Critical and Miscellaneous Essays* (London, 1896–9), iv.77–8.   [14] Lukács, *Historical Novel*, 38.

and sorrows, crises and confusions, the complex being of the age is portrayed.

Neale read some of Scott's Waverley novels in his youth (NJ 13.7.36, 29.10.36), and they seem to have provided him with ideas for the shape of his own novels, although there are some important differences. Like Scott, Neale included themes of revolution, war, violence, transition, and decay; but, unlike Scott, he continually emphasized religious issues. Neale built his tales around central characters—some major historical figures, others products of his imagination—who undergo a series of trials, whether physical or mental, before emerging as victors. Neale's protagonists consistently perform deeds of faith, which eventually lead to a higher level of holiness, at which point the stories end. These men and women are sure of purpose, never stray from their staunch Christian faith, and their destinies are inevitably realized from the outset of the narrative. Neale's tales do not contain the kinds of serious confrontations found in Scott, between parents and children, lover and beloved, or old friends, which serve to carry historical collisions between warring factions deep into personal relationships. Yet, despite these differences, there are elements in Scott's novels which provided Neale with inspiration. The most influential of Scott's works, not only in terms of observable structure, but also in relation to Neale's orientalism, is *The Talisman* (1825).

Scott's tale is set in the Holy Land, thereby placing it in the category of an oriental novel. Brantlinger describes it as 'an early nineteenth-century Western (perhaps we should call it an Eastern)', with Christian knights on horseback waging war against infidel Saracens on horseback, for domination of the Holy Land.[15] The Christians whom Scott presents—including the hermit Theodorick—are all Western, thus related to his own experience. Their customs and rituals are European, and there are no signs of Orthodox Christians, who were living in the Holy Land at the time, but with whom Scott would have had little or no direct acquaintance. What he does portray, however, are the life and customs of the Saracens, and their

[15] Brantlinger, *Rule of Darkness*, 142.

king, Saladin / Sheerkohf. The Muhammadans are consistently pictured as being at odds with the Christian forces, and although the novel ends peacefully, the Crusaders and Saracens part as enemies.

Neale's 'Easterns' display the stereotypic emphasis on Muslim cruelty and sensuality which were standard features of such novels in the nineteenth century. This view was not gleaned from personal experience by either Scott or Neale. Scott admits that he laboured 'under the incapacity of ignorance', and that his only acquaintance with Saracens was through the *Arabian Nights*. He therefore collected information from British travellers who had been to the East, extended their routes beyond 'The Grand Tour', and seen for themselves the 'struggles for freedom against a Mahomedan tyrant'. Scott noted that his literary inspiration for orientalism was drawn from Southey's *Thalaba the Destroyer* (1801); Byron's oriental poems, including 'The Giaour' and 'The Bride of Abydos' (1813); and Thomas Hope's *Anastasius* (1819). He believed that as a result of his researches he was able to provide his readers with 'the genuine costume of the East'.[16] Said is appalled by such statements, and points to the enormous liberties taken by oriental novelists:

It is as if, on the one hand, a bin called 'Oriental' existed into which all the authoritative, anonymous, and traditional Western attitudes to the East were dumped unthinkingly, while on the other, true to the anecdotal tradition of storytelling, one could nevertheless tell of experiences with or in the Orient that had little to do with the generally serviceable bin. But the very structure of Scott's prose shows a closer intertwining of the two than that. For the general category in advance offers the specific instance a limited terrain in which to operate: no matter how much a single Oriental can escape the fences placed around him, he is *first* an Oriental, *second* a human being, and *last* again an Oriental.[17]

Said's statements also apply to Disraeli, who travelled to the East in 1830-1; while in Greece he remarked: 'For a week I

---

[16] W. Scott, Introduction to *The Talisman* (Edinburgh, 1887), 3-4.
[17] Said, *Orientalism*, 102.

was in a scene equal to anything in the Arabian Nights,' and from Cairo he wrote: 'My eyes and mind yet ache with a grandeur so little in unison with our own littleness.'[18] The second quotation is particularly important, for it points to the effect of his pilgrimage on his political consciousness; the feelings intensified in later years, when he firmly believed in reducing the East to the level of a material possession in the quest for empire. By the time Disraeli wrote *Tancred* (1847), the favourite of all his novels, the territorial imperative had become compelling, so that the novel, says Said, 'is not merely an Oriental lark but an exercise in the astute political management of actual forces on actual territories'.[19]

In the cases of both Neale and Scott, the methodology employed to make Eastern ideas and practices intelligible to an interested but fundamentally alien readership derive from the same root—Romanticism. This movement was, in a sense, the product of the eighteenth-century Enlightenment; yet Romanticism and Enlightenment followed divergent paths. In *The History of Scottish Literature* Andrew Hook surveys the impact of this period and its ideas on the larger context, in a way which is apposite to oriental novels and their historicism:

The eighteenth-century Enlightenment everywhere promoted the values of reason, objectivity, moderation and tolerance; it celebrated the life of the mind. But its very success, and the progressive social and material ideals it advanced, inevitably set in motion a countermovement. . . . In one of its essences at least, romanticism repudiated the rationalism of the Enlightenment.

Paradoxically, the Scottish Enlightenment itself contributed to the emergence of romanticism both inside Scotland and beyond. . . . The Scots thinkers' interest in a more rational and analytical study of man and society inevitably led them back to examine such questions as the origins of human society, how civilization developed, the movement from one stage in social progress to the next. . . . In turn, this emphasis on the past structures of human society helped to bring about a situation in which those who found the modern, enlightened world somewhat unexciting and uninteresting could begin

---

[18] Quoted in B. R. Jerman, *The Young Disraeli* (Princeton, NJ, 1960), 114, 126.   [19] Said, *Orientalism*, 169.

to look back to the past, and find there modes of life and experience infinitely more appealing than those of the mundane present.[20]

By its very nature the historical novel blends the author's perception of history with the conventions of fiction. Neale's characters, like those of Scott, were inevitably involved in some crisis, the circumstances of which were based on existing historical evidence; but the crisis was always resolved in the manner of romance. In the works of both writers, historical and imagined—but representative—characters interact in such a way as to give the drama breadth and the potential for development. The balance between factual and fictional is a difficult one to strike, and requires specialist research combined with a sense of the extent to which characters should be allowed to make their own decisions. George Eliot's *Romola* (1863), for example, involved historical research, which the novelist undertook when she and George Henry Lewes were in Florence; it resulted in a novel describing the life of a fictional Florentine community in relation to external political events. Although Eliot exhibited great care in historical detail, the story suffers, by comparison with *Felix Holt* (1866) and *Middlemarch* (1871–2), from an overabundance of minutiae, which detract from the overall impression, and seem to put a damper on the novelist's story telling.[21]

There exist in Victorian fiction far more examples of the other extreme, which is characterized by George Henry Lewes in the *Westminster Review* in 1846 as a 'bastard species' of novels, loose imitations of Scott, and 'crammed for' in history books. He laments:

For the domestic novel a man needs knowledge of character, power of truthful painting, pathos and good sense. For the art-novel he needs imagination, style and a knowledge of art. For the roman intime he needs a mastery over mental analysis, passion and lyrical feeling. For the satirical novel he needs wit and knowledge of the world. But for the historical novel, as it is generally written, he needs no style,

---

[20] A. Hook (ed.), *The History of Scottish Literature*, 2 (Aberdeen, 1987), 309.
[21] Eliot needed a familiar setting for her imagination to be given its fullest scope. *Romola* is a dead weight in that Renaissance Italy was very foreign to her; the improvements in *Middlemarch* were a result of returning to a familiar setting.

no imagination, no fancy, no knowledge of the world, no wit, no pathos.²²

Neale's novels are not of this type. He had a sound historical knowledge and creative imagination, pathos, and some fancy, though little wit. His work suffers, however, from excessive reliance on his power of invention. We have already seen how Neale fabricated arguments in the absence of historical detail in order to form a more complete narrative in his *History of the Holy Eastern Church*. In certain cases he applied the same method to his historical fiction, in order to complete the picture, at the expense of historical accuracy.

The above raises important questions about whether the past is knowable. From his Marxist perspective on this problem, Lukács sums up some of the difficulties involved:

The question always depends upon the extent to which the present is known, the extent to which the contemporary situation can clearly reveal the particular trends which have objectively led to the present; and, subjectively, it depends on how and to what extent the social structure of the present, its level of development, the character of its class struggle, etc., further, inhibit or prevent knowledge of past development.²³

The depiction of 'reality', then, is dependent not only on the individual novelist, but also on the age in which he or she writes. There are no easy answers to the problems posed; but a listing of them demonstrates how closely an author's perception of history depends on his own historical milieu. It is important to recall this relationship when considering why Neale's fiction took on the particular form it did.

An outline of Neale's method is provided in his *Annals of Virgin Saints* (1846), a collection of short biographies designed to interest women readers in early and medieval Church history; it was also a call for the restoration of Anglican religious communities. In the preface he spoke about attempting to catch the spirit, rather than paraphrasing the actual words, of these saints:

²² G. H. Lewes, review of T. L. Hunt's *The Foster Brother* and *Whitehall*, *Westminster Review*, 45 (Mar. 1846), 34; quoted in Sanders, *Victorian Historical Novel*, 170. Cf. Balzac's criticism of Latouche's *Leo*, in which the latter is accused of 'incompetence' due to 'heaping up of facts' (Lukács, *Historical Novel*, 43).   ²³ Lukács, *Historical Novel*, 200.

> It is hardly needful to remark that... these Lives are derived from the original acts or biographies. From these they have been carefully and most faithfully translated; with an endeavour, however, rather to catch their spirit, than to paraphrase their words. For it is certainly truer,—as giving a truer idea of the times,—to describe a real scene by means of an imaginary conversation... than by a spiritless version of the historian's words.[24]

This is defensible as part of a plan to create an interesting narrative, while adhering to accepted historical fact; Neale, however, exceeded these self-imposed limits. His historical novels and stories concern heroic deeds for Christ, miracles, and uncompromising Christian belief. He wrote them primarily to bolster the faith of his readers, in an age which was experiencing change on an unprecedented scale, and, as a consequence, was increasingly pervaded by religious doubt. Some of his narratives relied heavily on unscientific resolutions to conflicts; these he thought necessary to defend:

> It is a mark of the age in which we live, that it refuses to believe in the truth of any historical account, unless time, place, persons and circumstances are explicitly and accurately stated. The slightest anachronism, real or imagined, which in the course of years may have insinuated itself into an ancient story, throws it into disrepute, and exposes its believers to the charge of credulity. Hence popular traditions, which almost always contain much that is true, and are hardly ever free from something that is false, are disregarded and despised:—hence ecclesiastical legends, more especially when they involve the miraculous, are laid aside with a smile of pity and contempt. It was not so in bygone days. Our fathers were content to derive edification from the sum of a tale, sundry details of which were perhaps falsified or corrupted: they did not reject the whole because of its parts, but they gave honour to the parts because of the whole. The world has long since declared which is the wiser habit of thought:—true wisdom, more especially true historic wisdom, is now-a-days made to consist in doubting every thing. An Apostle has taught us otherwise: love,—and what is true love but true wisdom? —if she beareth all things, believeth all things also.[25]

Such statements seem out of place in Neale's day and for his readers who, as he himself says, had an attitude to history

---

[24] [Neale] 'A Priest of the Church of England', *Annals of Virgin Saints* (London, 1846), p. x.   [25] Ibid. 1–2.

different from their forebears. His plea for acceptance—if only feigned—of the miraculous is allowable for a children's story such as 'The Manx Fisherman' in *Deeds of Faith*, in which Michael, on discovering a leak in his boat, prays to God to spare his life, and then finds the hole miraculously stopped up by a dogfish. Similarly we are ready enough to accept the scene from 'The Boulder of Val' de Passos' in *Lent Legends* (1855) in which Maria and her child emerge unscathed from their house, which was crushed, with them still inside, to such an extent that only the 'smallest splinters' remained.[26] But such miraculous occurrences appear also in his tales for adults, where he could be accused of trying to smooth over historical ambiguities for the sake of his narrative, in a way which hardly inspires confidence.

Neale's fiction is historical, in the tradition of Scott; but it is also religious. This second factor makes him not merely a novelist who wanted to teach history, or even one who wanted his readers to see in the past parallels to their own times, but a polemicist, battling against High-and-Dry Churchmanship, Evangelicalism, and religious doubt. The religious novel became for Neale a vehicle for propaganda. As a High Anglican he was part of a tradition which included such novelists as William Gresley (1801–72), Francis Paget (1806–82), Charlotte Mary Yonge (1823–1901), and Elizabeth Missing Sewell (1815–1906).[27]

In the world of the High Church novel Scott's influence may again be felt. Both Newman and Keble attribute to Scott the creation of a cultural mood favourable to a national religious revival. In an article in the *British Critic* in 1839 Newman wrote of Scott: 'During the first quarter of this century a great poet was raised in the North, who . . . has contributed by his works . . . to prepare men for some closer and more practical approximation to Catholic truth.'[28] In 1838 Keble, in the same publication, wrote: '[Scott's] rod, like that

---

[26] J. M. Neale, *Lent Legends* (London, 1905), 76.
[27] Wolff identifies most of the High Anglican novelists as Oxford men or their Oxford-influenced women relatives or parishioners (*Gains and Losses*, 113).
[28] J. H. Newman, 'The State of Religious Parties', *British Critic*, 25 (Apr. 1839), 400.

of a beneficent enchanter, has touched and guarded hundreds, both men and women, who would else have been *reforming* enthusiasts.'[29]

Both Newman and Keble imply that Scott had made conservatism romantic, inspiring new respect for the old order and the old faith. Events such as the passing of the Catholic Emancipation Act and the Reform Act, which rocked the Church of England in the 1830s, convinced Newman, Keble, and their followers that what was required was a renewed emphasis on holiness and antiquity. Scott, who had contributed to the popularity of the cult of the Middle Ages, influenced adherents of the Oxford Movement in their search for the Catholic roots of their Church.[30] Neale, who was attracted by this appeal to the past, embodied his beliefs in fiction; he was thus able to put flesh and blood on the skeletons of his historical characters, but in the form of a polemical novel.

Neale encompassed various concerns in his fiction (depending on the audience, whether children or adults), the religious and political events of his day, as well as the particular period in Church history which he was examining. His oriental tales had various settings, including Russia, Georgia, Constantinople, and Greece; all these were firmly set within the boundaries of the Orthodox Church. *Theodora Phranza* and *The Lazar-House of Leros* set out ostensibly to educate, but in reality focus on a present condition by recalling the circumstances of the past; the others were written with the sole purpose of teaching Eastern Church history. Sometimes the protagonists were major historical figures, like Cyril Loukaris in *The Lazar-House of Leros*; in other cases the focus was on fictional characters, like Richard Burstow in *Theodora Phranza*, who interact with characters drawn from history and play their own small part in its progress. The themes and methods vary; but there is one concern which predominates in Neale's

---

[29] J. Keble, 'The Life and Writings of Sir Walter Scott', *British Critic*, 24 (Oct. 1838), 473. Ostensibly Keble's article is a review of Lockhart's *Memoirs of the Life of Sir Walter Scott* (1838); however, he uses Lockhart only to show that there were in Scott's character and writings elements of the Catholic ethos which was at the heart of Tractarian polemics.

[30] Keble said that Scott 'indulged himself ... in a kind of imaginative regret for the departure of those heroic days from his own native soil and home' ('Life and Writings of Scott', 442).

historical fiction and which merits special consideration for what it reveals about the character of Neale, as well as his place within a larger nineteenth-century tradition: his treatment of death and martyrdom.

The Victorians' obsessive interest in death was widely reflected in both the imaginative literature and the theology of the period.[31] In 1840 the annual death rate per 1,000 persons in England and Wales was 22.9; as regards infants, out of 1,000 live births, over 150 died within the first year, a figure that remained fairly constant until the turn of the century. These figures have important implications for Neale who, in addition to experiencing the death of his father during his Evangelical childhood, must have heard many sermons on the subject.[32]

The kind of Evangelical background that Neale came from was important for Victorian views of death overall. In the question of attitudes to death, Rowell links Romanticism with Evangelicalism: both saw it as 'possessing a peculiar poetry of its own, and the emotions which it aroused were taken as revelatory of truth about the human condition'.[33] If Romanticism saw death as the occasion for significant emotion, Evangelicalism endowed it with moral significance. The deathbed became for the Victorians the place where the elect testified to their faith and demonstrated their trust in God. Some, like Henry Venn, whose *Complete Duty of Man* (1812) became a standard Evangelical work of moral guidance, urged parents to let their children have experience of Christian deathbeds:

---

[31] For recent critical discussions of the subject, see M. Wheeler, *Death and the Future Life in Victorian Literature and Theology* (Cambridge, 1990), and R. Barecca (ed.), *Sex and Death in Victorian Literature* (London, 1990). It is interesting to note that Newman identified Jeremy Taylor's *The Rule and Exercises of Holy Dying* (1651) as one of 'the most popular books in our Church' (*Lectures on the Prophetical Office of the Church*, (London, 1837), 397).

[32] Recall, too, how his mother reminded him of his own mortality when he asked her in his youth about Jesus as Lamb. Neale's experience of death in his own family was far from unusual. Rowell (*Hell and the Victorians*, 12) claims that by the time a child reached the age of 10, it was likely that he would have experienced at least one death in his family, and quite possibly more. [33] Ibid. 7.

If an opportunity could be found of bringing your child to the bedside of a departing saint, this object would infinitely exceed the force of simple instruction. Your child would never forget the composure and fortitude, the living hope and consolation painted on the very countenance of the Christian; nor his warm expressions of love, and gratitude to the Saviour, for a heaven of peace within, and assurance of pardon, instead of gloomy thoughts and foreboding apprehensions, or stupid sensibility to any future existence, the general case of dying men.[34]

Concern over being in a state of grace was widespread, and found adherents in Queen Victoria and Prince Albert. As a consequence of the death of the Queen's mother, the pair read together a book entitled *Heaven Our Home*, which portrayed the Celestial City as an 'etherialised, luminous, material habitation', where there would be a reunion of friends, and was emphatic on the point that those already departed were much concerned with those still on earth.[35]

The 'death-bed cult', to use Jay's term,[36] engendered certain devotional exercises of preparation for death among Victorians. These included laying oneself out as a corpse for a few moments, going through the rite of extreme unction mentally, and assisting imaginatively at one's own funeral.[37] These practices were seen as necessary because the faithful, on the point of death, were said to be acutely aware of their proximity to the Judgement seat. Some Evangelicals, such as the Claphamite Legh Richmond, counselled, 'Let it be your *sole* business here to prepare for eternity.'[38] This remark helps to explain Charles Simeon's lifelong habit of regarding himself as a dying man. Simeon's practice was well known, and prompted Neale to record in his journal on the day of Simeon's

---

[34] H. Venn, *The Complete Duty of Man* (1812), 308–9; quoted in Rowell, *Hell and the Victorians*, 7–8.
[35] Report in the *Northern Whig*; summarized in Rowell, *Hell and the Victorians*, 9–10.
[36] E. Jay, *The Religion of the Heart* (Oxford, 1979), 157.
[37] Information from Rowell, *Hell and the Victorians*, 165. Cf. Mark Twain, *The Adventures of Tom Sawyer* (1876), in which Tom attends his own funeral. While the scene is an amusing one, it shows that Twain was well aware of the religious tradition that is being considered here.
[38] T. S. Grimshawe, *Memoir of the Rev. Legh Richmond*, 274–5; quoted in Jay, *Religion of the Heart*, 158.

death, 'The day he has been preparing for for fifty-six years has come at last' (NJ 13.11.36).

It has already been noted that Neale grieved over the death of Charles Simeon in 1836. Neale too was affected by the deathbed cult, and, though Simeon abhorred the idea of a dying scene, preferring to be alone, his devoted follower Neale, wishing to glean some pearls of wisdom from his hero's eleventh hour, was at pains to collect the pertinent information. On 6 November 1836 Neale transcribed verbatim into his journal a report of Simeon's state from the Evangelical's biographer, William Carus:

I think you would like to hear what Mr Carus has been telling us, in his rooms, about Mr Simeon. I do think at this moment Mr Simeon must be the happiest man in the world! I will give you Mr Carus's own words:—

'I went to him after chapel this morning, and he was then lying with his eyes closed. I thought he was asleep, but after standing there a little while he put out his hand to me. I said, "The peace of God, which passeth all understanding, shall keep your heart and mind". He said nothing. I said again, "They washed their robes, dear sir, and made them white in the blood of the Lamb; they were clean, quite clean—I know it". He shut his eyes for a few minutes, and when he opened them I said, "Well, dear sir, you will soon comprehend with all saints, what is the breadth, and length, and depth, and height, and know the love of Christ, which passeth knowledge, that ye may—" 'He tried to raise himself, and said, after his quick manner, "Stop! stop! you don't understand a bit about the text; don't go on with it—I won't hear it—I shall understand it soon!" After a little while he said, "Forty years ago I blessed God because I met one man in the street who spoke to me, and, oh, what a change there is now!" I mentioned some other text to him; he was then so faint that he could hardly speak, but he whispered, "I think—death—silence". He had often spoken to me on this subject before, and I knew what it meant—he always expressed a wish to be alone when he died, not praying, but meditating, and not even to be interrupted with texts of the Bible. "Well, then, sir," I said, "we will not pray for you, we will only praise God". At that he seemed to be very much pleased. Then he employed himself in giving away sundry little presents, such as his gold-headed cane, and so-forth; and then he said, "There's one bottle of wine, the Lachryma Christi, in my bin; bring that to me and raise me up. Now may God's mercy continue to me the same firm trust as I now have in the tears of Christ shed for me (referring to the Lachryma Christi). I want nothing more. I can only use the language of my namesake, 'Lord, now lettest Thou Thy servant depart according to Thy word' ". He has not said anything since but lies meditating.' (NJ 6.11.36)

Neale's account demonstrates not only Simeon's rejection of some elements of the deathbed custom; more importantly, it shows the dogged persistence of Carus to fill the scene with a sanctity which he thought befitting a man of Simeon's stature. Carus was appealing to popular tradition, and from the above report it is clear that Neale was aware of and sympathized with these rituals.

A clear example from literature of the Evangelical attitude to death is found in Legh Richmond's *The Dairyman's Daughter* (1810), which is more of a tract than a religious novel, and was based on the author's own experience.[39] After Elizabeth's death, Richmond gazes meditatively on her earthly remains, and thinks:

The blood circulates no more: the eye has lost its power of seeing, the ear of hearing, the limbs of moving. Quickly a thought of glory breaks in upon the mind, and we imagine the dear departed soul to be arrived at its long wished-for rest. It is surrounded by cherubim and seraphim and sings the song of Moses and the Lamb on Mount Sion. Amid the solemn stillness of the chamber of death, imagination hears heavenly hymns chanted by the spirits of just men made perfect. In another moment, the livid lips and sunken eye of the clay-cold corpse recall our thoughts to earth, and to ourselves again. And while we think of mortality, sin, death and the grave, we feel the prayer rise in our bosom,—'O let me die the death of the righteous, and let my last end be like his!'

If there be a moment when Christ and salvation, heaven, and hell, appear more than ever to be momentous subjects of meditation, it is that which brings us to the side of a coffin containing the body of a departed believer.[40]

The key word for Richmond—and more generally for Evangelicals—was meditation.

---

[39] Maison considers *The Dairyman's Daughter* to be one of the forerunners of the Victorian religious novel (*Victorian Vision*, 89).
[40] L. Richmond, *The Dairyman's Daughter* (Edinburgh, 1850), 111–12. Maison makes an interesting generalization: 'No Evangelical writer could resist a good wallow in the deathbed scene' (*Victorian Vision*, 92).

The High Church tradition of death may be represented by the work of John Warton, who in 1827 published his three volumes of *Death-bed Scenes*, which were read by Pusey as a young man.[41] The following extract depicts the death of a Mr Waring:

> Mr Waring . . . was stretched upon the bed of death, and now almost a lifeless corpse. His eyes were closed; his face was black and ghastly; his throat gurgled horribly, as the breath forced a passage through it. I seized his hand, and pressed it. He opened his eyes convulsively, and shut them instantly. He attempted to speak but no intelligible sound escaped from his lips. Nevertheless his mind was manifestly not yet gone; and I hoped that he still possessed the sense of hearing. I knelt down, therefore, and began in a loud and solemn tone the most beautiful, affecting, and divine prayer, which is prescribed for the sick at the point of their departure. His lips moved, as if he were trying to accompany me. This sign of God's gracious goodness towards him, in the midst of his dreadful agony, for a moment overpowered me, and of necessity I stopped. He began to speak, and I put my head close to catch his words. He said, 'It is very comfortable to me; and that was all which I could distinctly understand. . . .' When he had entirely ceased, I resumed the prayer; his lips moved again for a short time, and then became motionless altogether. I grasped his hand, and asked him, if he died in the faith of Jesus Christ. He gave me no sign. Unwilling to witness his last moments, I withdrew; ejaculating to Heaven a petition for the Salvation of his soul, and [was] at length relieved by tears.[42]

The account of Mr Waring's death is important to the Tractarian understanding of eschatology, of which Neale was an adherent. In the 1830s and 1840s Pusey, Newman, Neale, and others extended to the future life the emphasis which they placed on the doctrine of the Church and the necessity of sanctification. Rowell notes that in an eschatological context the doctrine of the Church was developed through a stress on the communion of saints, and the call to sanctification led to a gradual acceptance of some kind of purgatory.[43] The revival of prayers for the dead—of which Neale approved—was associated with both these themes.

---

[41] Rowell, *Hell and the Victorians*, 8. Newman also had a copy of Warton's *Death-bed Scenes*, which is still in his library at the Birmingham Oratory.
[42] Quoted in Rowell, *Hell and the Victorians*, 8.   [43] Ibid. 90.

The early Tractarian understanding of the communion of saints was drawn both from the older High Church tradition and from the Fathers, but it was set within the framework of a seriousness shared with Evangelicalism and a sharp awareness that the drama of salvation was set against the ultimate choices of heaven and hell. This idea is evoked in Newman's *The Dream of Gerontius* (1865) which, although written ostensibly from the Roman Catholic viewpoint, draws on writers from all Christian denominations. Gerontius's soul balances on the point of death, and, aided by the prayers of friends and of the saints, struggles through to an act of faith, is escorted across the river to be purged, and finally shares in the adoration of the Heavenly Host. This was Newman's picture of an ideal Christian death, with Gerontius as the good—though not exceptional—Christian, who, because of his faith, is saved. The poem sums up, according to Rowell, much that Victorian believers wished to affirm about the future life.[44] The context of a personal eschatology, in which Newman painted his picture, was the frame which Neale used as well.

The individualizing tendency is also characteristic of Pusey, who speaks of death as a means of grace, whereby God offers man the chance of communion with Him; therefore he can describe death as 'that almost sacrament, when God's mercy and grace were particularly evident'. This idea enabled him to soften the popular doctrine of hell, which implied that few were saved.[45]

Neale is even more specific than Pusey concerning death as a sacrament. In a sermon of 1864 preached to his Society of St Margaret entitled 'Deus meus et omnia' he said: 'And, oh, what change, what most miraculous change, must that great Sacrament of Death have wrought on us, that the very glory which we could not, in its slightest manifestation, behold and live, we shall then only live, because we do behold!'[46]

Although, as in his hymns, Neale's eschatology concentrates on the joy of heaven, there are also signs of Tractarian severity:

---

[44] Ibid. 90, 160.
[45] E. B. Pusey, *What is Faith as to Everlasting Punishment?* (1880); quoted in Rowell, *Hell and the Victorians*, 112.
[46] J. M. Neale, *Sermons on the Apocalypse, the Holy Name and the Proverbs* (London, 1871), 107.

God's reward is offered to men who work out their own salvation. Every Christian must undergo some test of faith, because all are tainted by original sin. The trials which individuals undergo are varied; but they are epitomized, according to Neale, by the sufferings of the martyrs, who have come closest to the Beatific Vision. In a sermon for Holy Week entitled 'If We Suffer with Him', Neale explained the experience of the martyr, to whom all Christians should look for the key to salvation:

> We all know how our very nature shrinks from pain. Not that all dread it equally.... But still, all do dread it; and no doubt, in and by itself, pain is very dreadful. But then see what it is, and what it has done. It is that without which it is impossible to enter into the kingdom of heaven; it is that which all the spirits of the just men now made perfect have borne, and have borne bravely, before they could have done with it for ever. It is that which GOD's most gracious servants, the Martyrs, have endured in a still greater measure. They who were torn to pieces by evil beasts, dragged asunder by wild horses, burnt in the furnace, cut to pieces by knives, hung by one joint for days together in agony,—all these have known pain in a degree in which we probably may not be called to know it.... 'If we suffer we shall also reign with Him'. It follows that, if no suffering, then also no crown.[47]

The example of suffering martyrs who were recompensed in a life beyond death became for Neale an important theme in his ministrations, and on a more popular level in his novels and short stories, where he gave the theme fuller rein by bringing the historical figures to life—and then putting them to death—in order to create a vision of heaven which had implications for life on earth.

The power of Christian martyrs is evident throughout Neale's fiction. These shining examples of true faith in the face of adversity, and the eventual—often violent—death of the individual symbolizes the supreme sacrifice which a Christian can make. This idea is given extended treatment in *The Lazar-House of Leros*, in which Cyril Loukaris, Neale's hero from his *History of the Holy Eastern Church*, is held up

---

[47] J. M. Neale, *Readings for the Aged* (London, 1878), 132–3. See also Neale's sermon 'Why are ye fearful?', in *Sermons on the Apocalypse*, 281–6, for the sufferings of the martyrs as presented to the sisters of St Margaret.

as the epitome of living and dying according to one's principles. Neale said that few will attain the level of the martyrs, either in belief or in suffering; but he suggested that his readers try to emulate them in their own small way. He opened up the possibility for human upsurge and heroism among the masses, should they be given the opportunity; although he derived this theme from Scott, he restricted such acts to a Christian context.

Neale dwelt on the grisly details of the deaths of his martyrs in order to excite feelings of terror in his readers. The appeal to such emotions had been popularized by such writers as Matthew Gregory Lewis (1775–1818), author of *The Monk* (1796) and *Tales of Terror* (1801). The former was a three-volume Gothic novel for adults, containing scenes of torture, murder, rape, and the supernatural.[48] The latter, a collection of children's tales in verse with colour illustrations, was also designed to excite terror. In his version of 'Little Red-Riding-Hood' Lewis graphically depicts the wolf's attack on the grandmother:

> He pac'd the bed-room nine times three,
> And then devour'd poor grand-mummie!
>
> He dash'd her brains out on the stones,
> He gnaw'd her sinews, crack'd her bones;
> He munch'd her heart, he quaff'd her gore,
> And up her lights and liver tore!![49]

Both *The Monk* and *Tales of Terror* passed through numerous editions by the end of the nineteenth century (fourteen and four respectively), thus supporting the idea that the macabre had by Neale's day become an accepted part of both adults' and children's literature.

In his novels and tales from the 1840s Neale exercised a certain degree of propriety in his descriptions of death. The anonymously published *Annals of Virgin Saints* (1846) was a collection specifically designed for a female readership, whose

---

[48] Neale was also fascinated by the supernatural; in 1847 he published (anonymously) *Communications between the Seen and Unseen World*, a series of discourses on approaching death, family apparitions, haunted places, and witchcraft.

[49] M. G. Lewis, 'The Wolf-King; or, Little Red-Riding-Hood', in *Tales of Terror* (London, 1801), 25.

special needs regarding an education in Church history, he believed, had been neglected.[50] Some of the women die natural deaths; others, like St Cecilia, are put to death almost painlessly by Neale, who says that she 'triumphed gloriously in the . . . conflict' and died as a 'Christian hero'.[51] In the case of Saints Mary and Flora he also exercises restraint: 'They were carried to the place of punishment, where they knelt down, and made the sign of the Cross; and so received the stroke which, severing their heads from their bodies, united their souls to Him Whom they had loved.'[52]

Neale was aware that the inclusion of too many grisly details was likely to displease. Yet on occasion he was not averse to sensationalism. Thus he records in some detail the martyrdom of St Potamiaena, who was slowly lowered into a cauldron of boiling pitch:

> The fire was already blazing, and the melting pitch gave out its clouds of smoke. Potamiaena . . . looked at the apparatus of torture more unconcernedly, it seemed, than the spectators. Raised by a frame and pulley over the heated mass, the populace watched in hope that when her sandals touched the pitch, her courage would fail, or at least that her cries would manifest her pain. But this was the Jordan which, when her feet, like the priests of old, should be dipped in its brim, was to testify to the strength of GOD, not the weakness of man. Far from uttering a cry, she gave no sign of pain, and with cruel slowness, was lowered into the cauldron, so that more than an hour passed before her triumph was completed by her putting on immortality.[53]

This account is more detailed and dramatic than the previous two; yet Neale spared his audience many of the grisly details of the slow death. The pain experienced by Potamiaena is sanitized for the reader. Neale would have us believe that the martyr was actually wearing sandals, and that she was silent throughout the ordeal. Martyrdom is, in one sense, cruelty sanctified; the torture here depicted is rendered 'acceptable' by Neale so as not to offend the sensibilities of the women readers for whom the story was written.[54]

[50] Neale also had in mind the restoration of religious life in the Anglican Church, which he helped to effect in the 1850s.
[51] Neale, *Annals of Virgin Saints*, 29.   [52] Ibid. 234–5.
[53] Ibid. 37.
[54] For Victorian attitudes to the word 'torture', see E. Peters, *Torture* (Oxford, 1985), 151.

In later years more and more of Neale's tales concerned martyrdom. There is a pronounced atmosphere of sentimentality surrounding the deaths which Neale depicts. Before dismissing these scenes as overdone or cloying, particularly to our sensibilities, we should remember that the Victorians had a different understanding of what Thackeray refers to as 'sacred tears'. Kaplan, in his book on sentimentality in Victorian literature, points out that 'most Victorians believed that the human community was one of shared moral feelings, and that sentimentality was a desirable way of feeling and of expressing ourselves morally'.[55] Their attitudes were based on eighteenth-century views about human nature evoked by such leading figures as the third Earl of Shaftesbury, Francis Hutcheson, Adam Smith, and David Hume: that human beings are innately good, that the source of evil is malignant social conditioning, and that the spontaneous, uninhibited expression of the natural feelings is admirable, and serves as the basis for successful human relationships. Neale's heroes and heroines, like those of Dickens, represent an ideal of goodness which is a product of innate moral sentiments; both novelists hope, particularly in their depictions of death, that their audiences will respond to a moral sentiment shared between author and reader, with 'a depth of feeling that will validate the artistry of the dramatization as a moral force for individual rebirth and for communal health'.[56] Neale believed that his martyrdoms were morally instructive, and had extraordinary corrective potential; his main interest was not in accurate representation of such deaths, but in creating a world within his fiction which embodied the moral paradigms that he believed are an integral part of human nature.

The martyrological novel, with its grisly description of instructive death, was becoming a genre unto itself by the middle of the nineteenth century, with important contributions by Charles Kingsley (*Hypatia*, 1852–3), Nicholas Wiseman (*Fabiola*, 1854), and Newman (*Callista*, 1855). In all these novels there is the feeling that the authors enjoyed painting portraits of Christian heroes in their final moments of glory; Neale was no exception. By 1850, when he published *Deeds of Faith*, he noted with an air of happiness in his introduction:

[55] F. Kaplan, *Sacred Tears* (Princeton, NJ, 1987), 3.   [56] Ibid. 40.

It is indeed pleasant to think of those blessed spirits, now before the throne of the LAMB, who yet once dwelt in the bodies of sin and infirmity like ourselves. They and we are still knit together in one communion and fellowship: they have an interest in us and we in them. When we tell of what they wrought on earth, we must remember that we may one day hope to hear it from themselves in their Home and ours. Then we shall know better what they did and what they suffered.[57]

In another collection, *A History of the Church for the Use of Children*, part I: *From the Day of Pentecost to the Council of Chalcedon* (1853), Neale included more details about the instruments of torture, and even an illustration of the apparatus, with the following explanation of its workings:

Of all the instruments of torture by which the martyrs were tried, one of the most terrible was that kind of rack called the *equuleus*, or *little horse*. You have a view of it on the opposite page. The martyr was first stretched to the utmost on the crossbeam above; then that beam opened, and allowed the body to fall through, resting all the weight on the hands and arms. And this torture was but the beginning of further tortures; such as red hot plates, pincers, torches and the like.[58]

Such drawings and descriptions of torture were evidently accepted as part of writing about death and its horrors. This particular illustration was reproduced by the *Churchman's Companion* in its notice of new books.[59]

The most interesting of Neale's descriptions of martyrdom appears in *Lent Legends* (1855), in a story entitled 'The Sacrifice of Onnontague'. The heroine is a converted Canadian Indian, and her manner of death is noteworthy not only for the grisly details which Neale had hitherto avoided, but also

---

[57] Neale, *Deeds of Faith*, 11.
[58] Neale, *History of the Church for Children*, part I, 84–5.
[59] *Churchman's Companion*, 14/79 (July 1853), 62. This High Anglican publication, in which many of Neale's tales first appeared, explained the sentiments which actuated such depictions of martyrdom: 'Perhaps there are few means better calculated to strengthen faith in our holy religion than the history of the martyrs' sufferings,—who were, indeed, obedient to that command, and obtained grace to claim that promise,—who were so firmly rooted in the faith of CHRIST, that neither torture nor death could frighten them for confessing the truth they believed' (*Churchman's Companion*, 21/125 (May 1857), 356).

for its portrayal of non-Christians, whose brutality and pitilessness seem unbounded. The heroine, Margaret, an Indian convert, is captured by her tribe and tortured in the belief that she will renounce her faith. The cruelty of the Indians is highlighted by Neale through the actions of their chief, the Black Vulture, who is also Margaret's father; he himself tortures her, and displays no paternal affection whatsoever:

> The chief seized Margaret's right hand in his own, and with a sharp Indian knife tore one nail after another from the quick flesh.
> 'Now,' said he, 'pray to your GOD.'
> '*I will*,' replied the Martyr. And making the sign of the Cross, she said, 'In the name of the FATHER, and of the SON, and of the HOLY GHOST. Amen.'
> 'Give me her other hand,' cried the Black Vulture. 'Now,' he said, when he had wreaked vengeance on that also,—'now pray to your GOD.'
> '*I will*,' answered the Martyr again. 'LORD JESUS, Who didst not come to call the righteous, but sinners to repentance, call me to Thyself.' At a sign from the chief, the Indians leapt on their captive, with loud yells, tore her clothes from her, struck at her with their knives, buffeted her, maimed her with their hatchets, till ... it seemed a marvel ... that she should still breathe.
> . . . .
> You would not have the heart to hear,—at least I have not the heart to tell,—what this servant of GOD had the courage to bear. The Indians roast their prisoners at a slow fire; and then, when life is plainly going, they set them free, bid them run, and so stone them to death.[60]

The 'good taste' which Neale claimed to be showing in not describing Margaret's end is ironic, both in light of what has gone before and what he alludes to immediately afterwards. The degree of cruelty displayed here surpasses that in all his other portraits of martyrdom. His view of the Indians does not differ significantly from his portrayal of the Muslims, the opponents of the Eastern Christians in his oriental novels, who, in Neale's own day, controlled the lands in which many Orthodox lived. Reports from the East indicated that Ortho-

---

[60] Neale, *Lent Legends*, 99–100. 'The Sacrifice of Onnontague, A.D. 1693' first appeared in *Churchman's Companion*, 14/82 (Oct. 1853), 303–14, in 'The Children's Corner'.

dox Christians were being persecuted by their Islamic governors; the latter were therefore fiercely disliked by Neale. Unlike Scott's Saracens, who believe in chivalry, fair play, mercy, and even respect for the Christian religion, Neale's Muhammadans are cruel, sly, unprincipled, lecherous, and show no pity towards believers in Christ. Interestingly, like Scott, Neale had probably never met a Muslim; nor could he attest from personal experience to the character of North American Indians. These non-Christians differ in Neale's tales from the Romans, who not only had the capacity for sympathy with Christians, but in some instances came to believe in Christ themselves, and even died as martyrs, as in *The Farm of Aptonga* (1856). In Neale's oriental tales, by contrast, the Muslims almost never convert, and are stereotypically portrayed as persecutors and tyrants.

By the time Neale wrote *Theodora Phranza*, he had behind him the tradition of Walter Scott and the historical novel. He also inherited conventions of the religious novel, which emphasized death and martyrdom in sentimental terms. He believed that emulation of the martyrs would lead to a place in the kingdom of heaven; the deeds of these Christian heroes and heroines became for him an important theme in his fiction. With all this behind him, he presented to his audience tales of the Eastern Church, in the hope that he would bring to life for his readers a Christian communion of which the West was mostly ignorant, and from whose history important lessons—and, in certain cases, meaningful parallels—could be drawn.

Chapter 9

Theodora Phranza

NEALE's first full-length novel set in the Christian East was originally published in parts in the *Churchman's Companion* in 1853–4, and then as a single volume in 1857.[1] Judging from opening statements in the preface, written for the 1857 edition, Neale ostensibly wrote *Theodora Phranza* to give 'a fair view of the period when the Eastern and Western Churches were for the last time brought into formal alliance' (TP, p. i). From this stated purpose one might envision a novel, following *A History of the Holy Eastern Church*, which attempts to further the cause of unity by looking back to a time when East and West co-operated for the ultimate good. This scheme would place the novel in the tradition of Scott, with the past reinforcing the present—and, more importantly, future—considerations for *rapprochement* and mutual understanding.

Yet there were larger and more immediate implications which precluded considerations of the future, and which affected not only the small party in Britain in the 1850s interested in reunion, but Neale's readers from all Christian communions. His preface continues:

> The prophecy that the Ottoman possession of Constantinople should not extend beyond four hundred years was widely circulated and implicitly believed before the fall of that city. That the late war has to a certain extent fulfilled it, no one can doubt who, like myself, is convinced that, let whatever dynasty succeed to the possession of the Byzantine Empire, the sands of Turkish domination are now very fast running out. (TP, p. i)

The war to which Neale referred was the Crimean War (1853–6). In the above passage Neale alluded to the 'Eastern Question',

---

[1] This discussion of Neale's novel appeared previously—in a somewhat altered form—as 'Theodora Phranza; or, Neale's Fears Realized', *Victorian Review*, 15/2 (Fall 1989), 1–14, and is reproduced here by kind permission of the Victorian Studies Association of Western Canada.

which concerned the various European powers vying for supremacy over what was then a weak, crumbling Ottoman Empire. Britain's interest in the region led to her becoming involved in the war; and this situation in turn led Neale to write *Theodora Phranza*, a polemical novel which focused on the state of Orthodox Christians under Ottoman rule.[2]

For the fall of Constantinople Neale claimed as his sources various Byzantine historians whose names he barely mentions in his notes. One source which does stand out, which would have been read by many of Neale's audience, was Edward Gibbon's *The Decline and Fall of the Roman Empire* (1776–88) (TP 3).

Gibbon consistently portrayed Christians in an unflattering light, and the Church as vindictively destroying all the positive aspects of the Roman Empire, while assimilating its worst vices. An example of Gibbon's criticism is his assessment of the early Christian martyrs, whose number, he claimed, was 'very inconsiderable'; he also believed that the Roman magistrates used their power 'much less for the oppression than for the relief and benefit of the afflicted church' (D&F ii. 28, 27). Gibbon was also critical of the early Christian attitude to martyrdom in St Cyprian's day (third century); he claimed that individuals were advanced towards their fate by bishops who were anxious for immortality of another kind:

It is not easy to extract any distinct idea from the vague, though eloquent, declamations of the Fathers, or to ascertain the degree of immortal glory and happiness which they confidently promised to those who were so fortunate as to shed their blood in the cause of their religion. They inculcated with becoming diligence that the fire of martyrdom supplied every defect and expiated every sin; that, while the souls of ordinary Christians were obliged to pass through

---

[2] Chapman incorrectly cites 1848 as the original year of *Theodora Phranza's* serialization (*Faith and Revolt*, 167); this error causes him to miss the importance of the Crimean War to Neale's inspiration for the novel. The editor of the *Churchman's Companion* introduces the tale by highlighting 'the interest which at the present moment attaches itself to Constantinople, and to the question of the future fate of the Ottoman Empire' ('The Editor's Desk', *Churchman's Companion*, 14/79 (July 1853), 60). Chapman's error seems to have been based on Neale's statement in the preface, 'The following story was written nine years ago' (TP p. i). This statement appears to be in conformity with the tradition of the 'nine years recommended by Horace' (HEC 13) of HEC. The bulk of *Theodora Phranza* was, in fact, written in 1853.

a slow and painful purification, the triumphant sufferers entered into the immediate fruition of eternal bliss, where, in the society of patriarchs, the apostles, and the prophets, they reigned with Christ, and acted as his assessors in the universal judgment of mankind. The assurance of a lasting reputation on earth, a motive so congenial to the vanity of human nature, often served to animate the courage of the martyrs. (D&F ii. 33)

These views were certain not to find favour with such novelists as Newman, Kingsley, or Neale.

Newman, who, as Allchin believes, paid little attention to the Eastern Church because of Gibbon's presentation of Byzantium,[3] tried to discredit the Gibbonian position in a sermon of 1832 entitled 'The Contest between Faith and Sight'. He condemned the temptation which induced men to think themselves gods, so 'intoxicated by their experience of evil' that they 'think they possess real wisdom, and take a larger and more impartial view of nature and destinies of man than religion teaches'.[4] Of Gibbon in particular Newman says: 'For his great abilities, and, on the other hand, his cold heart, impure mind and scoffing spirit, [he] may justly be accounted as, in this country at least, one of the masters of a new school of error, which seems not yet to have accomplished its destinies.'[5]

Kingsley was equally concerned to criticize Gibbon's view of early Christians. As he puts it in the preface to *Hypatia*:

And thus an age, which, to the shallow insight of a sneerer like Gibbon, seems only a rotting and aimless chaos of sensuality and anarchy, fanaticism and hypocrisy, produced a Clement and an Athanase, a Chrysostom and an Augustine; absorbed into the sphere of Christianity all which was most valuable in the philosophies of Greece and Egypt, and in the social organization of Rome, as an heirloom for nations yet unborn; and laid in foreign lands, by unconscious agents, the foundations of all European thought and ethics.[6]

Kingsley's comments are more pointed than Newman's, and indicate the kind of refutation possible in a polemical, reli-

---

[3] See last part of ch. 1, n. 13.
[4] J. H. Newman, 'The Contest between Faith and Sight', in *Sermons, Chiefly on the Theory of Religious Belief* (London, 1843), 114; preached 27 May 1832.
[5] Ibid. 115.
[6] C. Kingsley, *Hypatia; or, New Foes with an Old Face* (London, 1968), 6–7.

gious, historical work of fiction, which was more direct than in a sermon or essay. Not only did the preface find fault with Gibbon's account, but Kingsley's whole novel was an attempt to show that while the Church of Alexandria was destined for destruction, she concurrently sowed the seeds of the Reformation. While Newman referred to Gibbon's *Decline and Fall* as 'the celebrated work of an historian of the last century'[7] Kingsley referred to Gibbon not only by name, but also as a 'sneerer'. The difference in presentation of Gibbon may be accounted for by the peculiarities of the personalities of Newman and Kingsley, or by the fact that Newman's comments appeared in a sermon; but in their novels, where criticisms could be more shaded and subtle, they both used the Church of the first centuries to modify the picture which readers had picked up from *The Decline and Fall of the Roman Empire*.

Like Newman, Neale respected Gibbon's ability; he noted in *Theodora Phranza* that Gibbon 'says well' of the Varangians —that is, he described their origin accurately (TP 3)[8]—and in *A History of the Holy Eastern Church* that Gibbon's researches concerning Hagia Sophia were 'pertinent' to his ecclesiological study of that Church (INT 232). Although Neale was never openly critical of *The Decline and Fall*, he certainly could not have favoured Gibbon's portrayal of Eastern Christians.

The difference in portrayal of two eras in Eastern Church history will suffice to show the difference between Neale and Gibbon. First, regarding Cyril of Alexandria (d. 444), whose times were chronicled in Kingsley's *Hypatia*, Neale recognized the Patriarch of Alexandria's faults, saying that some of his early 'hasty and violent' acts, such as his sacking of the Jewish quarter of the city, 'were by no means worthy of his character or his dignity'; yet his final judgement was that Cyril's 'noble defence of the perfect Divinity of our Redeemer ... rendered his memory precious to the Church' (INT 226). Gibbon was less gracious towards Cyril,

---

[7] Newman, 'Contest between Faith and Sight', 115.
[8] The original serial edition of *Theodora Phranza in the Churchman's Companion* did not include notes; they were added to the single-volume editions from 1857 onwards.

describing his zealous persecution of the Jews as a 'promiscuous outrage' (D&F v. 13). The difference between the two writers lies in their regard for the Alexandrian Christians: Neale tried to be fair, pointing out faults as well as merits; whereas Gibbon was apt to depreciate those whom he saw as having contributed to the destruction of classical civilization. In the forcibly exiling the Jewish community, Cyril ensured, says Gibbon, that Alexandria 'was impoverished by the loss of a wealthy and industrious colony' (D&F v. 13).

A second comparison may be made between the descriptions of the fall of Constantinople in 1453. Here again Gibbon treated the Eastern Christians with disdain, and placed the blame for the sack of their city squarely on their shoulders. He was particularly critical of the perceived reluctance of the citizens to defend their city in its last hours: 'I can suppose, I could almost excuse, the reluctance of subjects to serve on a distant frontier, at the will of a tyrant; but the man who dares not expose his life in the defence of his children and his property has lost in society the first and most active energies of nature' (D&F vi. 430). He then compared them with the Romans and the Christians of the first centuries, whom he had treated in earlier books of *The Decline and Fall*: 'The primitive Romans would have drawn their swords in the resolution of death or conquest. The primitive Christians might have embraced each other, and awaited in patience and charity the stroke of martyrdom. But the Greeks of Constantinople were animated only by the spirit of religion, and that spirit was productive only of animosity and discord' (D&F vi. 431). Neale, by contrast, emphasized that the religion of the Greek defenders was the source of their courage and fighting spirit. His portrayal was part of a display of the fervent, unwavering faith of Orthodox Christians, which motivated them in their deeds of faith and ultimately led to the sacrament of death and to glorious martyrdoms.

Although Kingsley and Neale differed from Gibbon in their view of the Church and the part played by the rise of Christianity in the progress of history, both seem to have used Gibbon as a source for their novels. Kingsley certainly used *The Decline and Fall*, and even reread it in the course of writing *Hypatia* to determine where his own unflattering emphases should fall.⁹ While Gibbon never saw the ultimate destiny of Alexandrian society fulfilled in the conversion of the Goths and in the Reformation, there were many points of contact between *Hypatia* and chapter 47 of *The Decline and Fall*.

In a similar vein, Neale and Gibbon never agreed on the character of the faith of Constantinople's defenders; yet their accounts displayed many similarities. Gibbon used as one of his main sources for the last days of Byzantium the work of the Greek historian Georgios Phranza, who was *protovestiarios*, or great chamberlain, to the Emperor Constantine Palaeologus and Neale's protagonist. With only minor variations Neale's account follows that in chapters 67 and 68 of *The Decline and Fall*. Towards the end of a distinguished diplomatic career, Phranza is sent to find a consort for his emperor. He is chosen by Constantine for this mission because of his rapport with foreign courts and also because the Emperor valued his opinion and treated him 'with the warm confidence of a friend' (D&F vi. 415). A Georgian princess is finally chosen, and Phranza returns to Constantinople. The embassy is significant, for according to Gibbon it represented 'the last days of the Byzantine empire' (D&F vi. 414); it is at this point that Neale's story begins.

Theodora Phranza opens in November 1452, with a banquet in honour of the recently returned Phranza. Present are the characters who will direct most of the action: Manuel Chrysolaras, a Greek noble; Sir Edward de Rushton, a Greek acolyth of the Empire of English descent, and Phranza himself. The mood is ominous because of the imminent arrival of Cardinal Isidore, the papal legate, who is to participate in an act of union between the Roman Catholics and the Orthodox. The Emperor Constantine and his friend Phranza both see that in their present distress such a union is a necessity if they are to receive succour from the Pope in the impending attack on Constantinople, which Chrysolaras says is 'a city worth dying for' (TP 8). Whereas Gibbon sees the act of union as 'a last trial of flattery and dissimulation' (D&F vi. 431),

---

⁹ Information from Sanders, *Victorian Historical Novel*, 124.

Neale is initially neutral, not revealing his own beliefs; but he puts into the mouth of Phranza the following speech, which denounces those who are opposed to the scheme: 'If the difference seems so irreconcilable to any one,—if the Latins seem so thoroughly to have apostatized, that death without them is better than union with them,—act as your conscience tells you: only then leave the city. We have no such scruples; have them for yourself, if you will, but do not weaken our arms by spreading them around us' (TP 8).

Neale then presents the opposing view through the Greek monk Gennadius, who preaches to the people: 'Do not ruin your cause, do not profane your faith, do not alienate your GOD, by accepting the assistance of these Azymites'—that is, the Roman Catholics, who used unleavened bread for the Eucharist. In a note Neale describes this difference as 'one of the bitterest causes of dispute between the two Churches' (TP 8).

Thus the scene is set. Neale presents the two major conflicts in his novel: the animosity between the Orthodox and the Turks, which leads to the siege of Constantinople, and the opposed religious and political motivations of the Latins and the Greeks. By the end of *Theodora Phranza*, both these problems have been dealt with, but in different ways. In the resolution of the first, the Muslims capture the city, which results in the fall of the Byzantine Empire and continued persecution of Orthodox Christians under Turkish rule. In the second, while there are no firm resolutions of the differences between Eastern and Western Christians, the end is not a gloomy one, because hope is offered from the third centre of Catholic Christendom: England.

Having introduced the two problems, Neale proceeds towards their solutions by entering into the substance of his narrative. He introduces the two romances which are to provide the motivation for acts of heroism: Euphrasia Chionatis, daughter of the Exarch of Silviri, is in love with Manuel Chrysolaras, who is meanwhile betrothed to Phranza's daughter Theodora. Chrysolaras manages to convince Phranza that he should break off his engagement to Theodora so that he can marry Euphrasia. Theodora in turn falls in love with Edward de Rushton, and the romantic crisis is settled; their initial entanglement bonds the four together, thereby allowing for their collective fate at the end of the novel.

The love between Theodora and de Rushton helps to effect—at least on a personal level—a union between East and West. Neale wanted to show that the animosity between Eastern and Western Christians, while prevalent on an official level, did not necessarily penetrate to the hearts of individuals. De Rushton, described by Neale as 'the pride of Western chivalry' (TP 23), of English parentage, in pursuit of Theodora's hand 'fondly... hoped to perform some chivalrous action for the empire or the Emperor, which might justify the Western stranger in asking the Oriental heiress to be his bride' (TP 24–5). Their eventual marriage is used by Neale as a symbol of the potential for unity which exists between East and West.

Theodora Phranza, whose name constitutes the title of the novel, is the central character not on account of her actions, but rather because of what she represents; she is the embodiment of Constantinople, who is desired not only by Chrysolaras and de Rushton, who represent the forces of good, but also by the forces of evil, here represented by the Grand Duke Leontius, a Greek traitor in the service of Ali Pasha, commander of the Turkish forces. For his part in the conquest, Leontius demands Theodora as his prize. Thus the struggle for Constantinople is paralleled by the quest for Theodora Phranza. Neale implies that he who carries off Theodora will also thereby have captured the essence of Byzantium.

Before the fate of the empire is sealed, Neale outlines the character of the conquerors. Gibbon brands the Sultan 'the great destroyer', with a 'savage and licentious nature', whose passions 'were at once furious and inexorable; that in the palace, as in the field, a torrent of blood was spilt on the slightest provocation' (D&F vi. 417, 418); Neale's assessment of the Turks and their leader is similar. As in the case of the North American Indians, he concentrates on the cruelty of the aggressors. In order to discover the whereabouts of Lieutenant Contari, the Turks capture his beloved Eudocia and torture her; the following is Neale's account:

'Will this serve the turn?' said Habib, returning with such a piece of wood as he had been ordered to bring.

'Excellently,' cried Walid, taking out his dagger, and carving each end to a blunt point. 'Now carry her to yonder tree. The rope, Omar.'

Eudocia was carried to the tree. 'Now,' continued Walid, 'tie me the rope round both her hands in a running noose, and draw her up to that branch.' The command was obeyed—not without a shriek of terror from the sufferer, or a silent prayer from the Priest. Walid next fixed the piece of wood upright in the ground, and under Eudocia; and then, taking off her sandal, desired the men who held the rope to lower her till the ball of the great toe should rest on the blunt point. 'That will do,' he said. 'Now make it fast. I never knew woman that endured that for five minutes.'

'You may make me shriek out,' cried Eudocia, 'for I am abundantly weak,—but never tell.'

. . . .

From the lips of the sufferer there burst such a long, piercing shriek that even some of the Janissaries started at the sound.

. . . .

'I will not tell,' gasped Eudocia: and in another moment uttered another shriek, more prolonged, more heart-piercing than the former. (TP 149)

Eudocia is rescued before she has revealed her lover's whereabouts; but until then, Neale is intent on exposing the tyranny of the Muslim forces, thereby giving some idea of the cruelty which they later display more fully.

Before the siege begins (6 April 1453), Neale returns to the act of union, which was anticipated from the outset of the novel. Although the plan appears to be favoured by Constantine and Phranza, Neale makes it clear that he himself does not approve of it. In describing the state of the religious parties in the city, his own sentiments emerge:

The general hatred which was felt to any idea of union with the Latins seemed, instead of being diminished by the pressing urgency of such a step, to derive strength and bitterness from the very fact of its being inevitable. The popular voice was louder than ever against the Azymites; the religious of both sexes . . . preached day and night against such a contamination of Eastern Orthodoxy; the last of the Greeks were exhorted to suffer the worst, even to death, rather than be freed by means accursed in themselves, and bringing a curse on others. (TP 88)

He does not stop here; later he portrays the Orthodox uttering curses against the Roman Catholics as the result of seeing a portentous comet:

'Saw ye ever the like of this?' said Theodosius, the wheelwright, to his gossip, the butcher at the corner of S. Irene's lane.

'Once, neighbour, once,' said he; 'and that was the year before the accursed Council of Florence.'

'Ah! ah! it is clear enough!' cried Peter the sacristan; 'it is the damnable doctrine of these Latins, that the sky itself rebukes. Mercy on us! mercy on us! what have we lived to see!'

'Oh, infamous Azymites! Oh, blasphemous Double-processionists!' sighed Pattelari, the schoolmaster; 'the Turks, the Turks, say I, a thousand times rather than the Pope!'

'Ah, my masters; this spawn of hell, this Cardinal Isidore, is to celebrate next week in the Great Church,' cried the butcher. (TP 175).[10]

Neale's historical imagination is here working splendidly. There is a real dilemma: it was unlikely that the Greeks would have favoured a papal mission; yet they despised the Turks. Neale is distancing himself, considering both sides of this difficult question in order to explore why Constantinople fell.

Cardinal Isidore's celebration in Hagia Sophia is accorded only a paragraph, which is surprising, given the attention which the event received in the first chapter; but the brevity of the account indicates that Neale held out no hope for its success:

On the twelfth of September, 1452, the False Union of the two Churches took place. Cardinal Isidore offered Pontifical High Mass, according to the Roman rite, in the Church of S. Sophia: and the schism, from that time became more determinately embittered than ever. The great church was deserted. The conforming Priests were suspended. Those that had communicated ... were put to penance at the approaching Lent. The siege, now known to impend, was hardly talked of: the Azymite and Processionist controversies were in every one's mouth; Cardinal Isidore could not leave his mansion without a guard; the monk Gennadius issued his instructions and thundered

---

[10] It should be noted that while Neale's dialogue seems unrealistic, it was entirely acceptable to Victorian readers, who were used to a certain amount of rhetoric and melodrama in fiction. The dialogue can also be seen as a mild satire on the anti-papal prejudices of the less well-educated members of Victorian society. Pattelari's exclamation concerning 'Double-processionists' is an attempt by Neale to convey the disdain with which he believed the Orthodox regarded the procession of the Holy Spirit from the Father and the Son, affirmed in the Western Church through the words of the Nicene Creed. The Orthodox regard this tenet as a fundamental error, and an impasse to intercommunion. See ch. 3, n. 16.

forth with the authority of a Pontiff; Constantine and Phranza were known to submit to the Union merely from motives of expediency; the monks were actively engaged against it: everywhere was polemical discussion and religious invective. (TP 186-7)

Neale's version agrees with that of Gibbon, who acknowledges that neither Constantine nor Phranza was sincere in this 'occasional conformity' (D&F vi. 432), and that this feigned acceptance of Isidore, a representative of 'the most odious of heretics and infidels' (D&F vi. 433) led to the Emperor's being deprived of the affection and support of his subjects. The 'False Union', as Neale and Gibbon claim, was an important factor in the fall of Constantinople.

Russia's position concerning the Council of Florence is relevant to Neale's presentation in *Theodora Phranza*. On hearing that the resolution welcoming reunion of the Churches had been accepted on the Pope's terms, a council of Russian bishops repudiated the decision. When Constantinople fell to the Turks in 1453, Russian Orthodox Christians saw this as divine punishment for capitulating to the Latin Church. Moscow, which was liberated from the Mongols in 1453 and attained the status of a patriarchate in 1589, became the 'third Rome', and thereafter retained the belief that she had some special right to Constantinople.[11] This was also Neale's belief; his perception of Tsar Nicholas's aims in the Crimean War— that is, the conquest of Constantinople—represented the fulfilment of Russia's destiny.

The second half of *Theodora Phranza* chronicles the siege of Constantinople and the end of the Byzantine Empire. Neale leaves behind the divisions between Eastern and Western Christendom to focus on the details of battle and on the Muhammadan conquerors. The account of the siege is largely faithful to Gibbon. Neale describes the city's defences, the Greek blockade of the harbour against attack, the arrival of

---

[11] Seton-Watson, *Russian Empire*, 31. He also notes that towards the end of the 18th cent., Empress Catherine II (1729-96) devised a plan for expelling the Turks from Europe and establishing her second grandson, Constantine, on a Greek throne in Constantinople (46). Information on the Council of Florence from Cross and Livingstone (eds.), *Oxford Dictionary of the Christian Church*, 518-19. See also N. Zernov, *Eastern Christendom* (London, 1961), 190-2.

the five Genoese ships, the Turkish circumvention of the blockade by transporting ships overland, and the final assault in which the city falls and the Emperor is killed. Neale supplements these events by following the fates of his protagonists, who for him are more important than the doomed city.

First he describes the marriage in Hagia Sophia—Neale's idea of the perfection of Eastern Church architecture—of de Rushton and Theodora according to the Orthodox Rite. The scene is important, for it binds together indissolubly the Englishman with the woman who symbolizes the Byzantine Empire. Their fate reflects what Neale envisions for the two nations.

The mood of the second half of *Theodora Phranza* alternates between happiness and melancholy. Joyous events, such as Theodora's marriage, are intermingled with mournful events, such as the death of Eudocia, as Neale attempts to show the confusion which reigns in Constantinople. Most pitiful of all is the execution of the Greek and Italian prisoners by the Turks within sight of the city walls, because of Constantine's refusal to concede to Muhammad II's demand for absolute surrender.

In the death of the prisoners Neale returns to his frequent theme of martyrdom. Though this subject is allotted only one line in Gibbon's account (D&F vi. 440), Neale devotes ten pages to the deaths of characters whom he has either briefly or more fully sketched for his readers (TP 294–305). He uses the fact that there were both Greeks (that is, Orthodox Christians) and Italians (Roman Catholics) among the prisoners to endow their death with a greater significance than was given to the act of union. In Hagia Sophia both the Latin and the Greek prelates joined in prayer in what Neale called the 'False Union'; but on the walls of Constantinople, Cardinal Isidore and the Archbishop of Chalcedon join to pronounce absolution over their flocks. The riotousness and discord with which Isidore was received in the church there gives way to silent acceptance. Neale is implying that whereas before the two ecclesiastics represented the dissension which stemmed from the Council of Florence, now, facing impending death and martyrdom, which for Neale were the occasion for the ultimate display of Christian faith which all should emulate, East

## Theodora Phranza

and West were united, with the Cardinal and Archbishop 'advancing together, neither yielding precedence to the other' (TP 299). Recalling the branch theory, this scene had implications for Neale's own day.

The cruelty of Muhammad II is emphasized by Neale, first through the zeal with which the executions are conducted and then in the Sultan's refusal to desist, even if this would mean Constantine sparing his more numerous Turkish prisoners a similar fate:

'I grieve,' said the Emperor, 'that Mahomet's cruelty should have brought this fate upon you; but, as surely as those men die, so surely is your doom sealed. But I would spare you and them, if I can: and to that end, one of you shall have free licence to go to the Sultan, and tell him what I have now said. You, fellow, you are young; we give you your life on condition of your taking your message, faithfully. Will you do this?'

'I will, may it please your Majesty.' (TP 304)

The message of mercy is conveyed; but the Sultan refuses, and the executions are carried out.

Although it is made clear that the deaths have a marked effect on the spectators, Neale exercises restraint in his account. The Christian prisoners are approached by a *mufti* and a janizary, the former proposing apostasy as an alternative to death, the latter, on receiving a refusal, beheading his victim:

When the proposal of apostasy was made to him he shook his head and smiled; but spoke not.
'God have mercy on his soul!' cried the Cardinal, when the fatal blow was given; 'for he hath died a martyr!'
'Amen,' said Sir Edward de Rushton. (TP 304)

The most affecting martyrdom is that of Gabriel Notaras, son of the great logothete, who stands on the wall next to the Emperor as he watches his son's execution:

He [Gabriel] had evidently, from the first, suffered more than his brethren, and some were even anxious lest, in the last moment of his life, he should fall away. Not so the Archbishop, who had known him from his youth.
'A moment more,' he said to the Logothete, 'and his pain will be over. Do not cover your eyes: see, he is looking at you!'
Gabriel Notaras looked up at his father for the last time: their eyes

met, there came a beautiful smile over his countenance; and the next moment he had done with the siege and its miseries for ever. (TP 304)

The martyrdoms shook the crowd; but what was even more emotive was the apostasy of the nephew of Gennadius, Isidore Chalcocondylas:

The spectators saw, with some surprise, that the brief question of the Mufti was succeeded by others; that presently the Janissary withdrew; that a short conversation followed, when the young Greek arose, and retired into the tent.

'He hath apostatized! he hath apostatized!' burst from the crowd; and neither the presence of the Emperor, nor of the Archbishop could hush the yell of derision and rage that ran along the walls. The prisoner next in order turned round, and spat on the place where Isidore had been kneeling; and then, folding his arms, bowed his head to the sword, and with his companion on the other side, closed the catalogue of victims. (TP 304–5)

This combination of martyrdom and apostasy is not repeated elsewhere in Neale's work. In other tales the purpose of martyrdom was to inspire in the onlookers—and readers—a sense of courage which would lead to performance of deeds of Christian heroism. Ostensibly this is the case in *Theodora Phranza* as well; but because the fall of Constantinople is the unavoidable end of the story, the apostasy injects a note of sadness and helplessness, and places some of the blame for the fall of Byzantium on the Christians themselves—both Latins and Greeks—whose faith was not united against the common enemy. This message is pertinent to the 1850s, when Eastern and Western Christians were again divided in their attitude to what Neale considered the Islamic aggressor.

The assault on the city then enters its final phase. Neale muses on the last night of calm the Byzantine Empire would ever know:

A night and a morning, and the destinies of the great city will have been accomplished; the long line of its princes will have ceased for ever; its heroic actions and its dark crimes have passed away from real existence.... But yet, on that fair evening, it existed; its Emperor and its princes were a living reality; its churches were unprofaned; its monasteries inviolate; it retained the impression of primeval times, and, amidst the changing West, exhibited the stamp of the immutable East. (TP 332)

In this sympathetic description of the city, Neale reiterates his overall impression of the Christian East: it was for him an unchanging reality, the supreme example of how the Christian faith of the first centuries—the spirit of which he was trying to recreate in Victorian England—could be preserved, even though the world around was experiencing change and development.

Neale is also sympathetic towards the Emperor and—unlike Gibbon—towards those who defend Constantinople. He is certain that in performing this final deed of faith they win for themselves a place in the kingdom of heaven. To emphasize this point he gives Constantine a speech at the last Council of the Empire which is filled with pathos and a reassurance of the hearers' destiny:

Nobles of Constantinople! it is we whom GOD has called by every tie of blood and honour to take care that, in its fall, this city shall not shame the glories of its earlier days. As in the life of a private man the last moments confirm its honour or its disgrace,—as the behaviour of a few hours may tarnish past glory, or go far to redeem past shame,—so it is with us. . . . It is in our power to show that the blood of martyrs and of warriors which has from age to age been poured forth for this city, has not been shed in vain. . . . This is the task, then, which GOD calls us to-morrow; not to conquer,—which we cannot,—but to endure,—which we can; and by enduring, to win for ourselves immortal renown in this world, and, as I well trust, everlasting glory in that which is to come. Think, then, that to-morrow thousands of just men made perfect, who have departed from this city to their reward, will be spectators of the conflict. Think that they will be ready to receive your spirits, and to carry them to your own happiness. Think that they are still invisibly with us,—nerving our arms, strengthening our hearts, putting wisdom into the weakminded, and courage to the timorous; and that, as they are with us now, so to-morrow we may hope to be with them. (TP 370–1)

This exhortation, which sounds like one of Neale's sermons, reiterates his ideas on death and martyrdom. The city will surely fall; but there is a ray of hope which shines on the defenders: because of their deeds of Christian faith performed in the last hours of the Byzantine Empire, they are assured of a reward in the Celestial City. By extension, Neale reminds his readers that emulation of the martyrs will lead to a place next to them at the close of earthly existence.

The ensuing battle, which Neale describes as 'a Babel of broken orders, hurried exhortations, shrieks, screams, execrations, shouts' (TP 382), results in the inevitable sack of the city and the dispersal of 60,000 Constantinopolitan inhabitants throughout the Ottoman Empire. According to Gibbon, Phranza is sold into slavery, and subsequently redeems himself, while his daughter dies in the seraglio (D&F vi. 449). Neale's version differs with respect to the fate of Theodora: she and her husband, de Rushton, escape to England, and are later joined by Chrysolaras and Euphrasia; there Theodora bears a son, whom she names Constantine.

Neale's surprise ending, which is unhistorical, embodied his private hope for the future of East–West relations. By sending Theodora to England and naming her son after the martyred Emperor, Neale established links between England and Constantinople which, the reader is to suppose, have remained firm during the intervening 400 years from 1453 to 1853. Neale's belief in the Catholicity of the Church meant that there were strong ties between the Anglican and Orthodox Churches in theology and doctrine; his own stand on the *Filioque*, concerning which he adopted the Eastern view, was one example of the connections which he sought to establish. *Theodora Phranza*, then, set out to prove that this East–West link was an enduring one, and that the Anglican Church —or England generally—had a special role to play in its maintenance.[12]

The great majority of British Christians regarded the Crimean War as a great campaign to subdue the 'evil' Russians. In attempting to catch the atmosphere of the nation, Tennyson, in *Maud*, sends the hero off at the end to fight in the

---

[12] Kaplan notes that marriage is sometimes used by Victorian authors to represent the victory of the moral sentiments: 'Society provides the ritual affirmation of its belief that the moral sentiments may be enriched in a special union which symbolizes that all division and discord can be made whole and harmonious. For the Victorians in general, an art that embodied such harmonies was not a compromise with popular taste or commercial demand but an affirmation of the inseparability of aesthetic and moral vision' (*Sacred Tears*, 109).

Crimea.[13] Webb had expressed to Neale support for the British cause, and in a letter of 1854 Neale made clear his conflicting sentiments on the Eastern War: 'I disagree with you *toto caelo* about the war, thinking it the most wicked that has of late years been, except Napoleon's Campaigns. Nevertheless, I hope for good too, if there could but be a free Church of Constantinople.'[14]

Neale was sympathetic to the reports then circulating in England concerning the cruelties inflicted on some of the thirteen million Christians—most of them Orthodox—under Ottoman rule. Extracts from a pamphlet entitled *History of the Origin of the War with Russia*, which contained some of these reports, gives an idea of the information available concerning Turkish persecution of Christians:

Vice-consul Baratti, writes, Scutari, June 1st, 1853, 'All the desperate characters have raised their heads again, and acts of rapine and robbery, are very frequent at the expense of the Christians. *Omar Pasha, the governor of this province is a Mussulman*, and sees with perfect indifference, all the excesses. The Christians who are exposed to the vengeance of their enemies, live in a continual state of alarm.'

. . . .

The following is an extract of a Proclamation of the Christian subjects of the Porte in Epirus, in March, 1854:

'The cruel bondage under which we, the population of Grecian Epirus, have laboured for upwards of four centuries, is not known to the Sovereigns and people of Christendom. Tyrannical fury has spared neither life nor property, nor left us any kind of liberty. God created us men in his own image and similitude; whereas we are treated like beasts. The temples of our ancestral faith have been a thousand times impiously polluted and despoiled; the graves of our forefathers opened, and their bones frequently cast into the fire; the honour of our wives and children continually outraged; so that our breath alone remains to us, and that but to augment our sufferings. . . . Cumulated oppressions, insults, and dishonour, sacrifice of life without end, spoliation upon spoliation, and all the dreadful woes of Hades itself, are written in our book of life.'

---

[13] The extent to which the war penetrated the British imagination is indicated by the classical scholar Jane Ellen Harrison (1850–1928), whose first toy was a box of bricks and soldiers marketed as 'The Siege of Sevastopol' (J. E. Harrison, *Reminiscences of a Student's Life* (London, 1925), 9).

[14] *Letters*, 225; dated 12 June 1854, from Sackville College.

Here are some extracts from the letters of Consul Saunders, March, 1854:

'Among other cases brought forward was one where a mother had her son and daughter bound up before her eyes and menaced with frightful tortures, boiling oil being prepared to pour upon them for this purpose, unless a large sum of money, which the family was supposed to possess, were immediately consigned, while the unfortunate mother, producing every species of valuable which she could collect, was with difficulty able to satisfy the rapacity of those ruffians, who eventually decamped with a large booty. It should be observed, that the parties concerned in the outrages are mostly wealthy Mussulman proprietors, who scruple not to commit every species of atrocity on such occasions.'[15]

Such reports, emphasizing Turkish oppression in the 1850s, and Neale's own historical researches into Christian suffering under Islamic rule were combined in his presentation of Muhammad II's forces in *Theodora Phranza* as cruel, unrelenting, avaricious conquerors. Their siege of Constantinople represents the crushing of Greek Christian resistance to Islam, and Neale was happy to draw the inference that the modern Greek Church needed its Russian champions.[16]

The anonymous *History of the Origin of the War with Russia* claims that the instigator of the Crimean conflict was the Turkish Sultan, who, on the advice of the French, rearranged the system of ecclesiastical authority over the holy places in Palestine. His granting the Roman Catholic minority exclusive possession of several spots which they had earlier shared with the Greeks roused the indignation of Tsar Nicholas.[17] The causes were in fact more complicated, although Orthodox rights at the holy places were an important consideration. The larger problem which sparked the controversy was the 'Eastern Question', which was the name given to the problems caused by the weakness of the Ottoman Empire in the mid-nine-

---

[15] Anon., *History of the Origin of the War with Russia*, (London, 1855), 27–8.

[16] Neale might have heard of Turkish persecutions from Popov, who— despite the dismissal of his embassy's diplomatic staff—was allowed to remain in Britain to care for the spiritual needs of the Russian prisoners of war captured in the Baltic campaign and ferried to Lewes, in Sussex (information from Popov's biographical details in Bradsky (ed.), 'Materials', *Khristianskoe chtenie*, Apr. 1904, 597).

[17] Anon., *History of the Origin of the War with Russia*, 4.

teenth century and the rivalry between its potential successors, which included Russia, France, Austria, and England.

Tsar Nicholas I, who has been described as the 'crowned gendarme'[18] on account of his militaristic nature and unrelenting spirit, was a stronger advocate of war than the Turkish Sultan. Anticipating imminent anarchy in Constantinople and 'an early dissolution of the Turkish Empire', the Tsar, in a letter to Lord Aberdeen, suggested that his armies might 'temporarily' occupy the Turkish capital; but the British Prime Minister made it clear that his government wanted no territorial aggrandizement at the expense of Turkey.[19]

Initially Nicholas did not want an open conflict; he attempted a diplomatic 'show of strength' at Constantinople, so that his embassy might 'recover the degree of influence it had earlier exercised' at the Porte.[20] The point of contention was the rights of Turkey's Christian citizens; and Menshikov, the Tsar's envoy, was authorized to use 'threatening or friendly language' to secure a convention recognizing Russia's right to protect them.[21] The Russian diplomat presented his government's list of requests at Constantinople on 5 May 1853; it was assumed by the Turks, British, and French that Russia sought a protectorate over all Orthodox subjects of the Sultan, both in Europe and in Asia. It was this document which transformed the conflict from diplomatic harangue into war.

Although the Greek Christians' spiritual leader was the Patriarch of Constantinople, the latter was subject to Turkish control: he was enthroned by the Turkish government, and, although he possessed some secular authority, it was subject to the good graces of the Sultan. One of the Tsar's aims was to free the Christians from such manifestations of Turkish authority and from the persecutions which occurred in many parts of the Ottoman Empire.

Turkey formally declared war on Russia on 5 October 1853. Nicholas, in rousing his subjects to arms, used religious motivation to stir Russians to side with him in their common,

---

[18] A. Palmer, *The Banner of Battle* (London, 1987), 254. See also Seton-Watson's assessment of Nicholas I in *Russian Empire*, 199–202, where the Tsar is dubbed the 'Gendarme of Europe'.
[19] Palmer, *Banner of Battle*, 15.
[20] Tsar's comment to Nesselrode; quoted in ibid. 19.   [21] Ibid. 16.

sacred cause. First he emphasized the role Russia was destined to play in the defence of Orthodox Christians:

> It is known to all our faithful subjects that the defence of the Orthodox Religion was, from time immemorial, the vow of our glorious forefathers. From the time that it has pleased Providence to entrust to us the hereditary throne, the defence of those holy obligations inseparable from it was the constant object of our solicitude and care. But to our great grief, recently, in despite of our efforts to defend the inviolability of the rights and privileges of our Orthodox Church, various arbitrary acts of the Porte have infringed those rights, and threaten at last the complete overthrow of the long-perpetuated order so dear to Orthodoxy.

Then, in his declaration of war, he spoke more specifically of the need to take up arms: 'We are firmly convinced that our faithful subjects will join the fervent prayers which we address to the Most High, that His hand may be pleased to bless our arms in the holy and just cause which has ever found ardent defenders in our pious ancestors.' Finally, six months later, by which time France and England had entered the war, the Tsar complained that although the European powers were predominantly Christian, they had allied themselves with their enemy against the Orthodox faith:

> Russia fights not for the things of this world, but for the Faith. England and France have ranged themselves by the side of the enemies of Christianity against Russia fighting for the Orthodox Faith. But Russia will not alter her Divine mission. May the Almighty assist us to prove this by deeds. And in this trust, taking up arms for our persecuted brethren professing the Christian faith, we will exclaim, with the whole of Russia, with one heart, 'O Lord, our Saviour, whom have we to fear? May God arise, and may His enemies be dispersed!'[22]

Such exhortations show that the Russian people were called to fight not only for their Emperor or their country, but for the Orthodox Church.

Popov's reports to the Holy Governing Synod put the Tsar's pleas in a slightly different light. As early as January 1846 the

---

[22] Quoted in anon., 'Mr Kinglake's Crimea', *Christian Remembrancer*, 46 (1863), 454. In a letter to his sister Anna, the Tsar said that to wage war against the Turks was 'a holy vocation to which Russia is ... called' (quoted in Palmer, *Banner of Battle*, 24).

Russian chaplain stated his conviction that it was Russia's destiny to take possession of Constantinople. In a demarcation of the 'true' path of Christian growth from the 'false', he outlined four points of fundamental importance: first, the preservation of the 'fundamental, original idea of Christianity'; second, the 'unceasing continuation of the principles on which the development of Christianity was based'; third, the 'power of assimilation', whereby various opinions would eventually merge into one (he uses the analogy of physical materials being absorbed into the blood of the human being who consumes them); fourth, 'an early, prophetical indication of the forms that the future development of Christianity will take', an example of which was the prophecy that 'Tsargrad', as Popov calls Constantinople, would one day belong to Russia.[23] Here Popov uses the prediction regarding the fate of the Turkish capital as an example of the future path which Russia —and the Orthodox Church—should take.[24]

Popov's vision was influenced by the Slavophilism of his mentor, Khomiakov, who was convinced of Russia's just cause in the Crimean War.[25] In a letter to a friend in 1854 Khomiakov outlined what he perceived to be the pervasive Russian sentiments concerning the war, including Russian sympathy for Christians in Turkey, opposition to British and French support of the Sultan, and belief in the glorious position of which Russia was assured as a result of her taking up arms:

Russia is contributing to a rebirth of the peoples forgotten by the rest of the world. In the interests of charity, sympathy and consolation we daily and consistently offer assistance to our long-suffering broth-

[23] Kline points out that *Tsargrad*, or 'King City', the medieval Russian name for Constantinople, was a calque on the Greek *Basis polis* ('Queen City'), with the secondary meaning 'City of the Tsar' ('Russian Religious Thought', 191).

[24] Report no. 6, in Brodsky (ed.), 'Materials', *Khristianskoe chtenie*, Apr. 1904, 611. It should be noted that while many perceived the capture of Constantinople to be the Tsar's ultimate goal, Nicholas himself did not; he could not accept any occupation or domination of Constantinople by the British or French, but he himself did not wish to take the city. His words, in a letter to the Austrian Emperor Franz Joseph, attest to his position: 'I shall never cross the Danube, and everything between the river and the Adriatic shall be yours' (quoted in Seton-Watson, *Russian Empire*, 310).

[25] Cf. the remark by Dostoevsky, also a Slavophil, in his *Diary of a Writer* (June 1876): '*Sooner or later Constantinople must be ours*' (quoted in Kline, 'Russian Religious Thought', 191; emphasis original).

ers under Mussulman domination.... God has endowed us with the responsibility of saving our brothers who are the blood of our blood and the heart of our heart. The war, in one respect criminal, is in another holy.

. . . .

Public opinion is moved on this point: Russia feels that justice may be applied by force on a nation which comprehends neither justice, nor compassion, nor fidelity to promises. England and France, under the pretext of maintaining a balance of European power—which is not threatened—have upheld Turkey's infidelity. Without offering anything in place of the guarantees which we have sought, except perhaps vague promises for the future; showing no respect for our feelings, without consideration for the most simple workings of humanity, they have enlivened the hopes of Turkey by their alliance and aid; they have reawakened Mussulman courage, and have fanaticised their passions. England and France alone are responsible for the oppression, ignominy, pillage, murder and rape, in short, all the sufferings and miseries inflicted on our brothers in Bosnia, Bulgaria, Anatole and Romilly, which the Turks have perpetrated in our justly reclaimed lands—and this page will never be erased from their histories.

. . . .

Russia has armed herself. Her decision resembles the action of a man who has consulted his heart, followed his conscience, and emerged in the belief that he would be negligent in his duty if he did anything other than what his soul-searching had dictated.

. . . .

War has been declared. Who shall emerge triumphant? No one knows what God has decreed. Yet we have no doubt about who is truly victorious. We have already triumphed by having raised arms for such a sacred cause: for suffering humanity, Christians oppressed by the Koran, purity of virgins, chastity of women, lives of men, freedom of religion and the development of the intellect. This glory is assured for us and cannot be wrenched from our grasp.[26]

While the orientalist Neale may have sympathized with Russia's motivations on a religious level, there were other considerations which he disregarded, but which proved key

---

[26] Birkbeck (ed.), *Russia and the English Church*, 167, 168, 169, 172. Khomiakov sent a copy of this letter, in French, to William Palmer in the hope that the latter would publicize its contents as an insight into Russian thoughts on the Crimean War. For further information on Khomiakov and Slavophilism, see Zernov, 'Alexei Stepanovich Khomiakov'.

factors in Britain's decision to enter the war. Britain's motivations were as complex as Russia's, but may be simplified as follows. In the eyes of the British the Tsarist state machine had become a menace to Western civilization. Businessmen deplored the incursion of Russian traders in the Far East, central Asia, and the eastern Mediterranean. Many political groups had complaints—genuine or feigned—against Russia. Finally, a restless national pride gripped large sections of the population.[27] France, Sweden, and Austria also had grievances against the Tsar—although the last two never entered the war. The allies—principally Britain, France, and Turkey—agreed on 'Four Points', which became the aims of the campaign: a European guarantee over the Danubian principalities, rather than a Russian protectorate; free navigation of the Danube; revision of the 1841 Straits Convention, so that the movement of warships through the Dardanelles and Bosphorus would be regulated in the interests of the balance of power in Europe; and, finally, Russia's renunciation of any claim to exercise a protectorate over the Sultan's Christian subjects.[28] Of these four points, Neale was most displeased with the last; indeed, it was his primary motivation for writing *Theodora Phranza*.

There were those in the British government who were reluctant to enter into a war with Russia. Among them was Gladstone, who dutifully supported the cabinet in its decisions, but was sympathetic to Russia's religious motivations in entering the war against Turkey. In a speech to the House of Commons in 1855 he asked Members of Parliament to consider the thoughts of the Russian troops in the Crimea:

Let any honourable gentleman put himself in the place of the Russian soldier.... Against whom is he fighting? Against the Turks—against the hereditary enemies of his race—against those whom he is taught to consider the hereditary enemies of his religion—and finally, and as respects all the Allies, against the invaders of his soil. If there are two motives which can act with overpowering might upon the human heart—if there are two incentives which can draw forth out of a man all the power and energy of which he is possessed, are they not these—first, that he is fighting against the enemy of his

---

[27] Palmer, *Banner of Battle*, 9.   [28] Ibid. 78.

religion; and secondly, that he is defending his own soil; and are not these the very motives which the Russian soldiery and people have at present to work upon them?

Gladstone supported his claims with a Russian account from Sebastopol of the religious devotion of the Tsar's army in the time of war:

On [June] the 20th the burial of the dead was continued, but towards evening the flag of truce was removed and the bombardment recommenced, but much more feebly than before. The same day a *Te Deum* was sung in the church of St Vladimir in celebration of our happy success, and the soldiers who attended wore the same clothes which they had worn in the struggle, and not a single coat was to be seen there which was not dyed with blood. In the evening the whole garrison of Sebastopol received the Sacrament. Osten-Sacken, with his staff, received it first, and the rest of the troops in succession.

He then issued a caveat to the British government to search their souls for the justice of their cause:

You may say that it is fanaticism, but at any rate it is not hypocrisy.... It is a sign of that character, partly passive, but capable of being roused by circumstances to a high and persevering activity, which has enabled Russia to occupy so prominent a position in the affairs of the world, which will never, I am convinced, enable her to become formidable to you so long as your cause is just, but which it must be worth your while to consider when you begin to doubt of its justice.[29]

Although Gladstone never strayed from the government's official position, he understood Russian religious motivations in the Crimean conflict and—although to a lesser extent than Neale—asked his listeners to consider the opposite viewpoint.

The war, in which approximately 20,000 British, 100,000 French, and countless Turks died, is thought to have cost the

---

[29] W. E. Gladstone, *Speech of the Right Hon. W. E. Gladstone... on the War and the Negotiations* (London, 1855), 19, 20. Palmer notes that Count von der Osten-Sacken, the senior Russian general inside Sebastopol, was an extremely devout Baltic German, who regularly interceded for the Almighty's blessing on Russia's army (*Banner of Battle*, 208). Interestingly Khomiakov intimated to Palmer that he 'should be glad, if I could be assured that Gladstone does not approve of this guilty and wicked war' (letter of 1854 in Birkbeck (ed.), *Russia and the English Church*, 165).

Russians the lives of 450,000 men.[30] For Neale, the Tsar's troops were the real heroes of the war, performing deeds of Christian faith for their beloved Emperor, which would earn them places in the kingdom of heaven. Like his defenders of Constantinople in *Theodora Phranza*, the Russian soldiers in the Crimea endured, and in their martyrdom earned a victory which surpassed those of the British and French troops. Neale expressed his feelings in a poem commemorating 'The Battle of the Alma', fought on 20 September 1854, in which the Russians suffered their first major setback. The martyred soldiers speak:

> Though outnumbered, outmanœuvred,
>   something comforts us within,
> Whispering: It is sometimes nobler
>   to be conquered than to win:
>
> Nobler to be conquered, fighting
>   for each home and wife and pet,
> Nobler to be conquered, leaving
>   names our land will not forget,—
>
> Than, for greed of gold or glory,
>   on the hard won field to say,
> GOD Himself approves aggression,
>   for to Him we owe the day.
>
> France and England sing *Te Deum*,
>   that *Te Deum* so disgraced,
> For the homes by you made homeless,
>   for the hearths by you laid waste:
>
> And to serve both GOD and Mammon,
>   —this world's gain, but that world's loss,—
> High above your very Altars
>   wreathe the Crescent with the Cross:
>
> There remains a dreader Judgment
>   where this wrong shall be repaid;
> Juster scales than those of glory
>   where this battle shall be weighed.
>
> On the Vigil of S. Matthew
>   Russian lips shall ever pray

---

[30] Palmer, *Banner of Battle*, 244.

> For the men that died by Alma,
>   when the Crescent won the day.
>
> Courage, brethren! France's tyrant,
>   through the good path oped by you,
> May yet havew his Saint Helena,
>   Alma yet her Waterloo![31]

Neale epitomized the battle as one in which the Cross, symbolizing the allied forces of England and France, had allied herself with the Crescent, which represented the Turks. He also saw France—not England—as the mortal enemy of Russia; but the two nations joined in a battle against the Tsar's army, in which they promoted Turkish interests, gained gold and glory for themselves, and, as a result, perpetuated the subjugation of the Orthodox. In December 1854 he wrote angrily to Webb: 'About the Russian war I feel so strongly that I had rather not write.... We are fighting to ensure the perpetual slavery of Turkish Christians.'[32] Neale was part of a minority who defended the Greek Christians—and the Russians—during the Crimean War.[33] His views were familiar to those around him, including his children; his daughter Agnes wrote a series of verses on Sebastopol, in which she praised the Tsar: 'And when he next does slay the Turks/May I be there to see his works!'[34] Neale believed that the British government was in error about the conflict; yet he hoped that 'this time two years I shall be in the majority'.[35] His hope for a reversal accounts for the relative sympathy with the British expressed in 'The Battle of the Alma'.

But his wish was not fulfilled: Sebastopol was evacuated, and the Russians defeated, thereby losing their status as the

---

[31] J. M. Neale, 'The Battle of the Alma', in *Sequences, Hymns and other Ecclesiastical Verses* (London, 1866), 99–101.

[32] *Letters*, 231; dated 9 Dec. 1854, from Sackville College.

[33] Charles Kingsley accused the Anglo-Catholics as a whole of supporting Russia. In a letter to Tom Hughes he writes: 'I always knew that the Puseyites, for superstitious feelings about "The Crescent and the Cross" disliked the war ... be sure that there is a strong Russian feeling among the Puseyites, just because they hanker after the Greek Church *faute de Rome*' (quoted in Chapman, *Faith and Revolt*, 103). Neither Kingsley nor Chapman substantiates this claim.

[34] *Letters*, 231; letter to Webb, dated 4 Dec. 1854, from Sackville College.

[35] *Letters*, 231; dated 9 Dec. 1854, from Sackville College.

strongest power on the European mainland. The Congress of Paris in 1866 ensured that Russia was not officially recognized as the protectress of Turkish Christians. It seems that the allied powers thought that the *Firman*, or decree, issued in Constantinople, promising an improved status for non-Turkish and Christian subjects, was sufficient. The British position was made clear as early as 1855, when Gladstone said that he anticipated 'no obstacle' from the Russians concerning the concession of the fourth 'Point'.[36] The allies also knew of Tsar Alexander's manifesto of 1856, proclaiming that an act of Providence had fulfilled 'the original and principal aims of the war. From now on, the future destiny and rights of all Christians in the Orient are assured. The Sultan solemnly recognized them ... Russians! Your efforts and your sacrifices were not in vain. The great work is accomplished!'[37]

The Turkish proclamation was not sufficient, however; before the end of the decade there were riots at the holy places in Jerusalem, and Christians were being slaughtered in Syria, Lebanon, and the Arabian peninsula. It seems that the allies thought that the guarantee of safety for Christians did not merit explicit inclusion in the Treaty of Paris. Neale's fears had become realities.

[36] Gladstone, *Speech on the War*, 8.
[37] W. Baumgart, *The Peace of Paris*, 1856; quoted in Palmer, *Banner of Battle*, 239–40.

Chapter 10

The Lily of Tiflis

IN his next oriental novel, issued anonymously in 1859, Neale moved some 1,000 kilometres east of the Crimea, to Georgia. *The Lily of Tiflis* was the first of his nine contributions to John Henry Parker's 'Tales Illustrating Church History': a series of short novels chronicling outstanding or memorable ecclesiastical events from all ages.[1] The novel concerns the martyrdom by the Persians of St Susanna in 466.[2] Neale's source for the tale seems to have been Plato Jossilian's *Church History of Georgia* (St Petersburg, 1843), of which he obtained a manuscript translation from Richard Blackmore; but as he himself said in *A History of the Holy Eastern Church*, the annals of the Georgian Church are 'deplorably inaccurate and ignorant', thus making it difficult to ascertain dates, places, or names. He did note, however, that the Muhammadan Caliphs did not 'occasion much devastation' in Georgia 'till Mirvan [Neale's Meruan], the last Prince of the House of Ommiyah, led his hordes into that country'. It was during this reign of terror that 'a countless host of martyrs ... contended for the Faith; among whom S. Susanna ... is the most illustrious' (INT 61–2).

Why Neale chose the Church of Georgia for his setting is uncertain. Founded by St Nina in the fourth century, the Church remained for a long time dependent on the Patriarch of Antioch, finally becoming autocephalous in the eighth century. It is possible that Neale wanted to reaffirm the

---

[1] Neale's contributions, all anonymous, to this series were: *The Exiles of Cebenna* (1859); *The Lily of Tiflis* (1859); *The Lazar-House of Leros* (1859); *The Quay of Dioscuri* (1860); *The Sea Tigers* (1860); *Lucia's Marriage* (1860); *Larache* (1861); *The Daughters of Pola* (1861); and *Dolores de Gualdini* (1866).

[2] Neale's St Susanna should not be confused with St Shushanik, the account of whose life is the oldest surviving work of Georgian literature.

connection between the Anglican and Eastern Churches: both Georgia and England considered St George to be their patron saint. In addition, atrocities were committed in Georgia in the late eighteenth century, concerning which Neale would have been sympathetic. In 1783 Georgia became a protectorate of Russia; the latter was committed to defend the former and to uphold the authority of the Georgian monarchy. In 1795 the Persian ruler Aga Muhammad Shah captured and sacked Tiflis, and massacred the population, including some Russian subjects.[3] The Georgian Church, like the Constantinopolitan, had experienced persecution, and her faith—in Neale's perception —had never faltered, despite pressure from both within and without. In *Essays on Liturgiology and Church History* (1863) Neale spoke of the Georgian Church as 'a Church which resisted the artifices of Nestorians, Jacobites, and Armenians, produced countless martyrs under the invasions of Turks, Persians and Tartars, and formed the nucleus of a mighty empire during the thirteenth and fourteenth centuries.' His crowning epithet for the Church in Georgia was the title 'ever-orthodox', which conveyed the ideas of strict retention of traditional doctrine, fervency of faith, and the ability to withstand and eventually conquer her oppressors.[4] The last two of these ideas are special concerns in Neale's novel.

Most of the narrative is taken up with the sack by Meruan of Tiflis, modern Tbilisi, which Neale calls 'the Windsor of Georgia' (LOT 5). The Muhammadans in *The Lily of Tiflis*, like those in *Theodora Phranza*, succeed because they temporarily overcome nature: they divert the river Sivan by means of a dam built on Mount Ali Ghez. Most of Neale's narrative is concerned with the military campaign and sketches of Georgian scenery and landscape. Concerning the latter feature

---

[3] Seton-Watson, *Russian Empire*, 61.
[4] Neale, *Essays on Liturgiology*, 200. Information on Georgian Church history from Ware, *Orthodox Church*, 177. The word 'autocephalous' is applied to those churches which are self-governing and independent, including the four ancient patriarchates (of Constantinople, Alexandria, Antioch, and Jerusalem) as well as Russia, Greece, Georgia, Cyprus, etc. The annals of the Georgian Church must have been considered a potentially interesting subject not only for English readers, but for Russians as well: *The Lily of Tiflis* was translated into Russian in 1859, and, according to Neale, proved 'a perfect hit' (letter to Webb, in *Letters*, 311; dated 11 July 1859, from Sackville College).

there is an anecdote told by one of Neale's daughters concerning her father's powers of description:

> I remember, when staying at Cambridge with my father and mother in 1861, we were asked to lunch in King's College by George Williams, Oriental scholar and traveller. In the course of conversation he asked, 'By the way, Neale, when were you in Georgia?' My father replied, 'Never'; at which he expressed great surprise, remarking that he thought from the descriptions in *The Lily of Tiflis* that my father must have been out there.[5]

Neale's main concern, however, was martyrdom. As in *Theodora Phranza*, the Muslims are the fierce, cruel aggressors, advancing to terrorize the Church in Georgia: 'Never was Church so persecuted; sometimes by the fire-worshippers of Persia; sometimes by the Arian followers of Mobedach; sometimes by the Monophysites of Armenia; but chiefly the hordes of Mahometan conquerors' (LOT 6). Immediately following the capture of Tiflis there is neither pillaging nor bloodshed as in the siege of Constantinople. Instead, there is a gloomy, ominous calm, during which the Caliph's troops 'keep very fair discipline' (LOT 70). The Christians are apprehensive, however, because Meruan, whom Neale has earlier shown to be a tyrant, has not yet arrived. Susanna fears the Persian commander, and says to her husband, Prince Alexander, 'It makes me shudder when I think of him.... Pray, pray let us beware of him.' Being a soldier, the Prince is more stoical, and replies, 'If we are in his power, he is in God's' (LOT 71). In order to calm her, he points out that although they have suffered humiliation in defeat, they are safe, as are their children.

The children, Tamar, Nina, and the baby Ketevan, play an important part in producing the desired emotional effect on Neale's readers. The novel opens with the tender scene of three small children sleeping comfortably. At the time Neale does not disclose why he has begun with this description; he immediately shifts to the battle. Only towards the end does the reader realize that the vignette is taken from the night before Meruan's arrival, when Alexander comforts Susanna by

---

[5] Comment by Neale's daughter, appended to a letter dated Christmas Day, 1857, from Sackville College; in *Letters*, 300–1.

The Lily of Tiflis

saying, 'here we have our pets safe and sound: (Do you know, I really think that the baby is grown!)' (LOT 71). This tenderness stands in contrast to the fate which awaits them at the hands of Meruan.

In the morning the storm-clouds which follow the calm begin to gather. The viceregent Meruan arrives, calls Queen Susanna to him, and offers her a bargain: if she surrenders herself to Meruan for one night, then Tiflis shall be restored to the Christians. The following exchange reveals the virtue of the Christian woman and the vice of her Muslim captor:

'Nothing—nothing that you can say can move me to regard you otherwise than I do now, with horror, and contempt, and abhorrence that I cannot express. This from the Viceregent of the Prophet! Advice to dishonour a husband,—to sin against God,—to commit a crime that even your own law would punish with death!'

'Well,' said Meruan, 'you have my offer. Grant me this one thing, and make what conditions you will for your husband and yourself . . . your palace and kingdom shall be restored to you, and who, save ourselves, need know what a price was paid for it?' (LOT 74)

As in *Theodora Phranza* Neale clearly distinguishes between Christians and Muslims. Here the latter are pictured as transgressors of their own faith when it suits them. In another instance of laxity Neale notes that Motassem, a Persian general, has no qualms about drinking a glass of wine, because he was 'never too particular in obeying the laws of the Koran' (LOT 34).

As a result of Susanna's refusal, her husband is thrown into prison; she is returned to her apartment in the palace. Then begins her most painful trial; but whereas in previous tales, tortures endured for the sake of Christianity were exclusively physical, here Neale combines physical with mental torment of an unusual kind in describing a deed of faith. Susanna is chained to a wall; her youngest daughter Ketevan is then brought in:

A child's wail in the passage. A carpet was spread on the other side of the room, and poor little Ketevan, screaming with fear, was brought in by a soldier. She held out her little arms to her mother—imploring, with the inarticulate words of infancy, to be taken to her. The baby was then laid down on the carpet, a very light chain fastened round one of its ankles, and stapled in like manner to the wall. (LOT 77)

Because of the restraints, Susanna is unable to suckle her baby. She is then informed that she will not be allowed to feed her child until she has rung a bell placed by her; but ringing the bell would mean concession to Meruan's demand to join his harem. What follows is worthy of quotation, for in it Neale creates the most pathetic, moving scene in all his fiction:

'O God!' cried Susanna, as the door closed . . . and was immediately locked and barred—'give me grace to bear this bitter, bitter trial! O my baby, my own darling baby, how can I see you dying before my very eyes, and not help you?' She threw herself down by the side of her couch, covered her face with her hands, and, with sobs that quite shook her frame, called on God for help.

For a little while the infant, relieved from its immediate alarm, was quiet, and then fell asleep; and the mother prayed as earnestly, but more composedly. Half-an-hour—an hour—and hour-and-a-half went by, and still Ketevan slept on. It wanted but a little to mid-day . . . when with a start and a scream the baby woke.

And then came the mother's trial indeed. The poor little one saw her, stretched out its tiny arms, made every infantine effort to get to her, while the big tears of hunger stood in its eyes, and its screams were heart-breaking. For six hours the Christian Queen endured: sometimes hiding her face in a silent agony of sorrow, sometimes lavishing the tenderest words and phrases of that tender Georgian language on the poor little unconscious creature. Sometimes it seemed as if the struggle would be too much for her mind. 'O Lord Jesus,' she almost shrieked out, 'I will do anything, I will bear anything for Thee—Thou knowest it, O Lord—Thou canst see into the very depths of my heart—but have I any right to murder my infant?' And then a long pause of silence, broken only by the baby's wailing. 'O my own, my darling one, shall I never feel those dear little soft lips again? will you never draw your little life again from your poor mother? O God, if it be thy will that I should be thus tried, take my poor little baby out of the world! Thou wast Thyself a baby once, Thou knowest what hunger is. I do not ask Thee to spare me, only to deliver my infant from this misery.'

About six, two of Meruan's attendants entered the apartment, bringing a table and a small but sumptuous repast, and proceeded to set it down by the Queen.

Oh how she pleaded with them! 'Look! here are jewels: take them all! I promise you never to inform who has them—I promise you gold to your very heart's desire, if you will only bring her to me for ten minutes! As you were born of women yourselves, you cannot be men if you can look on such a sight and not be moved! For that God's sake whom we both worship, oh do, do, *do*.'

But to all her entreaties the cold, polite answer, 'We should wish to oblige you, Madam, but we dare not!'

And so she was left again to that sore agony. The child's wailing was lower now; the mother fondly hoped that its strength was already beginning to pass. But it pleased God to try his saint to the uttermost. (LOT 78-80)

The way in which mother and child suffer is important, for it demonstrates Neale's sensitivity to societal standing in the construction of his narrative (similarly, Theodora Phranza never suffers physical hardship). The scene also—perhaps unintentionally—softens the reader's impression of the Muslims, whom Neale generally portrays in a most unfavourable light. The Queen may be tortured mentally, but she suffers on a couch, and her baby starves to death on a specially provided carpet. It seems that Neale is making the scene acceptable to a culture for which questions of class were so central.

At this point Neale leaves the pathetic scene of the dying child and desperate mother, and shifts to Meruan's chamber. The Viceregent is perplexed by Susanna's stubbornness in refusing food; he is advised by Hafiz, an apostate, to send her for counselling to the patriarch Eustathius, who, he predicts, will advise her not to commit suicide. The prelate fulfils this prediction; but Susanna is motivated by her maternity: ' "You know not what you ask," cries Susanna, almost angrily. "My baby starving before my very eyes, and I to feast!" ' (LOT 81). She then intimates to him that she is troubled by what she believes is a failure by Jesus, the 'Martyr of martyrs', to sympathize with her grief and suffering on a human level. Eustathius offers comfort by explaining the nature of Jesus's own torment: 'Our Lord on the cross did take upon Himself, by His own almighty power, all the individual sufferings of His people to the end of the world; and that, as much more fully and perfectly than they suffer, as His human nature was perfect above theirs. Think of this, and the more you think of it, the more comfort it will give you' (LOT 82).

Whereas in other novels Neale's martyrs suffer their fates resolutely, here, through Susanna, he explores the psychological nature of suffering. Susanna's torment is more believable—and therefore more 'human'—than, for example, Margaret's in 'The Sacrifice of Onnontague'. The Queen's maternal instincts, those with which Neale's readers would readily associate, place her suffering on a comprehensible level. This is his most successful depiction of Christian torment, in which he reaches a deeper, more mature level of presentation of this dominant theme in his fiction.

Susanna's psychological dilemma is the point of greatest tension in The Lily of Tiflis; what follows is expected, and welcome by comparison. Neale spares his readers the details of Ketevan's death, only alluding to them: 'I have not the heart to go through the hours of that sad night: to tell you how sometimes the poor infant lay comparatively still, moaning its little life away; how sometimes its shrieks and cries pierced to the very heart of the mother; how gradually, towards morning, its strength and its cries grew hoarser, and its moanings lower' (LOT 83).[6] He emphasizes instead her spiritual departure from earthly existence, building to the crescendo with which the novel reaches its climax: 'A more glorious illumination now was that which was about to burst on those poor little dying eyes.... The guardian angel had fulfilled his charge, and was presenting Ketevan before the throne of God as the protomartyr of this persecution' (LOT 84–5). Ketevan's ascent to heaven is accompanied by bright sunshine and relief for Susanna, who realizes that she has made the right moral decision, and that her period of mental strife is now over.

Most of Neale's martyrs die in the knowledge that they have accomplished deeds worthy of a place in the kingdom of heaven; not so the infant Ketevan. Her slow, painful death serves as an example for her family of the cruelty of their Muslim captors, and prepares them for what they too must undergo; in a larger sense Neale is alluding to Christian persecution under Islamic rule, which continued in 1859. The

---

[6] Cf. the death of Agnes's baby in M. G. Lewis's *The Monk* (London, 1796), iii. 149–51. Like Susanna, Agnes is chained to the wall.

scene also draws upon the familiar theme of the dying child, all too familiar to Neale's Victorian readers.

After this climax Neale spends an additional chapter immortalizing Ketevan, who is now known to be the 'Lily' of the title. For this purpose he translates his reader to the monastery of the Studium, or Stoudion, in Constantinople, one of the centres of Greek hymnody, and which he praises in these words: 'All the learning, all the talent, all the literary power of the Eastern Church is here laid up as in a treasure house' (LOT 86). He focuses particularly on the hymnologist Theophanes (759–818), who, according to Neale, 'holds the third place among Greek Church-poets' after St John Damascene and Cosmas the Melodist (HEC 92). Most of his compositions were celebrations of the Eastern martyrs; Neale notes that Ketevan has been immortalized in a canon by Theophanes commemorating the Georgians who died for the name of Christ. He does not translate these verses in *Hymns of the Eastern Church*; nor, indeed, are they in current use in the Georgian Church.[7] But Neale says that thus was Ketevan's memory preserved: 'The living, burning words which fall from the old man's quill will be a portion of the inheritance of the Eastern Church for ever, and another proof that out of the mouth of babes and sucklings God has ordained praise' (LOT 87–8).

Neale might have done best to end the novel at this point, after bringing the action to a painful climax, then providing a satisfactory conclusion in Ketevan's ascent into the kingdom of God and her immortalization in a canon by one of the most famous Eastern hymnographers. But for the sake of rounding out his tale, he chronicles the fates of Alexander, Susanna, Tamar, and Nina. The Prince of Georgia is said to have been poisoned; Susanna and Tamar are beheaded together; and Nina is taken to Baghdad to join Meruan's harem. The details of these fates are hastily sketched, and the novel ends with Susanna 'reckoned among the Martyrs' (LOT 94).

The *Lily of Tiflis* was not polemical in the way that *Theodora Phranza* was, except in its emphasis on the Muslim capacity

---

[7] A diligent search was made with the kind assistance of Archimandrite Moir; but no canon fitting Neale's description was found.

for cruelty to Christians. Its aim—and that of the series to which it belonged—was to illustrate Church history. This Neale did, primarily in his account of the battle for Tiflis; the theme and setting appealed to English and Russian readers alike. Yet there were more fundamental elements in his novel: the depiction of human suffering and the psychological difficulties involved in certain moral decisions. It is in the exploration of these questions that Neale's protagonist comes closest to achieving Forster's roundness of character,[8] and it is this that, despite the hurried ending, makes *The Lily of Tiflis* his most successful oriental novel.[9]

[8] E. M. Forster distinguishes between 'flat' and 'round' characters. Flat characters are types or caricatures, creations which we cannot turn round and be presented with new aspects; in their purest form they are constructed round a single idea or quality. See *Aspects of the Novel* (Harmondsworth, 1990), 73–81.

[9] In one of Neale's scrapbooks there is a highly favourable review of *The Lily of Tiflis*. It says: ' "The Lily of Tiflis" is . . . the most thrilling in pathetic interest, the most perfect in artistic style, the loftiest and clearest in its teaching, of any of the series [*Tales Illustrating Church History*] that have yet appeared. Very picturesque are its descriptions of scenery, very lifelike its conversations and minor details; most graphic and touching are its incidents, most heart-stirring its final catastrophe. It would be difficult to praise too highly this brilliant sketch. . . . "The Lily of Tiflis" is an admirable example of the way in which a story taken from the lives of the Christian laity, and depending for its chief interest on its delineation of human loves, hopes, and fears, may be made to illustrate Church history' (MS 3112, fo. 129 [publication name and date unknown], Lambeth Palace Library).

Chapter 11

The Lazar-House of Leros

NEALE's last full-length Eastern novel was published in 1859, shortly after *The Lily of Tiflis* and as part of the same series. He tells two interconnected stories: one, with a historical basis, concerns the last years of Cyril Loukaris, or Lucar, Neale's hero in *The Patriarchate of Alexandria*; the other, which is fictional, follows the life of Sophia, a young girl from Leros, who becomes a Sister of Charity.[1] These stories fuse together two important themes in Neale's work and life: the vindication of an Eastern prelate who, Neale believed, had strong ties with the Anglican Church, and the promotion of Anglican nursing sisterhoods, one of which Neale had founded several years before writing this novel. Placing these concerns in a fictional framework accomplished two aims: in the case of Loukaris, it allowed Neale to place in his hero's mouth words which he might not actually have spoken, but which Neale could use to plead the Patriarch's case; whereas Sophia gave Neale a vehicle for psychological exploration of the motivations behind the religious life, in an effort to make it acceptable—and perhaps attractive—to his readers.

The novel opens in 1635 on the island of Leros in the Aegean Sea. Cyril has recently been deposed from his see, and has gone into exile. From the outset Neale articulates his sentiments concerning the Patriarch:

Poor Cyril Lucar! there is hardly a sadder history in the annals of the Church than his.... Originally a priest in Egypt, then Patriarch of Alexandria, he had bitterly lamented the fearful ignorance which

---

[1] It should be noted that the term which Neale uses to describe the community on Leros, 'Sisters of Charity', is not to be confused with the Roman Catholic order of that name. The term is not used by Orthodox communities. Neale was projecting his own idea onto Eastern experience, in an effort to employ a name that Western readers would understand.

prevailed in his Church, and his whole soul revolted against its enforced slavery to Mahometan tyrants. In an evil hour he had become acquainted with Calvinist divines, his superiors in learning, in civilization, in tact: he valued their friendship; he considered the differences between them and himself as immaterial; he sympathized with them in their opposition to Rome. When he was made, first guardian of the vacant see of Constantinople, and then Patriarch, he was brought into more immediate opposition with the Jesuits, and with those of the Eastern Church who were disposed to Latinise; and among the latter, Cyril Contari was his most bitter opponent. Offering an enormous bribe . . . to the Sultan . . . Anthemius of Adrianople was raised to the throne of Constantinople, and Cyril Lucar banished to Rhodes. (LHL 7–8)[2]

The Turkish galley which was taking him there put in at Leros, where most of Neale's action is set.

Neale does not intend the novel to be a reiteration of Loukaris's history; the summaries of Loukaris's activities, which appear at several points, briefly encapsulate his account in *A History of the Holy Eastern Church*, albeit combining them with some personal views which he considered it best to omit from the earlier work. These accounts serve as prefaces to Neale's primary concern in bringing Loukaris into *The Lazar-House of Leros*: the presentation of the personal, human side of the Patriarch. As Neale pointed out in his *History*, Loukaris was partly to blame for his own demise; but the Patriarch's intentions, Neale believed, were honourable and not at variance with his Orthodox faith. Yet he thought that Loukaris was victimized by various parties, and that his depositions and death were a result of the conflict among religious, political, and commercial interests at Constantinople in the seventeenth century. After providing some necessary background and elucidating his own position, Neale turns to the private side of Loukaris.

On his arrival on Leros, the Patriarch is greeted by the principal priest, Theopemptus. They tour the island, and come to the Lazar-house, or hospice for lepers, which is run by a

---

[2] The usual transliteration of the Patriarch's surname is Loukaris; this will be used here except in quotations from Neale, where his own 'Lucar' will be preserved.

small community of 'Basilian' nuns[3]—Sisters of Charity, as Neale calls them, reminiscent of his own Society of St Margaret. Loukaris, the gentle, caring ecclesiastic, wishes to visit the hospice to offer pastoral care, but is warned by the gatekeeper that those who enter can never leave. The point is driven home by the inscription from Dante over the portal: 'Abandon all hope, ye who enter here!' Loukaris has no choice but to return to the city.

He stays with Theopemptus, and meets the other protagonist: the priest's daughter Sophia. The prelate's first words are, 'Your name, my child, . . . must needs be a sad one to an Archbishop of Constantinople.' In his musing he continues: 'Yes, it reminds me of that holy and beautiful house where our fathers worshipped—more to be lamented than the Jewish temple for that was burnt, but not profaned; this serves every hour to the miserable worship of the false prophet' (LHL 14). Hagia Sophia, the epitome of Eastern Church architecture in Neale's opinion, is again recalled. In view of Sophia's later circumstances, Neale here prepares for her embodiment of what he considers one of the shining lights of the Orthodox faith: its monastic life. Sophia the Sister of Charity comes to symbolize the staunch faith and commitment of the Orthodox, which in turn is represented by Hagia Sophia, to which the citizens of Constantinople ran for succour when their city fell (TF 343–6). Loukaris also mentions the Islamic faith, which will play a part in Neale's tale, and which in Loukaris's day— as in Theodora's and Susanna's—brought Eastern Christians under its yoke.

The Patriarch is not idle during his visit to Leros. First he is asked to conduct the marriage ceremony for Theopemptus's other daughter. Then he is informed that Sophia has expressed a desire to become a Sister of Charity at the lazaretto rather than at a convent. Loukaris gives encouragement, describing ministry to the lepers as 'a great work' and 'so high a calling'

---

[3] The rationale for Neale's use of the world 'Basilian' is that same as for his use of 'Sister of Charity': he wished to employ a name that Western readers would understand. The Orthodox do not use the term 'Basilian' to describe their religious, though Orthodox monks follow the rule of St Basil. See ch. 11, n. 1.

(LHL 15, 16). He talks to Sophia about her perceived vocation. After seeing that she is firm in her conviction and that she realizes the suffering which the new life will entail, he grants her his blessing, saying, 'Now that I have given your sister to an earthly bridegroom, I feel I have more right to plead that you may give yourself to a Heavenly One' (LHL 21). After accomplishing this work, Loukaris leaves Leros for Rhodes.

Sophia's first action is to give thanks for the fulfilment of her desire; this she does in her room, before an icon of the Saviour. Icons, which Neale presents at the beginning and end of Sophia's new life, are an element in Orthodox devotion which he has not previously explored in his fiction. Even in his *General Introduction*, where he considers the minutiae of Eastern ecclesiology, Neale discusses the iconostasis, not the icons themselves; he explains only that 'the iconostasis derives its name from the icons there depicted' (INT 192). But even in this vignette of Sophia giving thanks in her room, he does not enter into the details of Orthodox reverence for icons. His reticence stems from his desire to present the Eastern Church—a relatively unknown branch of Christianity as far as his readers are concerned—in a favourable light; and by avoiding icons, he spared himself the possibility of being accused of portraying image worship, which some Anglicans, among them Bishop Gilbert Turner of Chichester, perceived as a Romanist practice.

Because of the Bishop's prohibition, Neale could say little under his own name concerning the prelate's attitudes. But when Turner issued a pamphlet in 1852 condemning the incumbent of St Paul's Church, Brighton, for image worship, Neale felt that he had to speak out; he therefore published an anonymous letter, entitled *Pictorial Crucifixes*, in which he reproved the Bishop for promoting teaching which was 'perilous to the salvation of those poor, to whom, above all others, the Gospel is preached'. In no uncertain terms Neale chided Turner for his insufficient knowledge of the poor:

Now, your Lordship's complete and unconcealed ignorance, that to a large number of the poor, (those namely, who reached adult age before the establishment of Sunday or National Schools), the Gospel can only be preached by means of pictures; this, I say, is one among other proofs that you never yourself were intimately acquainted with the labours, and therefore could never acquire the experience of a Parish Priest.

He illustrated the Bishop's 'ignorance' through the reaction of a labourer to Turner's sermon in East Grinstead Parish Church: 'When I afterwards inquired... whether he had not been pleased with your Charge, his reply was, He had no doubt it was very good, but how should be understand such fine long words?'

What Neale advocated was the use of images for the instruction of the poor. If properly employed, visual aids such as the crucifix could produce significant results:

> I will give you an example which occurred in my own parish, and only last year. There was a labourer at least as well educated as most of his class, who lived near the Church, who was a constant attendant there, who was an occasional communicant. This man, on Good Friday, happened to be in the cottage while a visitor of his own rank was explaining to his child some prints on the subject of our LORD's Passion. After listening for some time:—'What,' he exclaimed, 'you don't mean to say, that they fastened him up with nails to a Cross alive?' On being reminded that it was so indeed, he continued; I give his very own words: 'Poor thing, how it must have hurt Him!' Now, here was a case in which a man who had heard lesson after lesson, and sermon after sermon, for forty or fifty years, was most completely ignorant of the way in which our Salvation was brought to pass, but for one of these pictorial crucifixes which your Lordship considers unscriptural, would have remained so to his dying day.[4]

Likewise in *The Lazar-House of Leros* Neale supported the use of images for religious instruction. Icons, of course, were not part of his English readers' tradition; yet he hoped that they would appreciate the parallel. In order to emphasize the point, he had to assign to the icons added significance; this he did in his relation of Sophia's death.

After giving his heretofore serious tale a taste of the picaresque through the capture of Theopemptus's son Constantine by pirates, Neale returns to Sophia, who deems herself ready for what she calls in the words of the twenty-third Psalm, her journey 'down into the valley of the shadow of death' (LHL 29). A strange, ecumenical induction ceremony takes place,

---

[4] [J. M. Neale], *Pictorial Crucifixes* (London, 1852), 3, 7, 8–9.

involving Roman Catholics, Orthodox, and Muslim Turks. As Sophia climbs the mountain of St Lazarus, at the top of which lies the hospice, she stops at three altars. Each time she is questioned about her intentions. The first is presided over by the proto-Pope, the second by the hegumen (abbot) of a monastery in the city, and the third by the Orthodox Bishop of Naxos. Of the last of these, Neale, with ecclesiological interest, says, 'Vested for the Liturgy, he wore those gorgeous robes, compared with which the splendour of the Latin Church is but dimness' (LHL 35).

Neale's catalogue of the bishop's vestments forms part of a technique which he occasionally uses in his fiction. At various points in his narrative he inserts brief sketches of rituals, doctrines, vestments, or ornaments which are peculiarly Orthodox. In *Theodora Phranza* he attempts such a description in the marriage scene of Theodora and de Rushton in Hagia Sophia; but the effect is marred by brevity. In *The Lazar-House of Leros*, by contrast, Neale uses the technique extensively, first in the marriage ceremony of Theopemptus's daughter, then in the brief scene involving Sophia and the icon, and later in the ceremony of her induction. Neale continues concerning the Bishop's vestments and the surrounding ecclesiastical furnishings:

The alb and phelonion, and stole glittered with precious stones— though it was whispered... that the rapacity of Turkish exactions had been met by the substitution of glass for some of the larger brilliants—and on his right side he wore the epigonation—for which the Western Church has no equivalent—intended to symbolize the warfare with Satan, and correspond to that verse, 'Gird thee with thy sword upon thy thigh, O Thou most Mighty.[5] In front of the altar, and to the right of the Bishop, was a lectern, elaborately carved, in teak-wood—and on this lectern lay open a manuscript of the Gospels: it was bound in oak, backed with hog-skin of an enormous thickness, studded with gems; and the clasps, and corners, and scutcheons, of pure silver, were stamped with the impress of the Panaghia [sic] and other saints. (LHL 35)[6]

[5] This verse is said by Orthodox priests on putting on the *epigonation*.
[6] *Panhagia*, 'All Holy One', is a name by which the Virgin Mary is known in the Greek Orthodox Church, and is the one almost always used in ordinary speech. Neale's peculiar transliteration of the word is *Panaghia*; see also INT 942.

Other aspects of Orthodoxy are conveyed through asides to the reader, such as that concerning the Lent provisions for the lazar-house: 'You must remember that the discipline of the Eastern Church was so terribly strict, as not even in the case of illness, such as that of St Lazarus, to relax the obligation or the kind of fasting' (LHL 46), or through Neale's notes, such as the one appended to Sophia's exclamation about the *Triodia* ('How richly they are bound! and what glorious clasps!'): 'The Triodion contains the offices of the Eastern Church from the Sunday of the Pharisee and Publican, that is, the Sunday before Septuagesima, till Easter-day inclusive' (LHL, 47).[7] Some explanations, like this last one, are perhaps unnecessary, or are clumsily inserted; nevertheless, these attempts at elucidation of Orthodox ritual form an interesting aspect of Neale's novel. Not only was he sketching Church history, but he was concurrently describing some of the minutiae of the ecclesiology, doctrine, and observance of a communion with which most of his readers were unfamiliar.

Neale's descriptions of Orthodoxy were not always accurate. In his attempt to relate Eastern ecclesiology to the more familiar Western arrangement, however, Neale sometimes misleads. Thus, in the scene in which Sophia—who changed her name to Agatha on taking the nun's habit—goes to the church to pray for her brother Constantine, he says that she prayed 'before the icon of the Panaghia [*sic*] on the rood-screen' (LHL 54).

There is an interesting fusion of traditions at one point in the novel, a Western form being used to illustrate an Eastern rite. Athanasia, a girl of 17, dies in the hospice, and during the Eastern funeral office, when the mourners in turn kiss the corpse, the 'Stichera of the Last Kiss' are sung. The translation of these verses, which Neale quotes in full, is in fact his own hymn 'Take the last kiss,—the last for ever', which he published three years after *The Lazar-House of Leros* as part of *Hymns of the Eastern Church*. The later version differs only in the substitution of the masculine pronoun for the feminine in the novel.

---

[7] Neale is mistaken: the *Triodion* does not include the offices for Easter Day.

> Take the last kiss,—the last for ever!
> Yet render thanks amidst your gloom.
> She, sever'd from her home and kindred,
> Is passing onwards towards the tomb:
> For earthly labours, earthly pleasures,
> And carnal joys, she cares no more:
> Where are her kinsfolk and acquaintance?
> They stand upon the other shore.
> Let us say, around her press'd,
> Grant her, Lord, eternal rest!
>
> (LHL 64)

The hymn is included for two reasons. First, as in *Hymns of the Eastern Church*, it demonstrates, through a Western hymnological form, that the Orthodox Church and its rites are not as foreign to British sensibilities as they might at first seem; as has been shown, this process of familiarization was Neale's purpose throughout his collection of Greek hymns. Secondly, the inclusion of this hymn in his novel represents part of the many-sided approach which Neale took to give his readers a better understanding of the Eastern Church. This process of education in *The Lazar-House of Leros* resembles an experiment: whereas in his hymn collection Neale was dealing with only one aspect of Eastern tradition, and therefore using one literary form for its transmission, here he is unsure about which presentation will be most effective, so he tries many different techniques, in the hope that one or more will appeal to the reader's sensibility.

The novel then turns to the demise of Cyril Loukaris. If there were doubts about Neale's feelings for the Patriarch, he now dispels them: 'Poor Cyril Lucar! I confess that, notwithstanding all his faults (and they were not few) I have a strong regard for him' (LHL 66). After describing the difficult situation with which Loukaris had to contend on his fourth and last reinstatement to the patriarchate, he places the blame for Loukaris's apparently heretical statements in the *Confession of Faith* (1629) on the Dutch and French Calvinists, who were 'most eager to prove that the sentiments of the Greek Church on the Blessed Eucharist coincided with their own'; they therefore 'wrung from him a confession of Faith containing several expressions which seemed to run contrary to the

Catholic belief on the mystery'. Sir Thomas Rowe, the British ambassador in Archbishop Abbot's time who aided in Loukaris's first reinstatement, is also snubbed by Neale for coaxing the Patriarch to provide tangible proof of his approval of reformed theology. Archbishop Laud, another of Neale's heroes, is praised, however, for trying to put a stop to 'the coqueting which had been carried on with the foreign Protestant communities'. Those who are given the harshest treatment by Neale are the Jesuits, who, he claimed, 'had determined, since Cyril, to use their own expression, rose after each deposition like a cork out of the water, to procure that kind of deposition which would not be terminable till the Resurrection' (LHL 67).

This kind of harsh, pointed criticism is not found in his *History of the Holy Eastern Church*, where he records, in more guarded terms, that 'His enemies, finding that the banishments of Cyril did not advance their own views, determined on his death' (ALX ii. 453). Such differences in Neale's accounts of Loukaris point to a more personal view in *The Lazar-House of Leros*, one which would have been outside the realms of historical propriety and fact in his *History of the Holy Eastern Church*.

Neale then returns to the private Loukaris, who, while walking with his domestic chaplain, Paisius, through Constantinople, meets Theopemptus's son Constantine. The boy relates the story of his kidnapping, travels, imprisonment, and, currently, his enslavement to Musa Pasha, governor of Constantinople. The Patriarch promises that he will try to effect the boy's release. Constantine departs, after Neale has presented a benevolent Loukaris, who has not forgotten the kindness of Theopemptus and now wishes to do all he can for Constantine.

Loukaris continues his walk, reaching Hagia Sophia, the fate of which he had earlier lamented in the company of Sophia/Agatha. The following conversation ensues between Loukaris and Paisius:

'How beautiful it is!' said the Patriarch, but rather to himself than to his companion—'how beautiful it is!' as they came in sight of the dome of St Sophia, 'my own cathedral; I marvel whether it will ever be restored to the worship of the Orthodox Church.'

'Of a surety it will be,' replied Paisius. 'I firmly believe in the old prophecy, that four hundred years will see the extinction of the Mahometan rule.'

'It may be so,' replied the other, 'for even now, methinks, one can see that this great empire is tottering.' (LHL 69)

Neale reiterates his expectation, first expressed in the 1857 preface to *Theodora Phranza*. He foresees the weak Ottoman Empire crumbling, and that his—and Loukaris's—beloved church will be restored to its sacred purpose. In 1859 Neale had not rescinded his hope for Christian freedom in the Turkish dominions, despite the outcome of the Crimean War and the Treaty of Paris.

Neale continues with his version of the Patriarch's private thoughts. He gives Loukaris an apologia, in which his actions and statements are justified to the reader:

All my life long Rome has shewn me her worst and unkindest side; it may be that the Protestants have shewn me their best. I have not knowingly and wilfully gone beyond what our Eastern Church tolerates at least; but this I willingly acknowledge, that I have stated our doctrines so far as to make them as little offensive as possible to the reformed communions.... If I should be taken away from this world—and God cannot call me sooner than I am willing to go—I hope there will be some one who will do justice to my memory. (LHL 70)

Loukaris's last wish is fulfilled in the above passage, which sums up Neale's thoughts about his hero. Because of what he has already admitted about Loukaris's faults, his death—which Neale does not consider a martyrdom—seems believable and pathetic, yet almost a welcome end to a life which has known so much strife.

The murder of Loukaris is connected to the fictional portion of *The Lazar-House of Leros* through Constantine, who overhears his master saying that Cyril of Beroea, Loukaris's rival, has bribed the governor to commit the crime while pretending to take the Patriarch into retirement on the Prince's islands. All this would be done in order to proclaim the rival as the undisputed Ecumenical Patriarch. Constantine hurries to tell Loukaris, and manages to do so just as the prelate is about to set sail. Loukaris, however, tired of torment, sees no alternative but to get into the boat and accept his fate with calm resolution. Once at sea his conductors hand him his death-warrant, strangle him, and throw his body overboard.

For Constantine, because of his courageous and beneficent effort, there is surely a heavenly reward. For Loukaris, says Neale, there is no way of knowing for certain because of his chequered career. He does, however, leave his readers with his private thoughts on the fate of Loukaris's soul:

Let us hope that all his weaknesses, which were many, his mistakes, which we can see plainly enough, his sins, which history has taken especial care to record, were not in the last moment of his life regarded by the great Judge in Whose presence he was about to pass. Let us hope that his many and earnest prayers—for even his enemies could speak of his well-known devotion—then rose up for him, and cried to the throne of God; that his alms, which had been most abundant, delivered him from death and purged away all sin, fought on his side better than a sword or a strong spear; that his deep humility and repentance when he had seen himself to be wrong, was accepted for those faults likewise, for which, had he known them to be faults, would have offered them also. 'If Thou, Lord, shouldest be extreme to mark what is amiss, who may abide it?'
. . . .
For my own part, when I think of the troubles that were about to fall on his Church, I cannot doubt that the righteous was taken away from the evil to come. I firmly believe that, notwithstanding his errors, of him too it might be said, 'The souls of the just are in the hand of God, and there shall no torment touch them.' (LHL, 86-7)

Neale's own assessment and hopes for the Patriarch are not forced on the reader: the latter is left to form his own opinion after weighing the evidence with which he has been presented. Neale's reserve on this point is also seen in *The Patriarchate of Alexandria*, where he says that 'we utterly reject the ... idea that he died as a Saint and a Martyr'; yet,

Considering what he did and what he suffered, the strength of his enemies, the weakness of his friends, the power of his early associations, the unkindness and unfairness of Rome, the bitterness of his persecutors, his own meekness, and patience, and great humility, and using towards him that charity of judgment which we should ourselves desire, we are justified in believing, that, notwithstanding his many errors, —

After life's fitful fever, he sleeps well. (ALX ii. 455)

In both *The Lazar-House of Leros* and *A History of the Holy Eastern Church* Neale wanted to vindicate a man who was perceived by some to be a heretic, but to him was a hero, who displayed many human failings, but had many outstanding qualities as well.[8]

The Loukaris strand, while an integral part of Neale's plan for the novel, is nevertheless a sub-plot, and occupies a secondary position when compared with the Sophia strand. Loukaris is denied access to *The Lazar-House of Leros* of the title; he is therefore excluded from about one-third of the narrative. The hospice is reserved for Sophia (now Agatha) and for her martyrdom, with which the novel ends.

That Agatha will soon die becomes apparent shortly after her acceptance into the sisterhood. She befriends Fatima, a Muslim girl who has come to the lazaretto with leprosy. Agatha hopes for her conversion; but Neale steps in to explain that it was a dangerous aspiration: 'You must remember that, for the most part, the spirit of the Eastern Church had been so thoroughly crushed in the islands of the archipelago, that to hold her own was the height of her ambition; while to make converts, entailing as it did such fearful consequences, was considered quite out of the question' (LHL 59). With this warning Neale marks the beginning of the end for Agatha. His comments also help to explain the lack of Muslim conversions in his other stories. The Muhammadans, cruel aggressors in Constantinople and Tiflis, would surely, Neale implies, make life harder than it already was for the Christians under their control if conversions from Islam were widespread.

[8] There are parallels in Victorian fiction to Neale's treatment of Loukaris. Bulwer Lytton, in *Rienzi, the Last of the Tribunes* (1835), *The Last of the Barons* (1843), and *Harold, the Last of the Saxon Kings* (1848), and Harriet Martineau, in *The Hour and the Man*, both use the historical novel as a means of initiating a re-evaluation of a particular personage, hitherto looked upon unfavourably. Simmons points out that in *Rienzi* Lytton was primarily concerned with salvaging the Tribune's character from the 'superficial and unfair' treatment by Gibbon; also, in *The Last of the Barons* he criticized David Hume (in the notes to the novel) as 'hasty', 'inaccurate', and 'more than ordinarily incorrect' (*Novelist as Historian*, 43). Although *Hypatia* and *Theodora Phranza* also sought to redress the balance of history in light of Gibbon's unfavourable presentation, in those novels there is not as marked an emphasis on the individual historical figures and the vindication of their characters as there is here in *The Lazar-House of Leros* and in the novels of Lytton and Martineau.

The Lazar-House of Leros alternates between Loukaris and Agatha. When Neale next returns to the lazaretto, it is to cement the bond between Fatima and Agatha. At first the two girls form 'a striking contrast with each other' (LHL 71), not only because of Fatima's affliction compared with Agatha's good health, but also because of their different religions. But this soon changes: Fatima is baptized; Agatha is made her godmother; and the Turkish girl takes Agatha's former name, Sophia. Thus the ties which bind them together—in life as well as in impending death—are complete.

The end of the novel is near. Neale completes the Loukaris sub-plot with the Patriarch's pathetic death; but before switching to Agatha, he interjects: 'When I first began this story I did not mean that it should be half so melancholy a one as it has turned out. It seems as if I had nothing but death to write about, and I cannot hold out any hopes to you that its conclusion will be at all more cheerful' (LHL 87).[9] In light of what we have seen so far of Neale's fiction, this comment seems strangely out of place: most of his stories either end in death or present death as the predominant theme. His self-consciousness concerning *The Lazar-House of Leros* is a result of his experimentation in combining more complex themes than ever before: propaganda for the religious life, apologetics for Cyril Loukaris, various presentations of Orthodox Church doctrine and practice, and finally martyrdom. The last of these themes, which Neale had developed to a finer point than the others—and because of its desirability as a standard Victorian fictional set piece—was the most fitting one with which to end.

Fatima (now Sophia) grows gradually weaker as a result of her disease, and finally expires after being given the sacrament of extreme unction. Her short-tempered, violent brother, Ali Bey, appears at the lazaretto, having been told by an informer that Fatima died as a Christian. Neale notes that

[9] Neale continues: 'What can I do for you? why this: I will promise that the next story I tell you of the Eastern Church shall be a far more cheerful one. I have, as the drapers say of their ribbons, a large assortment; you shall have a brighter colour next time' (LHL 87). Neale never kept the promise concerning the Orthodox Church; his subsequent 'Tales Illustrating Church History' were set in the West; but the novel which followed *The Lazar-House of Leros*, *Lucia's Marriage* (1860) did have a happier ending.

conversion was a capital offence in those days, not only for the Muslim concerned but also for any one who assisted in it—in this case Agatha and the hegumene. The latter confronts Ali Bey, and on learning that his source was the report of an informer, says: 'That they have done this thing gives me the honour of martyrdom; they deliver me from the slow and tedious death which is coming upon me, and translate me in a moment to that land of which we are even now denizens, to which belong our hope and our love.' (LHL 90–1).

At this point Agatha, seeing that the Turk is going to kill the hegumene, steps forward, saying that it was she who led Fatima towards conversion. She is shot, but does not die instantly; rather, she is taken to her room, where she dies alone, as is the custom for religious of the Orthodox Church. The icon, which has played a part in Agatha's religious devotion before, is again presented here: the deathbed ritual involves suspending it before Agatha's eyes, so that her 'last glance may rest on the image of the Crucified' (LHL 93).

Agatha's death is described too hurriedly by Neale, when compared with that of Loukaris. It seems that after his apology for dwelling on melancholy subjects, he wishes to end the novel as quickly as possible. If Neale had spent more time describing Agatha's martyrdom, the effect on the reader would have been more pronounced. The death scene is weak when compared with those of Loukaris, Susanna, Ketevan, or the prisoners outside the walls of Constantinople. There are, however, some important points to be made about what Neale was trying to do in his ending.

One consideration is that, like Legh Richmond in *The Dairyman's Daughter*, he may have been drawing on personal experience in describing Agatha's death. He might have had in mind Amy Scobell, a sister of his own Society of St Margaret, who died of typhus in November 1857.[10] The lives of the members of Neale's community were in real danger from the infectious diseases transmitted by those for whom they cared. Sister Miriam cites cases from the 1850s in which the nuns developed whooping cough, typhus, and scarlet fever; some of

---

[10] Neale's memoranda on Sr. Amy's last hours are recorded in Sr. Miriam, 109d–13d.

The Lazar-House of Leros

them continued to care for their patients despite the inherent peril to themselves.[11] Their determination in duty and in benevolence resembles that of Neale's Agatha.

In these severe trials the sisters said that they drew their strength from their founder and chaplain, Neale. He wrote them letters of counsel and encouragement, visited them when he could, and ensured that they were provided with basic comforts while engaged in 'cottage nursing'. In one instance, on seeing that a sister's sleeping place leaked badly when it rained, despite his order for repairs, Neale got up on the roof and did the job himself. Such deeds earned him these praises from Sister Miriam: 'That was one of his especial gifts: the power of lifting people up above their natural selves, and heartening them to do heroic acts.'[12] Given the esteem in which Neale was held by his community, there may have been something of Neale's character in his portrayal of Cyril Loukaris as encouraging Sophia to enter the lazar-house of Leros and become a Basilian nun.

The kind of nursing sister which Neale makes Agatha out to be is echoed in a sermon which Neale delivered to his community in 1857; it emphasized the potential for leadership and guidance among religious: 'Dear Sisters, each of you must be God's appointed light in the sorrow of others. "That we may be able to comfort them who are in any trouble with the comfort wherewith we ourselves are comforted of God." There it is. It is to a sad, dark, cold world that you go out: and in that world, what is the very vocation of a Sister of Mercy, but to give comfort and light?'[13] In her care for the lepers, Agatha provides comfort; in converting Fatima, she teaches the Turkish girl to see the light.

In his portrayal of Agatha and her community, Neale may also have been drawing on reports of the Russian nursing sisters who served in the Crimean War. The Russian Sisters of Mercy[14] faced much greater danger than their British or

---

[11] Sr. Miriam, 318b–19b; see also Anon., *Doing the Impossible* (East Grinstead, 1980), 17–20.
[12] Sr. Miriam, 320b.
[13] J. M. Neale, 'The Virtuous Woman', in *Sermons Preached in a Religious House*, ed. J. Haskoll (4 vols., London, 1869–74), ii. 407.
[14] Russian Sisters of Mercy are nothing to do with the Roman Catholic order of that name.

French counterparts: whereas Florence Nightingale and her assistants worked in the comparative safety of the Bosphorus, Alexandra Stakhovich and her order of the Exaltation of the Cross tended the wounded in the besieged city of Sebastopol. Both Russian and Allied nurses worked in an atmosphere rife with typhus and other diseases; but the Russian sisters ran the additional risk of working under battle conditions. On account of their dangerous circumstances, they were singled out for special treatment by Neale: 'If England sent her Sisters of Mercy, if France despatched her *Soeurs de la charité*, to Scutari and Balaclava, both France and England saw Russia encourage her Basilian nuns to stand ankle-deep in blood in the hospital at Sebastopol during the awful cannonade that preceded the fall of its southern side.'[15] Agatha's courage was of the same kind.[16]

The threat to Agatha's life culminates in her death from the fatal gunshot. In her death she performs a double act of faith: first, she saves the life of the hegumene by accepting responsibility for Fatima's conversion; then, in her martyrdom, she assures herself a place in the kingdom of heaven by dying for what she believed, undaunted by the imposing figure of the Turk. She is a hero in Neale's eyes; but his account of her fortitude is marred by its brevity.

Neale supplements the martyrdom and his personal concerns with a brief deathbed scene. Such a lingering demise is unusual for a writer who prefers to kill his characters quickly;[17] but, picking up on a technique which was evolving in Scott, Neale uses an icon, which has twice before been mentioned as the focus of Agatha's prayers, as the narratological device which interprets the Eastern plot for the intelligent Western reader. At this important moment he does not attempt to describe

---

[15] Neale, *Essays on Liturgiology*, 257.

[16] It should be noted (in connection with Russia) that after the Crimean War two Russian ladies were sent by the Orthodox Church to East Grinstead to learn about nursing religious. They returned to Russia, hoping to found communities along the same lines as St Margaret's (information from anon., *Doing the Impossible*, 57).

[17] See Lukács, *Historical Novel*, 63–4. Ketevan's slow death is not of the same type as Agatha's: the infant, who at such an early age possesses the powers neither of speech nor of understanding, is incapable of acting in a deathbed scene of the type which has previously been described.

the 'image of the Crucified'—even though Agatha's eyes are riveted to it. Perhaps fear of accusations of image worship were at the root of his reticence. The solitary death in the Orthodox tradition differs from the experiences of Neale's readers. But Neale uses this to show his Victorians audience, for whom the moment of death was so important, how Orthodox tradition could differ completely from Western in this point, yet be equally edifying and profound.

The Lazar-House of Leros is a many-faceted novel. It is complex in structure and ambitious in its aims. As a vehicle for promoting the religious life it is a success, because of Agatha's firm resolution to join the sisterhood, her acts of charity in the hospice, and, as a reward, her success in converting Fatima and assurance of a place in the kingdom of heaven. As an apologetic for Cyril Loukaris's life and actions the novel is also a success, because of its consistent portrayal of the Patriarch's character, its honesty concerning his faults, and the candid, personal remarks by Neale himself. As a presentation of various aspects of Orthodox tradition, however, it is only a qualified success: there is no pattern to the points considered, and the methods used are various, including notes, interjections, stray comments made by characters, and detailed description. The ending, as we have seen, is unsatisfying, and detracts from the effect of the successes on the reader.

Yet *The Lazar-House of Leros* is a highly original work. Subtitled *A Tale of the Eastern Church in the Seventeenth Century*, the novel ventures on to territory not previously explored by Victorian novelists. Neale may not have been wholly successful in his attempt to familiarize readers with the Orthodox tradition, but the task was difficult, and his attempt remarkable.

Chapter 12

Short Stories

NEALE's two shorter pieces, 'Erick's Grave' (1845) and 'The Story of S. Metrophanes of Voronej' (1850), preceded the three works already considered. They are included in this discussion for two reasons: for the sake of completeness and as early examples of orientalism in Neale's fiction.

'Erick's Grave' appeared in a collection entitled *Triumphs of the Cross: Tales and Sketches of Christian Heroism*. It is set in Russia at an unspecified time, and concerns a servant, Erick, who is travelling in a sledge with his master, Baron Jaroslav, and the master's family. Before reaching their destination, they observe a pack of wolves following them. Gradually the animals approach the sledge, and the mood becomes tense. The Baron has a gun; but he could not hope to kill all the wolves. The pack suddenly attack the party; the Baron fires, and the animals grow fiercer. Finally Erick, realizing that the wolves will not be satisfied until they have a victim, volunteers to jump from the sledge and keep the animals occupied, while the Baron and his family make for the next village. He takes the gun and jumps; the master, who is racing away, hears a single shot, and then the growling of the wolves, which gradually fades.

On reaching the village, Baron Jaroslav and his family praise God and give thanks for Erick, who sacrificed himself for them. He has no grave, for he was devoured by the wolves; but Neale thinks it unimportant that his earthly remains have no resting-place. What is important is the soul of the man, which returns to its Maker at the time of death. But Erick is not forgotten on earth: the Jaroslav family will preserve his memory for his unselfish Christian act.

There is a moral to this tale: 'And what are you to learn from this story? What but this? If there have been found those who were willing, for their friends' sake, to give up the dearest thing they had, even their life, will you not be ashamed at your selfishness in being unwilling to give up the very smallest trifle for those you love? It is all very well to *read* of the Triumphs of the Cross, but when will you *show* them?'[1] As in his other tales concerning deeds of Christian faith, Neale advocates his readers' emulating these heroes in their own small way, thereby ensuring for themselves a place in the kingdom of heaven.

'Erick's Grave', though set in the Christian East, does not distinguish clearly between Eastern and Western traditions, and as a result, questions may be raised concerning its status as a tale of the Orthodox Church. The story appeared in a collection which treated tales of Christian heroism in a wider sense: triumphs of the Cross in the context of the universal Church. The message—the emulation of Christian martyrs—is not confined to a specific tradition, and is of the kind which appeared in many of Neale's published works. But the story is significant, because it is the only one of Neale's oriental tales which is not set within the confines of history; it therefore falls within the realm of what Wright, in *Theology and Literature*, calls 'narrative theology'.[2]

'Erick's Grave' is Christian faith proclaimed in a narrative form; as such, it perhaps distinguishes itself as a tale specifically of the Russian Orthodox Church. Pascal, in *The Religion of the Russian People*, considers a phenomenon which would help to explain why Neale's tale is not only Orthodox, but also Russian: the *podvig*, or 'exploit'. This is Christian heroism which sometimes culminates in total sacrifice, thereby fulfilling the precept laid down in the Gospel, 'Greater love hath no man than this, that a man lay down his life for his friends' (John 15: 13). The example is cited of a child's nurse, 70 years old, who saved her charge from a carriage rushing towards them by lying on top of the child, so that her body was crushed and trampled by the horses, while the infant survived. Pascal explains that such deeds are not limited to Russians; what is particularly Russian, though, is 'the sense

---

[1] J. M. Neale, 'Erick's Grave', in *Triumphs of the Cross* (London, 1845), 173.
[2] Wright, *Theology and Literature*, 83.

that the Gospel is there to be put into practice. More than most peoples the Russians are scandalized by disparity between teaching and conduct.'³ This elucidation helps to explain Neale's moral in 'Erick's Grave', where he asks the reader when he will *show* (Neale's emphasis) the triumphs of the Cross. It is perhaps the Russian idea of *podvig* which Neale wished to present in his tale.

In his other short story, 'The Story of S. Metrophanes of Voronej', Neale added more flesh to the frame of an Eastern setting by using a historical basis. Set again in Russia, in 1710, the tale describes the final stages of construction of a small palace of Peter the Great near the city of Voronej, where the Emperor had established shipyards for strengthening his navy. Metrophanes, first Bishop of Voronej, is summoned for a consultation by Peter to the palace, in front of which the monarch was erecting statues of heathen divinities—among them Venus and Mars. The Bishop refuses the invitation, saying that he will not cross the threshold until the statues are removed. Fearing the wrath of the Emperor, Metrophanes begins to prepare in earnest for death, and orders the bells to be rung for evening service. When Peter hears them, he sends to enquire why they are being rung; on learning that the Bishop has ordered it so that he may celebrate vespers for the last time and thus better prepare himself for death, Peter laughs as if it were a joke, and orders the offensive statues to be removed.

The substance of Neale's account came either from Muraviev's *History of the Church of Russia* (1842) or from the latter's source for the anecdote, Demetrius of Rostov's *Lives of the Russian Saints* (1836, published only in Russian). The main outline of the story is the same in all three; but Neale, while acknowledging Metrophanes' notability as 'a zealous and uncompromising maintainer of the doctrines of the Church, in defence of which he was ready to have laid down his life', in Muraviev's words,[4] concentrated instead on the statues and the effect produced on the populace. He wished to emphasize their feelings of horror at the prospect of pagan

[3] P. Pascal, *The Religion of the Russian People* (London, 1976), 33.
[4] Mouravieff, *History of the Church of Russia*, ed. W. Palmer, trans. R. W. Blackmore (Oxford, 1842), 258. For Muraviev's account of the 'idol episode', see pp. 401–2.

images being placed at the portals of a Christian emperor's palace. Some snippets of conversation are recorded:

> 'Is he really going to set them up?'
> 'Are they really and truly idols?'
> 'I am sure they are. They used to worship them a hundred years ago.'
> 'I shall go—I am afraid to stay.'
> 'Perhaps he is going to break them up.'
> 'No, by S. Jonah, look! he is pointing to where they are to stand.'

(SSM 96)

Neale tries to convey the fear which Orthodox Christians had of what he calls 'images'. In addition to speeches by various characters, he inserts an explanatory paragraph:

I must tell you that the Eastern Church has so great a fear of breaking the Second Commandment, that not even in churches are the images of Saints allowed. We here are so sadly used to read and hear of heathen gods and goddesses, whose lives were an abomination—we are so used to see their images or their features, that we can hardly imagine the horror which those Russian peasants felt when they saw these statues of Venus and Mars, and learnt that they were idols. (SSM 95)

It is surprising that Neale does not distinguish an 'image'—by which he means a statue—from an icon. The words are different in the Greek Septuagint version of Exodus 20: 4, the key text, which forbids the making of *eidola*. The word *eikon* is used in Deuteronomy 4: 16; but a Greek would think of *eidola* first as the forbidden or pagan object of worship.[5]

The avoidance of discussion of icons or only brief allusion to them—examples of which have been examined above—is also apparent here. After this explanation of the Orthodox abhorrence of 'images'—even of saints—in their churches, Neale proceeds to a description of the cathedral where Metrophanes is Bishop, and notes that 'the walls were covered with curious little pictures of Saints, all from the East'; this is followed by a catalogue of these holy figures. The 'little pictures' are icons; yet Neale does not label them as such.

---

[5] The Authorized Version does not distinguish, using 'graven image' in both Exod. 20: 4 and Deut. 4: 16.

The rest of the story concerns Metrophanes' refusal to attend a feast held by Peter, despite a direct request to do so. The prelate's action is a form of protest to the plan to erect the pagan statues. Realizing the trouble he has caused, Peter removes the statues, and the story ends happily.

In a tale like *The Lazar-House of Leros* Neale's failure to explain the role of icons in Orthodox worship can be attributed to his fear of being accused of promoting image worship. But in 'The Story of S. Metrophanes' it is less excusable, because it was Neale's express purpose to show how the Orthodox disapproved of statues, or 'images'. His reticence about this subject in his fiction stands in contrast to his private attitude. Neale was proud of his own small collection of icons, which he received from the Russians in appreciation of his researches into the Christian East, as he intimated to Webb: 'I wish you could see my glorious *Icons*. One, of the TRINITY under the shape of the three Angels appearing to Abraham—it is, you know, from the Troitzkoi-Sergievsky Monastery—is the most highly finished thing I ever saw.'[6] A discussion of icons would have been most appropriate, in the causes of both intellectual honesty and avoidance of confusion; for the reader is bewildered by Neale's claim that 'images' are forbidden in Orthodox churches, followed by a catalogue of 'curious little pictures of Saints' in the cathedral.

The tales are varied; they include successes, qualified successes, and failures. As with his other fiction, they represent a remarkable attempt to reach out beyond the academic or church-going communities addressed in his *History of the Holy Eastern Church* and his translations of Greek hymns, to further his aims of achieving a better understanding of this relatively unknown branch of Catholic Christendom and of allowing his readers to see in her a reflection of their own religious tradition.

[6] *Letters*, 311; dated 26 Feb. 1860, from Sackville College.

EPILOGUE

The Legacy of Neale

It is clear to anyone who has studied the development of the Anglo-Catholic revival that Neale played a significant role in the process of change both within and without the Anglican Church. As a nineteenth-century intellectual figure, Neale fits into a pattern which by the time of his death had already begun to dissolve—that of the highly competent amateur, a gentleman rather than a player, whose life of creativity and scholarship was funded by private means and by the Church, rather than by a career in professional scientific or academic institutions. Indeed, his public life was the very reverse of a specialist's, being an essentially practical and polemical one, concerned with the transformation of Anglican art, architecture, and liturgy and with the creation of a new religious order, and, indeed, more generally with the broadest issues in the national culture.

This book has treated Neale's career only in so far as it relates to his activities as an interpreter of Byzantium and Eastern Orthodoxy to the Victorian England of his day. He found in Orthodoxy a powerful weapon against Rome and for the High Church tradition in the Church of England. He significantly strengthened that tradition in the realms of both scholarship and devotion, by demonstrating the international existence and extraordinary achievement of another form of non-Roman Catholic Christianity and by enriching the English Church's worship and imaginative life through incorporation of the poetry, history, and hagiography of the neglected third of the Christian world.

In tracing the quest for *sobornost*, Neale's work has been firmly placed in the context of Western attitudes to the Orient, to Islam, and towards Russia in particular, which is a matter of great contemporary concern. The changes being experienced by Church, State, and society in Eastern Europe are of monumental proportions, and the possibility for interaction between East and West, on a wide variety of levels, is immense. In treating other traditions with reverence and understanding, it is possible to emerge from researches and communication with a lucid understanding that the 'harmony' or 'conciliarity' inherent in *sobornost* involves the creation of an atmosphere of mutual respect which allows for the maintenance of individuality and distinctness and the exchange of spiritual gifts.

Neale was deeply sensitive to the ways of Orthodoxy, and, in attempting to familiarize a British reading public with her traditions, he adopted 'Oriental views, feelings, and, even, perhaps, prepossessions' (ALX i, p. xvi). He attempted to challenge the pervasive Western attitude towards the East: that of 'we–they', or 'over here–over there'. Yet the traditional orientalist stance persists: the East is still perceived as static and in need of help and instruction. Westerners still believe in their cultural superiority, and persist in making sweeping generalizations and pronouncements about Eastern culture and society. In a Christian context in particular, the West must, in the tradition of Neale, divest itself of its cultural baggage, and take up a stance similar to his, by orientalizing itself, in order to appreciate more fully a part of the Church long neglected, but containing essential truths and paradigms of Christian strength—particularly as manifested in the face of opposition and oppression.

The chronological approach adopted in this book, moving through an analysis of historical narrative, hymns, and novels, reflects the growth in Neale's understanding of his subject, and serves to document the state of mind out of which works of imaginative power and genuine popular appeal emerged. In writing *A History of the Holy Eastern Church*, Neale engaged in painstaking (if occasionally erroneous) groundwork, analyzing Orthodoxy's historical, theological, and doctrinal developments. The volumes which emerged represent a domestication of Orthodoxy for British readers, and purport to show that Eastern Church doctrine and practice are less alien to Western Christians than they might at first seem. The adaptation of Eastern hymns was the next logical step, encapsulating oriental ideas in a recognizably Western mould, and one which encouraged the use of Eastern compositions as an accepted element of British church worship. The works of fiction provided him with an opportunity for communicating Orthodox Church history and theology in a form which required neither specialized theological knowledge nor religious commitment, and in which popular themes and motifs ensured marketability. This gradual widening of his approach points to a carefully orchestrated plan to bring this ancient branch of Christendom closer to the experience of Western readers.

In producing his orientalist works, the wider aim of *sobornost* was constantly in Neale's mind. His publications may be seen as an attempt to construct a bridge between two communions and ways of life, across which avenues of dialogue might be established. His primary concern was to overcome barriers and misconceptions which had become canonical. He realized that the cause of unity required more than academic investigation: it demanded the discarding of prejudices and presuppositions and the adoption of a state of mind in which the full benefits of shared experience could be enjoyed. Once this atmosphere has been created, the 'glorious mass of theology' and 'huge treasure of divinity' (HEC, p. xli) embodied in both Eastern and Western traditions may be shared.

GLOSSARY

Canon A series of 8 odes, each made up of a number of *troparia*. The canon occurs at matins after the reading of the Psalter and of Psalm 50. Originally at this point in matins, the 9 scriptural canticles were sung, with a short refrain inserted between the verses. St Andrew of Crete (7th–8th cent.) established the practice of expanding these short refrains into *troparia* celebrating some particular theme such as repentance (as in St Andrew's own 'Great Canon'), the feast or saint of the day, Jesus, the *Theotokos*, or the departed. Gradually the custom of reading the actual biblical text largely disappeared. As a result the *troparia* of the canon are now usually recited by themselves, accompanied by a short invocation, such as 'Glory be to Thee, O God, glory to Thee' or 'Most Holy Theotokos, save us'. The sole biblical canticle still sung in full is the *Magnificat*. In present practice there is no 2nd ode in the canon, except on various days in Lent; thus the canon, which theoretically contains 9 odes, has in reality only 8. Normally more than one canon is prescribed to be read at matins: on Sundays, 4; on normal days, 3; on Great Feasts, usually 2, but occasionally only 1. In reading canons, ode 1 of the 1st canon is read; then ode 1 of the 2nd, 3rd, etc. canon; then ode 3 of the 1st canon, etc.

Canticle A prayer or poetical composition of biblical origin, other than the Psalms. The 9 biblical canticles appointed for use at matins are as follows: (1) the Song of Moses at the Red Sea (Exod. 15: 1–19); (2) the Song of Moses in Deuteronomy (Deut. 32: 1–43); (3) the Song of Hannah (1 Sam. 2: 1–10); (4) the Song of Habakkuk (Hab. 3: 2–19); (5) the Song of Isaiah (Isa. 26: 9–20); (6) the Song of Jonah (Jonah 2: 3–10); (7) the Song of the Three Holy Children (3–34) (in the Septuagint Dan. 3: 26–56); (8) the *Benedicite* (S. of III Ch. 35–66) (Septuagint, Dan. 3: 57–88a, plus some non-biblical verses); and (9) the Song of the *Theotokos* (*Magnificat*, Luke 1: 46–55) and the Prayer of Zacharias (*Benedictus Dominus*, Luke 1: 68–79). Apart from the *Magnificat*, all these canticles are now usually omitted, except during Lent.

Easter Known as the 'Feast of Feasts' or, in Greek, *lampra* ('the brightest day of all'). It is the pre-eminent festival in the Orthodox Christian year. It is preceded by a long period of repentance, fasting, and preparation, extending over 10 weeks, encompassing 22 days of preliminary observance, 40 days of the Great Fast of Lent, and finally

Holy Week. Balancing this period there follows after Easter a season of 50 days of thanksgiving, concluding with Pentecost. The Easter midnight service, with its climactic chant of 'Christ is risen from the dead', is a supremely joyful evocation of the Resurrection, the event which typifies for the Orthodox the redemption issuing from the Cross.

Epigonation A square or rhomboid vestment suspended by one of its corners from a ribbon which hangs either from the girdle or from across the left shoulder of the celebrant. It reaches down to the right knee, and hence it is called *epigonation* (on the knee). Originally, it was worn only by bishops, later by archimandrites as well and, in recent times, by married priests holding one of the higher ecclesiastical distinctions. The *epigonation* symbolizes a spiritual sword, and points to the scared obligation of the celebrant to communicate the word of God correctly and truthfully, thereby slicing through the adverse powers of Satan. The *epigonation* is also used as an instrument for the transmission of grace by the bishop, when he recites a prayer of absolution over an Orthodox believer.

Ephymnia Short interjections introduced into the Psalms during the second period of Orthodox hymnody (5th–7th cents.), and forming the basis of the *troparion, sticheron, ypakoë,* and *kathisma,* q.v.

Exapostilarion A *troparion* occurring at the conclusion of the canon at matins and frequently developing the theme of Christ as the light of the world.

Great Feasts After Easter, which is known as the 'Feast of Feasts', the Orthodox recognize 12 Great Feasts, divided into two groups. The 5 'Feasts of the Mother of God' are as follows: (1) the Birth of the *Theotokos* (8 Sept.); (2) the Entry of the *Theotokos* into the Temple (21 Nov.); (3) the Meeting of Our Lord (2 Feb., Western Candlemas); (4) the Annunciation of the Mother of God (25 Mar.; Western Lady Day); (5) the Dormition of the Theotokos (15 Aug., Western Assumption). The 7 'Feasts of the Lord' are as follows: (1) the Exaltation of the Cross (14 Sept.); (2) Christmas (25 Dec.); (3) Theophany (6 Jan.); (4) Palm Sunday (one week before Easter); (5) the Ascension of Our Lord (40 days after Easter); (6) Pentecost (50 days after Easter); (7) Transfiguration (6 Aug.). As can be seen, 3 out of the 12 are movable, forming part of the annual Easter cycle, whereas the remainder belong to the cycle of the *Menaia*. It should be noted that while the Orthodox Churches of Constantinople, Alexandria, Antioch, Cyprus, Greece, Romania, and Poland have been using the Gregorian calendar since 1923, the Orthodox Churches of Jerusalem, Russia, Serbia, Bulgaria, and Georgia use the Julian calendar, with the result that they celebrate their ecclesiastical feasts 13 days later. The divergence over calendars does not, however, affect the dating of Easter, which is calculated on the basis of the spring equinox.

Homokatalexia A term referring to lines of liturgical verse which have exactly the same word ending. It must be clearly distinguished from rhyme, which does not require such precise correspondence.

Homotonia A term referring to lines of liturgical verse in which the metrical accents coincide.

Iconostasis The screen of icons separating the sanctuary from the *naos* (nave) of an Orthodox church and pierced by three doors: a central one, called Beautiful Gate, or Royal Gate, which has painted on it an icon of Jesus and is used by the officiating clergy; and two other doors, one on each side of the Royal Gate, which are smaller, decorated with icons of the archangels Gabriel and Michael, and are used by the altar-boys and non-officiating clergymen.

Irmos A term applied to the opening stanza in each ode of the canon. In the original Greek text, all the remaining *troparia* in the ode follow the same rhythm as the *irmos*. It acts as a linking verse, joining together the theme of the biblical canticle, which the ode of the canon was originally designed to accompany, and the theme of the feast or commemoration of the day, which is developed in the *troparia* that follow.

Isosyllabia A term referring to lines of liturgical verse which have the same number of syllables.

Katavasia The concluding stanza in an ode of the canon, so named because originally the members of the choir came down from their stalls on either side and stood in the centre of the church to sing it. Sometimes the *irmos* is repeated as *katavasia*, but on Sundays and certain feasts the *katavasia* at the end of each ode is specially appointed according to the time within the liturgical year.

Kathisma A term signifying either (1) each of the 20 sections into which the Psalter is subdivided in the Orthodox Church or (2) a short *troparion* sung or read during matins at the end of each *kathisma* of the Psalter.

Kontakion Originally a long poem, designed for singing in church, consisting of a short preliminary stanza, followed by some 8 to 14 strophes, each known as an *oikos*. In time the *kontakion* was replaced by the canon, and in today's liturgical books all that remains is the brief preliminary stanza, followed by the first *oikos*. These are to be found between canticles 6 and 7 of the canon at matins.

Glossary 271

Liturgy A term used by the Orthodox specifically to denote the Eucharist (unlike the West, where the term is often used to signify public worship in general).

Menaia The twelve volumes (one for each month) which contain the services for the fixed feasts throughout the year, from 1 Sept. (the beginning of the ecclesiastical year) until 31 Aug. It corresponds to the *proprium sanctorum* in the West.

Naos The nave, set apart for the laity. The word is believed to derive from the Latin *navis* (ship), a symbol for the Church of Christ.

Octoechos The liturgical book containing the variable portions for the daily offices throughout the week. Eight series of offices are provided, 1 for each of the 8 tones of Byzantine church music; and within each series there are 7 sets of services, 1 for each day of the week. Throughout the year, the services proceed week by week through the various tones: on the Sunday of St Thomas (the 1st after Easter) the sequence begins with Tone 1, and proceeds through the different tones until Tone 8 is completed; the offices for Tone 1 are then resumed, and so on through the sequence.

Ode One of the 9 (in practice 8) subdivisions of the canon. It consists of from 8 to 30, or even more, stanzas all structurally alike (although 14 seems to be the ideal number). The single stanza is called the *troparion*; its length varies from 3 to 13 lines. All the *troparia* are composed on the rhythmical pattern of a model stanza, the *irmos*. An ode is either built on the pattern of an *irmos* specially composed for it or follows the metre of an *irmos* already used for another ode.

Oikos The stanza that follows the *kontakion*, between canticles 6 and 7 of the canon at matins.

Panhagia 'All holy one'; the name by which the Virgin Mary is known in the Greek Orthodox Church, and the one always used in ordinary speech.

Parakletike Another name for the *octoechos*, q.v.

Pentekostarion The liturgical book containing the hymns and readings for the season from Easter Sunday to the Sunday of All Saints (the Sunday after Pentecost).

Photagogikon 'Hymn of light'; another name for the *exapostilarion*, q.v.

Sticheron A brief liturgical hymn that follows a verse (*stichos*), which is usually a psalmic or other scriptural passage. They occur particularly at vespers, between the closing verses of 'Lord, I have cried', and at matins, between the concluding verses of lauds.

Synaxis A gathering for the purpose of worship. The term was used by the early Christian writers in place of 'synagogue' in order to distinguish between Christian and Jewish assemblies.

Theotokion A *troparion* or *sticheron* in honour of the *Theotokos*. The last of any series of *troparia* or *stichera* usually takes the form of a *theotokion*.

Theotokos Greek for 'God-bearer', the chief title ascribed to the Blessed Virgin Mary in the theology and worship of the Orthodox Church.

Triodion The liturgical book which contains the services for the Great Fast of Lent, beginning where the *Octoechos* leaves off, on the Sunday of the Publican and Pharisee (the 10th before Easter), and ending on the Saturday of Holy Week. Many canons in the *Triodion* contain only 3 canticles or odes, hence the title of the volume.

Trisagion The words 'Holy God, Holy and Mighty, Holy and Immortal, have mercy on us'. They are usually repeated 3 or more times, and occur in the Liturgy, in matins, and in almost every office, as part of the short petitions preceding the Lord's Prayer.

Troparion A short hymn celebrating a liturgical event, a commemorated saint, etc. Many were written in praise of the Virgin Mary. This word is now commonly used to denote a 'stanza' of Orthodox religious poetry. It applies particularly to the *apolytikon* ('troparion of the feast' or 'troparion of the day') or to the stanzas of a canon.

Ypakoë A troparion sung at matins on Great Feasts and Sundays. On Great Feasts it usually occurs after canticle 3 of the canon; on Sundays it comes at the end of the reading of the Psalter. The Sunday ypakoë is also read at the midnight office on that day, after the canon to the Trinity.

BIBLIOGRAPHY

1 MANUSCRIPTS

Journal of Benjamin Webb, MSS Eng. Misc. d. 475, e. 406–43, f. 97–9, Duke Humfrey's Library, Bodleian Library, Oxford.

Letter to E. B. Pusey from B. Pontiatin, 19 Feb. 1865, from Christ Church, Oxford; Pusey Papers, Pusey House, Oxford.

Letters and papers of John Mason Neale, MSS 1750 (fos. 114–43), 2677–84, 3109–18, 3120 (fos. 31–82), Lambeth Palace Library, London.

Reports of churches surveyed by members of the Cambridge Camden Society, MSS 1977–93, Lambeth Palace Library, London.

Transcriptions of Benjamin Webb's journal relating to John Mason Neale, 1839–66, made by Canon P. G. Ward in 1951; MS 3595, Lambeth Palace Library, London.

Transcriptions of the journals of John Mason Neale for 1836–8 and 1851–2, in the possession of Leon Litvack.

Transcriptions of the journals of John Mason Neale for 1838–44, MSS 3107–8, Lambeth Palace Library, London.

Leppard, M. J., 'Summary Bibliography of Works of and about John Mason Neale' (East Grinstead, 1969–).

2 WORKS BY J. M. NEALE

Agnes de Tracy: A Tale of the Times of S. Thomas of Canterbury (London, 1843).

Annals of Virgin Saints (London, 1846). Published anonymously under the pseudonym 'A Priest of the Church of England'.

Ayton Priory; or, The Restored Monastery (Cambridge, 1843).

Carols for Christmastide (London, 1853).

Carols for Eastertide (London, 1854).

Church Enlargement and Church Arrangement (Cambridge, 1843).

Communications between the Seen and Unseen Worlds (London, 1847). Published anonymously.

The Daughters of Pola: Family Letters Relating to the Persecution of Diocletian, now translated from an Istrian MS (London, 1861).

Deeds of Faith: Stories for Children from Church History (London, 1902). First published in 1850.

Dolores de Gualdini: A Tale of the Portuguese Revolution of 1640 (London, 1866). Published anonymously.
English History for Children (London, 1845).
'English Hymnology: Its History and Prospects', *Christian Remembrancer,* 18 (1849), 302–43.
Essays on Liturgiology and Church History (London, 1863).
The Exiles of Cebenna: A Journal Written during the Decian Persecution, by Aurelius Gratianus, Priest of the Church of Arles; and now done into English (London, 1859).
The Farm of Aptonga: A Story for Children of the Times of S. Cyprian (Burntisland, 1869). First published in 1856.
A Few Words of Hope on the Present Crisis of the English Church (London, 1850).
A Few Words to Church Builders (Cambridge, 1841).
A Few Words to Churchwardens on Churches and Church Ornaments, No. 1, Suited to Country Parishes (Cambridge, 1841).
A Few Words to Churchwardens on Churches and Church Ornaments, No. 2, Suited to Town and Manufacturing Parishes (Cambridge, 1841).
'The *Filioque* Controversy', *Christian Remembrancer,* 48 (1864), 468–502.
'Greek Hymnology', *Christian Remembrancer,* 37 (1859), 280–316.
Herbert Tresham: A Story of the Great Rebellion (London, 1843).
Hierologus; or, The Church Tourists (London, 1843).
A History of Greece for Young Persons (London, 1845).
A History of the Church for the Use of Children, Part I: From the Day of Pentecost to the Council of Chalcedon (London, 1853).
A History of the Holy Eastern Church: General Introduction (2 vols., London, 1850).
A History of the Holy Eastern Church: The Patriarchate of Alexandria (2 vols., London, 1847).
A History of the Holy Eastern Church: The Patriarchate of Antioch, ed. George Williams (London, 1873).
The Holy Eastern Church: A Popular Outline of its History, Doctrines, Liturgies and Vestments (London, 1870). Published anonymously under the pseudonym 'A Priest of the English Church'.
The Hymnal Noted (London, 1851).
'The Hymnal Noted', *Ecclesiologist,* 12 (1851), 11–16.
Hymni Ecclesiae, a Breviariis quibusdam et Missalibus Gallicanis, Germanis, Hispanis Lusitanis, desumpti (Oxford and London, 1851).
'Hymns and Hymnals', *Christian Remembrancer,* 46 (1863), 105–44.
Hymns for Children (London, 1843).
Hymns for the Sick (London, 1843).

Hymns of the Eastern Church (London, 1862; 2nd edn., 1863; 3rd edn., 1866).
'Intercommunion with the Eastern Church', *Christian Remembrancer*, 47 (1864), 455–70.
Introduction to the History of the Holy Eastern Church, Appendix: *A List of All the Sees in the Holy Eastern Church* (London, 1851).
Larache: A Tale of Portuguese Church in the Sixteenth Century (London, 1861).
The Lazar-House of Leros: A Tale of the Eastern Church in the Seventeenth Century (London, 1916). First published in 1859.
Lent Legends: Stories for Children from Church History (London, 1905). First published in 1855.
Letter on 'The Hymnal Noted', *Ecclesiologist*, 13 (1852), 22.
The Life and Times of Patrick Torry, D.D., with an Appendix on the Scottish Liturgy (London, 1856).
The Lily of Tiflis: A Sketch from Georgian Church History (London, 1917). First published anonymously in 1859.
Lucia's Marriage; or, The Lions of Wady Arabah: A Story of the Idumaean Desert (London, 1860).
(trans.), *Mediaeval Hymns and Sequences* (London, 1851).
'Modern Studies of the Eastern Church', *Christian Remembrancer*, 40 (1861), 224–50.
'New Translations of Eastern Liturgies', *Christian Remembrancer*, 50 (1865), 420–36.
Notes, Ecclesiological and Picturesque, on Dalmatia, Croatia, Istria, Styria, with a Visit to Montenegro (London, 1861).
Occasional Sermons, Preached in Various Churches (London, 1873).
'"On the History of Hymnology": A Paper Read before the Ecclesiological/Late Cambridge Camden Society, on Monday, June 23rd, 1851', *Ecclesiologist*, 12 (1851), 241–50.
Pictorial Crucifixes: A Letter to the Lord Bishop of Chichester, by a Priest of the Diocese (London, 1852). Published anonymously.
'Proposal for a Noted Hymnal and an Explanation of the Gregorian Note', *Ecclesiologist*, 11 (1850), 174–83.
The Quay of Dioscuri: A History of Nicene Times; written in Greek by Macarius, Merchant of Tunnies and Palamydes, and now translated from Two Alexandrian Manuscripts (London, 1860). Published anonymously.
Readings for the Aged, Selected from Sermons Preached in Sackville College Chapel (London, 1878).
The Sea Tigers: A Tale of Mediaeval Nestorianism (London, 1916). First published anonymously in 1860.
Secession: A Sermon Preached in the Oratory of St Margaret's, East Grinstead, November 18, 1859 (London, 1868).

Selections from the Writings of John Mason Neale, D.D. (London, 1884).
Sequences, Hymns and other Ecclesiastical Verses (London, 1866).
Sequentias ex Missalibus Germanicis, Anglicis, Gallicis, aliisque medii aevi collectae (London, 1852).
Sermons for the Church Year (2 vols., London, 1876).
Sermons on the Apocalypse, the Holy Name and the Proverbs (London, 1871).
Sermons on the Blessed Sacrament: Preached in the Oratory of S. Margaret's, East Grinstead (London, 1871).
Sermons Preached in a Religious House, ed. J. Haskoll (4 vols., London, 1869–74).
Shepperton Manor: A Tale of the Times of Bishop Andrewes (London, 1845).
Songs and Ballads for the People (London, 1843).
Stories from Heathen Mythology and Greek History for the Use of Christian Children (London, 1905). First published in 1847.
Stories of the Crusades: De Hellingley and the Crusade of S. Louis (London, 1905). First published in 1846.
Theodora Phranza; or, The Fall of Constantinople (London, 1857). First published in serial form in *Churchman's Companion*, 14 (1853), 1–22, 81–105, 161–81, 241–78, 321–58, 401–27; 15 (1854), 1–23, 81–105, 161–85, 241–69, 321–42, 401–27; 16 (1854), 1–19, 81–99, 161–76, 241–60, 321–39, 401–19.
Triumphs of the Cross: Tales and Sketches of Christian Heroism (London, 1845).
Twenty-Three Reasons for Getting Rid of Church Pues (London, 1841).
The Two Huts: An Allegory (London, 1856).
(trans. and ed.), *Voices from the East: Documents on the Present State and Working of the Oriental Church, Translated from the Original Russ, Slavonic and French, with Notes* (London, 1859).
[and Littledale, R. F.], *Commentary on the Psalms* (2 vols., London, 1860, 1868). Vol. 1, published in 1860, was Neale's own work; vol. 2, published posthumously in 1868, was completed by Littledale.
[and Littledale, R. F. (eds.)], *The Liturgies of SS. Mark, James, Clement, Chrysostom and Basil, and the Church of Malabar; Translated, with Introduction and Appendices* (London, 1859).
[and Russell, J. F.], *Hints for the Practical Study of Ecclesiastical Antiquities for the Use of the Cambridge Camden Society* (Cambridge, 1840).
[and Webb, B. (eds.)], *The History and Fate of Sacrilege*, by Sir Henry Spelman (London, 1846). Editors said to be 'Two Priests of the Church of England'.

[and Webb, B. (trans. and eds.)], *The Symbolism of Churches and Church Ornaments: A Translation of the First Book of the Rationale Divinorum Officiorum by William Durandus, Sometime Bishop of Mende, with an Introductory Essay, Notes and Illustrations* (Leeds, 1843).

3 OTHER WORKS

Adey, L., *Class and Idol in the English Hymn* (Vancouver, 1988).
——, 'Great Aunt Tilly's Beautiful 'Ymns: A Victorian Religious Sub-Culture', *Wascana Review*, 12/1 (Spring 1977), 21–47.
——, *Hymns and the Christian 'Myth'* (Vancouver, 1986).
Ahmed, A. S., 'Jeans for Me, Robes for You', *Guardian Weekly*, 143/2 (15 July 1990), 21.
Allchin, A. M., 'An Anglican View of Anglican–Orthodox Contacts', *Eastern Churches Quarterly*, 15/1–2 (1963), 56–60.
——, 'Grundtvig's Catholicity', in *N. F. S. Grundtvig: Theolog og Kirkelaerer* (Copenhagen, 1983), 42–53.
——, 'Grundtvig's Translations from the Greek', *Eastern Churches Quarterly*, 14/1 (1961), 28–44.
——, 'The Hymns of N. F. S. Grundtvig', *Eastern Churches Quarterly*, 13/3–4 (1959), 129–43.
——, 'N. F. S. Grundtvig: The Spirit as Life-Giver', in *The Kingdom of Love and Knowledge: The Encounter between Orthodoxy and the West* (London, 1979), 71–89.
——, *The Silent Rebellion: Anglican Religious Communities, 1845–1900* (London, 1958).
Anonymous, 'The Conversion of St. Vladimir; or, The Martyrs of Kief: A Tale of the Early Russian Church', *Tales Illustrating Church History, 5: Eastern and Northern Europe* (London, 1871).
——, *Doing the Impossible: A Short Historical Sketch of St Margaret's Convent, East Grinstead, 1855–1980* (East Grinstead, 1980).
——, 'E. I. Popov', in *Entsiklopedichesky slovar* (St Petersburg, 1891–1907), xlviii. 562.
——, *A History of the Origin of the War with Russia, Drawn Up from the Parliamentary Documents* (London, 1855).
——, 'Mr Kinglake's Crimea', *Christian Remembrancer*, 46 (1863), 447–67.
——, 'Oriental Ecclesiology', *Ecclesiologist*, 13 (1851), 5–15.
Anson, P. F., *The Call of the Cloister: Religious Communities and Kindred Bodies in the Anglican Communion* (London, 1955).
——, *Fashions in Church Furnishings: 1840–1940* (London, 1965).

Arnold, M., *Culture and Anarchy: An Essay in Political and Social Criticism* (London, 1869).
Barreca, R. (ed.), *Sex and Death in Victorian Literature* (London, 1990).
Beckford, W., *The History of Caliph Vathek* (London, 1868). First published in 1786.
Birkbeck, W. J. (ed.), *Russia and the English Church during the Last Fifty Years, Volume I, Containing a Correspondence between Mr William Palmer, Fellow of Magdalen College, Oxford, and M. Khomiakoff, in the years 1844–1854* (London, 1895).
Blackmore, R. W., *A Doctrine of the Russian Church, being the Primer or Spelling Book, the Shorter and Longer Catechisms, and a Treatise on the Duty of Parish Priests* (Aberdeen, 1845).
Bolshakoff, S., 'Patristic Foundations of Khomyakov's Theology', *Eastern Churches Quarterly*, 10/5 (Spring 1954), 233–7.
Boyce, E. J., *'Good Bye': A Few Lessons from the Life of the Late Warden, Addressed to the Brethren and Sisters of Sackville College, East Grinstead* (London, 1867).
——, *A Memorial of the Cambridge Camden Society* (London, 1888).
Brandreth, H. R. T., *Unity and Reunion: A Bibliography* (London, 1945).
Brantlinger, P., *Rule of Darkness: British Literature and Imperialism, 1830–1914* (Ithaca, NY, 1988).
Brodsky, L. (ed.), 'Materials Concerning the Question of the Anglican Church: Reports by the Rev. E. I. Popov to Nicolai Alexandrovich Protasov, Procurator of the Holy Governing Synod', *Khristianskoe chtenie*, Apr. 1904, 596–613; May 1904, 730–47; June 1904, 878–93.
——, 'Materials Concerning the Question of the Anglican Church: Reports by the Rev. E. I. Popov to Alexander Petrovich Tolstoy, Procurator of the Holy Governing Synod', *Khristianskoe chtenie*, June 1905, 888–905; July 1905, 112–32; Sept. 1905, 393–408.
Bulgakov, S., *The Orthodox Church* (Crestwood, NY, 1988).
Burke, E., *Reflections on the Revolution in France*, ed. C. C. O'Brien (Harmondsworth, 1982).
Burton, R. F. (trans.), *The Kama Sutra* (London, 1883).
—— (trans.), *The Perfumed Garden* (London, 1886).
——, *Personal Narrative of a Pilgrimage to El-Madinah and Meccah* (3 vols., London, 1855–6).
——, *A Plain and Literal Translation of the Arabian Nights' Entertainments, now Entitled The Book of the Thousand Nights and a Night, with Introduction, Explanatory Notes, and a Terminal Essay upon the History of the Nights* (London, 1885–6).
Byron, G. G. N., *The Bride of Abydos: A Turkish Tale* (London, 1813).

——, *Childe Harold's Pilgrimage* (2 vols., London, 1819). First published in 1812–18.

——, *The Giaour: A Fragment of a Turkish Tale* (London, 1813).

Cameron, J. M., 'John Henry Newman and the Tractarian Movement', in *Nineteenth Century Religious Thought in the West*, ed. N. Smart, J. Clayton, P. Sherry, and S. Katz (3 vols., Cambridge, 1985), ii. 69–109.

Carlyle, T., *Past and Present* (London, 1978).

——, 'Sir Walter Scott', in *Critical and Miscellaneous Essays* (5 vols., London, 1896–9), iv. 22–87.

Chadwick, O., *The Victorian Church* (2 vols., London, 1971).

Chapman, R., *Faith and Revolt: Studies in the Literary Influence of the Oxford Movement* (London, 1970).

Chateaubriand, F. R. de, *Itinéraire de Paris à Jérusalem et de Jérusalem à Paris, en allant par la Grèce, et revenant par l'Egypte, la Barbarie, et l'Espagne* (Paris, 1811).

Chatfield, A. W., *Songs and Hymns of the Earliest Greek Christian Poets, Translated into English Verse* (London, 1876).

Christoff, P. K., 'Christianity and the Church—"Sobornost" ', in *An Introduction to Nineteenth-Century Russian Slavophilism, 1: A. S. Xomjakov* (The Hague, 1961), i. 137–71.

Church Hymnary Revision Committee (eds.), *The Church Hymnary*, 3rd edn. (Oxford, 1973).

Clark, K. M., *The Gothic Revival* (London, 1928).

Clarke, B. F. L., *Church Builders of the Nineteenth Century: A Study of the Gothic Revival in England* (New York, 1969).

Clarke, W. K. L., *A Hundred Years of Hymns Ancient and Modern* (London, 1960).

Clendenin, F. M., 'Neale and Childhood', *Living Church*, 19 Jan. 1918, 398.

Close, F., *Church Architecture, Scripturally Considered, from the Earliest Ages to the Present Time* (London, 1844).

——, *The 'Restoration of Churches' is the Restoration of Popery: Proved and Illustrated from the Authenticated Publications of the 'Cambridge Camden Society': A Sermon, Preached in the Parish Church, Cheltenham on Tuesday, November 5th, 1844* (London, 1845).

Clow, W. M., 'A Hymn of the Cross', in *The Cross in Christian Experience* (London, 1909), 294–305.

Cooke, W., and Webb, B. (eds.), *The Hymnary: A Book of Church Song* (London, 1872).

Covel, J., *Some Account of the Present Greek Church, with Reflections on their Present Doctrine and Discipline; particularly in the*

Eucharist, and the Rest of their Seven Pretended Sacraments (Cambridge, 1722).

Cross, F. L., and Livingstone, E. A. (eds.), *The Oxford Dictionary of the Christian Church* (Oxford, 1974).

Davey, C., *Pioneer for Unity: Metrophanes Kritopoulos (1589–1639) and Relations between the Orthodox, Roman Catholic and Reformed Churches* (London, 1987).

Disraeli, B., *Tancred; or, The New Crusade* (3 vols., London, 1847).

Drain, S., *The Anglican Church in Nineteenth Century Britain: Hymns Ancient and Modern (1860–1875)* (Lewiston, NY, 1989). Revised version of 'A Study of *Hymns Ancient and Modern*, 1860–1875' (Ph.D. thesis, London, 1979).

Duffield, S. W., *English Hymns: Their Authors and History* (London, 1886).

Edmunds, C. C., 'The Sisterhood of St Margaret', *Living Church*, 19 Jan. 1918, 393–4.

Elias, N. M., *The Divine Liturgy Explained: A Guide for Orthodox Christian Worshippers* (Athens, 1984).

The English Hymnal (London, 1979).

Every, G., 'The Legacy of Neale', *Eastern Churches Review*, 1/2 (Autumn 1966), 142–5.

Faber, W. F., 'Dr Neale's Hymns', *Living Church*, 19 Jan. 1918, 392–3.

The Festal Menaion, trans. Mother Mary and K. Ware (London, 1969).

First Report of the Eastern Church Association (London, 1866).

Flaubert, G., *Salammbô* (Paris, 1863).

——, *Voyage à Carthage* (Paris, 1858).

——, 'Voyage en Orient', in *Oeuvres complètes*, ed. B. Masson (2 vols., Paris, 1964), ii. 549–705. First published in 1849–51.

Florovsky, G., *Aspects of Church History* (Belmont, Mass., 1975).

——, 'The Orthodox Churches and the Ecumenical Movement Prior to 1910', in *A History of the Ecumenical Movement, 1517–1948*, ed. R. Rouse and S. C. Neill, 2nd edn. (London, 1967), 171–215.

Forster, E. M., *Aspects of the Novel* (Harmondsworth, 1990). First published in 1927.

Fox, A., 'Keble and Neale: Their Place in Church History', *Hymn Society of Great Britain and Ireland Bulletin*, 6/5 (no. 107) (Sept. 1966), 83–97.

Francis, E. K. (trans. and ed.), *Keble's Lectures on Poetry, 1832–1841* (2 vols., Oxford, 1912).

Frost, M. (ed.), *Historical Companion to Hymns Ancient and Modern* (London, 1962).

Gabriel, Sr., *John Mason Neale, 1818–1866* (Hove, 1981).
Gales, R. L., 'Christian and Romantic', in *Studies in Arcady, and Other Essays from a Country Parsonage* (London, 1910), 405–25.
——, 'A Tractarian Minstrel', in *Studies in Arcady, and Other Essays from a Country Parsonage*, 2nd ser. (London, 1912), 333–41.
Gibbon, E., *The Decline and Fall of the Roman Empire* (6 vols., London, 1979).
[Gillet, L.] 'A Monk of the Eastern Church', *Orthodox Spirituality: An Outline of the Orthodox Ascetical and Mystical Tradition* (London, 1978).
Gladstone, W. E., *Speech of the Right Hon. W. E. Gladstone, M. P. for the University of Oxford, on the War and the Negotiations, in the House of Commons, on the 3rd of August, 1855* (London, 1855).
Harrison, J. E., *Reminiscences of a Student's Life* (London, 1925).
Helmore, F., *Memoir of the Rev. Thomas Helmore, M.A.* (London, 1891).
Helmore, T., *The Psalter Noted* (London, 1849).
Higginson, J. V., 'John Mason Neale and 19th-Century Hymnody—His Work and Influence', *Hymn*, 16/4 (Oct. 1965), 101–17.
Holroyd, J. E., 'Victorian Hymn-Writer's Gothic Zeal', *Country Life*, 1 Dec. 1966, 1518–20.
Hook, A. (ed.), *The History of Scottish Literature*, 2: *1660–1800* (Aberdeen, 1987).
Houghton, W. E., *The Victorian Frame of Mind, 1830–1870* (New Haven, Conn., 1979).
Hugo, V., *Les Orientales* (Paris, 1829).
Huntingdon, G., 'John Mason Neale', *Newbury House Magazine*, 1928, 350–60.
Hymns Ancient and Modern for Use in the Services of the Church, with Appendix (London, 1868).
Jay, E. (ed.), *The Evangelical and Oxford Movements* (Cambridge, 1983).
——, *The Religion of the Heart: Anglican Evangelicalism and the Nineteenth-Century Novel* (Oxford, 1979).
Jenkyns, R., *The Victorians and Ancient Greece* (Oxford, 1980).
Jensen, N. L., et al. (eds.), *A Grundtvig Anthology: Selections from the Writings of N. F. S. Grundtvig (1783–1872)*, trans. E. Broadbridge and N. L. Jensen (Cambridge, 1984).
Jerman, B. R., *The Young Disraeli* (Princeton, NJ, 1960).
Johnson, S., *The History of Rasselas, Prince of Abyssinia* (London, 1838). First published in 1759.

Jowett, W. (ed.), *A Memoir of the Rev. Cornelius Neale, M. A., to which are Added his Remains, being Sermons, Allegories, and Various Compositions in Prose and Verse* (London, 1835).

Julian, J. (ed.), *A Dictionary of Hymnology, Setting Forth the Origin and History of Christian Hymns of All Ages and Nations* (London, 1907).

Kaplan, F., *Sacred Tears: Sentimentality in Victorian Literature* (Princeton, NJ, 1987).

Keble, J., *The Christian Year* (London, 1895). First published in 1827.

——, 'The Life and Writings of Walter Scott', *British Critic*, 24 (Oct. 1838), 423–83.

Kinglake, A. W., *Eothen, or Traces of Travel Brought Home from the East* (London, 1918). First published in 1844.

Kingsley, C., *Hypatia; or, New Foes with an Old Face* (London, 1968). First published in 1852–3.

Kline, G. L., 'Russian Religious Thought', in *Nineteenth Century Religious Thought in the West*, ed. N. Smart, J. Clayton, P. Sherry, and S. Katz (3 vols., Cambridge, 1985), ii. 179–229.

Labrunie de Nerval, G., *Voyage en Orient* (Paris, 1848–51).

Lamartine de Prat, M. L. A. de, *Souvenirs, impressions, pensées et passages, pendant un voyage en Orient (1832, 1833) ou notes de voyageur* (Paris, 1835).

Landow, G. P., *Victorian Types, Victorian Shadows: Biblical Typology in Victorian Literature, Art and Thought* (London, 1980).

Lane, E. W., *An Account of the Manners and Customs of the Modern Egyptians* (2 vols., London, 1836).

——(trans. and ed.), *The Thousand and One Nights, Commonly Called the Arabian Nights' Entertainments* (London, 1839–41).

Langford, H. W., 'The Non-Jurors and the Eastern Orthodox', *Eastern Churches Review*, 1/2 (Autumn 1966), 118–31.

Lawrence, J., 'William Palmer of Magdalen and the Russian Orthodox Church: A Centenary Tribute', *Sobornost/Eastern Churches Review*, 2/1 (1980), 80–2.

Lawson, M. S. (ed.), *Collected Hymns, Sequences and Carols of John Mason Neale* (London, 1914).

——(ed.), *Letters of John Mason Neale, D.D.* (London, 1910).

The Lenten Triodion, trans. Mother Mary and K. Ware (London, 1978).

Lewis, M. G., *The Monk, A Romance* (3 vols., London, 1796).

——, *Tales of Terror, with an Introductory Dialogue* (London, 1801).

Liddon, H. P., *The Life of Edward Bouverie Pusey, D.D.* (4 vols., London, 1893–7).

Lindhardt, P., *Grundtvig: An Introduction* (London, 1951).

Littledale, R. F., *Offices of the Eastern Church* (London, 1863).

Litvack, L. B., 'All for Love: John Mason Neale and the Perth Deanery Refusal', *Church of England Historical Society Journal*, 32/1 (Mar. 1987), 5–21. Reprinted in *Churchman*, 101/1 (1987), 36–48.

——, ' "Come, Ye Faithful, Raise the Strain": Victorian Experiences of Hymns', in *A Collection of Treatises on Languages and Literature*, Tokushima Bunri University, 6 (Mar. 1989), 41–66.

——, 'The Greek Hymn Translations and Adaptations of N. F. S. Grundtvig and J. M. Neale', *Hymn Society of Great Britain and Ireland Bulletin*, 12/10 (no. 183) (Apr. 1990), 182–7.

——, 'Theodora Phranza; or, Neale's Fears Realized', *Victorian Review*, 15/2 (Fall 1989), 1–14.

—— (ed.), 'Towards Reconciliation: A Report on the Anglican Church by a Russian Priest', *Sobornost/Eastern Churches Review*, 9/2 (1987), 23–40.

Lough, A. G., *John Mason Neale*, Oxford Prophets Series, 12 (London, 1983).

——, *John Mason Neale: Priest Extraordinary* (Newton Abbot, 1976).

——, *The Influence of John Mason Neale* (London, 1962). Revised version of 'The Influence of John Mason Neale' (Ph.D. thesis, London, 1961).

Lukács, G., *The Historical Novel*, trans. H. and S. Mitchell (Harmondsworth, 1981).

Maison, M. M., *The Victorian Vision: Studies in the Religious Novel* (New York, 1962).

Martineau, H., *Eastern Life, Past and Present* (3 vols., London, 1848).

Mill, J. S., *Autobiography*, ed. J. Stillinger (Oxford, 1971). First published in 1873.

Miller, E. C. jun., *Toward a Fuller Vision: Orthodoxy and the Anglican Experience* (Wilton, 1984).

Miriam, Sr., *John Mason Neale: A Memoir* [articles from *St. Margaret's Magazine*, 1887–95, bound together in 1 vol.] (East Grinstead, 1895).

Mitchell, J., *Scott, Chaucer, and Medieval Romance: A Study of Sir Walter Scott's Indebtedness to the Literature of the Middle Ages* (Lexington, Ky., 1987).

Mouravieff, A. N., *A History of the Church in Russia*, ed. W. Palmer, trans. R. W. Blackmore (Oxford, 1842).

Mozley, J. B., *A Review of the Baptismal Controversy* (London, 1862).

Neale, V., 'Recollections of Dr Neale', *Living Church*, 19 Jan. 1918, 395–8.

Newman, J. H., *Apologia pro vita sua*, ed. M. Ward (London, 1979).

——, *Callista: A Sketch of the Third Century* (London, 1881). First published in 1855.

——, *Lectures on Certain Difficulties Felt by Anglicans in Submitting to the Catholic Church* (London, 1850).
——, *Lectures on the Present Position of Catholics in England: Addressed to the Brothers of the Oratory* (London, 1851).
——, *Lectures on the Prophetical Office of the Church, Viewed Relatively to Romanism and Popular Protestantism* (London, 1837).
——, *Loss and Gain: The Story of a Convert* (London, 1848).
——, *Parochial and Plain Sermons* (8 vols., London, 1875).
——, *Sermons, Chiefly on the Theory of Religious Belief, Preached before the University of Oxford* (London, 1843).
——, 'The State of Religious Parties', *British Critic*, 25 (Apr. 1839), 395–426.
—— (ed.), *Tracts for the Times* (3 vols., London, 1833–41).
——, and Keble, J. (eds.), *Remains of the Late Rev. Richard Hurrell Froude* (London, 1838–9).
Nias, J. C. S., *Gorham and the Bishop of Exeter* (London, 1951).
Norman, E., *The English Catholic Church in the Nineteenth Century* (Oxford, 1984).
Occasional Paper of the Eastern Church Association, no. 1 (Sept. 1864).
Ollard, S. L., *A Short History of the Oxford Movement* (London, 1915).
——, and Cross, F. L., *The Anglo-Catholic Revival in Outline* (London, 1933).
Palmer, A., *The Banner of Battle: The Story of the Crimean War* (London, 1987).
Palmer, W., *An Appeal to the Scottish Bishops and Clergy, and Generally to the Church of their Communion* (London, 1849). Published anonymously.
——, *A Harmony of Anglican Doctrine with the Doctrine of the Catholic and Apostolic Church of the East* (Aberdeen, 1846).
——, *Notes of a Visit to the Russian Church in the Years 1840, 1841*, ed. J. H. Newman (London, 1882).
Papadeas, G. L. (ed.), *Greek Orthodox Holy Week and Easter Services* (Daytona Beach, Fla., 1985).
Pascal, P., *The Religion of the Russian People* (London, 1976).
Patrinacos, N. D., *A Dictionary of Greek Orthodoxy* (Pleasantville, NY, 1984).
Patterson, F. A., et al. (eds.), *The Works of John Milton* (18 vols., New York, 1931–8).
Pearson, C. B., 'Hymns and Hymn-Writers', in *Oxford Essays* (London, 1858), 145–79.
Pereira de Figueredo, A., *Tentativa Theologica: Episcopal Rights and Ultra-montane Usurpations*, trans. E. H. Landon (London, 1847).

Perry, D. W., *Hymns and Tunes Indexed by First Lines, Tune Names and Metres, Compiled from Current English Hymnbooks* (London and Croydon, 1980).
Peters, E., *Torture* (Oxford, 1985).
Phillips, C. S., 'Hymns of the Eastern Church', in *Hymnody, Past and Present* (London, 1937), 27–46.
Pocknee, C. E., 'Hymnody in the Eastern Churches', *Hymn Society of Great Britain and Ireland Bulletin*, 7/9 (no. 123) (Jan. 1972), 169–72.
——, 'Hymnody since the Oxford Movement', *Hymn Society of Great Britain and Ireland Bulletin*, 3/2 (no. 59) (Spring, 1952), 22–6.
Pollard, A., *English Hymns*, 'Writers and their Work' series no. 123 (London, 1960).
Prickett, S., *Romanticism and Religion: The Tradition of Coleridge and Wordsworth in the Victorian Church* (Cambridge, 1976).
Pusey, E. B., *The Articles Treated on in Tract 90 Reconsidered and their Interpretation Vindicated in a Letter to the Rev. R. W. Jelf, D.D.* (Oxford, 1841).
——, *A Letter to His Grace the Archbishop of Canterbury, on some Circumstances Connected with the Present Crisis in the English Church* (Oxford, 1842).
Reeves, J. B., *The Hymn as Literature* (New York, 1924).
Ricaut, P., *The Present State of the Greek and Armenian Churches* (London, 1679).
Richmond, L., *The Dairyman's Daughter* (Edinburgh, 1850). First published in 1810.
Ridley, K., 'A Pioneer in Reunion—William Palmer', *Sobornost*, 18 (June 1939), 9–18.
Rouse, R., 'Voluntary Movements and the Changing Ecumenical Climate', in *A History of the Ecumenical Movement, 1517–1948*, ed. R. Rouse and S. C. Neill, 2nd edn. (London, 1967), 309–49.
Routley, E. R., *Christian Hymns Observed* (Oxford, 1982).
——, *An English-Speaking Hymnal Guide* (Collegeville, Minn., 1979).
——, *A Panorama of Christian Hymnody* (Chicago, 1979).
Rowell, G., *Hell and the Victorians: A Study of the Nineteenth-Century Theological Controversies Concerning Eternal Punishment and the Future Life* (Oxford, 1974).
——, *The Vision Glorious: Themes and Personalities of the Catholic Revival in Anglicanism* (Oxford, 1983).
Said, E. W., *Orientalism* (Harmondsworth, 1985).
Sanders, A., *The Victorian Historical Novel, 1840–1880* (London, 1978).
Savas, S. J., *Hymnology of the Eastern Orthodox Church* (New York, 1983).

———, *The Treasury of Orthodox Hymnology: Triodion* (Minneapolis, 1983).
Scott, W., *Count Robert of Paris* (Edinburgh, 1898). First published in 1831.
———, *The Talisman: A Tale of the Crusaders* (Edinburgh, 1887). First published in 1825.
Seton-Watson, H., *The Russian Empire, 1801–1917* (Oxford, 1967).
Shaw, P. E., *The Early Tractarians and the Eastern Church* (Milwaukee, 1930).
Simmons, J. C., *The Novelist as Historian: Essays on the Victorian Historical Novel*, Studies in English Literature, 88 (The Hague, 1973).
Stanley, A. P., *Lectures on the History of the Eastern Church, with an Introduction on the Study of Ecclesiastical History* (London, 1894).
Steegmuller, F. (trans. and ed.), *Flaubert in Egypt: A Sensibility on Tour* (London, 1972).
Storringtonian, 'John Mason Neale, D. D., Hymnologist', *Sussex County Magazine*, 1928, 459–61.
Sutherland, J., *The Longman Companion to Victorian Fiction* (London, 1988).
Tamke, S. S., *Make a Joyful Noise unto the Lord: Hymns as a Reflection of Victorian Social Attitudes* (Athens, Oh., 1978).
Taylor, J., *The Rule and Exercises of Holy Dying* (London, 1869). First published in 1651.
Tennyson, G. B., '"So Careful of the Type?"—Victorian Biblical Typology: Sources and Applications', in *Essays and Studies* (London, 1984), 31–45.
———, *Victorian Devotional Poetry: The Tractarian Mode* (Cambridge, Mass., 1981).
Thackeray, W. M., *Notes of a Journey from Cornhill to Grand Cairo, by way of Lisbon, Athens, Constantinople, and Jerusalem: Performed in the Steamers of the Peninsular and Oriental Company* (Chicago, n.d.). First published in 1844.
Thodberg, C., 'Grundtvig the Hymnwriter', in *N. F. S. Grundtvig: Tradition and Renewal: Grundtvig's Vision of Man and People, Education and the Church, in Relation to World Issues Today*, ed. C. Thodberg and A. Thyssen, trans. E. Broadbridge (Copenhagen, 1983), 160–96.
Tomlinson, G., *Report of a Journey to the Levant, Addressed to the President of the Society for Promoting Christian Knowledge* (London, 1841).
Towle, E. A., *John Mason Neale, D.D.: A Memoir* (London, 1906).

Trappes-Lomax, M., *Pugin: A Mediaeval Victorian* (London, 1932).
Turner, F. M., *The Greek Heritage in Victorian Britain* (New Haven, Conn., 1981).
Van Allen, W. H., 'John Mason Neale', *Living Church*, 19 Jan. 1918, 390–1.
Vischer, L. (ed.), *Spirit of God, Spirit of Christ: Ecumenical Reflections on the Filioque Controversy* (London, 1981).
Ware, K., 'Metropolitan Philaret of Moscow (1782–1867)', *Eastern Churches Review*, 2/1 (Spring 1968), 24–8.
——, *The Orthodox Way* (London, 1979).
Ware, T., *The Orthodox Church* (Harmondsworth, 1963).
Watson, J. R., *The Victorian Hymn* (Durham, 1981).
Wellesz, E., *History of Byzantine Music and Hymnography* (Oxford, 1961).
Wheeler, M., *Death and the Future Life in Victorian Literature and Theology* (Cambridge, 1990).
Williams, G. (ed.), *The Orthodox Church of the East in the Eighteenth Century, Being the Correspondence between the Eastern Patriarchs and the Nonjuring Bishops, with an Introduction on Various Projects of Reunion between the Eastern Church and the Anglican Communion* (London, 1868).
Williams, I., *The Altar, or Meditations in Verse on the Great Christian Sacrifice, with Numerous Illustrations* (London, 1847).
——, *The Baptistery, or the Ways of Eternal Life* (London, 1842).
——, *The Cathedral, or the Catholic and Apostolic Church in England* (Oxford, 1838).
Wiseman, N., *Fabiola; or, The Church of the Catacombs* (London, 1854).
Wolff, R. L., *Gains and Losses: Novels of Faith and Doubt in Victorian England* (New York, 1977).
Wright, T. R., *Theology and Literature* (Oxford, 1988).
Zernov, N., 'Alexei Stepanovich Khomiakov', *Sobornost*, 10 (June 1937), 3–12.
——, *Eastern Christendom: A Study of the Origin and Development of the Eastern Orthodox Church* (London, 1961).
——, *The Russians and their Church* (London, 1978).

INDEX

(Note: all publications are by Neale unless otherwise stated)

A Few Words of Hope on the Present Crisis of the English Church (1850) 24
A Few Words to Churchwardens, no I (1841) 11
A great and mighty wonder 145, 173
A History of the Church for the Use of Children (1853) 204
A History of Greece for Young Persons (1845) 176
A History of the Holy Eastern Church: General Introduction (1850) 24, 61, 76, 78–80, 119–20, 123, 125, 129–31, 135, 137–40, 144, 154, 246
A History of the Holy Eastern Church: The Patriarchate of Alexandria (1847) 18, 70, 81, 243, 253
A History of the Holy Eastern Church (1847: 1873) 13, 18, 34, 53, 58–9, 73, 75–88, 91, 94, 102, 190, 200, 207, 210, 234, 244, 251, 254, 264, 266
Abbot, George, Archbishop of Canterbury 85, 251
Aberdeen, G. H. G., Lord, British Prime Minister 225
acrostic 124
Akathist hymn 13, 105–7, 109–10
Albert, Prince Consort 195
Alexander II, Tsar of Russia 233
Allchin, A. M. 53–4, 57, 95, 98, 209
Anatolius, St 145, 149
Andrew of Crete, St 109, 123, 129–30, 146, 149
Anglicanism and Orthodoxy 18, 37–54, 73, 77–86

Anglo-Catholicism of Neale 4–5, 8, 14, 19, 23–5, 33–4, 54–6, 61
Annals of Virgin Saints (1846) 190, 201
Anson, P. F. 11, 13
antiquarianism 182–4
of Neale 4
Apologia pro vita sua (Newman) 40–1
apostasy 219–20
architecture 5–6, 9, 80, 125, 218, 245
Gothic 9–10
Neale and 6–8, 58, 60–1, 218, 245
Arnold, Matthew 176–7
Arsenius, Metropolitan of Thebais 38
Art thou weary, art thou languid 114, 149, 167–73
Ayton Priory (1843) 30

Baker, Henry 33
Barberi, Dominic 108
Battle of the Alma, The (1866) 231–2
Beatitudes 170
Benedicite 104, 111
Benedictus Dominus (Prayer of Zacharias) 105, 111, 142
Bernard of Cluny 117
Bouvy, E. 105
Boyce, Edward 7–8, 15
branch theory 40–2, 45, 52, 62, 65, 72, 219
Brantlinger, P. 186
Brodsky, L. 51
Burton, R. F. 66, 68
Byron, G. G., Lord 187

Cambridge Camden Society 8–15, 17, 20–1, 56, 80

Cameron, J. M. 41
canon 60, 109–14, 116, 124–5, 129, 142–3, 155, 159–60
Canon for Christmas Day (Cosmas the Melodist) 111–13
canticles, biblical 110–11, 132–3, 135, 137, 141–3, 155, 160, 162, 166
Carlyle, Thomas 172, 183, 185
Carols for Christmastide (1853) 30
Carols for Eastertide (1854) 30
Carus, William 2, 10, 196–7
centos of Neale 114, 144, 154, 161, 163, 166–7
Challis, James 6
Chalmers, Thomas 100
Chapman, R. 5
Chatfield, Allen William 172
childhood of Neale 1–2
Christian, dost thou see them 144, 146, 152, 172–3
Church Enlargement and Church Arrangement (1843) 12
Church of the Fathers 42, 54, 58, 65
Clark, Kenneth 14
Clarke, B. F. L. 9
Close, Francis 20–1
Collier, Jeremy 38
Come and let us drink of that New River 134, 146
Come ye faithful, raise the strain 114, 147, 152–3, 173
Commentary on the Psalms (with Littledale) (1860: 1868) 34
Comparison of the Differences betwixt the Eastern and Western Churches, The (Philaret) 48
Comte, Auguste 183
Constantine Palaeologus, Emperor of Byzantium 212
Constantinople 224–5, 227
 fall of 208, 211, 213, 217–18, 220, 222
Cosmas the Melodist 109, 111–14, 145, 149, 154–62, 165–6, 169, 174, 241
Council of Florence 217–18

Covel, John 63
Crawley, Neale in 16
Crimean War 32, 207–8, 217, 222–5, 227–32, 252, 257
Cyril of Alexandria, St 210–11

Dairyman's Daughter, The (Richmond) 197
Dalton, James 2
Davey, C. 86
de la Warr, Earl 21–2
death 86, 181, 194–5, 198, 207, 221, 241, 256
 Neale and 196–7, 199, 201–4
 in Orthodoxy 259
Decline and Fall of the Roman Empire, The (Gibbon) 208
Deeds of Faith: Stories for Children from Church History (1850) 182, 192, 203
Demetrius of Rostov 262
Dickens, Charles 184, 203
Disraeli, Benjamin 68, 187–8
Dream of Gerontius, The (Newman) 199
Durandus, William 12, 17

Easter, festival of 122–3, 125, 131–44, 170
Easter canon (John Damascene) 98, 124
Eastern Church Association 33, 88
Ecclesiological Society 28, 118
Ecclesiologist, The 11, 20–1, 28
ecclesiology 7, 9, 12, 14–15, 18, 20, 24, 56, 61, 91–2, 183, 249
 Eastern 79–80, 86, 246
ecumenism 33, 44, 101, 175, 177
education of Neale 2–3, 15
Eliot, George 189
Enlightenment 188
Eothen, or Traces of Travel Brought Home from the East (Kinglake) 66, 69
Erick's Grave (1845) 181, 260–2
eschatology 198–9
Essays on Liturgiology and Christian History (1863) 78–9, 235

Euchologion 149
Evangelicalism 4, 194, 197, 199
Every, G. 80
Exaltation of the Cross 258

Farm of Aptonga, The (1856) 206
Father of Peace, and God of Consolation 99–100, 106, 145
Fierce was the wild billow 149, 172–3
Filioque 38, 222
Flaubert, Gustave 68–9, 71, 81, 92
Florovsky, G. 38, 42, 49
Forster, E. M. 242
Fox, Adam 14, 34
Froude, Richard Hurrell 5–6

Gaskell, Elizabeth 184
Gentili, Luigi 108
Georgia, Church of 234–6
Germanus, St 149
Gibbon, Edward 208–12, 214, 217–18, 221–2
Gillet, Lev 104, 175
Gladstone, W. E. 229–30, 233
Gnosticism 102–3
Golden Canon of Easter (St John Damascene) 131, 143
Gorham judgement 23–5
Great Canon (St Andrew of Crete) 123, 129–31
Greek culture 176–7
Gregory of Nazianzus 107
Grundtvig, Nikolaj Frederik Severin, comparison of Neale and 95–100
Guildford, Neale in 15–16

Hagia Sophia (Instanbul) 210, 218, 245, 251–2
Hardy, Thomas 184
health of Neale 16–18, 20–1, 32
Hellenism 103, 177
Helmore, Thomas 28, 30
heroism 181, 201, 220, 261
Hook, Andrew 188

Hope, Thomas 187
Horologion 149, 151
Houghton, W. E. 171, 183
Howley, William, Archbishop of Canterbury 44–5
Hutton, Thomas Palmer 21–2
Hymnal Noted, The (1851; 1854) 28–9, 113, 117–19
Hymni Ecclesiae (1851) 27
hymnologist, Neale as 24–9, 86–8, 183, 241, 249–50, 266
  see also translator, Neale as
Hymns Ancient and Modern 28, 33, 152, 154, 166
Hymns of the Eastern Church (1862) 1, 33, 91, 94, 101, 105, 108, 113–14, 116–17, 121–3, 127, 130–1, 134–5, 137, 139–40, 143–4, 152, 154, 167–8, 172, 174–5, 177–8, 241, 249–50

Iconoclastic Controversy 59, 109–10, 125
iconostasis 80–1
icons 38, 60–2, 246–7, 256, 258, 263–4
  Neale and 109, 125, 264
image:
  light as 140
  use of 156–7, 160, 162–3, 167, 170, 246–7
  worship 259, 263–4
Immaculate Conception, concept of 107–8
imperialism 64–5, 67, 78
In days of old, on Sinai 149, 154–67, 173
Islam:
  Neale and 50, 70–1
  persecution of Christians 75, 84, 187, 205–6, 208, 213–15, 219–20, 223–5, 236–7, 239–42, 245, 252, 254
  supposed sexuality of Muslims 68–71, 92, 187
  Western attitude to 92, 265
Italohellenes 109

Index

James II, King 38
Jay, E. 195
Jesu, Name all names above 151, 173
Jesuits 84, 251
Jews 210–11
John Damascene, St 98, 109, 114, 124, 131, 134, 142–3, 146–9, 154, 159, 241
Joseph of the Studium, Archbishop of Thessaloniki 109, 124, 148, 150–1
Jossilian, Plato 234
Jugie, Martin 48
Julian, J. 166–7

Kaplan, F. 203
Keble, John 26, 192–3
Khomiakov, Alexei Stepanovich 49–50, 227
Kinglake, Alexander W. 66–7, 69, 92
Kingsley, Charles 184, 203, 209–11
Kline, G. L. 49
Knezevitch, Stephen 92
Kritopoulos, Metrophanes 82, 84–6

Landow, G. P. 156
Laud, William, Archbishop of Canterbury 251
Lazar-House of Leros, The (1859) 91, 181, 193, 200, 243–59, 264
legacy of Neale 265–7
Lent Legends (1855) 192, 204
Let our choir new anthems raise 150, 173
Let us rise in early morning 137, 146
Lewes, George Henry 189
Lewis, Matthew Gregory 201
Lily of Tiflis, The (1850) 91, 181, 234–43
Littledale, Richard F. 91, 172
Liturgies of SS Mark, James, Clement, Chrysostom and Basil, and the Church of Malabar, The (1859) 91, 96–7
liturgy, Neale and 96–7, 144

Loukaris, Cyril 81–6, 193, 200, 243–4, 250–1, 253, 259
Lukács, Georg 184–5, 190

macabre 201–2, 204
Madeira, Neale in 17–19, 54, 56–7
Magnificat (Song of the *Theotokos*) 104, 111, 142, 166
Maison, M. M. 184
Manning, Henry 24
martyrdom 86, 181, 194, 200–5, 207–8, 211, 218–22, 231, 236, 240, 255–6
Mary II, Queen 38
Mary, Mother 126, 155
Mary, Virgin:
  Neale and 106, 166–7
  as *Theotokos* 13, 105–7, 110, 142, 166–7
Mediaeval Hymns and Sequences (1851) 27, 113, 118–19
medievalism of Neale 6
meditation 197
Menaion 104, 120, 124, 126, 145, 149–50
Menshikov, Alexander 225
metre 117, 143, 152, 155
Metrophanes of Smyrna 151
Mill, John Stuart 183
Mill, W. H. 28
Miller, jun., E. C. 44
Milton, John 128–9
Miriam, Sr 256–7
Monk, The (Lewis) 201
Montalembert, Charles, Count 17, 56–7, 62
mortality of Christ 136, 138, 140, 158–9
Muhammad Shah, Aga 235
Muraviev, Andrei Nikolaievich 47, 58, 108, 262

narrative theology 261
Neale, Agnes, daughter of Neale 16, 29, 232
Neale, Cornelius, father of Neale 1
Neale, Sarah Norman (née Webster), wife of Neale 16

Index

Neale, Susanna, mother of
  Neale 1–2
Newman, John Henry 5, 7, 19, 24,
  40–1, 45, 51, 55–7, 108, 161,
  192–3, 198–9, 203, 209–10
  comparison with Neale 3–4
Nicholas I, Tsar of Russia 94, 217,
  224–6, 229, 231–2
Nightingale, Florence 258
Nina, St 234
Nonjurors 37–40, 42, 50
North American Indians 204–6,
  214
*Notes Ecclesiological and
  Picturesque, on Dalmatia,
  Croatia, Istria, Styria, with a
  visit to Montenegro* (1861) 67,
  79, 92
*Notes of a Journey from Cornhill
  to Grand Cairo*
  (Thackeray) 66–7
novel:
  historical 185–6, 189, 207
  historical and religious 32, 181,
    184, 192–3, 207
  travel 65–8
nursing sisterhood 30–2, 243,
  256–8

O happy band of pilgrims 33, 114,
  150, 168, 172–3
O wondrous type, O vision fair 164
Octoechos 104, 124, 149–51, 167
Oldknow, Joseph 92
Orient, Western attitude to 265–6
orientalism 64–6, 72, 86
  Neale and 63, 65–6, 72, 74,
    186–7, 260
Orthodoxy 70, 211, 250, 256
  and Anglicanism 18, 37–54, 73,
    77–86
  death 259
  Easter festival 122–3, 152–3
  festivals 144
  history 75–6, 78
  hymnology 60, 102–16, 123–4,
    129–31, 143, 156, 166, 170–2,
    175, 178

  icons 61
  image worship 263–4
  Neale and 12, 37, 50, 53, 59,
    83–4, 91–4, 120–2, 248–9,
    265–6
  in Russia 37, 217, 226–7, 261–2
  Scripture 158–9
  sin 136
Orthodoxy Sunday 125
Overton, J. H. 25–7
Oxford Movement 4–5, 8, 25, 44,
  54, 98, 193

Palmer, William 45–50, 52, 54,
  58–9, 62
Paradise 125–9
Parker, John Henry 32, 234
Pascal, P. 261
Patrinacos, N. D. 105, 107
Pearson, William 15
Pentekostarion 104, 124, 131,
  146–51
Penzance, Neale in 17
Pereira de Figueredo, Antonio 57
Perry, D. W. 173
Peter the Great, Tsar 38, 49
Philaret, Metropolitan of
  Moscow 48–9, 93–4, 159
Phranza, Georgios 212
Pictorial Crucifixes (Neale,
  published first anon.)
  (1852) 246–7
Pinkerton, Robert 48
Pocknee, C. E. 177–8
podvig, concept of 261–2
Popov, Eugene Ivanovich 51, 59,
  93–4, 120–1, 174–5, 177, 226–7
priest, Neale as 15–16
Protasov, Count, Chief
  Procurator 46–8, 51
psalms 97, 103
Pugin, Augustus 5–6, 9
Pusey, Edward Bouverie 7, 30, 43,
  51, 198, 199

Raise thine eye a little way 171
Ricaut, Paul 63
Richmond, Legh 195, 197, 256

Romanism 5, 13, 20, 21, 24, 40–1, 43, 49, 55, 73, 77–8, 84–5, 93, 106–8, 176, 208, 246
 anti- 53–4; of Neale 56–8
Romanos the Melodist, St 105, 110
Romanticism 5, 188–9, 193–4
Rouse, R. 101
Routley, E. R. 118, 173
Rowe, Sir Thomas 251
Rowell, G. 13, 42, 59, 61, 194, 198–9
Royal Asiatic Society 64
Russell, William 2
Russia 233, 235
 Crimean War 207–8, 217, 222–5, 227–32
 fame of Neale in 94
 Orthodoxy in 37, 217, 226–7, 261–2
 Western attitude to 265
Russian Sisters of Mercy 257

Sackville College, Neale at 21–3, 30–1, 34
Sacy, Antoine Isaac Silvestre de 114–16
Safe home, safe home in port 114, 150, 168, 172–3
Said, Edward W. 64–5, 115, 187–8
Salammbô (Flaubert) 69
salvation 136, 199–200
Sanders, A. 182, 184–5
Savaites 109
Savas, S. J. 102–3, 110, 131, 166
Scobell, Emily (Sr Amy) 31, 256
Scott, Sir Walter 5, 184–9, 192–3, 201, 206–7, 258
scriptural hymns 104, 110, 162
Sebastopol, Crimea 230, 232, 258
secessions 19, 24, 38, 41, 55–7, 109
sentimentality 203, 207
Sequentias ex Missalibus Germanicis, Anglicis, Gallicis, aliisque medii aevi collectae (1852) 27
sexuality of Muslims, supposed 68–71, 92, 187
Shaw, P. E. 42

short stories of Neale 91, 260–4
Simeon, Charles 2–3, 10, 195–7
Slavophilism 49–50, 227
Société Asiatique 64, 115
Society of St Margaret 26, 30–1, 34, 245, 256–7
Song of Habakkuk 104, 111, 135, 162
Song of Hannah 104, 110, 133, 160
Song of Isaiah 104, 111, 136, 137
Song of Johah 104, 111, 138
Song of Moses 104
 in Deuteronomy 110
 at Red Sea 110, 132, 155
Song of the Three Holy Children 111, 138, 142
Southey, Robert 187
Stakhovich, Alexandra 258
Stand on thy watch-tower 135–6, 146
Stars of the morning 150, 173
Stephen the Sabaite, St 167
Stories from Heathen Mythology and Greek History for the Use of Christian Children (1847) 176
Story of S. Metrophanes of Voronej (1850) 181, 260, 262–4
Street, George Edmund 34
Studites 109
Studium, Constantinople 109, 241
suffering 159, 170–1, 224, 240, 242
Sumner, Charles Richard, Bishop of Winchester 16
superiority of West over East 64–6, 68, 266
Sutherland, John 32
symbolism 4, 11, 13–14, 59–61, 125

Take the last kiss,—the last for ever 249–50
Tales of Terror (Lewis) 201
Talisman, The (Scott) 186
Tennyson, Alfred, Lord 222
Thackeray, William Makepeace 66–7, 70, 92, 184, 203

Index

The abyss of many a former sin 144, 148, 152, 173–4
The choirs of ransomed Israel, see *In days of old, on Sinai*
The day is past and over 33, 149, 159, 172, 174
The Day of Resurrection 33, 131–3, 143–4, 146, 152, 172, 174
Theoctistus of the Studium 151
Theodora, Byzantine Empress 125
Theodora Phranza (1853–4; 1857) 32, 91, 181, 193, 206–33, 235–7, 239, 241, 248, 252
Theodore, Abbot of the Studium 109, 147–8
Theophanes, St 147, 241
Those eternal bowers 149, 174
Thou hallowed chosen day! 140, 147
Thou New Jerusalem, arise and shine 142–3, 147
Tolstoy, A. P., Chief Procurator 59, 174
Tomlinson, George, Bishop of Gibraltar 43
Towle, E. A. 26
Tractarianism 4–5, 10, 20, 25, 40–2, 44–5, 55, 57, 98, 183, 198–9
Transfiguration 140
translator, Neale as:
 of Greek hymns 13, 25–6, 33, 86, 94, 96, 98–102, 109, 113–15, 119–21, 124–8, 130–4, 141, 143, 154–5, 158, 162, 167–8, 170, 172–3, 177–8, 264
 of Latin 25–7, 29, 117–19
travel, Neale and 79
Treaty of Paris (1866) 233
Triodion 104, 121–3, 125–7, 129, 131, 146–8, 249

Turner, Ashurst Gilbert, Bishop of Chichester 22–3, 31, 246–7
Turner, F. M. 176
Two Huts, The (1856) 32
typology 8, 156–67

ultramontanism 56–8

Vardisanis 103
Venn, Henry 194
Victoria, Queen 195
Victorian attitudes 86, 103, 156–7, 159, 169, 171, 176, 182–3, 194, 199, 203, 295
Voices from the East (1859) 107–8

Wake, William, Archbishop of Canterbury 39–40
Ware, Kallistos (Timothy) 60, 123, 126, 130, 133–6, 155, 158, 171
Ware, T. 60, 123, 130
Warton, John 198
Watts, Isaac 26
Webb, Benjamin 8, 12, 16, 18–19, 26, 28, 55–6, 109, 118, 223
Wellesz, Egon 132
Wesley, Charles 26
Who from the fiery furnace saved the three 138, 147
Wilberforce, Robert 24
William III, King 38
Williams, George 75, 87
Wiseman, Nicholas 203
Wright, T. R. 261
writer, Neale as 13, 17, 21, 32, 50, 76, 86–8, 181–3, 186, 188–94, 200–1, 203, 206
 see also publications by name

Zara, island of 92–3
Zernov, N. 50, 60